Russia and America

From Rivalry To Reconciliation

Russia and America

From Rivalry To Reconciliation

EDITORS

George Ginsburgs,
Alvin Z. Rubinstein,
and Oles M. Smolansky

M.E. Sharpe INC. Armonk, New York • London, England

Library of Congress Cataloging-in-Publication Data

Russia and America : from rivalry to reconciliation / edited by George Ginsburgs,
Alvin Z. Rubinstein, and Oles M. Smolansky.
    p.   cm.
Includes bibliographical references.
ISBN 1-56324-284-2 (c).—ISBN 1-56324-285-0 (p)
1. United States—Foreign relations—Russia (Federation)
2. Russia (Federation)—Foreign relations—United States
I. Ginsburgs, George.
II. Rubinstein, Alvin Z.
III. Smolansky, Oles M.
E183.8.R9R88   1993
327.47073—dc20
93-15877
CIP

Printed in the United States of America

Contents

Preface

In the 1990s the United States and Russia find themselves at a watershed: the Cold War is over; the Soviet Union has been dissolved and replaced by fifteen independent nation-states; communism is discredited; and security for the two great powers is more a function of domestic reform than external threat. As we move into the post–Cold War era, U.S. and Russian leaders need to rethink basic assumptions about security, about foreign policy priorities, and about essential political alignments.

Moscow and Washington need to reconceptualize their relationship. Although no longer the hub of a vast imperial system, Moscow is the capital of the Russian Federation, the largest of the fifteen republics to emerge to independence as a result of the USSR's demise. By virtue of its possession of a preponderance of the former Soviet Union's nuclear and conventional forces, it is the most powerful, and it is the richest in resources. The Russian leadership under President Boris Yeltsin is committed to the return of Russia to Europe, to ending the isolation from the West that was a dominant feature of the period of Soviet rule. This process started under Mikhail Gorbachev, whose acquiescence to decommunization in Eastern Europe, reduction of Soviet forces in the area, and agreement to German reunification were intended to foster the Europeanization of Moscow's policy. In the interest of pursuing a "common European home," Gorbachev had implicitly accepted the dismantling of the common socialist alliance.

However, there has always been a certain ambivalence toward Europe among Russia's ruling elite. In the mid-nineteenth century, two competing conceptions crystallized: Slavophiles versus Westernizers. The Slavophiles believed in the superiority and historical mission of Russia's Byzantine, Eastern Orthodox, autocratic tradition; they exalted messianic nationalism, unity of the Slavs, and expansion across the Eurasian land mass. The Westernizers argued that Russia was part of Europe, albeit at a less advanced economic and political stage of development; they espoused liberalization of society and a constitutional system modeled on the British experience. Both of these currents of thought are very much alive in the Russian Federation today. The outcome of their competition will affect the kind of domestic order and foreign policy that Moscow develops and that the United States can support.

A number of Western observers have correctly noted that the return of Russia to Europe is by no means a foregone conclusion. Russian nationalism is one potentially destabilizing uncertainty. Another source of discord is opposition to Yeltsin's commitment to a market economy and an end to the statist-style society of the past. Ethnic separatism, which was instrumental in undermining Gorbachev's reform efforts, could well erupt into civil war and precipitate a return to a repressive political system.

The immediate problem for the United States is how extensive a commitment to make to the transformation of Russia and its integration into the Western-dominated international order. In March 1992, former President Richard Nixon called Yeltsin "the most pro-Western leader in Russian history. Under those circumstances then, he deserves our help. . . . We have to realize that if Yeltsin fails, if freedom fails, the new despotism which will take its place will mean that the peace dividend is finished, we will have to rearm, and that's going to cost infinitely more than would the aid that we provide at the present time."

Russia needs an American policy, and America needs a Russian policy. Certainly, international security and stability depend on the ability of Russia and America to forge an essentially cooperative relationship. These essays, which were originally presented at a conference at the University of Pennsylvania on February 18 and 19, 1993, seek to analyze a range of critical issues that go to the heart of the relationship between Russia and the United States. The focus is primarily on developments in Yeltsin's Russia and on their implications for U.S.-Russian relations.

To enhance our understanding of the erratic process of change that is taking place in Russia, we arranged for Russian, Ukrainian, and Uzbek scholars to comment on the essays of the American participants. These comments are included at the end of each section of this book. We hope that the total package will prove a welcome addition to the emerging assessment of the evolving Russian-American relationship.

The conference could not have been held without the support of a number of institutions, whose encouragement we gratefully acknowledge: the Department of Political Science and the Center for Russian and East European Studies of the University of Pennsylvania; the Institute of National Strategic Studies, National Defense University, and its director, Alvin H. Bernstein; the Earhart Foundation; and the Foreign Policy Research Institute.

George Ginsburgs
Alvin Z. Rubinstein
Oles M. Smolansky

About the Editors and Contributors

Donald D. Barry is director of the Center for International Studies and University Professor of Government, Lehigh University. His areas of interest are post-Soviet law and politics and American administrative law. Barry edited *Toward the "Rule of Law" in Russia? Political and Legal Reform in the Transition Period* and is coauthor of *Post-Soviet Politics: The Fall of the USSR and the Rise of the Successor States*, both published in 1992.

Nina Belyaeva is president of the Moscow-based Interlegal Research Center, an independent think tank. She has written on the emerging multiparty system in Russia and helped draft legislation for the Russian parliament. In 1993 she was an adjunct fellow at the Center for Strategic and International Studies and a visiting fellow at the United States Institute of Peace.

Yaroslav Bilinsky is professor of political science and international relations at the University of Delaware. The author of *The Second Soviet Republic: The Ukraine After World War II*, as well as numerous articles on Soviet politics, he is now writing a second book on Ukraine.

William C. Bodie is director of executive communications at Northrop Corporation (Los Angeles). He was formerly a senior fellow at the Institute for National Strategic Studies at the National Defense University and chairman of the Manhattan Institute Seminar on International Affairs. His articles and reviews have appeared in *The Wall Street Journal*, *The National Interest*, *Orbis*, *Problems of Communism*, *Freedom at Issue*, *World Affairs*, and *Strategic Review*.

George Ginsburgs is Distinguished Professor of Foreign and Comparative Law at the Law School, Rutgers University (Camden). He has written extensively on Soviet legal affairs, the legal systems of the Communist regimes of Eastern Europe and Asia, and international relations. His most recent publications include *The Soviet Union and International Cooperation in Legal Matters*, published in two volumes in 1988 and 1992.

Viktor L. Israelyan, a graduate of the Diplomatic Academy in Moscow, served as a professor of international diplomacy during most of the 1960s. He joined the Ministry of Foreign Affairs in 1968 and was granted the rank of ambassador in 1971. In 1988 he rejoined the Diplomatic Academy. His Russian-language publications include *The Anti-Hitler Coalition* (also published in English and French), *The United Nations and Disarmament*, and *Diplomats Face to Face*.

Igor Ivanovich Lukashuk, a senior scientific staff member at the Institute of State and Law, Russian Academy of Sciences, since 1985, has published more than 200 works on international law, including *The Functioning of International Law*, published in Russian in 1992. He has participated in the work of numerous international organizations and since 1978 has served as a member from Ukraine on the permanent chamber of the Arbitration Court at The Hague.

Rajan Menon is Monroe J. Rathbone Professor of International Relations at Lehigh University. He is the author of *Soviet Power and the Third World*, coeditor of *Limits to Soviet Power*, and contributor to numerous journals and edited volumes. His current research is on security issues in Central Asia and imperial decline.

Sergo A. Mikoyan, chief researcher at the Institute of Peace Studies, is currently a visiting researcher at Georgetown University. He has written extensively on international relations, political science, and history, particularly on Latin America, Russia, India, and the United States, and is widely published in English.

Martha Brill Olcott is a professor of political science at Colgate University. Author of *The Kazakhs*, she also edited *The Soviet Multinational State* and S.P. Poliakov's *Everyday Islam: Religion and Tradition in Rural Central Asia*, both published by M.E. Sharpe. Olcott has published numerous articles in academic books and journals, including *Problems of Communism*, *Foreign Policy*, *Current History*, and *Foreign Affairs*.

Robert J. Osborn, professor of political science at Temple University, is the author of two books and numerous articles on the Soviet Union and the politics of the post-Soviet republics. He is currently working on a joint Russian-American project that will examine the roots of ethnic conflict in both countries.

Nicolai N. Petro is assistant professor of political science at the University of Rhode Island. He was founding director of the Center for Contemporary Russian Studies at the Monterey Institute of International Studies and served as special assistant for policy in the Office of Soviet Union Affairs at the U.S. Department of State and as visiting political attaché at the U.S. Embassy in Moscow, 1989–90. He has written extensively on Russian politics and is currently working on a book about Russian political culture.

Oleg G. Pocheptsov is chairperson of the department of Communication and Cultural Linguistics, Kiev University, and visiting scholar at the University of Pennsylvania's Annenberg School of Communications. He has written extensively in Ukrainian and Russian on linguistics and philology.

Alvin Z. Rubinstein is professor of political science at the University of Pennsylvania. His published works include *Soviet Foreign Policy Since World War II* (4th ed., 1992), *Red Star on the Nile*, and *Soviet Policy Toward Turkey, Iran, and Afghanistan.* His book *Moscow's Third World Strategy* was awarded the Marshall Shulman Prize of the American Association for the Advancement of Slavic Studies.

Leonid Rudnytzky is professor of Germanic and Slavic literatures at LaSalle University in Philadelphia and director of the University's Central and Eastern European program. Since 1990 he has also been president of the Shevchenko Scientific Society. His publications include numerous studies on Ukrainian cultural history.

Oles M. Smolansky, University Professor of International Relations at Lehigh University, is a native of Ukraine. His published works include *The Soviet Union and the Arab East Under Khrushchev, The USSR and Iraq: The Soviet Quest for Influence*, and numerous book chapters and articles in professional journals. His book *The USSR and Iraq* was awarded the Marshall Shulman Prize of the American Association for the Advancement of Slavic Studies.

Henry Trofimenko is a professor at the Diplomatic Academy of the Russian Ministry for Foreign Affairs, as well as an analyst at the Institute of the USA and Canada, Russian Academy of Sciences. He has been a visiting professor at several American universities and has written extensively on U.S. foreign policy and global strategy. His works include *U.S. Military Doctrine* (1986) and *USSR–U.S.: Half a Century of Peaceful Coexistence* (coauthor, 1983).

Dilbar Turabekova is an associate professor in the department of philology, Tashkent State University in Uzbekistan. Trained at the Institute of Foreign Languages in Moscow, she has extensive experience as a translator as well as in teaching language and literature.

David T. Twining is a U.S. Army colonel and director of the program on Eurasian Independent and Commonwealth States at the U.S. Army War College, Carlisle, Pennsylvania. He is the editor of *Beyond Glasnost: Soviet Reform and Security Issues* and author of *Strategic Surprise in the Age of Glasnost* and *The New Eurasia: Guide to the Republics of the Former Soviet Union*.

A

RUSSIA AND AMERICA IN THE POST–COLD WAR WORLD

New Russia and the United States

Victor L. Israelyan

In Russian policy toward the United States, three approaches or tendencies can clearly be distinguished. The proponents of the first—let us, for the sake of convenience, call them "America-centrists"—were inclined to see the United States as the sole partner and potential ally of Russia. They sometimes fetishized American experience and the life-style, economic order, and political system of the United States. If in years past Communist ideology interpreted the policy of the United States—domestic and foreign—only in a negative sense, so now "America-centrists" began to treat it, as a rule, in a positive vein. "Well, in America this question is decided thus and so . . ." Or "Americans in an analogous situation act in this way." Such arguments were, in their view, the most persuasive in any dispute.

Proponents of the second tendency—"America-phobes"—took the diametrically opposite point of view, according to which the United States was the main culprit for the collapse of the Soviet Union and bears the bulk of the responsibility for all the hardships that have befallen the Russian and other peoples of the former Soviet Union. They were convinced that the grandeur of Russia, its renaissance, and perhaps also the restoration of the USSR were possible only through opposition to the United States. They believed that if it were not for the "American fifth column" in the USSR in the guise of Gorbachev, Shevardnadze, and company, America would have had a snowball's chance in hell of winning the Cold War.

Finally, the champions of the third approach—the idealists—operated on the premise that Russia's relations with the United States must develop on the same terms and principles that would govern her relations with all the other states of the West. Recognizing the paramount role of the United States in world affairs and duly appreciating the pluses and minuses of American democracy, they saw no reason to assign priority to Russian-American relations. Russia was open to friendship and cooperation with every state, with all states, and it had no adversaries—such was the philosophical platform of this wing.

3

Yeltsin and the United States

And what about President Yeltsin? What place did he assign to Russia's relations with the United States? To begin with, he considered that the deep chasm that had developed between states "which until just recently were titled 'superpowers' must be liquidated."[1] To that end, Yeltsin initiated a whole series of practical steps which were intended to help remove all the remnants of hostility from the Cold War period. First, there were Russia's unilateral steps and the Russian-American agreements in the field of strategic arms reduction, which were unprecedented in scope and unusual in form—the Washington "framework agreement." He also expressed Russia's readiness to join in ascertaining the fate of American POWs who might be on Russian territory, and he backed several political initiatives of the Bush administration. Some of these steps, particularly in the area of arms limitation and reduction, prompted sharp criticism in Russia. On the whole, though, Yeltsin's line for radical change in the relations between Russia and the United States bore fruit.

In the course of 1992, the principal documents of Russian-American relations —the Camp David declaration by the presidents of Russia and the United States of February 1 and the Russian-American Partnership and Friendship Charter adopted during the Washington summit on June 17—recorded qualitative shifts in the character of the relations between the United States and Russia. The first document served notice that the two states "do not consider each other as potential antagonists."[2] The second already went considerably further, declaring that "proceeding from mutual trust and respect as a basis for their interrelationship, they [Russia and the United States] develop relations of partnership and friendship."[3] All this gave Yeltsin grounds to declare with satisfaction at the joint session of the U.S. Congress in June 1992 that "the partnership and cooperation of the two largest democratic states in order to strengthen democracy is a truly great goal."[4]

At the same time, Yeltsin did not stake everything on the priority of Russian-American relations; nor did he accentuate their uniqueness, as practically all the leaders of the Soviet Union had done during the whole course of the postwar period. For instance, in an interview given to the radio station Deutschlandfunk, he said: "We adopt the best that there is in progressive countries—Germany, France, the United States, England, Japan—both from the point of view of technology and that of people's living standard, their culture."[5] In another interview, with the newspaper *Komsomol'skaia pravda* shortly before his visit to Washington, Yeltsin underscored the European direction of Russia's policy. "Russia has from time immemorial been with Europe," he said, "and we must integrate into the European institutions: the Council of Europe, the Common Market; we must enter the political and economic unions."[6] And in the fall of 1992, speaking on the vectors of Russian diplomacy: "The Russian Federation's foreign policy must be a full-scale foreign policy with multiple vectors. While developing our relations with western countries—the United States, Germany, Great Britain, Italy—we must work with equal diligence along the eastern salient—with Japan, China, India, Mongolia."[7]

The Russian president's position, then, draws on elements of the first and third approaches mentioned above.

Russia, the New World Disorder, and the Post–Cold War World

What are the prospects for the different approaches to Russian-American relations within Russia's social circles and corridors of power? What would be the effect on the United States and Russia, as well as on the rest of the world, of each of these approaches?

It is probably easier to answer these questions by referring to the approach of opposition to and confrontation with the United States. The whole sorry history of Soviet-American relations during the Cold War provides ample evidence of what this leads to. The confrontation of the two superpowers created a permanent threat to all mankind.

Returning to it under the new conditions, which find Russia (as distinct from the Soviet Union) without military or economic—to say nothing of political—parity with the United States, promises Russia no gain. Use of the only trump card which Russia retains—the nuclear arsenal that still exists—would mean suicide. Attempts to resurrect the image of the United States as enemy, saddling Russian foreign policy with Cold War stereotypes, would be marked adventurism.

An equipoise in Russia's relations with all the countries of the West, including the United States—and indeed with the entire world—on the basis of mutual advantage and due care for the interests of all the members of the global community and in the name of the flowering of democracy and civilization, no doubt sounds ideal. It is also not clear what the stability of such relations would rest on.

In the decades after World War II, the strategic parity between the United States and the USSR became a prerequisite for political stability. A rough balance of power was maintained between NATO and the Warsaw Pact. When the Berlin Wall came down and communism in the Soviet Union and in Eastern Europe began to collapse, the longest era of stability in Europe in the twentieth century ended. Until then, the West Europeans were safely protected from the Soviet military threat by the American security umbrella. That stability, built on balance of power, was not replaced by any new order or system of international security. Regrettably, the Cold War was replaced not by peace based on a balance of interests and the harmonious development of international relations, but by a new world disorder.

Amid the ruins of the postwar world order, and especially in Eastern Europe and the former Soviet Union, many hotbeds of the most intense conflict have sprung up, some of which have escalated to prolonged wars between new state entities (former Yugoslavia, the Transcaucasus, and other regions). The phenomenon of enthnocentrism, which was characteristic of the sociopolitical development of mankind in the twentieth century and led to the liquidation of colonialism and multinational empires (Austro-Hungary, the USSR), began manifesting itself in aggressive, violent form. With regard to the state unity of the Soviet Union and many of its former republics, Gorbachev's slogan of "freedom of choice" backfired. Post–Cold War reconstruction requires new concepts of international relations; world leaders, statesmen, and political theorists have offered their vision of the new world order. One of the first to do so was Mikhail Gorbachev, who couched his concept in the attractive form of "new thinking." In numerous speeches, especially at the UN General Assembly in 1988, he painted a beautiful picture of the future harmonious evolution of the world. He stressed that further global progress was possible through the quest for a universal consensus in the movement toward a new world order which would be based on a balance of interests and the freedom of choice in a nonviolent world. Gorbachev believed that this was a requisite for building an international system capable of coping with the formidable economic, ecological, political, and other problems facing humanity.

Shortly after Gorbachev, President Bush started talking about the new world order. He, too, did not miss the opportunity to use the UN rostrum to paint cheerful vistas for the establishment of such an order. Just as Gorbachev's, Bush's views were very general, except for one significant difference. Whereas Gorbachev, in accordance with his "new thinking," assigned to the Soviet Union the role of one of the chief guarantors of and vital participants in the future world order, Bush found no room in it for the Soviet Union, which disappeared from the political map of the world, or for its successor—Russia.

To be fair, we must note that the president never did allocate roles for future participants in the new world order; he emphasized only the special interest of the United States in its establishment. Many other leaders also spoke in favor of the new world order in general terms. In sum, they called on the world community to move toward a world based on the rule of law, in which national security would be buttressed by a system of collective security with effective conflict-resolution and peacekeeping functions performed by multilateral institutions—above all, by a reorganized and strengthened United Nations.

This view, however, was not shared by many others. Given the existence in human society of antagonistic classes, the leaders of the world's surviving communist regimes obviously do not believe in the possibility of harmony in international relations. Nor do the dictators of a number of Third World countries with totalitarian regimes. Furthermore, many political theorists predict a return to the traditional power politics of the past. They say that the major powers—the United States, Germany, Western Europe, Russia, China, Japan, and India—will seek to assert themselves in their own regions and compete for influence in other areas of the world. Michael Sandel of Harvard University writes: "The end of the Cold War does not mean an end of global competition between the superpowers. Once the ideological dimension fades, what you are left with is not peace and harmony, but old-fashioned global politics based on dominant powers competing for influence and pursuing their national interests."[8]

The international life of the last few years gives every reason to expect that, at least in the foreseeable future, the development of world politics will follow the course traced by Sandel. It would be illusory to assume that the acuteness of ethnic conflicts will abate in short order and the process of atomization of international relations will follow a bloodless path, that North–South contradictions will soften, and, finally, that the world will be guaranteed against forms of totalitarianism, including one with a communist pigmentation. Hardly.

New conflicts, disputes, and potentially dangerous situations will affect the security interests of all powers, some of them to a greater degree, some to a lesser. For example, conflicts in the region of the Commonwealth of Independent States definitely will affect the policy of Russia more than the policy of other great powers. Furthermore, it strikes us that in the post–Cold War period, competition in the spheres of economics and technology may exacerbate the clash of interests between the leading industrial states. This would hardly contribute to the harmonization of relations, conflict-free coexistence, and entente.

Finally, such expressions as "universal human values" and "civilized world" have gained wide currency in the contemporary political lexicon. There is no doubt that there is much to recommend them. But their widespread use must not in any way overshadow or level all the diversity of culture, tradition, religion, and ideology in human society. The growing enthnocentrism in the world only emphasizes that diversity. It was especially noticeable in the case of the disintegration of the Soviet Union, which previously had appeared to be a monolithic community. In the face of the existence of different civilizations, the achievement of mutual understanding and consensus on the many questions of contemporary intercourse is an extremely complicated task.

The new world order, or more precisely, the post–Cold War world, will take shape through the aggregation of common values, coinciding interests, and agreements on the one hand, and, on the other, distinctions, contradictions, and divergences—just as in any stage of human history. Its stability will be insured by a balance of power—or, rather, by the balance of influence. Time will tell how the new balance looks, what its components will be and how long it survives.

I want to emphasize that the balance of power will not display the traditional character of power being determined by the military strength of a state. The military factor in world politics has already receded, and the economic factor is taking its place. In the future, its role will further decline: the power of a state will be determined not by guns, but by butter. Future confrontations and struggles between major powers or their aggregates are hardly likely to assume a military character, especially when any future war between great powers with modern types of weapons spells suicide. After all, even given the most profound political, ideological, and other contradictions, neither the Soviet Union nor the United States ever risked resorting to the use of the military factor in their confrontation, although in some instances they came close to doing so (the Cuban missile crisis, the October 1973 Arab-Israeli war).

The strengthening of political authority in the world, the expansion of spheres of influence, and the conquest of new markets will be effected with the help of economic levers. The military superpowers of the post–World War II world will be replaced by economic superpowers.

The United States, Russia, and the New Balance of Power

In March 1991, President Bush hailed Desert Storm as the beginning of a new order. He seemed to suggest that the United States ought to lead the post–Cold War world as the only surviving superpower and universally recognized master authority.

The disintegration of the other superpower did mark an end to the bipolar world system, and hegemony quite naturally passed to the United States. But this is a temporary role. Just as it took approximately ten years following the end of World War II for the bipolar world to take its shape, so it will take no less time to determine the new balance of power in the post–Cold War world. During this transitional period, the United States most probably will continue to exercise the power of the leader and master the intricacies of massive international interdependence. Coincidentally, a new balance of power will be taking shape in which the United States will no longer be the dominant authority, but one of the chief components of the political structure that will replace the bipolar world of the Cold War.

One can expect that the development of international life will cross two stages. During the first stage—the transitional one—the outlines of the interests and capabilities of the primary states in the post–Cold War environment will emerge. The states will rub against each other, so to speak, find the most advantageous partners, separate top priorities of international life from matters of secondary importance, elaborate effective solutions to new problems (ecology, enthnocentrism, etc.), sketch long-term prospects for their domestic development, and so forth. In time, these processes will determine the character and particular features of the second stage—a stable equilibrium of power which will reflect the blocs, or groupings, of states in the economic, political, and military spheres. The stability of international life, just as in the past, will depend on the balance of power which crystallizes in the course of the transitional phase.

During the first stage, Russia, just like many other states, will strive to develop broad, balanced relations with all countries, among them the United States.

Such an approach is natural, especially when one takes into account the instability of the political situation in Russia. With the stabilization of the domestic situation and the first positive results of economic reform, the foreign policy orientation of Russia will also be clearly set. Stabilization in the other countries of the former Soviet Union will likewise serve to stimulate the engineering of a new balance of power. Russia will become a natural participant in whichever of the blocs that will earn it the greatest economic and political profits. " 'All together' is not a paying proposition for Russia: whatever bloc it joins, that bloc will support it"—such is the opinion of the well-known Russian public figure Gavriil Popov.[9]

If Russia takes the path toward democratization and consistent economic reform, her cooperation with the United States in the long term is considerably more attractive in view of the ensemble of strategic, political, economic, and other interests. I share the standard arguments in favor of Russian-American cooperation, with the sole reservation that the time is not yet ripe for allied relations. Russia must first stabilize her domestic situation, must put her relations with the former republics of the Soviet Union on a firm good-neighbor footing; and the United States must make up its mind whether its leadership and hegemony are imperative or whether it is ready to explore other alternatives for the post–Cold War world order.

In a nutshell, Russian-American relations are in a state of transition whose duration will in large part be determined by the farsightedness of the political leaders of Russia and the United States and the skill of American and Russian diplomacy.

How the Americans Saw the
Second Russian Revolution

I was afforded the opportunity to observe the American reaction to the dramatic events in the Soviet Union firsthand, having arrived in the United States at the very climax of the 1991 August putsch. Interest in our affairs was terrific. Television and the newspapers were filled with reports from Moscow and other Soviet cities. In the past, when I had served as a Soviet diplomat in the United Nations, I was often called upon to address American audiences. But never before did news from the Soviet Union attract so much attention as it did in 1991. The disintegration of the Soviet Union, the Gorbachev-Yeltsin confrontation, the emergence of some fifteen new states, the names of many of which Americans had a hard time pronouncing—all this was breathtaking.

Overall, I got the impression that Americans were not overjoyed by the news of the demise of the Soviet Union; they were not gloating. Some expressed anxiety about the consequences of the USSR's disintegration; some even expressed sympathy, although, as a rule, the defeat of communist ideology was greeted with great satisfaction.

The greatest importance was attached to the position of the American leadership. There was no dearth of good wishes for the democratic transformations in Russia and the other republics from the president, the secretary of state, and other U.S. officials. "The United States recognizes and welcomes the emergence of a free, independent and democratic Russia headed by its courageous president, Boris Yeltsin," stated President Bush in his television address to the country on December 26, 1991.[10] After his first meeting with Yeltsin in January 1992, the American president reported with satisfaction that "we met not as adversaries, but as friends."[11] Secretary of State Baker echoed the president, repeatedly proclaiming America's support for Yeltsin's efforts in the democratization of Russia. "The democratic government of Russia no longer represents a direct and permanent threat to the United States," he said in his appearance before the Senate Foreign Relations Committee on April 9, 1992.[12] Other officials in the Bush administration spoke in the same vein.

However, interest in the events in Russia and other states of the former Soviet Union soon waned. Life followed its course, pushing forward new problems and conflicts. Bloodshed on the territory of the former Soviet Union—in Nagorno-Karabakh, Georgia, Tajikistan, and other places—became a routine feature of international life. It is striking how little attention the topic of Russian-American relations began to draw in 1992, and how meager were the practical steps taken by the American administration to infuse them with dynamism and give effect to the ententes reached at the two summits of Bush and Yeltsin in 1992.

In the course of the electoral campaign, the "Russian theme" was banished to the wings. For many months, the two main candidates, Bush and Clinton, crisscrossed the land, delivered speeches, gave interviews, and appeared on television —and only rarely was mention made of the former superpower where events had occurred that have been described by Librarian of Congress James Billington "as one of the most serious policy problems of our lifetime."[13] In the campaign platform of the Democratic Party of the United States, only a few lines were devoted to the former Soviet Union in the paragraphs dedicated to the problem of "promoting democracy" in the world. Furthermore, the word "Russia" does not appear there at all. True, in his main speech at the Democratic Party convention, Clinton twice mentioned Russia, but only in passing and in the most general terms.

Even granting the priority of economic and other domestic concerns in the United States, such obviously diminished attention is hard to justify in view of the series of new global problems that were erupting in the wake of the disintegration of the Soviet Union. Naturally, the phenomenon prompted sharp criticism by prominent American political scientists and Sovietologists. Already back at the end of 1991, the director of the Harriman Institute at Columbia University, Robert Legvold, referring to the dramatic events in the Soviet Union, wrote in his article "While We Sleep": "Through all of this, we do nothing. Nothing. From Tokyo to the White House, from Congress to our intellectual centers. We sink our heads in the sands of self-preoccupation."[14]

The whole world knows Richard Nixon's critical assessment of Bush's policy toward Russia. Nixon, whose authority in the field of Soviet-American relations very likely has no equal, voiced unhappiness with the tempo of American-Russian cooperation throughout 1992. Shortly after Clinton's victory, Nixon wrote in *The New York Times*, "But as was the case during the campaign, the most important issue since the end of World War II has received minimal attention." And further on in the same article, he emphasized that "the collapse of Boris Yeltsin's pro-Western, democratic Russian Government would have a greater impact on the American economy than anything the new administration could do at home."[15]

Senator Sam Nunn, appearing on the CBS program "Face the Nation" on November 15, 1992, also voiced dissatisfaction with the fact that America was too absorbed in its own problems and did not pay enough attention to relations with Russia; as a result, the United States was, in his opinion, in the absurd situation of having helped Gorbachev's communist regime substantially more than it was now helping Yeltsin's democratic one.[16]

Given the leading role of the United States in world affairs during the entire postwar period, the rather stormy political life of America in 1992 revealed an obvious discrepancy between the tremendous new responsibility of the United States as the sole superpower on the one hand and, on the other, Washington's limited, belated, and inadequate response to the challenge that the disintegration of the Soviet Union posed for the world community. "The causes of this discrepancy are numerous"—as the participants of the working group on U.S. Diplomacy Toward the Commonwealth of Independent States wrote in their report —"but a major impediment to action has been a failure on the part of U.S. leadership adequately to define and then explain to the American people our long-term security interests in the former Soviet Union."[17] One cannot but agree with this conclusion.

American Political Scientists Define the U.S. Stand Toward Russia

American political scientists, together with business people and representatives of the administration, have staged a series of conferences, round-table discussions, and seminars devoted to the topics of the long-term security interests of the United States and the American positions toward Russia and other states of the former Soviet Union. I had the pleasure of taking part in the Eighty-first American Assembly, on the topic After the Soviet Revolution: Implications for U.S. Policy, and in the working group of the Institute for the Study of Diplomacy of Georgetown University, as well as several others.

What was unique was the unanimity among the participants in their appraisals of the events in the former Soviet Union. The end of the communist order and the dissolution of the USSR were seen as landmark events in the greatest revolution of the twentieth century. The same consensus greeted the intention of Russia and other members of the Commonwealth of Independent States (CIS) to launch themselves resolutely on the path to democratic development. Finally, all the participants underlined the tremendous importance of the dissolution of the Soviet Union for the fate of the world and particularly for the United States. The organizers of the conferences sought to frame visions of the post–Cold War world and so to advance the discussion of how the United States might seize this historical opportunity. "Let's not lose this historic chance"—those words I heard from many participants in these discussions.

The American experts clearly saw the complexity and instability of the situation in Russia and the other states of the former Soviet Union and premised their analysis on two basic alternative routes it could take: either further destabilization with unpredictable consequences or gradual consolidation of democratic transformations. "If Mr. Yeltsin fails, we will again live in a dangerous world with the threat of nuclear war hanging over our heads. The wave of freedom sweeping the world will ebb and we could get caught in the undertow"—this is how Richard Nixon in his article "Save the Peace Dividend" articulated the first alternative.[18]

American experts saw the principal threat that a destabilizing process in Russia posed for the United States and the whole world in the growth of nuclear danger, including Russia's possession of strategic and tactical nuclear weapons, the presence of nuclear weapons in Ukraine, Belarus, and Kazakhstan, and the risk of nuclear proliferation and of more Chernobyls. Parallel to nuclear danger was the risk of the proliferation of other weapons of mass destruction—chemical and bacteriological weapons—and the technology to build them. The danger of a revival of an authoritarian state in Russia was also addressed. Such a development could encourage and strengthen the existing dictatorships and thus increase the potential for trouble that would profoundly affect the rest of the world.[19]

Another issue of serious concern was the rising ethnic tension and political breakdown in the region of the former Soviet Union, which could transform this region into one of permanent turmoil and violence, the effects of which could spill across borders and escalate into a genuine threat to the security of the United States and the entire world community.[20]

It was also noted that local conflicts in the regions of the former Soviet Union—such as those in Nagorno-Karabakh, Georgia, Abkhazia, Tajikistan—coupled with increasing economic difficulties, might send large numbers of people in flight toward the West, including the United States. In the long run, such large-scale emigration could endanger the stability of any Western state.[21] According to Murray Feshbach and Paul Goble, participants in the Institute for the Study of Diplomacy's working group, deterioration of the health situation in Russia and the other republics would have a deleterious impact on global health because of the potential spread of disease. As well, they claimed that environmental hazards in a destabilized Russia and other CIS countries would have global implications, especially for the United States and others in the northern hemisphere.[22]

Such are the perceptions concerning the dangerous consequences for the United States and the whole world of continuing uncertainty and destabilization in Russia. These views are voiced by experts, political scientists, and many of my American interlocutors interested in the situation in the former Soviet Union.

The second alternative—the consolidation of democratic transformations in Russia—was obviously more desirable. It corresponds to U.S. national security interests and the safeguarding of global stability. This conclusion was shared by all the participants in the discussions. In their opinion, such an alternative promised the United States great benefits:

• The threat of nuclear war between the two biggest military powers will be eliminated. The United States, in concert with Russia and other nuclear powers, would have the opportunity to create a reliable and effective barrier to the proliferation of nuclear arms and to move forward to a nuclear-free world.

• The reduced military threat to American security will lead to an assured reduction in defense spending, allowing the United States to transfer resources to other productive uses. "It has been projected that the United States over the next 10 years can save between $250 billion and $300 billion in defense expenditures if present trends continue," wrote Nixon in the aforementioned article in *The New York Times*.[23]

• While assisting Russia with democratic, economic, and political transformations, the United States helps to generate a world market for profitable trade and investment and economic growth that can be translated into jobs and income. In the view of the former U.S. ambassador to Russia, Robert S. Strauss, "The country [Russia] is important for us as an engine of our own economic transformation, and it can assist the West in dealing with all the '-isms' in the volatile, dangerous parts of the world."[24]

• The United States can succeed in the dismantling of confrontational military-based international relations and in the establishment of a cooperative international system consistent with the increasingly interdependent world only in close cooperation with Russia.[25]

James Billington summarized the benefits of American-Russian cooperation with these words: "Russia is important to the United States because: It is one of the few future Americas in the world; it is the greatest emerging market; it is important to the politics of the future, which will be based increasingly on culture and commerce rather than on military and political power."[26]

Operating from these economic, political, and security interests of the United States, American experts and political scientists came to the conclusion that it was necessary for the United States to procure comprehensive assistance for the democratic development of Russia. Effective measures must be undertaken to prevent the aggravation of American-Russian relations. In his interview with *Moscow News*, Zbigniew Brzezinski said: "This is why I think it is so important for the U.S. to help Russia undertake the political as well as economic changes it is now pursuing."[27]

Discussions of the implications of the Soviet Union's breakdown for U.S. policy produced, as a rule, summary recommendations. Some of them were sent to the American government and distributed widely. These recommendations spanned a wide range of questions: humanitarian aid; procurement of assistance in setting up democratic institutions; grants of economic, financial, and technical assistance; help in carrying out measures in the sphere of nuclear arms reduction and control; cooperation in the field of management and training of Russian businessmen in modern methods of running private companies and banks; development of cooperation with Russia in matters of resolving ethnic, religious, and regional conflicts; strengthening interaction with Russia in the United Nations and other international organizations.

In my opinion, all these proposals and recommendations—some large-scale, others dealing with particular issues—deserve serious attention. For example, I expressed the thought that it would be useful to amend the Internal Revenue Code special tax exemptions for American companies who wish to invest in Russia or any other CIS member. It seemed to me that it may be worthwhile to have a ten- to fifteen-year period during which all such U.S. companies would not be required to pay income tax on earnings derived from these operations. This would serve the dual purpose of stimulating U.S. economic growth while helping Russia. Another thought would be for the U.S. government to guarantee investments by American companies in Russia and the other republics. Neither proposal involves the direct expenditure of funds in Russia, but each is designed to encourage American companies to invest in these countries that so badly need the capital infusion and technical know-how that can be generated by American corporations instead of the government; at the same time, the creation of jobs in American industry would be fostered.

The American participants in the discussions came to yet another series of conclusions. First, help and assistance to Russia and other CIS members must be rendered on collective and cooperative terms by all the Western countries. Second, the United States must play the leading role here. "No coherent response to the challenges of the former Soviet Union is in the cards without a U.S. lead," declared the participants of the American Assembly. Third, the United States will not be able to play the role it must play if the American people are not convinced that deep engagement in Russian affairs is a sensible investment in their own national security and economic welfare. Finally, imperative and paramount prerequisites for furnishing assistance to Russia are the determination and readiness of Russia's own citizens to contribute the lion's share to the effort to create their new, democratic state. Plainly, all these conclusions are indisputable.[28]

Has the United States a Vital
Interest in Russia or Not?

And yet, many of these otherwise very substantive discussions did not provide an answer to what, in my opinion, is the key question: What place will Russia occupy in the long-term strategic plans of the United States?

A considerable number of proposals regarding various types of American aid and assistance to Russia were of a short-term nature. Their implementation would cover the transition to the post–Cold War world and further the stabilization of the political and economic situation in Russia. I share the view of Timothy J. Colton and Robert Legvold, who write in the conclusion to their book *After the Soviet Union*: "Often the issue is reduced to helping the new states or not and on what scale—helping them materially by providing various types of economic assistance or practically by sending an infinite variety of experts to teach them how to build new political, economic, and social institutions. This seems to us too narrow an approach."[29] In my opinion, Colton and Legvold have made a successful attempt to demonstrate "that the task is manifold and spread across different spheres."[30]

I have in mind, however, another dimension—not horizontal, but temporal. Mankind is moving from a bipolar to a multipolar world; a situation with one superpower is unlikely to be stable or permanent, and Russia will continue to exist as a major power in Eurasia's heartland. The question boils down not to whether Russia, after the transitional period of stabilization, will be a powerful or weak state. The choice, according to former Ambassador Strauss, is "between a strong inward-looking authoritarian state or a strong democratic state that participates in the world community." I would add that the choice will be far more complicated, inasmuch as the world community itself is unlikely to end up as a unipolar world, but is more apt to assume the shape of a community of groups of states with specific interests, cultures, different levels of development and capabilities, and so forth.

What choice will Russia make in such a world? What shared values—political, economic, cultural, and so on—will prevail in determining its place in the multipolar post–Cold War world? One can here imagine different scenarios: Russia–the United States, Russia–Western Europe, Russia–Germany, Russia–China, Russia–Japan, Russia–Third World. Combinations of these combinations are also possible.

One of the most likely is the Russo-German scenario. In its favor speak mutual economic interests, geographic proximity, a vast historical experience of coexistence—positive and negative. At the end of the eighties and the beginning of the nineties, Germany was the main economic partner of Russia and in the transition period laid a sound foundation for German-Russian cooperation over the long term. "You are closer to us," said Yeltsin at a meeting with representatives of the business circles of the Federal Republic of Germany in December

1992, "than the United States and Japan, even from a territorial point of view."[31]

The Russian-Chinese scenario has great potential as well. To such factors as the longest land frontier, approximately equal level of economic development, and many common social problems must be added the presence in Russia of a highly influential political platform of the champions of resurrection of socialism who will perceive in a Chinese-Russian alliance a good opportunity to "validate socialism."

We have already spoken of the advantages of and prospects for a Russo-American alliance. Each of the designated scenarios has its pluses and minuses. Under specific circumstances, each of them can become a reality. Much will depend on Russia, its development, and its policy. But no less will also depend on its partners—their vision of the post–Cold War world and their attitude toward Russia over the long term.

Robert G. Livingston, in his article "Let Germany Do It," argued that the United States has "no vital interest in Russia" and advised Washington "to ask the Germans to lead in aiding Russia."[32] Does this mean that the interests of the United States would be served by the transformation of the entire belt from Eastern Europe to the Urals into a zone of primarily German economic penetration? Would the United States wish to see Germany elevated to the status of a new superpower? I share the opinion of Ambassador Lukin, who considers that "the presence of a strong and friendly Russia will help Europeans avoid a 'Germanized Europe' and keep moving toward a 'Europeanized Germany'—an outcome more desirable for all concerned."[33] I believe that preventing a "Germanized Europe" is in the interests of the United States as well. Lukin reminds us in this connection that in the past Russia and the United States were drawn to each other by a fundamental strategic interest, namely, to prevent the emergence of a hegemonic regime in Europe.[34]

With regard to a Russian alliance with the Asian-Pacific region: Is the United States interested in having a situation where, after the settlement of existing disputes between Russia and Japan, the latter would have the opportunity of wide access to the extremely rich resources of Siberia and the Russian Far East and thus consolidate its leadership in many branches of the world economy? Would a successful, wide-ranging Chinese-Russian alliance, including the military-political sector, promote the maintenance of American influence in this region of the world? Russia is the heartland of Eurasia, endowed with enormous potential capabilities. According to Colton and Legvold, "If this heartland, an area of enormous natural wealth with skilled and talented people, can reach the point of economic take-off over the next ten to fifteen years, the well-being of Europe, Asia, and others, including the United States, in the twenty-first century will be considerably, maybe even immeasurably, enhanced."[35] History proves that the United States always attached utmost importance to the region of Eurasia, assigning it ultimate international priority.

So evidently, the responses to both scenarios will be no. Many of my interlocutors in university audiences, at various round tables, and in private talks spoke in that vein. Particularly threatening to the interests of the United States was the prospect that Germany and Japan would further strengthen their world positions by milking their special relations with the states of the former Soviet Union. An alliance based on close and broad cooperation between the United States and Russia was viewed as the antidote to that possibility.

The recommendations of the authoritative working group of the Institute for the Study of Diplomacy also noted the need for a strategic partnership of the United States with Russia and other states of the former Soviet Union. True, they skirted the question of the possible structures of the future multipolar world, although the discussions did touch on that subject.

In light of the fact that one of the authors of the idea of a new world order was President Bush himself, we may assume the likelihood that its contours were discussed in the upper echelons of power in Washington. Perhaps various models of a future multipolar world and the place and role of the United States in it, as well as that of other states, were also considered. It is more probable, though, that the 1992 electoral campaign pushed these questions into the background. In any case, Washington's belated reactions to several important events in Russia, the insignificant volume of aid rendered to Russia, the noticeably declining interest toward Russia in Washington (how otherwise can one explain the absence of an American ambassador in Moscow for several months?)—all this is testimony that a long-term U.S. strategic policy vis-à-vis Russia has not yet been enunciated in Washington.

The year 1992 was in many ways decisive for the fate of Russia, for the dynamics of the development of democratic processes there, and for the alignment of political forces. Much depended on the determination, precision, and concreteness of the positions of the United States with respect to Russia. Washington's dilatoriness in no way benefited Russian democracy and, in fact, contributed to definite vacillations in Russia's foreign policy course.

If one does not count the numerous declarations of friendship and good intentions, 1992 may be considered the year of missed opportunities. Whether the Clinton administration will succeed in retrieving lost ground and elect to follow a different policy toward Russia, only the future will tell.

Notes

1. *Diplomaticheskii vestnik*, 1992, nos. 11, 13.
2. Ibid., p. 12.
3. Ibid., 1992, no. 13–14, p. 8.
4. Ibid., p. 7.
5. *Ekho planety* (Moscow), November 1991, p. 48.
6. *Komsomol'skaia pravda*, May 27, 1992.
7. *Rossiisskie vesti*, October 19, 1992, p. 1.
8. See Robert S. McNamara, *The Changing Nature of Global Security and Its Impact*

on South Asia (Washington, DC: Washington Council on Nonproliferation, 1992), pp. 4–5.

   9. *Izvestiia,* July 31, 1992.
   10. *Diplomaticheskii vestnik,* 1992, no. 11, p. 14.
   11. Ibid.
   12. Ibid., p. 16.
   13. Working Group on U.S. Diplomacy Toward the Commonwealth of Independent States, Institute for the Study of Diplomacy, School of Foreign Service, Georgetown University (ISD), *First Interim Report,* June 1992, p. 1.
   14. *The New York Times,* December 10, 1991.
   15. Ibid., December 19, 1992.
   16. See *Izvestiia,* November 16, 1992.
   17. ISD, *First Interim Report,* p. 1.
   18. *The New York Times,* November 19, 1992.
   19. ISD, *First Interim Report; After the Soviet Union: Implications for U.S. Policy,* The Eighty-first American Assembly, April 23–26, 1992, Arden House, Harriman Institute, New York (American Assembly), p. 7.
   20. American Assembly, p. 7.
   21. Ibid., p. 8.
   22. ISD, *First Interim Report,* p. 15.
   23. *The New York Times,* November 19, 1992.
   24. Ibid., November 15, 1992, sec. 4, p. 19.
   25. American Assembly, p. 7.
   26. ISD, *First Interim Report,* p. 31.
   27. *Moscow News,* 1992, no. 27, p. 2.
   28. American Assembly, pp. 14–15.
   29. Timothy J. Colton and Robert Legvold, eds., *After the Soviet Union: From Empire to Nations* (New York–London: Norton, 1992), p. 191.
   30. Ibid.
   31. *Izvestiia,* December 17, 1992.
   32. *The New York Times,* March 21, 1992.
   33. V. Lukin, "Our Security Predicament," *Foreign Policy,* 1992, no. 88, p. 71.
   34. Ibid., p. 72.
   35. Colton and Legvold, *After the Soviet Union,* p. 188.

B

DOMESTIC DETERMINANTS OF RUSSIA'S FOREIGN POLICY

2

Constitutional Politics: The Russian Constitutional Court as a New Kind of Institution

Donald D. Barry

Introduction

As an institution, the Constitutional Court of the Russian Federation has no exact parallel in Russian or Soviet history. An effort in the 1920s to endow the USSR Supreme Court with the function of advising parliament with regard to the constitutionality of acts of state organs was stifled by the advance of Stalinism. The USSR Constitutional Supervision Committee, created at the end of the 1980s, was a more promising institution. Still only an advisory body, its decisions had considerable impact for two reasons: the committee came into being at a time when the Soviet Constitution and the institutions created by it were finally being allowed to influence political and legal operations; and the principle of separation of powers, which accorded independence and authority to the individual branches of government, was gaining acceptance.

These developments provided a promising basis for the creation of the Russian Federation's Constitutional Court, which was established in 1990 but did not commence work until late 1991. From the beginning, however, the Constitutional Court was thrust into the midst of political controversy. It is an institution whose role in law and politics is as yet largely undefined. The ultimate judgment on it will depend on how it handles the challenges it faces in its first several years of existence.

In examining the Constitutional Court of the Russian Federation and assessing its effectiveness as an institution, we shall briefly consider the following: the place of constitutions in the Soviet/Russian political system; the attitude toward the principle of separation of powers; constitutional control, and the USSR Supreme Court; and the USSR Constitutional Supervision Committee. We shall conclude with some observations on the implications of these developments for the broader picture: the possibility of a stable democratic political and legal system emerging in Russia, and what that means for relations with the democratic countries of the West.

From Stage Prop to Power Map:[1]
The Place of Constitutions in the
Soviet Political System

When Soviet constitutions had little real meaning—that is, throughout most of the seventy-five years of Soviet power—they could be safely ignored. Four national-level constitutions (and corresponding documents on the republic level) were adopted during this period. But no one mistook the fanfare associated with their promulgation (particularly evident with regard to the 1936 and 1977 documents) for genuine political activity. These were orchestrated rituals controlled by the political leadership, intended in part to demonstrate how firmly the leadership was in charge. If some of the provisions in these constitutions might have been interpreted as challenging the regime's prerogatives (e.g., the article allowing union republics freely to secede), the unwritten rules of Soviet politics prevented such challenges from being realized, or even publicly aired.

Alongside the formal constitutional document was a set of principles of political operation that actually governed the system. These principles have been described numerous times, but perhaps nowhere as cogently as by the late Tibor Szamuely. The "real constitution," according to Szamuely, "contains the actual rules of Soviet political life: the rules of Party management of the country, of *nomenklatura* and *Glavlit*, of the organization of elections and of the passport system, of doublethink and thought-crime (to use Orwellian shorthand). Every intelligent Soviet citizen is familiar with these rules and acts in accordance with them."[2] Thus, in spite of the superficial activity associated with the adoption of constitutions and the significant amount of attention paid to them by Soviet and foreign analysts, their importance for legal and political operations in the country was essentially nil.

This began to change in the late 1980s, when the attempt was made—largely by Gorbachev and his lieutenants—to endow some constitutional provisions with greater political significance. Convinced that the old governmental structures would not serve the ends of *perestroika*, Gorbachev set out to replace them with bodies that would be more responsive to and representative of the populace. His hope, apparently, was that the creation of these new bodies would persuade large segments of the population to support his efforts to remake the Soviet system into a more effective political and economic operation. To be sure, he did not intend to create a fully democratic system. Nor did he aim to diminish his control (or, at least in the beginning, Communist Party control) over the system or the process of change.

But when put into practice, some of the new structures and procedures either did not work as originally intended or were rejected by significant segments of the Soviet populace. In both cases, the intended level of central control was diminished, leading to incipient challenges to Gorbachev's (and the party's) position. Thus, for instance, when the idea of creating a congress of people's deputies was adopted at the Nineteenth Party Conference in 1988, it was assumed that local Communist Party organizations would control the nominations for parliamentary seats, even in contested elections. In many cases, however, it did not work that way. Further, the scheme for creating new state structures at the republic level supposed that each union republic would have a two-tiered legislature, as on the USSR level (a congress and a supreme soviet), and that a portion of the deputies would be chosen by social organizations rather than by popular vote. But there was such dissent about these arrangements that the USSR Constitution was changed to allow each republic to decide these matters for itself. In the end, all the republics except Russia opted for a one-tier legislature, and the practice of social organizations' choosing deputies was all but abandoned.[3]

Thus, where the Constitution formerly had no place in defining and distributing political power, now constitutional law became one of the loci of the new political controversies that came to the fore at the end of the 1980s. The new structures were created by the Constitution, their authority was defined by the Constitution, and they came to possess sufficient power to challenge the way in which traditional Soviet politics had been played. The importance of constitutional structures was further enhanced in 1990, with the creation of the USSR presidency. And in the same set of constitutional amendments that established the presidency, the Communist Party lost its legal monopoly on political power. In more than a formal sense, genuine constitutional politics had arrived on the Soviet political scene.

The plans to adopt a new constitution for the USSR never reached fruition, and, with the Soviet Union's demise, the focus on constitutional politics shifted to the republics. What was clear by this time was that constitutional provisions had joined a number of other issues (e.g., the rights of ethnic minorities and national territories, the nature and pace of economic reform) as matters of significant political controversy. And this is understandable: *real* constitutions have to do with the distribution of political power and with the rights of individuals and groups. These are matters on which the diverse forces in society strive to make their views felt. Where real political differences are still suppressed (e.g., Turkmenistan), a new constitution can be adopted quickly and easily.[4] Where controversy rages (e.g., Russia), adoption of a new document is correspondingly more difficult.

One of the other signs that constitutional law has become significant is the creation of a special organ to arbitrate disputes based on the Constitution. This body may take different forms, but the favored one in the former Soviet republics and Eastern Europe is a constitutional court.[5] Such courts have been established in several republics, but the Constitutional Court of the Russian Federation has so far been the most active and has received the most public notice. As suggested above, the establishment of Russia's Constitutional Court has benefited not only from this different attitude toward the Constitution but also from a commitment to the principle of separation of powers. After looking at the evolution of that doctrine, we shall examine two somewhat analogous predecessor institutions: the traditional Soviet-era arrangement for handling matters of constitutional interpretation, and the USSR Constitutional Revision Commission, which operated briefly at the end of the Soviet era.

Separation of Powers: Evolution of a Doctrine

The traditional Soviet view rejected the doctrine of separation of powers. It denied that the doctrine truly operated in "bourgeois" states and found it inappropriate for a Soviet-type system. A 1965 Soviet source stated that in spite of the delineation of a separation of powers in some Western constitutions, "in practice the principle has been realized in no bourgeois state, since every state amounts to a dictatorship of a particular class."[6] On the other hand, because all power in the Soviet Union was said to reside in popularly elected soviets, there could be no separation of powers: "The theory and practice of the socialist state system . . . proceeds from the principle of the full power of the people (the workers), carried out by the representative organs of the people."[7] Moreover, separation of powers was rejected on more basic ideological grounds. As another source put it, "Marxist-Leninist theory rejects the separation of powers as ignoring the class nature of the state."[8]

By the 1970s, Soviet spokesmen were allowing that a kind of division of labor between the representative bodies and the administrative bodies existed. But they staunchly denied that this had anything in common with the "notorious" separation of powers.[9]

With the changes in state structure in the *perestroika* period, however, the rejection of separation of powers became less defensible. Soviet jurists and others began mentioning the doctrine in favorable terms. Gorbachev even allowed himself to advocate a "separation of functions" (though he was speaking here of a separation between party and state activities) and, in discussing broad powers for the Constitutional Supervision Committee and ten-year terms for its members, he remarked that "we are creating our own socialist system of 'checks and balances.' "[10] Western analysts saw in the constitutional amendments of the late 1980s the beginnings of the introduction of separation of powers.[11]

This has been important for the institutions being examined in this chapter. It has meant not just long terms in office for members of the Constitutional Supervision Committee, but also a sense that their decisions, even though they were technically recommendations to the legislature, would carry weight. And when the Russian Federation took the further step of creating a true constitutional court, its members were given unlimited terms and its decisions were made final and unappealable. Thus, although the principle of separation of powers may not yet have been fully achieved, some of its features have provided the Constitutional Court sufficient protection to allow it to be an independent force in law and politics.

Constitutional Change and Supervision: The USSR Supreme Court in the 1920s

Until the creation of the Constitutional Supervision Committee in 1989, the principal institution for making judgments on the constitutionality of the acts of state organs was the parliament. This was true under the constitutions of 1918, 1924, 1936, and 1977.[12] The only partial exception to this arrangement occurred during the 1920s, when the USSR Supreme Court was given a limited right to advise parliament as to the constitutionality of certain acts. Under the 1924 Constitution and the 1929 Law on the Supreme Court, the court, at the request of the presidium of the USSR Central Executive Committee, was charged with providing opinions on the constitutionality of acts of the legislative bodies of the union republics and of the government of the USSR (the Council of People's Commissars). These opinions were strictly advisory, and Soviet sources differ in their assessments of the significance of this function.[13] Whatever its importance, the Supreme Court's advisory role did not last long. After the early 1930s, the court was seldom called upon for this function because, according to Soviet sources, the growth of the cult of personality made constitutional control and supervision irrelevant.[14] The 1936 Constitution eliminated the Supreme Court's role in this area, a position which the 1977 Constitution did not change.

The Constitutional Supervision Committee

As early as the 1970s, a number of Soviet jurists had cautiously put forward the idea of an independent agency of constitutional review. Only at the end of the 1980s, however, were conditions right for a proposal of this kind to succeed. What was then established was not a true judicial body but a committee loosely attached to the parliament.

Although the basis for the Constitutional Supervision Committee was established by constitutional amendments at the end of 1988, its actual creation was delayed for more than a year by a variety of political problems.[15] When it finally was established at the end of 1989, the committee's powers were somewhat restricted by further constitutional amendments. Under the law of December 23, 1989, the Constitutional Supervision Committee was to be composed of "specialists in the field of politics and law."[16] It addition to a chairman and a deputy chairman, it was to have twenty-five members, whose numbers would include one person representing each union republic. Several republics refused to participate, however, and so the committee never reached its intended number. Members were chosen by the Congress of People's Deputies for ten-year terms, arranged so that half the members would be replaced every five years.

The committee's jurisdiction was limited to normative acts of various kinds—draft laws and laws of the USSR, the constitutions and laws of the union republics, and other acts of general application such as decrees of the Council of Ministers or acts of individual ministries. The committee could not rule on particular cases and thus did not have a true judicial function. A conclusion of the committee that an act was not in conformity with the USSR Constitution or USSR laws led to that act's immediate suspension (only laws adopted by the USSR Congress of People's Deputies were exempted from this provision). The agency in question was then to bring the act into conformity with the Constitution or law, and, if it failed to do so within a specified period of time, the committee could take the matter to the Congress of People's Deputies. The Congress could reject the committee's conclusion only by a two-thirds vote of its total membership.[17] Those who favored a stronger constitutional review process were disappointed at the narrowness of the committee's charge and the cumbersome nature of its procedures.[18]

The committee's function was further weakened by protests from the republics. Several union republics saw the creation of the committee as a means to limit their sovereignty and objected strenuously to its operation. Therefore, a compromise was reached that removed the committee's jurisdiction over republican constitutions and other acts, except for provisions that affected the basic rights and freedoms of citizens. This compromise was written into a resolution accompanying the Law on the Constitutional Supervision Committee.[19]

In spite of these restrictions, the Constitutional Supervision Committee was an active body during the year and a half of its actual existence.[20] It reviewed a significant number of legal acts[21] and managed to capture a great deal of attention in the Soviet press and among the legal community, both at home and abroad. That it received such attention is not surprising: it was a new institution, of a kind that the Soviet Union had not had before; it seemed to have the potential for checking the exercise of improper official power, something that had been lacking in Soviet law and politics in the past; though not a court (although its chairman and others had urged almost from the start that it be transformed into a true court), it held out the promise of developing into a "third force" (*tret'ia vlast'*) that could mediate between the legislature and the executive branches in a newly popular separation-of-powers system. Moreover, it gained public notice because its members, and particularly its chairman, S.S. Alekseev, seemed always ready to thrust the committee and themselves into the public eye through interviews and other public statements. At least one Western analyst has criticized this behavior, particularly when it involved comments on matters pending before the committee.[22]

The decisions of the committee are a matter of record and have been examined by numerous analysts.[23] While judgments on its work vary, the committee has been given high marks for its decisions on individual and political rights. Its important rulings in this area included the invalidation of the practice of issuing secret legislation affecting citizens' rights;[24] a ruling that the restrictions on the freedom of movement and choice growing out of the legal provisions concerning residence permits (*propiski*) violated the Constitution and international human rights treaties;[25] an injunction as contrary to the Constitution against the President's decree regulating demonstrations in downtown Moscow;[26] a ruling that the compulsory treatment of alcoholics and drug addicts violated the Constitution and human rights treaties;[27] and a ruling that ministry decrees limiting ministry liability for the production of substandard goods violated consumer rights.[28]

On the other hand, some of its decisions, particularly those having to do with center–republic relations, were not greeted with such enthusiasm. For instance, when the Russian Republic adopted a law prohibiting the heads of government agencies from holding more than one position, either in government or in a social organization, President Gorbachev asked the committee to review the law. Its intent was clearly to prevent any Communist Party official from holding more than one high government position at the same time. With one dissent, the committee ruled that the law infringed the constitutional rights of governmental officials and social organization members.[29] In a second controversial opinion, the committee struck down laws of the Baltic republics and Moldova that sought to rescind the USSR regulations that gave military personnel preferred status in the acquisition of housing.[30] There was also a dissenting opinion in this case, and it is important to note that these were the only two dissents in the corpus of committee decisions.

Thrust into this highly charged atmosphere of the center trying to preserve its position and the republics seeking greater autonomy or even independence, the committee sided with the center. This no doubt damaged its credibility in some circles, as critics have asserted. But it is perhaps too much to expect, under the circumstances of the time, that the committee would have acted differently.

Further criticism of the committee focused on its lack of carefully reasoned opinions and the fact that a number of its decisions remained essentially unexecuted.[31] And, certainly, its attempt to demonstrate neutrality was damaged when its members spoke out on important political issues that were not before the committee (e.g., Chairman Alekseev's statement that it would be unconstitutional for certain republics not to participate in the March 1991 referendum on the preservation of the Union).[32] Finally, the committee's failure to take a strong stand at the time of the coup in August 1991 made it appear cowardly and ineffectual. No matter what after-the-fact rationalizations it made, its members had not shown the courage that many others had in opposing the unconstitutional acts of the coup plotters.[33]

How should one assess the record of the Constitutional Supervision Committee? Aside from its behavior during the coup, it is my belief that its work, on balance, rates a positive judgment. If its opinions were not well-reasoned, they were certainly a considerable advance over the boiler-plate decisions handed down for so long by Soviet judges. If the committee favored the union over the republics, this is more or less to be expected from a union-level body whose instincts would naturally be in that direction.[34] That some of its decisions went unimplemented and unenforced is hardly the fault of the committee. Judicial and judicial-type bodies often lack means for enforcing decisions and depend on the executive for this function. In the history of the United States, there are numerous examples of executive reluctance or refusal to enforce judicial orders. And, as will be shown below, the new Russian Constitutional Court has already faced one such situation in its short life.

Finally, it is certainly true that independent statements by committee members, outside the confines of the committee, carry considerable risk. They can suggest bias or prejudice, impairing the credibility of the body. Some of Chairman Alekseev's statements clearly fell into this category, and as a long-time jurist he should have known better. At the same time, members of judicial-type bodies may be able to use the prestige of their office to achieve positive ends with out-of-court statements. Needless to say, such statements need to be made with the appearance of scrupulous fairness. As will be discussed below, Russian Constitutional Court Chairman Zor'kin has made several such statements.

In sum, my assessment is to some extent in line with the view of former Committee Vice Chairman B.M. Lazarev, that critics of the committee had unreasonable expectations regarding its accomplishments.[35] Lazarev was referring largely to the legal limitations on the committee's jurisdiction. In addition, however, it is worth recalling that the creation of the Constitutional Supervision Committee was the first effort of its kind after seven decades of relentless insistence that an independent body of constitutional review not only was unnecessary but was downright alien to the Soviet system. Given this atmosphere, it is no wonder that the committee did not get it right the first time.

The several drafts of the treaty for a renewed union provided for a constitutional court to replace the Constitutional Supervision Committee. As noted above, Committee Chairman Alekseev and others had advocated the creation of a constitutional court for some time. This matter soon became a moot point, but even before the USSR's demise, the Russian Republic had decided to create its own constitutional court.

The Russian Constitutional Court

Origin and Legal Basis

The constitutional basis for the Constitutional Court of the Russian Republic was established by an amendment to the RSFSR Constitution of December 15, 1990.

The provisions of the amendment are extremely brief, leaving the essentials regarding the court's composition and operation to enabling legislation.[36]

Political disagreements delayed the adoption of the Law on the Constitutional Court until August 1991.[37] This detailed document, running to eighty-nine articles, is the legal basis for the court's present operation. Even with this law in place, however, it is clear that the debate over the Constitutional Court's role and powers is not yet settled. All the drafts of the Constitution of the Russian Republic so far published have contained much more detailed provisions on the Constitutional Court than are to be found in the existing Constitution, and these provisions have varied considerably from one draft to another.

The Law on the Constitutional Court is hardly a model of legislative drafting. Long and seemingly haphazardly organized, it contains some provisions that would appear appropriate for the internal documents of a court (e.g., how security for the court and the protection of its members are handled, in Article 86) and some that, in other countries at least, would seem so obvious that they would require no spelling out in a legislative act (e.g., that the expenses of the court are financed from the republic budget, in Article 85). That such seemingly petty details have been included in a parliamentary enactment perhaps testifies to the drafters' lack of experience in creating a law of this kind. More likely, it signals their effort to anticipate and overcome possible attempts to dilute the court's authority.

Under the act, the Constitutional Court has wide power to review international treaties as well as domestic normative acts (as adopted by, e.g., the parliament, the president, the Council of Ministers) and to suspend them, if they are found to be contrary to the Constitution. It is also authorized to review acts based on the application of the law, including those against individuals, and to declare such acts in violation of the Constitution. Decisions of the Constitutional Court on these questions are final and not subject to appeal or protest. In addition, the court is provided the authority to issue conclusions (*zakliucheniia*) on whether official acts conform to the Constitution. Although these conclusions can be rendered on a variety of issues, their main purpose, apparently, is to provide the court's opinion on the legality of the removal of high state officials such as the president.[38]

Article 1.2.3 of the law provides that the court "does not review political questions." Although the apparent intent of the drafters (to keep the court from becoming embroiled in petty political squabbles) is both understandable and reasonable, it is unlikely that this provision by itself will assure that end. By their nature, courts—especially constitutional courts—are inevitably faced with questions freighted with political significance. In the American legal system, no notable success has been made in delineating "political questions" from other legal questions, although courts have sometimes used the political-question doctrine to avoid reviewing cases.[39] In a like way, the Russian Constitutional Court might employ the provision to avoid rendering a decision. In this sense, the prohibition on reviewing political questions could be seen as increasing the court's discretion rather than, as some have suggested, restricting its authority.[40]

Under the law, the Constitutional Court is to consist of fifteen judges chosen by the Congress of People's Deputies. A candidate must be between the ages of thirty-five and sixty and is expected both to have extensive legal knowledge and to have worked at least ten years in the law. To enhance their independence, judges serve unlimited terms but cannot serve beyond age sixty-five. They are unremovable unless the size of the court is reduced by law, in which case they continue to receive full pay. On the other hand, a judge may be suspended from duty by a ruling of the Constitutional Court for any of a long list of reasons, including poor health, continued absence from court sessions, activities incompatible with a judge's position, and expressing of an opinion to the media on a pending case. A judge may lose his or her position on the court, also by a ruling of the Constitutional Court, not only upon reaching the age of sixty-five or by voluntarily retiring, but also for incapacity based on a court ruling or as a result of a legally valid court sentence against him or her.

The Court in Operation

The Russian Constitutional Court got off to a slow start. In August 1991, thirteen of the fifteen judges were named. The Congress was unable to agree on the last two appointees, who were to be chosen at its next session, and more than a year and a half later, the final two members still had not been named. But the law allows the court to commence work with two-thirds of its members present, and near the end of 1991, almost a year after the constitutional provision creating the court had been adopted, the thirteen judges had been sworn in and had chosen Valerii D. Zor'kin as their chairman.

The activity of the Russian Constitutional Court, in the public mind and in fact, has been dominated by the "Communist Party case." In terms of the court's establishing its own self-confidence and its reputation as a sound and respected institution, it is unfortunate that this difficult case came so early in its life. On the other hand, the publicity associated with this sensational case certainly focused public attention on the court, establishing the presence and importance of this new institution within the context of an evolving tripartite governmental system. The Communist Party case was accepted by the court only several months after it commenced operation. But even by that time, the court had rendered decisions on several important matters and had made efforts to demonstrate its presence in other, not strictly judicial, ways. This latter practice has continued even after the Communist Party decision and constitutes one of the interesting and largely unanticipated activities of the court.

Aside from the Communist Party case, certainly the most important decision of the court to date is one that went against President Yeltsin. In its first decision, in January 1992, it declared unconstitutional the president's edict that ordered the merging of the ministries of security and internal affairs. The court asserted that this was a violation of the principle of separation of powers, since the executive cannot create ministries or reorganize the executive branch.[41]

Apart from the decision itself, the case is notable for several other reasons. Prior to the decision, Chairman Zor'kin made more than one statement to journalists, to the effect that the president's edict was unconstitutional.[42] After the decision, Sergei Shakhrai, who had argued the president's case before the court, made statements implying that the executive branch might resist the decision's implementation.[43] Court Chairman Zor'kin then took his case to the public, through the press and in a televised session of the Supreme Soviet, at which Shakhrai also spoke.[44] In the end, Yeltsin canceled his edict and abided by the decision, but Zor'kin's off-the-bench comments showed how unsure he was of the court's authority. This behavior may be understandable for a new institution, particularly in connection with its first decision. The continued practice of extra-judicial commentary by court members, particularly Zor'kin, suggests a lingering doubt that the court has gained the respect of the other state organs.

More than two weeks after this case had been decided, the court issued a related decision having to do with the behavior of the newspaper *Rossiiskaia gazeta*. In the view of the court, the newspaper's coverage of the case seemed to suggest that, even after the court's decision, the president's edict was still in effect. The court issued a summons to its editor-in-chief, V.A. Logunov, to explain the newspaper's behavior. When Logunov did not appear, it handed down a decision fining him 500 rubles for disrespect to the court and ordering publication of *this* decision in *Rossiiskaia gazeta*.[45] The particular sensitivity of the court, its concern for establishing its authority, led it to seek to control the behavior of the press. By pushing the matter to the point it did, however, it also demonstrated its vulnerability as an institution.

Among other important decisions of the Constitutional Court were several in which it ruled against the activities of parliament. In the principal one of these, the court declared unconstitutional a law by which the parliament attempted to take over from the executive the functions of the State Committee on Competition and Antimonopoly Policies. The court ruled that these were functions of the executive branch. It took the occasion of handing down the decision to warn the president concerning delays in signing bills sent from the legislature.[46]

In addition to playing a mediating role between the executive branch and parliament, the court has rendered a number of decisions in another area, that of hearing complaints from individuals about violations of constitutional rights.[47] But it discovered the limits of its effectiveness in attempting to assert itself in the knotty area of federal relations. When Tatarstan decided to hold a referendum in March 1992 on the republic's independence, the Russian parliament asked the Constitutional Court to rule on the constitutionality of the referendum as well as on some earlier acts of Tatarstan that had pointed in the direction of independence. The court pronounced that key parts of the referendum, and of other documents adopted by the republic, were unconstitutional. Chairman Zor'kin went on television to explain the court's decision the same day that it was handed down, and later made further tough statements against the referendum and Tatarstan's subsequent actions.[48] Parliament issued a strong resolution urging President Yeltsin to enforce the court's ruling, stating that the results of the referendum would have no legal force. Yeltsin appealed to the Tatarstan parliament not to hold the referendum; then, when it was clear that it would take place, he urged voters to cast "no" votes. But he did not move to enforce the court's order or to keep the referendum from taking place. The vote in favor of statehood and independence won easily in heavy voting. Although Zor'kin spoke after the referendum about the possibility of impeachment and criminal charges being brought against Tatarstan leaders, in the end nothing was done—except to the prestige and authority of the Constitutional Court, the Russian parliament, and the Russian president.[49]

The Communist Party Case

The origin and legal basis of this "case of the century" are simple enough to describe—and are nearly the only simple matters connected with it. Thirty-six people's deputies of the RSFSR, most from the "Communists of Russia" faction of the parliament, petitioned the Constitutional Court in mid-November 1991 to declare unconstitutional three of President Yeltsin's edicts—that of August 23, 1991, suspending the activity of the RSFSR Communist Party; that of August 25, 1991, freezing the assets of the Russian and USSR communist parties; and that of November 6, 1991, banning these parties on RSFSR territory and seizing their assets. Before the initial hearings on this matter, the liberal deputy O.G. Rumiantsev and others submitted a petition, which amounted to a countersuit, asking the court to declare the Russian and USSR communist parties to be unconstitutional bodies. The court decided to combine the two petitions in a single case, and with that decision a highly political issue became even more politicized. Could the court have declined to hear the case on the basis of Article 1.2.3 of the Law on the Constitutional Court ("The Constitutional Court of the Russian Federation does not review political questions")? No evidence indicates that the court seriously considered this option, and, given the weightiness of the matters at issue, perhaps backing away from the case on this ground would have been an unacceptable alternative. But it is hard to conceive of a set of circumstances that would be more appropriate for the application of Article 1.2.3.

To a reasonable extent, the proceedings themselves were conducted as if the issues were truly legal rather than political, although some lapses from normal judicial decorum certainly took place.[50] But the reality of the political nature of the proceedings was lost on no one, and the behavior of participants in court, down to the seating arrangements in the gallery (communist supporters on the right, behind the party lawyers' bench, Yeltsin supporters or those holding neutral views on the left, behind the president's lawyers) reflected this understanding.[51] Rather than elaborate on the proceedings and the mass of evidence and expert testimony, this account will provide a short summary of the proceedings and concentrate on the decision itself.

The Communist Party case was of truly epic proportions, particularly in the context of recent Russian and Soviet court proceedings. From the original petitions until the decision was handed down, about twelve and a half months elapsed. The court sessions themselves were spread over five months. Fifty-two sessions were held, and forty-six witnesses were called, including some of the most significant personages of the former Soviet regime, such as Egor Ligachev, Nikolai Ryzhkov, and Aleksandr Yakovlev. Numerous experts gave testimony, and a mountain of documentary evidence, some of it obtained from secret Communist Party archives, was introduced.[52] The volume of evidence is made more impressive by a ruling that limited admissible documents to those from the period after March 14, 1990—the date of the repeal of Article 6 of the USSR Constitution. It is no wonder that the court needed several recesses—one for six weeks—to sort out the mass of data presented (and probably also to lower the tension level of the proceedings).

In the early stages of the proceedings, the court indicated its desire that Mikhail Gorbachev be called as a witness. But when Gorbachev expressed his reluctance to do so, the court "silently agreed" not to call him (the quoted words are those of Constitutional Court Judge Nikolai Vedernikov).[53] But after the late summer recess, the court determined that it was necessary to hear from Gorbachev and it issued a summons for him to appear. Thereby ensued a spectacular subplot to the trial. It provided renewed grounds for the Gorbachev–Yeltsin rivalry and temporarily diverted attention from the trial itself. Gorbachev refused to appear and was eventually fined by the court and prohibited from traveling abroad until he obeyed the summons. In response to Gorbachev's adamant stand, President Yeltsin ordered the takeover of the premises of the Gorbachev Foundation and of a country retreat that had been given to the foundation. Gorbachev countered by calling the hearing a "show trial" and characterizing himself as a "refusenik." At first he was denied permission to travel to Germany for the funeral of Willie Brandt, but finally, with negative world public opinion mounting and at the suggestion of President Yeltsin, the court gave its permission.

During the whole controversy, the Constitutional Court, through its press service, was issuing statements explaining why Gorbachev must testify. After Gorbachev's return from abroad, the court decided to stop trying to compel his appearance. But Chairman Zor'kin made a number of statements to the press and on television about Gorbachev, asserting, among other things, that he was acting "in the old totalitarian tradition" and that he had "virtually signed his own death sentence as a politician." He also stated that Gorbachev had "concealed much from the people" in connection with the Katyn affair (Polish military officers murdered in western Russia in the early 1940s). In reply, Gorbachev asked for television time to answer Zor'kin's statements. His characterization of Zor'kin's behavior bears quoting. Zor'kin's commentary, he said, "in itself represents not only a blatant violation of the ethics of legal proceedings, but also testifies to political excess, bears the imprint of political pressure, and thereby places the objectivity and independence of the chairman of the Constitutional Court under doubt."[54]

By the time the brouhaha over Gorbachev's testimony had trailed off to an indecisive conclusion, the Constitutional Court had nearly finished its proceedings. It soon retired for deliberations, with the announcement of its decision about a month away. When the decision was released, on the eve of an important meeting of the Congress of People's Deputies, it turned out to be a decidedly mixed result, amounting to neither complete victory nor complete defeat for either side.

The court's opinion was divided into five parts—the first three on the three Yeltsin edicts, the fourth on the constitutionality of the CPSU and the CP-RSFSR, and the fifth on several other relevant points.[55] The rulings on each of the president's edicts are multifaceted; what follows is a distillation of their major points. On the edict of August 23, 1991, which had suspended the activity of the Russian Communist Party, turned over its property to state agencies, and frozen its monetary resources, the court found the actions of the president to be in accordance with the Constitution. On the August 25 edict, nationalizing the property of the CPSU and the CP-RSFSR, the court adjudged the president's act unconstitutional. In terms of the import of this ruling, the court indicated later in its opinion that property matters such as these "may be resolved on general principles in accordance with legal procedure," that is, through the regular courts. Regarding the edict of November 6, the court ruled that banning the activity of the Communist Party in the Russian republic, as far as it applied to the leadership structures of the party, was in conformity with the Constitution. But it held that the primary organizations of the Russian Communist Party that were set up in local territories and did not operate as state structures should not have been banned.

On the question of the constitutionality of the CPSU and the CP-RSFSR (the issue the Yeltsin side asked the court to rule on), the court stated in Part IV of the opinion that since the CPSU had basically collapsed by September 1991, and the CP-RSFSR was not organized as an independent political party by that time, there was no need to rule on the issue. The last part of the opinion stated that the court's ruling went into effect immediately, was final, and was not subject to appeal; it noted, as indicated above, that the property issues reviewed should be resolved by the regular courts; and it provided instructions for publishing the court's opinion.

To sum up the major points in the decision:

1. Under the Constitution, the president was justified in suspending and then banning Communist Party activity. Although several articles of the Constitution were cited with regard to these rulings, the court made no effort to explain the reasoning by which it reached its conclusions.

2. Banning the territorial primary party organizations was unconstitutional. In connection with this assertion, the court hinted at the justification for banning the higher party organs. It stated that the primary territorial organizations "retained their social nature and were not changed into state structures." The court thus seemed, by implication, to embrace the primary assertion of the president's side: that the higher party organs *were* ruling state structures and did not constitute a real political party or association. Thus, under law, this part of the party could be banned. But one needs to strain to reach this conclusion, which the court never spelled out.

3. The taking of party property was unconstitutional, but such property would not thereby be automatically returned to the party. Return would have to be sought through the regular legal process. As many commentators have pointed out, not only is this a process that could take considerable time, but there is also a fundamental question as to whom such property might be returned. The old Communist Party is gone and several splinter parties have risen in its place.

4. Since the Communist Party in effect collapsed during the last part of 1991, the issue of its constitutionality had become moot.

It should be noted that two judges, Luchin and Ebzeev, dissented from the decision of the court and wrote separate opinions. Judge Luchin, at a press conference on the evening the decision was announced, set out the reasons for his dissent. The biggest problem with "the court's flawed, reprehensible decision," he said, is that the edicts that formed the basis of the case "were issued by an inappropriate person. The president did not have the right to issue those decrees." Luchin also opposed the combining into one case the petitions of the opposing sides, which he characterized as "judicial nonsense." In his dissent, he returned again and again to the political nature of the decision (e.g., "We acted not as legal experts but as politicians . . .").[56]

And this, to the author, is the key element of the case: If the nature of a case is basically political rather than legal, it will be extremely difficult for a court to render a decision that is well-grounded in law. Given what it had to work with, it is not surprising that the Constitutional Court's ruling was seen by commentators from all sides as basically political.[57] We commented above on the lack of reasoned explanations in the court's opinion, but no doubt this was at least in part deliberate: attempting to explain the court's reasoning would have politicized the decision even further.[58]

The decision was also widely seen as a compromise, a characterization that is hard to disagree with. Both sides got something and neither was confronted with the kind of complete defeat that might have caused great public uproar. As Otto

Latsis put it in *Izvestiia*, the court disarmed a political land mine of unpredictable force.[59] And judging from the overall response to the decision since it has been handed down, the Constitutional Court emerged from this difficult case with its credibility largely intact.

In conclusion, then, the decision was not an elegant one and it did little to advance the purely legal aspects of Russian constitutional law. But it did allow the political system to extract itself from an extremely difficult situation. "Hard cases make bad law"—so goes the old American legal aphorism. But in this instance it made good politics.

Off-the-Bench Behavior of Court Members

As *Izvestiia* noted, Constitutional Court Chairman Zor'kin gave an interview to a group of journalists "almost immediately after the decision was announced" in the Communist Party case.[60] As indicated above, dissenting Judge Luchin did the same. And Zor'kin's vigorous criticism of Gorbachev for refusing to testify, even as that issue was pending, has been reviewed earlier. These were not isolated incidents. Several instances of Zor'kin's commenting on cases, either pending or recently decided, have been noted in this chapter. The same penchant for extrajudicial commentary was seen with regard to USSR Constitutional Supervision Committee Chairman Alekseev. Should it be concluded, therefore, that such behavior is considered acceptable? At least with regard to commentary on pending matters, this does not appear to be the case. Gorbachev's comment in this regard, that Zor'kin's criticism of his refusal to testify violated judicial ethics and cast doubt on Zor'kin's ability to make an objective judgment, has already been noted. At least one Russian lawyer has publicly expressed the same view, quoting Zor'kin himself to show that the court's chairman fully realized the import of his extrajudicial remarks: "Maybe I'm breaking the law by revealing these cogitations of mine, so to speak, ... but I am leaning more and more toward the idea that, for all practical purposes, Gorbachev in the capacity he now occupies is becoming unnecessary to Russia."[61] It is hard to disagree with Zor'kin about the questionable legality of his behavior.

Article 20.3 of the Law on the Constitutional Court states: "A judge of the Constitutional Court of the Russian Republic does not have the right anywhere except at a session of the Constitutional Court of the Russian Republic to voice publicly his opinion on a question under review or accepted for review by the Constitutional Court of the Russian Republic before the adoption of a ruling by it on this question." As noted above, violation of this provision constitutes grounds for a judge's suspension. There can be little doubt, then, about the impropriety of Zor'kin's comments in such instances.

Two other kinds of off-the-bench behavior by Constitutional Court judges also merit mention. One is the public comment or statement *after* the decision has been issued and the other is the more general statement or activity having to do with affairs of the day not connected with a case before the court. As noted in the course of this analysis, postdecision statements to the press have been frequently made by Zor'kin. These might be interpreted as being designed to educate the public. On occasion they appear intended to apply pressure to other branches of the government, to assure that the court's decision will be implemented. Nothing in the law appears to prohibit such statements. Since talking with the press has become a routine activity with Zor'kin, it may be that it is now an accepted part of the chairman's role. In this early period of the court's existence, when it is trying to establish its authority and legitimacy, this function may well be justified. In the long run, however, prudence might suggest a more retiring role for the court and its chairman.

Of a completely different nature are extrajudicial actions on matters not before the court. At the time of the signing of the Federation Treaty in April 1992 Zor'kin found it appropriate to speak out about his concerns.[62] In June 1992, the Constitutional Court issued a statement (zaiavlenie) on what it called a "threat to the constitutional structure" of the state which it saw growing out of a number of problems facing the country.[63] This was followed by a television appearance by Zor'kin which expanded on the court's statement.[64]

But Zor'kin's most visible activity to date has been in connection with the controversy between the parliament and the executive branch at the end of 1992. Zor'kin made a widely praised speech at the beginning of the Seventh Congress of People's Deputies in which he appealed to the two sides to find a way out of the crisis.[65] Shortly thereafter, he published an article in Moscow News expanding on his speech before the congress. In it, he warned that "the Constitutional Court will not stand aloof watching how constitutional order in this country is perishing. In the last resort the court will call individual officials to account."[66] When the situation worsened and President Yeltsin threatened to call for a referendum to allow the public to decide between the president and the congress, Zor'kin stepped in and brokered an agreement between the two sides. He arranged and participated in consultations between Yeltsin and parliament speaker Khasbulatov, the result of which was a decree adopted by the congress that provided a compromise on a number of issues and called for a national referendum in April 1993 on the basic provisions of a new constitution.[67]

The immediate reaction to Zor'kin's intervention seemed to be generally positive. But it was not long before it began to be questioned. Although Zor'kin appeared to have acted alone, he claimed to have consulted daily with other Constitutional Court members, and that the positions he took were, in effect, those of the court.[68] If this is the case, then the Constitutional Court as an institution was involved in this very political controversy. Questions can be raised as to both the propriety and the wisdom of taking this role. On the first, there appears to be nothing in the Law on the Constitutional Court that permits this *judicial* body to engage in political bargaining of this kind. Zor'kin has tried to expand the court's mission by after-the-fact rationalizations,[69] but if the court is to undertake this kind of role it seems reasonable that it be written into the law. Would it be wise to expand the court's functions in this way? Probably not. Keeping the judiciary apart from the political fray is, in the long run, one of the most important guarantees of its continued authority and legitimacy.

One can understand why, in a critical situation such as the December crisis, the court would not want to be accused of the kind of timidity that characterized the USSR Constitutional Supervision Committee during the August 1991 coup. But in overstepping the bounds of its legal authority, the court may have damaged its credibility for the strictly judicial role that it will be called on to play in the future. Serge Schmemann has captured the nub of the long-term–short-term problem with the following comment made at the time of the December crisis: "It can be argued that a Chief Justice should not plunge into the heart of a political struggle between other branches of government. But that is in lands with an established sense of legality."[70] Let us hope that the times are not frequent when the Russian chief justice feels the need to attempt a repeat performance.

Conclusion

The success of the fledgling Russian democracy will not depend upon the existence or nonexistence of a constitutional court. There are a number of other features of democratic systems that Russia lacks, or is only beginning to acquire, that are of greater near-term importance.[71] But among the conditions required for the operation of a democratic system is a mechanism that provides genuine protection of constitutional rights and a means for preventing any authority, most particularly state agencies, from acquiring power beyond their constitutional mandate. As this essay has shown, the frozen authoritarianism of seven decades of Soviet rule precluded the development of institutions that could perform these tasks.

The USSR Constitutional Supervision Committee, though flawed in structure and hampered in its operation by the problems of the country and its ideological ties to the past, was a promising institution in many ways. It faced frankly a number of issues that confronted it and handed down some decisions that, for the time, showed considerable courage. While its critics found great fault with it, its accomplishments suggest, to this analyst at least, that with time and under the right conditions, it might have developed into an effective institution. In looking back at the dismal record of Soviet political institutions, the Constitutional Supervision Committee stands out for the positive contributions it made.

The Russian Constitutional Court has the advantage over the USSR Constitutional Supervision Committee of being a genuine judicial body that can render final and unappealable rulings. If the record of the first year of the court is a mixed one, there are, nevertheless, numerous bright spots. It has shown itself capable of both protecting individual rights and curbing excessive governmental power, considerable accomplishments in themselves.

Critics need to understand that new institutions, particularly judicial ones, with neither a tradition of independence nor a political constituency to provide support, face significant obstacles. The French Constitutional Council began as a rather docile body easily dominated by President Charles de Gaulle. Over the years, however, it has developed—in the words of one who has examined its work—into "a central player in the governing process of France."[72] It is not beyond possibility that Russia's Constitutional Court could come to occupy a similar place in the Russian system.

What is required to bring this about is for Russia to develop the other aspects of its political-social system that are generally associated with democratization. Western governments that seek to help this process through contributions to the development of the Russian economy and in other ways should understand that in creating the Constitutional Court, Russia has developed a bulwark against authoritarianism that has never before existed in its history.

Notes

1. The author is indebted to Aryeh L. Unger for these terms. See *Constitutional Development in the USSR* (London: Methuen, 1981), p. 1. Unger quotes Brezhnev as saying in 1977: "We have not created the Constitution as a stage prop." "Power map" is a term used by Ivo Duchacek to describe constitutions in his book *Power Maps: Comparative Politics of Constitutions* (Santa Barbara, CA: ABC-Clio, 1973).

2. Tibor Szamuely, "Five Years After Khrushchev," *Survey* 72 (Summer 1969), pp. 59–60.

3. Michael E. Urban, *More Power to the Soviets: The Democratic Revolution in the USSR* (Aldershot, England: Edward Elgar, 1990), p. 143.

4. *Moscow News* describes the 1992 Turkmen Constitution as tailor-made for the brand of authoritarianism practiced by President Niyazov, who also led the republic as leader of the Communist Party before the demise of the Soviet Union. *Moscow News*, 1992, no. 27, pp. 6–7.

5. See Herman Schwartz, "The New East European Constitutional Courts," *Michigan Journal of International Law*, vol. 13 (1992), p. 741.

6. *Entsiklopedicheskii slovar' pravovykh znanii* (Moscow: Sovetskaia entsiklopediia, 1965), p. 395.

7. Ibid.

8. *Iuridicheskii entsiklopedicheskii slovar'* (Moscow: Sovetskaia entsiklopediia, 1984), p. 313.

9. *Sovetskoe konstitutsionnoe pravo* (Leningrad: Leningrad University, 1975), p. 334. On this point see also Unger, *Constitutional Development*, pp. 94–95, 273.

10. *Izvestiia*, November 30, 1988, p. 1; *CDSP*, vol. 40, no. 48, pp. 6–7.

11. But not a fully developed system. Robert Sharlet referred to it as a "muted" separation of powers, "a work in progress." *Soviet Constitutional Crisis: From De-Stalinization to Disintegration* (Armonk, NY: M.E. Sharpe, 1992), pp. 94, 95. See also Stewart Goldman, "The New Soviet Legislative Branch," in Robert T. Huber and Donald R. Kelley, eds., *Perestroika-era Politics: The New Soviet Legislature and Gorbachev's Political Reforms* (Armonk, NY: M.E. Sharpe, 1991), p. 70.

12. Iu.L. Shul'zhenko, "K voprosu o sisteme organov konstitutsionnogo kontrol'ia v SSSR," *Sovremennyi konstitutsionalizm* (Moscow: Institute of State and Law, USSR Academy of Sciences, 1990), pp. 38–40.

13. After citing statistics on Supreme Court review of the constitutionality of state acts, N.F. Chistiakov concludes that "the activity of the Supreme Court in this field of constitutional supervision and control of legality had great significance and fully justified itself. This was temporary but extremely necessary work." *Verkhovnyi sud SSSR* (Moscow: Nauka, 1984), p. 26. B.N. Topornin, by contrast, states: "However, the participation of the USSR Supreme Court in carrying out constitutional control did not develop. On the one hand the Presidium of the Central Executive Committee sent them cases extremely rarely, and, on the other, the Court was more and more constricted in its initiatives." "Konstitutsionnyi kontrol': Idei i problemy realizatsii," *Teoriia prava: Novye idei*, issue 1 (Moscow: Institute of State and Law, USSR Academy of Sciences, 1991), p. 30.

14. Shul'zhenko, "K voprosu," p. 39; V.P. Kazimirchuk, "On Constitutional Supervision in the USSR," in W.E. Butler, ed., *Perestroika and the Rule of Law* (London: I.B. Tauris, 1991), p. 151.

15. On these problems and other matters connected with the establishment of the committee, see Herman Hausmaniger, "The Committee of Constitutional Supervision of the USSR," *Cornell International Law Journal*, vol. 23, no. 2 (1990), p. 287.

16. *Izvestiia*, December 26, 1989, p. 2; FBIS-SOV, February 7, 1990, p. 73.

17. For the details on overruling, depending on the legal act in question, see ibid., articles 19–22.

18. See the discussion in B.M. Lazarev, "Komitet konstitutsionnogo nadzora SSSR," *Gosudarstvo i pravo*, 1992, no. 5, p. 23.

19. *Izvestiia*, December 26, 1989, p. 2; FBIS-SOV, February 7, 1990, p. 70.

20. The committee held its first meeting on May 16, 1990. It disbanded on December 23, 1991.

21. Lazarev, "Komitet konstitutsionnogo nadzora," p. 24, says the committee "reviewed 29 questions." Alexander Blankenagel states that the committee "published 23 decisions." "Toward Constitutionalism in Russia," *East European Constitutional Review*, vol. 1, no. 2 (Summer 1992), p. 25.

22. Peter B. Maggs, "Enforcing the Bill of Rights in the Twilight of the Soviet Union," *University of Illinois Law Review*, 1991, no. 2, pp. 1052, 1063.

23. See, e.g., Blankenagel, "Toward Constitutionalism"; Lazarev, "Komitet konstitutsionnogo nadzora"; Maggs, "Enforcing the Bill of Rights"; Alexander V. Mishkin, "The Emergence of Constitutional Law in the Soviet Union," *New Outlook*, vol. 2, no. 2 (Spring 1991), p. 9.

24. *Vedomosti S''ezda Narodnykh Deputatov SSSR i Verkhovnogo Soveta SSSR* (hereinafter *Ved. SSSR*), 1990, no. 50, item 1080.

25. *Ved. SSSR*, 1990, no. 47, item 1004. And see the supplementary decision on this matter in ibid., 1991, no. 46, item 1307.

26. *Ved. SSSR*, 1990, no. 39, item 774.

27. *Ved. SSSR*, 1990, no. 47, item 1000.

28. *Ved. SSSR*, 1990, no. 47, item 1001.

29. *Ved. SSSR*, 1990, no. 47, item 1002.

30. *Ved. SSSR*, 1990, no. 47, item 1003.

31. Blankenagel, "Toward Constitutionalism," pp. 27–28; Mishkin, "Emergence of Constitutional Law," p. 11.

32. Mishkin, "Emergence of Constitutional Law," p. 14.

33. See the censored statement by the Constitutional Supervision Committee published in *Pravda*, August 20, 1991, p. 3; FBIS-SOV, August 28, 1991, p. 25; and Lazarev, "Komitet konstitutsionnogo nadzora," p. 25. For an assessment of the committee's behavior during the coup, including a review of its uncensored statement of August 20, see Maggs, "Enforcing the Bill of Rights," pp. 1059–61.

34. With regard to the events in Lithuania in January 1991, Committee Chairman Alekseev said shortly thereafter that the committee had no right to review the matter because what was at issue was not a normative act. But he made no secret of his personal view: "Everything that happened there occurred beyond the framework of law and beyond the framework of the Constitution. Whatever was committed by the Armed Forces and the so-called Committee on National Salvation stands outside the law." *Moscow News*, 1991, no. 4, p. 10.

35. Lazarev, "Komitet konstitutionnogo nadzora," p. 24.

36. Article 119 of the Constitution of the Russian Republic states that the Constitutional Court is chosen by the RSFSR Congress of People's Deputies, and that both the procedure for choosing the court and its activity will be defined by a law adopted by the congress. Article 165 adds that the Constitutional Court is the highest judicial organ of constitutional control in the Russian republic and that it consists of fifteen judges.

37. *Vedomosti S''ezda Narodnykh Deputatov i Verkhovnogo Soveta RSFSR* (hereinafter *Ved. R.F.*), 1991, no. 30, item 1017. An English translation may be found in FBIS-USR, September 10, 1991, p. 21.

38. This is the view of Constitutional Court Judge Ernest Ametistov as expressed in *Rossiiskaia gazeta*, April 27, 1992, p. 2; FBIS-USR, May 9, 1992, p. 19.

39. On this point, see Stephen D. Ford, *The American Legal System* (St. Paul, MN: West Publishing Company, 1970), chapter 5 on political questions, especially pp. 485–93.

40. See Carla Thorson, "RSFSR Forms Constitutional Court," *Radio Liberty Report on the USSR*, vol. 3, no. 51–52, p. 14.

41. *Izvestiia*, January 15, 1992, p. 1.

42. *Moskovskie novosti*, 1992, no. 1, p. 2; FBIS-SOV, January 8, 1992, p. 43; INTERFAX in English, December 26, 1991; FBIS-SOV, December 27, 1991, p. 39.

43. He stated that the court had made a political rather than legal decision and that the decision did not necessarily mean that the president's edict was invalid. "Vesti" newscast, January 15, 1992; FBIS-SOV, January 16, 1992, p. 39.

44. Moscow Russian Television Network, January 16, 1992; FBIS-SOV, January 21, 1992, p. 59; see also INTERFAX in English, January 15, 1992; FBIS-SOV, January 17, 1992, p. 37.

45. *Ved. R.F.*, 1992, no. 13, item 670.

46. *Ved. R.F.*, 1992, no. 27, item 1571.

47. See, e.g., the decision of June 22, 1992, on the complaint of several workers that they had been illegally discharged from their jobs. *Ved. R.F.*, 1992, no. 30, item 1809.

48. Moscow Russian Television Network, March 13, 1992; FBIS-SOV, March 16, 1992, p. 63; Ann Sheehy, "Tatarstan Asserts Its Sovereignty," *RFE/RL Research Report*, vol. 1, no. 14 (April 3, 1992), p. 1.

49. This review of events relies heavily on Sheehy, "Tatarstan."

50. One Communist people's deputy was banned from the court after an outburst in which he advocated the violent overthrow of the Russian government. Cited in Carla Thorson, "The Fate of the Communist Party of Russia," *RFE/RL Research Report*, vol. 1, no. 37 (September 18, 1992), p. 4. During the author's attendance at the court, a lawyer for the Yeltsin side had to be cautioned by the court for insulting remarks directed at his communist counterparts.

51. Some of these observations and others in the analysis of the case are based on the author's attendance at the October 12, 1992, session of the court and discussions of the case with a number of lawyers in Moscow.

52. Information in this paragraph is based in part on *Izvestiia*, December 1, 1992, p. 1.

53. Moscow Radio, July 23, 1992; FBIS-SOV, July 31, 1992, p. 8.

54. The account of the controversy over Gorbachev's summons to the Constitutional

Court is based largely on an FBIS-SOV supplement of October 23, 1992, "Constitutional Court on CPSU Legality." This supplement contains thirty-three articles or texts of broadcasts on the controversy, covering the period of October 7 to October 20, 1992. Also used was *The New York Times*, October 14, 1992, p. A7.

55. The text of the decision may be found in *Rossiiskaia gazeta*, December 16, 1992, p. 6; FBIS-SOV, December 30, 1992, p. 22.

56. *Nezavisimaia gazeta*, December 2, 1992, p. 2; *CDSP*, vol 44, no. 49, December 30, 1992, p. 12.

57. See, e.g., the set of analyses of the case collected in *CDSP*, vol. 44, no. 48, December 30, 1992, pp. 11–13.

58. Court Chairman Zor'kin hinted at this shortly after the decision was announced when he said that the decision was "the fruit of compromise." *Izvestiia*, December 1, 1992, p. 2.

59. Ibid.

60. Ibid.

61. *Nezavisimaia gazeta*, October 27, 1992, p. 1; *CDSP*, vol. 44, no. 43 (1992), p. 26.

62. See *Nezavisimaia gazeta*, April 4, 1992, p. 1; FBIS-SOV, April 6, 1992, p. 37; Moscow Programma Radio Odin, April 3, 1992; FBIS-SOV, April 9, 1992, p. 34.

63. *Ved. R.F.*, 1992, no. 27, item 1572.

64. Television First Program Network, June 28, 1992; FBIS-SOV, June 29, 1992, p. 37.

65. *Rossiiskaia gazeta*, December 3, 1992, p. 6.

66. *Moscow News*, 1992, no. 50, p. 3.

67. See Zor'kin's December 12 speech to the Congress, outlining the provisions of the decree. Radio Rossii Network, FBIS-SOV, December 14, 1992, p. 4. Also see the text of the decree as adopted, *Rossiiskaia gazeta*, December 15, 1992, p. 1.

68. *Rossiiskaia gazeta*, December 31, 1992, p. 3.

69. In addition to his statement, quoted above, to the effect that the court would not stand by and watch the constitutional order of the country perish, he has been quoted as stating: "But an institution of authority such as the Constitutional Court is first of all the defender of the constitutional structure, the preserver of the powers and that which firmly supports them. If, in our view, they err, then we should help them as an intermediary and well-meaning participant." *Rossiiskaia gazeta*, December 31, 1992, p. 3.

70. *The New York Times*, December 13, 1992, sec. 4, p. 2.

71. The literature on the qualities associated with democratic systems is large. Two sources that discuss the matter and cite numerous relevant writings are Giuseppi Di Palma, *To Craft Democracies: An Essay on Democratic Transitions* (Berkeley, CA: University of California Press, 1990), esp. chapter 1, "Rethinking Some Hard Facts"; Barry Holden, *The Nature of Democracy* (New York: Barnes and Noble Books, 1974), esp. chapter 4, "The Necessary Conditions of Democracy."

72. F.L. Morton, "Judicial Activism in France," in Kenneth M. Holland, ed., *Judicial Activism in Comparative Perspective* (New York: St. Martin's Press, 1991), p. 133.

_____ 3

Conservative Politics in Russia:
Implications for U.S.-Russian Relations

Nicolai N. Petro

The failure of the coup of 1991 marked the end of the close relationship that has existed for nearly seventy years between the Soviet regime and portions of the Russian intelligentsia. In just three days in August, many conservative intellectuals saw a fundamental pillar of their faith in the regime dissolve—the idea that a communist regime was essential for the survival of the Russian nation. Since then, the search for a new set of values has been the principal task of the intelligentsia, and now, a little over a year later, we are beginning to see the contours around which a new consensus on the political right is emerging.

Much of the analysis of post-Soviet Russian politics has focused on the "radical democratic" wing of Russian politics which triumphed that August. In this paper, however, I examine the much lesser known (and consequently more greatly feared) conservative alternative to the radicals which also emerged strengthened and reinvigorated from the coup.

Russian Conservatives Before 1991

Western reporting has often confused stalwart Marxist-Leninists with more traditional Russian nationalists. In fact, however, the two have been not only quite distinct, but often opposed.[1] Marxist-Leninists typically identified their priority as loyalty to the party and to ideology. During *perestroika*, party diehards like Nina Andreeva and Egor Ligachev argued that true communists were above all loyal to the "ideals of the October Revolution." These ideals were exemplified not only by Lenin but also by Stalin, albeit with some excesses. This form of conservatism, as Darrell Hammer correctly notes, should be termed "modified Stalinism," since it defends not only the historical achievements of the Soviet regime made under Stalin, but also the brutal necessity of achieving them.

Today, this view is held by only a small handful of political organizations at the fringes of the Russian political spectrum. They include groups like the All-Union Communist Party–Bolsheviks (VKP[b]) founded by Nina Andreeva, and the All-Russian Communist Workers' Party (RKPR), headed by Viktor Anpilov, economist Andrei Sergeev, and former editor of the CPSU's journal of theory, *Kommunist*, Richard Kosolapov. The former is a throwback to the early Stalinist era of the party, its name intended to evoke nostalgia for that bygone era. It advertises 35,000 activists, although others place the total membership at less than one thousand.[2]

In March 1992, these groups formed to become Russian Labor *(Trudovaia Rossiia)*. In a frank acknowledgment of the unpopularity of anything that smacks of communism, this group has dropped any mention of its ideology in its name but still calls for reconstituting the USSR and opposing capitalism and the privatization of national resources (especially land). They hope to organize a multinational constituency of small communist cells that will force the present regime out of office and restore socialism as the country's guiding ideology.[3]

In August 1992, communist groups held their first unity conference but were unable to agree on principles for unifying. Nevertheless, this conference did create two standing bodies to coordinate their positions and organize joint activities. One of their major ambitions is to seek legal recognition for a Russian communist party, so that it can obtain the property and funds sequestered by the government when it abolished the CPSU.[4] Opinion polls show that only three to five percent of voters support Russian Labor, hence the prospects for the resurrection of the Communist Party within Russia to anything like its former status appears exceedingly remote, and little more needs to be said about communism in Russia for the foreseeable future.[5]

There is, however, a broader conservative revival under way in Russia which is associated with anticommunist Russian nationalism. Moderate Russian nationalism seems to be undergoing a renaissance in the aftermath of the coup attempt and the disintegration of the USSR and in concurrence with popular discontent over the decline in living standards. This may seem odd given the collapse of communism, but it highlights what many Western observers have tended to overlook—the uneasy relationship between Russian nationalism and communism, which *perestroika* finally exacerbated. These "traditionalists," as Nina Andreeva disparagingly termed Russian nationalists opposed to communist values, can be divided into two constituencies: National Bolsheviks and Russophiles.[6]

The designation "National Bolsheviks" was first used by political writer Peter B. Struve at the time of the Revolution to identify those who saw communism as the next, inevitable epoch in Russian history. Fearing that further civil war would only serve to weaken Russia, National Bolsheviks accepted the legitimacy of the new communist regime, justified its historical victory, and tried to work within the new system to transform its more cosmopolitan, antinational characteristics.

They hoped that the Bolshevik regime would eventually adopt the characteristics of a Russian national state.

An important reason for the sympathy evinced toward the Bolsheviks by many intellectuals who did not share their ultimate objectives was that, in their own way, the Bolsheviks had tapped into the desire of the intelligentsia for a healing of the rift between the populace and the intelligentsia that had become so pronounced after Peter the Great. In his essay on the origins of Russian communism, Russian religious philosopher Nikolai Berdiaev argued that the Bolsheviks' struggle for total control coincided with the Russian intelligentsia's striving for wholeness. He argued that in bringing down the old "consecrated" Russian empire the Bolsheviks had created "an inverted theocracy" whose style approached that of Slavophilism.[7]

When he wrote this essay in 1937, Berdiaev was criticized for justifying the Bolshevik coup, but he is quite correct in identifying an important reason for the residue of support the regime maintained throughout its existence: in its efforts to transform society it could claim to be uniting society behind a unitary national-religious concept. Though the Bolsheviks openly disparaged many traditional Russian values, considering them subversive to their ultimate purpose of creating a "new Soviet man," many both in the Soviet Union and abroad convinced themselves that the initial antinational fervor would dim after they had consolidated power. The new leadership would then see the benefits of relying on traditional mainstays of Russian national and cultural identity.

These arguments attracted not only philosophers and writers, but also managers and leading members of the military. They appealed to political figures on both the left and right. Their most important political thinker was Nikolai Ustrialov, who thought of himself as a Slavophile. He emerged from the same political environment as Struve and Bulgakov, namely the right wing of the Constitutional Democratic Party.[8] At the same time, however, Ustrialov departed from contemporary neo-Slavophiles on the importance of religious beliefs. Like Danilevskii before him, he relegated religious belief to the personal sphere, claiming that what was practical in politics was moral. His opponents saw in this the root problem of politics and urged a public confession of belief and the subordination of politics to Christian standards. Whereas Struve, Bulgakov, and the thinkers of the Silver Age of Russian philosophy saw the Bolshevik destruction of the foundations of prerevolutionary society as an absolute evil, Ustrialov saw it as only a relative evil because it would ultimately enhance Russia's national greatness.[9]

The hostility between traditional Russian nationalism and the new regime has been downplayed by many Western analysts, since after 1934 Stalin selectively embraced tsarist symbolism and emphasized the Russian leadership in the new union. To many, both in Russia and abroad, this seemed to confirm the validity of the National Bolsheviks' analysis that the regime had finally succumbed to the pressures of nationalism. The notion that the Communist regime had now embraced the very same values that it had been trying so hard to eliminate came to dominate postwar Soviet studies in the United States.[10]

It is important to remember, however, that National Bolshevism originated as a grudging and purely utilitarian acceptance of Bolshevism. Its underlying appeal had been in the assumption that communism was only a temporary phenomenon that would inevitably be replaced by an idea more accurately reflecting the Russian character.[11] For its most prominent advocates, the survival of Russia demanded loyalty only to the state, not to its ideology. However, well before the Nazi invasion Stalin had effectively succeeded in manipulating this patriotic sentiment, converting tacit support into forced acceptance of his bloody transformations of society. Subsequent generations of Soviet scholars would disparage *smenovekhovstvo* as the wishful thinking of the outdated "class enemy."

The similarities of many contemporary Russian "nationalist" concerns to those of the *smenovekhovstvo* movement, however, are hard to overlook. Before the collapse of the USSR, prominent writers like Petr Proskurin, Vadim Kozhinov, Vasilii Belov, Iurii Bondarev, and Aleksandr Prokhanov all shared the notion that the Soviet regime ultimately reflected the Russian national interest and had become, in essence, the heir to the culture and values of the Russian empire. Today, one can add to this list the names of Eduard Volodin, Mikhail Antonov, Valentin Rasputin, Igor' Shafarevich, and Stanislav Kuniaev. For these intellectuals, the critical issue facing Russia today is its survival as a nation. Every effort must be made to preserve and strengthen her attributes of statehood (read "state power"). As a rule, this group favored a strong union and a strong centralization of authority. To the very last they believed that the old regime retained sufficient authority to accomplish these tasks. Once it lost this ability, however, it lost its only real attractiveness.

While National Bolsheviks stressed loyalty to the state because they believed that the USSR had become the Russian Empire, the other major exponents of intellectual conservatism, the Russophiles, urged disloyalty to the Communist state because of their belief that the USSR was the antithesis of Russia. They urged an end to Communist overlordship of Russia and called instead for a "spiritual renaissance" of Russia that would reject materialism and utopian solutions to political problems and above all restore Russia's religious and cultural heritage, which they viewed as a bulwark against modern totalitarianism.

Like the National Bolsheviks, Russophiles hold dear the concept of Russian greatness, but see it as the result of the recovery of Russian spirituality rather than the accrual of power to the state. Thus, whereas National Bolsheviks tended to applaud the Soviet Union's role in world affairs in opposition to the United States, Russophiles viewed the Soviet Union's expansive foreign policy interests as a sacrifice of Russian domestic interests for the sake of hollow aggrandizement. They favor isolationism rather than imperialism.[12] Their most prominent spokesman today is Aleksandr Solzhenitsyn, but alongside him one might mention longtime dissidents like Vladimir Osipov and Leonid Borodin, writer

Dmitrii Balashov, *Novyi mir* editor Sergei Zalygin, and academicians Igor Vinogradov, Sergei Averintsev, and Dmitrii Likhachev.[13]

Despite their differences, today's National Bolsheviks and Russophiles share a common terminology and certain common aspirations, which has led to confusion in the West. The most important similarity is the desire for a "rebirth of Russia" (*vozrozhdenie Rossii*). But this is interpreted quite differently by each group. For the National Bolsheviks a strong stable government is needed in order to restore the Russian empire. Since the powerful, coercive amalgam of communism has dissolved, they now search for an alternative that would guarantee Russia's survival as a multiethnic state. Their approach to Russian history and Russian culture (even Russian Orthodoxy) is largely a function of how each will serve that goal.

The Russophiles, by contrast, see a strong and stable Russian government as the byproduct of a revitalization of Russia's cultural and religious heritage. Russia will be resurrected as a multinational empire, they believe, because its culture has long been a source of attraction for neighboring peoples. Its tarnished ideals need only be burnished to once again provide a shining beacon to beckon to other nations. Echoing Jonathan Winthrop's famous image likening America to a "shining city upon a hill," Russophiles argue that Russia can once again become a cultural avatar for her neighbors, as she was for much of her history.

Understanding the similarities and differences between these two strands of modern Russian conservatism helps to explain the rapid collapse of intellectual support for communism and its ability to regroup so quickly under the banner of nationalism. By 1990, with *perestroika* and *glasnost'* in full swing, Russophile ideas were being widely aired and were having a considerable impact on National Bolshevik thought. The works of many previously banned anti-communists, most notably the works of Aleksandr Solzhenitsyn, were being published and receiving much favorable commentary.[14] Despite the growing attractiveness of Russophile ideas, however, many National Bolsheviks remained convinced that the survival of the union depended on the institutions, if not the ideology, of the CPSU.

The failure of the August coup, the indictment of the CPSU as a criminal conspiracy, and, finally, the dissolution of the USSR shattered all illusions on that score. It seemed for a while as if the radical democrats had emerged triumphant; but over the course of 1992 their popularity diminished while the strength of openly conservative and nationalist forces in Russia increased. The typical explanation has been to attribute the falling ratings of the "radicals" to the collapse of the economy, but this is only part of the story. The intellectual appeal of conservatism has been growing because the new center of gravity for conservative traditional Russian political thought is no longer communism but patriotism. By 1993, Russian conservatism had gone a long way toward distancing itself from its nationalist and Stalinist fringes and attracting moderates into a new and potentially powerful political coalition.

Russian Conservatism

At the beginning of 1992, there was still a rather clear division between supporters of President Yeltsin and groups left over from the old CPSU. Indeed, many of the president's closest advisers still viewed the struggle against these remnants as being paramount.[15] But while the communists have languished in political isolation, the coalition of seven proreform parties that united under the umbrella of Democratic Russia soon splintered into a number of currents.

The most significant split was the separation of the center-right or "conservative" political groups from the rest: the Democratic Party of Russia (led by Nikolai Travkin), the Constitutional Democrats–Party of National Freedom (*Kadety*, led by Mikhail Astaf'ev), and the Russian Christian Democratic Movement (*RKhDD*, led by Viktor Aksiutchits). These three broke off to form the coalition People's Accord (*Narodnoe soglasie*). From the outset, Astaf'ev explains, "Democratic Russia" was dominated by groups that saw Russia's heritage as an obstacle to westernization. But by joining this coalition and coming up with the name "Democratic Russia," the conservative parties hoped to encourage the remainder in the coalition to take a more benign view of patriotism and influence presidential policies and cabinet appointments. When it became clear, however, that the government was not about to share its authority with the coalition, they left.

The shock of the August coup and the disintegration of the USSR reinvigorated Russian conservatives in two ways. First, it proved conclusively to the National Bolsheviks that the old order simply had too few adherents to provide a strong and stable national government. They were reluctantly forced to reexamine their basic assumptions regarding the Soviet regime and Soviet socialism. Second, it forced a frank discussion of how much (and on what terms) anticommunist Russophiles would be willing to compromise with National Bolsheviks. The result was a series of soul-searching articles in the conservative media (*Den'*, *Nash sovremennik*, *Molodaia gvardiia*, *Narodnaia pravda*) and an often bewildering patchwork of coalitions, splits, and regroupings on the right among groups that would, at first glance, appear to have little in common.

In Russia today, many prefer to apply a simple economic litmus test in order to identify groups on the political spectrum. Thus, for example, groups that support a free market are termed "proreform" and characterized as being on the left, while those that favor continued nationalization are termed "antireform" and on the right. But these categories make little sense in a contemporary European or American context. Here, the left has come to be associated, not with rampant privatization, but with the pursuit of social equity through expanded government intervention. By contrast, this is precisely the role now claimed by the right in Russia.

To avoid such confusion, I prefer to go back to the most basic assumptions about human nature that have helped to define distinctive political expectations.

Thomas Sowell has termed such assumptions "visions" of human nature, and distinguished between "unconstrained" and "constrained" political visions, which roughly correspond to utopian political aspirations and political aspirations that reject utopianism.[16] The vehement rejection of anything that smacks of utopianism is especially characteristic of modern Russian conservatism. As a leading conservative politician, Viktor Aksiutchits, explains:

> The characteristic of "leftist" politics is a desire for radical transformations of the traditional structures of life, utilizing extremist and, consequently, militant means of struggle. The orientation of the "right," by contrast, presumes reliance on the traditional institutions of society, on their creative development; i.e., it relies not on revolution, but on dynamic evolution. . . .
> We are liberals in the sense that for us the rights and freedoms of the individual (who is created in the image of God), and the self-determination of social groups are paramount. But we are conservative in that we understand that only a strong, democratic state authority will be capable of protecting and guaranteeing these rights and freedoms.[17]

While Christian Democrats like Aksiutchits consciously draw upon the heritage of Russian religious philosophers of the early twentieth century (Ivan Il'in, Peter B. Struve, Father Sergei Bulgakov, Semën Frank among them), the other major conservative party, the Constitutional Democrats, seeks to reclaim the heritage of its prerevolutionary namesake, with one important difference—a refusal to embrace radical change for change's sake. They fault the pre-1917 Constitutional Democrat–Menshevik coalition for setting the stage for the Bolshevik coup, as their leader Mikhail Astaf'ev explains:

> The fact that the resurrected Kadet Party contains elements of conservatism can be easily explained. First, this is a natural response to the chaotic disintegration of the country. Second, we remember what the flirtation with political extremism and cooperation with ultraradicals once led to. Third, we have always been supporters of individual rights and personal freedoms, including the right to private property as the foundation of a market economy and contemporary democracy. In politics this is called neoconservatism, which corresponds to our view of the world.[18]

As successors to the Russophile strand of national thought, both the Constitutional Democratic and Christian Democratic parties stress their anticommunism. The main difference between them is the philosophical justification for the primacy accorded to individual liberty. As their names imply, the latter is a religious party that views liberty as emerging from a religious worldview, much like the Christian Democratic parties of Western Europe. The former, by contrast, sees liberty as anchored in secular institutions governed by the rule of law, like European conservative parties. The Christian Democratic Party claims 12,000–15,000 adherents nationwide, while the Constitutional Democratic Party claims 6,000–7,000 members.[19]

Nikolai Travkin's Democratic Party of Russia subsequently joined with Vice

President Aleksandr Rutskoi's People's Party of Free Russia (*NPSR*) and with Arkadii Vol'skii's Industrial Union to form another centrist coalition, the Civic Union. Although many of its leaders are sympathetic to the concerns of the conservatives, the Civic Union represents a loose centrist coalition of parliamentarians without any strongly defined ideology. They support a number of short-term changes to the current economic policy, but are reluctant to mount a wholesale challenge to President Yeltsin, preferring instead to be the government's "loyal opposition." Because of their close ties with the "new establishment," critics have tended to view the Civic Union as a last bulwark of support for the president, rather than as a political alternative to him.

Russian Statism

Further along the opposition spectrum, other groups have demanded that the president and his cabinet be replaced. These groups are labeled "red-browns" (a communist-fascist coalition) by their opponents and the "united left-and-right opposition" by their supporters. The most important coalition here is the parliamentary bloc Russian Unity (*Rossiiskoe edinstvo*), organized in April 1991. It is made up of five smaller factions: *Rossiia* (Sergei Baburin and Nikolai Pavlov), *Otchizna* (Boris Tarasov), *Agrarnyi soiuz* (Mikhail Lapshin), *Kommunisty Rossii* (Ivan Rybkin and Gennadii Saenko), and *Grazhdanskoe obshchestvo* (Mikhail Chelnokov). An overlapping group is the Russian National Assembly (*Russkii natsional'nyi sobor*), an interim coalition which included the heads of the Constitutional Democratic and Christian Democratic parties, Mikhail Astaf'ev and Viktor Aksiutchits, as well as former KGB General Aleksandr Sterligov and Central Committee apparatchik Gennadii Ziuganov. Ziuganov subsequently went on to head the openly confrontational National Salvation Front (*Front natsional'nogo spaseniia*), while Sterligov now heads the Council of National-Patriotic Forces and has attempted to distance himself from the Front since it was outlawed by Yeltsin on October 28, 1992.[20]

These coalitions represent one last attempt to salvage National Bolshevism. They are distinguished by the belief that Russia's very survival as a nation is threatened today just as it was in 1917, and that to survive she must maintain many old Soviet structures. In the press they are often referred to as *patrioty*, or *patrioty-gosudarstvenniki*, or simply *gosudarstvenniki* (statists). These terms highlight an emphasis on attributes of state power, and serve to distinguish them from the more moderate conservatives, commonly referred to in the press as *dempatrioty* (democratic patriots) or *gosliberaly* (statist liberals).

A common feature of extreme statism is rejection of and hostility toward the West, which is seen as an alien culture that seeks to take advantage of Russia's current turmoil. This theme often accompanies discussions of Russia as a *samobytnaia kul'tura*—an original culture with her own values, standards, and ideals that are opposed to those of the West (materialism, individualism, rapacious greed, spiritual emptiness). What the West cannot pressure Russia into conceding, it is trying to purchase; hence, the second axiom of the statists: "Russia should not be for sale!" Instead, it should develop its own distinctive economic model (neither capitalist nor socialist) which reconciles Russia's traditional concern for social justice with entrepreneurship. Interestingly, what is being rejected here is specifically American-style capitalism. By contrast, Japan and, more rarely, Sweden and Germany, are cited as examples of countries that have succeeded in the capitalist system while retaining their traditional cultural frameworks.

Statists also oppose any military or foreign policy concessions to the West. They believe that America is trying to separate Russia from her former Soviet allies, to dismember the USSR, and finally to dismember Russia herself so that she ceases to exist as a national entity. Their foreign and military policy does not appear to have any goal other than opposition to what the West, in particular the United States, supports. Thus nuclear disarmament is undesirable because it "plays into the hands" of the Americans; the new regime has "sold out" its former ally Iraq; and now Russia's "historical ally" Serbia—an "Orthodox nation"—is being sacrificed to Washington's ambition to establish a new world order in which Russia would become merely a territory for the extraction of mineral resources.

To oppose this Western conspiracy that is trying to finish the second time around what it failed to accomplish through the Bolshevik Revolution of 1917, some prominent statists, like the head of the Union for the Spiritual Rebirth of the Fatherland, Mikhail Antonov, argue openly for a new messianic idea—not the communist ideal alien to Russia, but an ideal true to Russia's tradition as a more moral, more just, more spiritual society.[21]

Radical democrats often argue that statists simply wish to restore communism or some analogous form of dictatorship based on narrow-minded nationalism that would end social and economic reforms and usher in a new cold war. They point to the rhetoric of the leaders of the Russian National Assembly and especially those of the National Salvation Front. In his decree outlawing this front, Yeltsin refers to it as "seeking to provoke disorder and destabilizing society for the accomplishment of their extremist political objectives, and creating anticonstitutional structures and illegal militarized formations."[22]

Others, however, look at the conservative political spectrum and point to the growing influence of its more moderate coalition partners—the Constitutional Democratic and Christian Democratic parties. They see this coalition not as a harbinger of dictatorship, but as the dawn of a historic reconciliation of patriotic forces long divided by communism. The symbols of their alliance are meant to evoke such an image. The emblem of the Russian National Congress, for example, shows a white horse, symbolic of the forces that resisted the Bolsheviks during the Civil War, frolicking together with a red horse, symbol of the accomplishments of the Soviet period.

Concern about the course chosen by the government has drawn these two very disparate political orientations into temporary alliance. For both, a strong Russia means a strong government capable of enforcing its decrees. Moderate conservatives and statists both view the radical democrats as utopian ideologues bent on transforming Russia at all costs. They accuse the radicals of controlling access to the media, refusing to compromise with the opposition, and being too dependent both on the West and on the old party *nomenklatura*. Moderate conservatives advocate private entrepreneurship and the rule of law, but they draw the line at destroying Russia in order to institute reforms. Finally, moderate conservatives and statists share a desire for a Russian national renaissance based on Russia's historical tradition rather than the importation of Western models and ideas. These similarities have led to a tactical alliance on the right, manifested in March 1992 during a conference of "patriotic" opinion leaders and cemented in the Political Declaration of Left and Right Opposition issued at the end of September 1992.[23]

Ultimately, however, this is an alliance of common aspirations but few shared values. While statists see some justification for the appeals of the August coup, for example, the leadership of the moderate conservative parties has denounced it as "criminal." The conservative parties emphasize the rule of law, constitutional guarantees, the primacy of individual rights over group rights, free markets, private property, and personal ownership of land, most of which are opposed by statists.[24] Perhaps just as important, while the conservatives acknowledge Russia's distinctive history, they stress that her population has aspirations analogous to those of people everywhere. These aspirations are expressed in parties analogous to those in other countries. Contacts with foreign groups like these should be expanded, say the conservatives, not contracted.

Given the significant divergence of views on fundamental matters, how can conservatives even begin to seek an alliance with statists? Very simply put: to gain influence. Conservatives believe they can accomplish two important objectives by forging a tactical alliance with statists. First, they hope to force the government to hold new elections in 1993, in which centrist parties will emerge as a stronger force at the expense of both the left and the right extremes. Second, they believe that they are having greater success in moderating the communist influence among the statists than they had in instilling a sense of patriotic sentiment among the radicals. Theirs might be called a policy of constructive engagement with groups further to the right, continuing the intellectual conversion of the National Bolsheviks that had been begun by the Russophiles.

Still, this coalition is tenuous at best. After initially joining the Congress of Civic and Patriotic Forces, the leadership of the Christian Democratic Movement has drawn the line at participating in the Sterligov's Russian National Congress or Anpilov's *Trudovaia Rossiia*. Within the Constitutional Democratic Party, the issue of whether to join the National Salvation Front is a personal choice. The head of the party, Mikhail Astaf'ev, advises the National Salvation Front and has taken on a more strident anti-Western tone after his most recent visit to the United States. By contrast, his young deputy Dmitrii Rogozin has termed the National Salvation Front dangerous and has called for a dialogue with the Civic Union and more centrist political forces.[25] The newly formed coalition Rebirth of Russia (*Vozrozhdenie Rossii*) indeed combines the younger political leaders of the Constitutional Democrats, Travkin's Democratic Party of Russia, and even the Russian Social Democratic Party.

Strengths and Weaknesses of the Right

Moderate conservatives are in a weak position in the present Congress of People's Deputies. They number fewer than a dozen deputies among a sea of former communists. At the same time, having burned their bridges to the radical democrats, their only chance of influencing policy seems to be in making intellectual inroads among the statists.

Despite their small numbers, aligning with the right rather than with the left appears to have borne some fruit. Although the Coalition of Left and Right Forces failed in its effort to oust all of Yeltsin's cabinet, it did succeed in making significant inroads on the president's authority. It is too early to say, however, whether this trend will continue or merely galvanize the president's supporters to organize themselves better in the future.

But while statists are a much larger group within the Congress of People's Deputies when compared to conservatives, this is the direct result of a Soviet electoral system that heavily favored the former party bureaucracy. In the aftermath of the August coup, many in this group are desperately in search of new ideas, and the most attractive worldview is provided by the moderate conservatives, descendants of the earlier Russophile dissidents. Under their influence, many statists have abandoned their earlier attempts to restore their alliance with communist forces.

Thus even the most unabashed statists now confess publicly the end of communism. For Aleksandr Sterligov, communism has "exhausted itself in our country . . . we believe we must resurrect true Russia, its cultural and historical values, its state structures."[26] For Sergei Baburin, the joint opposition is characterized by only three principles, "democracy [*narodovlastie*], patriotism and justice." Its goal is to overcome the contraposition between democratic principles and national traditions which has existed for centuries.[27] Even those on the right who would defend socialism in principle, like *Trudovaia Rossiia*'s Anatolii Denisov, seem to cling to it more out of desperation than ideological fervor:

> Although a majority of us prefer humanistic marxism, we reject conspiratorial tactics and any attempt to come to power by force, to seize power. . . .
> We count on the fact that public opinion leans to the center. We are centrists. We declare that we are centrists. We do not even have a firm ideology.

> We support socialism, but do not insist on the marxist model of socialism. We allow for peasant socialism. It is all the same to us how a person came to socialism—to the idea of social justice in society.[28]

The extent of this rejection was made apparent when the most prominent statist organizations (including the Russian National Assembly, the Christian Democratic Party, the Russian All-National Union, and the Union for the Rebirth of Russia) refused to join the National Salvation Front, deeming it excessively confrontational.[29] Drawing a line to the right and placing former Communist hard-liners beyond the pale of acceptable political discourse is a watershed in the evolution of the right as significant as the August 1991 coup attempt itself.

What worries many Western observers, however, is that the rise of Russian nationalism may be no better, ultimately, than communism. In times of crisis, Walter Laqueur has written, "the negative ugly aspects of Russia's past—tyranny, darkness and servitude—tend to overpower Russia's beautiful and harmonious features."[30] Eastern nationalism (as distinct from Western nationalism), he argues, is congenitally antiliberal, repressive of minorities, and prone to conflicts with its neighbors, and has a "generally destructive character."[31] Influential observers like Laqueur, Stephen Sestanovich, Richard Pipes, Henry Kissinger, and Peter Reddaway have compared the present political situation in Russia to the weak democracy of the Weimar Republic, which led just a few years later to the triumph of National Socialism.

The notion that just under the surface of reforms in Russia there lurks a fascist dictatorship waiting to pounce finds considerable support among the American media and academic observers. It was a prominent theme in the United States during Gorbachev's tenure, and it formed part of the rationale for the rather uncritical degree of support for him.[32] Today, many of the same voices tie the entire fate of the reform process to Yeltsin.[33] A common stereotype thus lingers in the approach of many influential American observers that blithely ignores the new realities of parliamentary politics in Russia. This stereotype is rooted in a deep skepticism that Russian history and political culture can provide any foundation for stable democracy. Russia's options, accordingly, are to choose between the collapse of democracy under the weight of Russia's authoritarian tradition and the collapse of democracy due to the resurgence of communist institutions.

There is much in the rhetoric of the conservative parties to support the worst suspicions of these pessimists. But in order to get a realistic picture of their political impact one must go beyond the rhetoric and examine the new context of Russian politics in the post-Soviet era. Here several factors have emerged that mitigate extremism.

First, there is the undeniable vitality of political pluralism. Even in the Congress as presently constituted, conservatives and statists together represent no more than 35 to 40 percent of parliamentarians. Even acting as a united bloc, they would find staunch opposition not only within the parliament, but from the executive branch, from the judicial branch, and from the media—dominated by radical democrats.

Second, there is the electoral and coalition-building process itself as it has developed during the past two years. In a seminal article on the process of political party formation in different cultures, Brent Steel and Taketsuga Tsurutani note that parties that stick closely to their ideological stances rarely manage to capture more than a fraction of the electorate, and hence they remain perpetually marginalized. By contrast, parties that recognize the value of coalition-building and flexible alliances are rewarded with political authority.[34] The remarkable fluidity of the coalition-building process in Russia testifies not only to the youth and lack of traditions among the new political elite, but also to the pragmatism of most members of parliament. The deputy chairman of the Constitutional Democratic Party, Dmitrii Rogozin, recently explained his party's reasoning:

> You are wrong to think that we have betrayed our fundamental principles. Although the opposition is indeed quite diverse, this is nothing strange—in all countries parliamentary parties at times form the most disparate coalitions. In the Spanish parliament, for example, communists not infrequently band together with phalangists, without shocking anyone. At the Russian Congress of People's Deputies we and the Christian Democrats together have no more than ten votes, while the communists and Baburin's "Rossiia" faction garner up to 500. By uniting we can bloc the passage of legislation that neither they nor we approve of. This does not mean, however, that we have forgotten our ideological differences and now hug each other in fraternal embrace.[35]

Since no single party is strong enough to dominate parliament, each must seek coalition partners and learn the deft art of political compromise. The noted exception to this—the National Salvation Front—confirms Steel and Tsurutani's rule.

Third, the ostracism of communist ideologues has become the defining characteristic of Russian politics. For conservatives like the Constitutional Democrats, anticommunism is a lesson learned from their pre-1917 history; for others, it is the basis for their existence. Whatever the reason, it fundamentally changes the center of gravity of the political spectrum, exerting pressure on even the most extreme statists to move toward the political and intellectual center. As parliamentary procedures and traditions stabilize, statists increasingly look to the center, rather than to the left, to find coalition partners.

Finally, the attraction of conservative Russophile thinking seems to extend beyond its numerical strength in the congress. A recent poll of membership of Travkin's and Rutskoi's parties conducted by the political science faculty at Moscow State University showed that 30 percent of members of Rutskoi's People's Party of Free Russia saw themselves as natural allies of the prerevolutionary Constitutional Democratic Party, while 28 percent saw themselves as intellectually closer to the Social Democrats (Bolsheviks and Mensheviks split roughly evenly). At the same time, among members of the Democratic Party of Russia, 37 percent saw themselves as kindred to the prerevolutionary Constitutional Democrats or even more conservative Octobrists, while 15 percent identified with the Socialist Revolutionaries (viewed as a party representing the peasantry), and almost none identified with Social Democrats.[36] This spill-over to other intellectual currents on the right helps to explain the considerable intellectual status of conservative political groups, far beyond their actual numbers.

Even more interestingly, opinion polls indicate that while only 10 percent of the populace would be prepared to support a "national-patriotic" political organization, up to 40 percent find the idea of a "Great Russia" (*velikaia Rossiia*) attractive. What offends voters are not the ideas, but the extremism exhibited by certain leaders of this orientation. Several observers have therefore speculated that if a popular, moderate political leader were to espouse the conservative agenda, it could become a dominant force in Russian politics.[37]

Russian politics has thus become, quite predictably, more conservative and nationalistic but not (as is often suggested in the West) because Russia is a "patrimonial" society, or has a longing for authoritarianism, or because of the peasant background of its population. The reasons have more to do with Crane Brinton's astute observation that after "the experience of a great revolution ... the patient emerges stronger in some respects from the conquered fever, immunized in this way and that from attacks that might be more serious."[38] There is deep and abiding disillusionment in Russian society today with any and all notions of social experimentation. In this respect, the radicalism of today's democrats is viewed with the same jaundiced eye as the radicalism of yesterday's Marxists.

This widespread disillusionment with politics and political ideals has spawned a strong desire to recover a sense of basic pride in self and national identity upon which to recreate valid, patriotic ideals for the future. For most people this is still a cultural and religious rediscovery first, whose concrete political manifestations have not yet begun to show themselves. As the authors of the conservative manifesto "To the Russian [*rossiiskoi*] Intelligentsia," point out, however, it is implausible that a healthy political ideal will emerge totally unconnected to patriotism.[39]

Implications for the United States

For the United States, the question of who will dominate on the right—statists or conservatives—has serious foreign policy implications. The answer provides a good indication of the prospects for improving relations between the United States and Russia.

The strategy of the moderate conservative parties is to seek early parliamentary elections. They hope to benefit from the current disillusionment with government policies as well as the continuing skepticism about communism. Their prospects seem bolstered by the fact that they were not even an organized presence in the first election, but might be dimmed by the lambasting they have received in the mainstream press for their alliance with the statists and the frictions this has caused among their own constituents.[40] Short of such an electoral realignment, however, conservatives are likely to maintain their tactical alliance with the statists, defending those issues which are dearest to them while yielding to them on those issues where there is the least at stake for Russia, most notably on issues of foreign policy. Russian foreign policy today is a perfect arena for grandstanding because, faced with economic collapse, there is so little chance that Russia will become involved in any external adventure.

Anti-Westernism costs so little politically because almost no one expects to see any significant Western economic assistance. Critics believe that in the pursuit of such aid, Foreign Minister Andrei Kozyrev has been in an unseemly haste to throw away whatever bargaining chips Russia had (unlike Ukraine, which, they point out, proposes to get a good price for every nuclear weapon it dismantles). Their attitude is not unlike that of many notable American politicians during the period of revolutionary upheavals in Europe during the mid-nineteenth century, when the most vituperative denunciations of the repression of liberty, and the most outrageous promises of support for the freedom of Hungarians and Greeks, were voiced in the U.S. Congress but with no expectation of fulfillment. When Henry Clay and Daniel Webster assumed their duties as secretaries of state, however, their pronouncements changed 180 degrees.[41] Similarly, the passionately anti-Western foreign policy rhetoric of the statists is largely for domestic consumption and should not be taken as an indication of the fully formed foreign policy views of a government led by the opposition.

Much more serious is the treatment of Russians in the former Soviet republics. This issue has the potential to poison our relations with Russia for many years to come, especially if, after years of manifesting concern for human rights in the USSR, the United States suddenly falls silent about human rights violations against Russians in these republics. Having opened the Pandora's box of human rights, we are now forced to deal with it lest our silence be interpreted as proof that all along U.S. policy was simply anti-Russian, not pro–human rights.

American interests would be well served by applying our human rights policy even-handedly in all the former Soviet republics. Beyond that, it would be wise to seek to establish contacts with local minority communities and with grievance committees in Russia and Ukraine that have been set up to deal with this complex issue. During my brief tour as visiting political attaché at the U.S. Embassy in Moscow, I found that simply displaying a modicum of concern for the plight of refugees and the new minorities reduced suspicions and opened the door to dialogue with conservatives on a number of other issues.

In the final analysis, just as the Russian right exaggerates Russia's moral superiority over the West, its critics (both inside and outside Russia) exaggerate the barrenness of Russia's democratic heritage. The unwillingness to identify any redeeming features in Russia's heritage has led some to conclude that it is "desirable for Russia to keep on disintegrating until nothing remains of its institutional structures."[42] Anything that delays or mitigates the process of disintegration (especially mentions of an effective central authority, national allegiance, or religious faith as integrative vehicles) are decried as veiled efforts to reconstitute the old regime. These sorts of prescriptions simply fuel the claims of the right that influential Western thinkers are advocating policies aimed at destroying Russia rather than helping to restore her. Indeed, the anti-Western diatribes of influential Russian conservatives are often just mirror images of those of their American counterparts, responding tit for tat to the presumed superiority of Western democratic institutions, economic values, tolerance for diversity, inherent peacefulness, and so on. Darrell Hammer's plea to do more to root out Russophobia in our public thinking is still very much apropos.[43]

There are, in addition, some small but highly symbolic gestures that would serve to put our post-Soviet policy toward Russia on the right track and deprive anti-Western critics of ammunition. One such step would be to repeal the Captive Nations resolution of 1959. This proclamation designates the peoples of the USSR as captives of "Communist Russia" and declares that the United States will offer support to all people seeking independence except the Russians. The resolution obviously stirs the ire of Russian nationalists and is often cited to prove the anti-Russian character of American policy; yet even after the fall of communism, efforts to repeal or amend this anachronistic bit of legislation have come up against the opposition of domestic ethnic constituencies who equate Soviet expansion and Russian imperialism.[44]

Most of all, however, it would behoove American analysts and policy-makers to become less obsessed with who is president of Russia and begin to pay greater attention to the vitality of the new Russian political spectrum. Our efforts in this regard are somewhat frustrated by uncertainty regarding the true depth of support for the various groups, but even so it is high time to take this pluralism and its impact on the formation of policy more seriously and stop tying the fate of democracy to one individual. Paying close attention to the diversity of Russian political thought would allow a more relaxed appraisal of the prospects of the opposition to Yeltsin and what its victory would mean to U.S.-Russian relations. As long as political pluralism is preserved and Marxist-Leninists are kept isolated, the remaining ideological, national, and religious extremes should slowly become tempered by the political process. True, the institutions that guarantee this are not yet fully formed, but the process for creating them has proceeded remarkably smoothly to date.

Political science tells us that the ideal scenario for political stability is for the center-left and center-right parties to emerge bolstered by future elections. But even the worst possible scenario—a weak center with two highly antagonistic extremes on the left and right—would not be too different from what we have today and which, despite its inadequacies, is making slow but steady progress.

More of the same might delay the enactment of important legislation but not, ultimately, prevent it.

This political process in Russia, we must remember, is little more than a year old. The process of political regeneration cannot be rushed; it must develop naturally and may take forms we in the West do not feel entirely comfortable with. A strong conservative movement in Russia strengthens democracy in the long run, if for no other reason than for the balances it gives to the excesses of the radical democrats. Rather than fight this balance, it would be far better to recognize that it contributes to pluralism and, ultimately, to the stability of Russian democracy.

Notes

1. This point has been made by, among others, John Dunlop, S. Frederick Starr, and Geoffrey Hosking. For the most systematic discussion see Darrell P. Hammer, "The 'Traditionalist' Opposition in Soviet Politics," Final Report on Contract No. 804–02 for the National Council for Soviet and East European Research, July 1990.

2. Valerii Vyzhutovich, "Kto doigryvaet partiiu?" *Izvestiia*, May 6, 1992, p. 3. Arkadii Dubnov, " 'Krasnyi' kon' na pereprave," *Novoe vremia*, no. 18, 1992, p. 6.

3. Recent articles on the RKPR and other communist groups include: Anna Ostapchuk, "Zashchishchat' KPSS bol'she nekomu," *Nezavisimaia gazeta*, September 5, 1992, p. 2; S. Terskaia, "Viktor Anpilov: Voznia vokrug person," *Narodnaia pravda*, 1992, no. 47 (December), p. 1; Mikhail Tiutev, "Na rodine Yel'tsina rodilas' programma bor'by s nim," *Megalopolis-Ekspress*, December 23, 1992, p. 15.

4. Ostapchuk, "Zashchishchat'," p. 2. For more information on these parties and all others, the most complete reference is the ten-volume *Rossiia: partii, assotsiatsii, soiuzy, kluby*, compiled by V.N. Berezovskii, N.I. Krotov, and V.V. Cherviakov (Moscow: RAU Press, 1991–92).

5. Iu. Soldukhin, N. Beliaeva, V. Lepekhin, Iu. Satarov, "Politicheskie sily Rossii— 1993 g.," p. 8 (a report prepared by Interlegal USA, New York).

6. Hammer, "Traditionalist Opposition," p. 9. Other terms used with reference to Russophiles include "pseudo-Slavophilism," "dissident Russian nationalism," "Russites," *neopochvennichestvo, vozrozhdentsy*, and "the Russian party." Frederick C. Barghoorn, "Russian Nationalism and Soviet Politics," in Robert Conquest, *The Last Empire: Nationality and the Soviet Future* (Stanford, CA: Hoover Institution Press, 1986); Susan Massie, "Is There a New Russian Spirit?" speech delivered at the Senator John Heinz Seminar, Council on Foreign Relations, December 3, 1986; and John B. Dunlop, "The Contemporary Russian Nationalist Spectrum," *Radio Liberty Research Bulletin*, special edition, December 19, 1988.

7. Cited in Hans Kohn, *The Mind of Modern Russia* (New Brunswick, NJ: Rutgers University Press, 1955), pp. 253, 255.

8. Mikhail Agurskii, *Ideologiia natsional-bol'shevizma* (Paris: YMCA Press, 1980), pp. 51–52, 74..

9. Agurskii, *Ideologiia*, p. 77.

10. Adam Ulam, "Russian Nationalism," in *The Domestic Context of Soviet Foreign Policy* (Boulder, CO: Westview Press, 1981), pp. 3–18. Cyril Black, *Understanding Soviet Politics* (Boulder, CO: Westview, 1986), p. 180–210. On the debate over the role of ideology in shaping Soviet foreign policy see especially "Ideology and Power Politics: A Symposium," in Alexander Dallin, *Soviet Conduct in World Affairs* (Westport, CT: Greenwood, 1976 repr. of 1960 ed.), pp. 37–74.

11. Hammer, "Traditionalist Opposition," pp. 10–11.

12. Nicolai N. Petro, "New Political Thinking and Russian Patriotism: The Dichotomy of Perestroika," *Comparative Strategy*, vol. 9, no. 4 (1990), pp. 351–70.

13. The most recent statement of their views is the appeal "To the Russian [rossiiskoi] Intelligentsia," signed by fourteen prominent political and cultural leaders, many of them close to *Novyi mir*. A short version first published in *Komsomol'skaia pravda*, September 27, 1992, and later more completely in *Rossiia*, as a response to the public letter of the "Independent Civic Initiative" signed by Iu. Afanas'ev, Leonid Batkin, V. Bibler, Elena Bonner, Iurii Burtin, Viacheslav V. Ivanov, and Lev Timofeev, which appeared in the newspaper *Demokraticheskaia Rossiia* one month after the coup.

14. Solzhenitsyn's rehabilitation began with literary critic E. Chukovskaia's articles "Vernut' Solzhenitsynu grazhdanstvo SSSR" and "Uchitsia terpimosti k zhivushchim" in successive issues (August 5 and 12, 1988) of *Knizhnoe obozrenie*. It can be considered completed with the publication of "Kak nam obustroit' Rossiiu" in *Komsomol'skaia pravda*, one of the country's largest circulation dailies, in September 1990.

15. For more on this point, see Nicolai N. Petro, "The Rising Star of Russia's Vice-President," *Orbis*, Winter 1993, pp. 17–18.

16. Thomas Sowell, *A Conflict of Visions* (New York: William Morrow, 1987).

17. Tat'iana Snopkova, "My—Liberal'nye konservatory," *Vek XX i mir*, 1991, no. 6, pp. 22–23.

18. L. Vlodavets and L. Ponomarev, "Nasha strana podpisala bezogovorochnuiu kapituliatsiiu," *Patriot*, 1992, no. 43 (October), p. 3.

19. "Viktor Aksiutchits," *Moskovskie novosti*, August 16, 1992, p. 11; Valentina Nikiforova, "Put' k istine," *Pravda*, January 7, 1992, p. 3; Anatoliia Kostiukova, "Kadety: Levyi marsh s pravoi nogi," *Megalopolis-Ekspress*, July 22, 1992, p. 22.

20. "Ukaz Prezidenta Rossiiskoi Federatsii o merakh po zashchite konstitutsionnogo stroia Rossiiskoi Federatsii," *Rossiiskaia gazeta*, October 30, 1992, p. 2. On Sterligov, see *Itogi* report of November 1, 1992, "My gotovy sotrudnichat' s Prezidentom," in *Russia & the CIS Today*, no. 1082 (November 2, 1992), p. 14.

21. Mikhail Antonov,"Na uzkoi doroge sektanstva," *Literaturnaia Rossiia*, 1992, no. 20, pp. 3–4; and "Nuzhna patrioticheskaia ekonomika, ili na puti k sviatoi Rusi," *Vek XX i mir*, 1992, no. 3, pp. 12–15.

22. "Ukaz Prezidenta," p. 2.

23. On the March conference see "Spravedlivost'. Narodnost'. Gosudarstvennost'. Patriotizm," *Literaturnaia Rossiia*, 1992, no. 11, p. 2. "Politicheskaia deklaratsiia levoi i pravoi oppozitsii," *Sovetskaia Rossiia*, September, 22 1992, p. 1.

24. "Programma Konstitutsionno-Demokraticheskoi Partii (Partii Narodnoi Svobody)," Moscow, n.d., personal copy. Excerpts of the program and resolutions of the Russian Christian Democratic Movement are available in the *Russian-American Review*, Summer 1990, pp. 12–17, published by the Congress of Russian-Americans in Washington, D.C.

25. *Novosti* report of November 6, 1992, reported in "Lider Kadetov ob tekushchem momente," *Russia & CIS Today: TV & Radio Monitoring*, no. 1093 (November 6, 1992), p. 7.

26. "Sterligov," *Russia & CIS Today*, November 2, 1992, p. 14.

27. V. Agafonov and V. Rokitianskii, "Tragediia perestroiki—tragediia nevezhestva," *Novoe Russkoe Slovo*, July 24, 1992, p. 9.

28. Report from television program "Molitva za otechestvo," reported in "Govoriat predstaviteli soveta narodno-patrioticheskikh sil," in *Russia & CIS Today*, no. 967 (September 18, 1992), p. 15.

29. For a discussion on the relationship between Christian Democrats and statists see

"Viktor Aksiutchits," *Moskovskie novosti*, August, 16, 1992, p. 11.

30. Walter Laqueur, "Russian Nationalism," *Foreign Affairs*, Winter 1992/93, p. 109.

31. Ibid., 112.

32. See, for example, A.M. Rosenthal, "The Cruel Delusion," *The New York Times*, May 31, 1990, A23; or Graham E. Fuller, former vice chairman of the CIA's National Intelligence Council, "When Gorbachev Fails . . . ," *The Washington Post*, September 24, 1989, p. B5.

33. In his final public remarks on "The MacNeil-Lehrer News Hour," January 6, 1993, outgoing CIA director Robert M. Gates reiterated that one could not overestimate Yeltsin's importance to the success of democratic reforms.

34. Brent Steel and Taketsuga Tsurutani, "From Consensus to Dissensus: A Note on Postindustrial Parties," *Comparative Politics*, January 1986, pp. 235–48.

35. Kostiukova, "Kadety," *Megalopolis-Ekspress*, July 22, 1992, p. 22.

36. Anna Poretskaia, " 'Grazhdanskii soiuz': vzgliady raznie, zato odinakovie interesy," *Nezavisimaia gazeta*, July 22, 1992, p. 2.

37. Iu. Soldukhin et al., "Politicheskie sily Rossii," p. 11; Nicolai N. Petro, "Toward a New Russian Federation," *The Wilson Quarterly*, Summer 1990, pp. 120; Richard Sakwa, "Christian Democracy in Russia," *Religion, State and Society*, vol. 20, no. 2 (1992), p. 162.

38. Crane Brinton, *The Anatomy of Revolution*, excerpted in Roy C. Macridis and Bernard E. Brown, *Comparative Politics*, 7th edition (Pacific Grove, CA: Brooks/Cole, 1990), p. 437.

39. *Komsomol'skaia pravda*, September 27, 1992. See also note 13, above.

40. Igor' Surikov and Vladimir Todres, "Aksiutchits i Astaf'ev teriaiut storonnikov?" *Nezavisimaia gazeta*, June 3, 1992, p. 2; Sakwa, "Christian Democracy in Russia," pp. 153–54.

41. Kenneth W. Thompson and Nicolai N. Petro, "Persistent Patterns in International Power," in *Institutions and Leadership*, Kenneth W. Thompson, ed. (Washington, DC: University Press of America, 1987), pp. 82–84.

42. Richard Pipes, "Russia's Chance," *Commentary*, March 1992, p. 30.

43. Hammer, "Traditionalist Opposition," p. 47.

44. Ibid., pp. 32–33.

4

Russia: Federalism, Regionalism, and Nationality Claims

Robert J. Osborn

Introduction

The news coming out of Russia's many regions and ethnic minority jurisdictions since the end of Soviet rule suggests developments that may pose important questions for U.S. foreign policy in the next few years and beyond. To what extent will U.S. policy be dealing with both Moscow and several dozen regional fiefdoms, each exercising the right to sign international treaties and carry on an independent foreign policy in certain respects? Will Washington find itself, for example, dealing with the risen ghost of the Far Eastern Republic of 1920–22, a piece of history that has already spawned a popular movement in that area? Or, to take a more realistic prospect, will U.S. aid and trade representatives find themselves choosing between the programs and wishes of Moscow's economic authorities and those of certain economically powerful regions? Will there be a quasi-independent Siberian government? Is there an international role for the already established regional authorities, each embracing between half a dozen and a dozen oblasts and republics, and most founded even before the breakup of the Soviet Union: the Great Urals Association, the Siberian Charter, the Far Eastern Association, the Black Soil Regional Association, and the Great Volga Association?[1]

There has been some discussion about the prospect for certain territories becoming "little dragons" along the lines of Taiwan or Singapore, for example Sakhalin under the administration of Valentin Fedorov. If this happens, will the United States and other economically interested nations be tempted to ignore Moscow and treat local administrations somewhat like sovereign governments? Will it be possible for the United States to coordinate its aid program and monitor loans if Moscow and its dozens of oblasts, republics, and national districts are mired in an endless struggle over who collects the taxes and who spends them? Would it not be easier and more fruitful for both the U.S. government and foreign investors to deal with a cooperative regional administration on the latter's terms, ignoring Moscow's bureaucracy and restrictions?

Multiethnic Russia—about one-fifth of its population is non-Russian—accords thirty-two of its non-Russian peoples a national territory in some form. These territories are in turn the basis for a large array of claims and struggles, struggles which in a few cases have turned violent. Will the ethnic disputes in the North Caucasus infect the rest of the vast Russian lands with violence? While we are worrying about Third World nations secretly acquiring discarded Soviet nuclear weapons, what about the Tatar Republic? And speaking of the Tatar Republic, what if this government feels pressed to realize its formal claim to separate statehood and demands diplomatic recognition from any country that wants a part in its oil economy? (As of early 1993, the Tatarstan regime appears to be on the point of settling its status within the Russian Federation on the basis of a separate treaty; nevertheless, it has reserved some options for future situations.) Yakutia, now the Sakha Republic, might bargain similarly with its extensive diamond-mining industry.

The main conclusion offered here is that the danger with Russia's republics and regions is not outright secession, but rather damaging disarticulation of a kind which could sap the authority of Moscow, making it less capable of, among other things, shaping a coherent foreign policy. This is in spite of the noisy proclamations emanating from some of the republics and regions, the ongoing "war of laws," and the widespread regional defiance of the Russian government's laws and directives. The cases in which Washington or individual American companies could be confronted with awkward political choices will likely be in ambiguous situations of central-local conflict: To what extent should the U.S. government cooperate with X republic, Y oblast, or Z regional association by supporting a local policy that is being pursued in defiance of Moscow?

However, the continued successful regional defiance of Moscow's writ could eventually—and perhaps "eventually" is only a few years away—produce a situation in which certain regions find the option of self-determination both attractive and practical. Such a development would be the result, first, of successful economic growth under regional auspices, including the development of foreign markets for regional products. It is not hard to imagine a region whose leaders and population have transformed the notion of breaking away from an interesting political fantasy to a serious economic possibility. Anyone who watched the rapid collapse of the Soviet government in 1991 attentively hardly needs to be reminded how short the path from an anecdote of the absurd to a mind-boggling reality can be.

In short, the Russian Republic all by itself could pose a series of specific dilemmas for the United States and the other industrial nations. These dilemmas, if not properly understood and treated with appropriate restraint, could seriously damage the Clinton administration's efforts to promote a cooperative relationship with the Russian Federation and to assist its economic recovery.

Today it is possible only to lay out the main lines of Russia's regional and ethnic developments. Predicting which regions will offer either serious problems or unusual opportunities for the United States is hardly possible, first of all because the dealings of local leaders among themselves and with Moscow are complex, and appearances are deceptive. Public stances and proclamations, including calls for separatism, can sometimes only be taken at face value. In the case of Tatarstan, for example, that government's various statements about the right to independent self-determination have turned out to be primarily a bargaining position. In part, however, these statements have been a way of acknowledging separatist sentiments in a portion of the republic's Tatar population.

The best key to evaluating developments in the regions is an analysis of the real interests of regional leaders. Such an analysis assumes, however, that the leadership of a given region is well enough organized to work its will. In the near future, economic circumstances and political developments in certain regions will definitely impel their leaderships to reduce their dependence on Moscow, to increase local control over their own economies, and, with time, to seek their economic and political security more and more in relationships outside Russia's vast territory.

First, we shall review the parts of Russia's changing constitutional and administrative framework which affect Moscow's control over its increasingly restive republics and regions. Second, we shall look at political relations between Moscow and the regions, particularly the efforts of Yeltsin's government to maintain political and administrative supervision. Next, we take a selective look at the political, economic, and ethnic components of movements toward greater regional autonomy. Finally, such conclusions, possibilities, and cautions as can be derived from these rapidly changing events will be outlined briefly.

The Constitutional and Administrative Framework

The Russian Republic was in name a federation from the very beginning of Soviet rule, starting with the RSFSR Constitution of 1918. In constitutional form, the Russian federal system differed from that of the Soviet Union. While the Soviet system was formally the creature of the republics (including the Russian Republic) that agreed in 1923 to form a union, the Russian Republic was the creator rather than the creature of the autonomous republics (ASSRs) within its territory. By the end of the 1980s, sixteen ASSRs shared Russia's land with forty-nine oblasts (provinces) and six krais (territories); and subordinate to certain of the oblasts and krais were five autonomous oblasts and ten okrugs (national districts).[2] True, the ASSRs were endowed with rights which went beyond those of the other territorial subdivisions. But as pillars of the federal structure, their position was hardly different from the position of the oblasts and krais.

The declarations of sovereignty by Russia's former autonomous republics (ASSRs) were an immediate consequence of the union republics' declarations of sovereignty. Both classes of declarations must be regarded first, as political bargaining positions at the beginning of debates over the Union Treaty and the new constitution for the Russian Federation.[3] As constitutional documents, the majority of the autonomous republics' declarations contain two kinds of assertions that undermine the philosophy of a federal system: first is that the laws of the republic hold primacy over those of both the Russian Republic and the (then existing) USSR; second is that the republic is a federal component of *both* the Russian Republic and the USSR. The latter claim has of course fallen by the wayside, and so far the republics within Russia have made no claim to individual membership in the Commonwealth of Independent States. Nevertheless, even as concerns their role within the Russian Federation, the declarations state or imply that the republics are the founders of the Russian federal system, just as the republics of the USSR were always regarded in constitutional form and philosophy as the founders of the Soviet system. This assumption has been rejected repeatedly by Yeltsin's advisers and supporters.

Actually, the first republic within the Russian Federation, the Bashkir ASSR, did join Russia via an agreement with Moscow that can be regarded as a bilateral treaty of federation, signed March 23, 1919. At the end of the Civil War, however, the Soviet regime unilaterally canceled some of the federal provisions of this treaty, and Bashkiria's nationalist leaders thereupon departed to join the Basmachi movement. But this was the first and last time such a treaty was signed by the Russian government. Just fourteen months later, the Bashkir ASSR was established a second time, by a Russian government decree, which had already become the standard procedure for creating autonomous republics in the RSFSR.[4] In constitutional form, the ASSRs were most definitely created by the central government and not by compact among sovereign states.

Oleg Rumiantsev, secretary of the Russian government's Constitutional Commission, has supported this view from the time the commission began its work: The republics did not join the Russian Federation, for they were already part of Russia; hence Russia's three federal treaties of March 1992 cannot be regarded as the equivalent of Gorbachev's failed Union Treaty, or of its 1922 predecessor.[5]

This constitutional background helps explain why sovereignty declarations of 1990 specifically rejected the notion of federal relationships established by central laws and decrees. They did so by specifying voluntary membership, plus the requirement that terms of membership be set by mutual agreement, including the proposed Union Treaty and a prospective Russian federal treaty. They acknowledge the existence of the USSR and the RSFSR, and their membership in both federations. The term "subject of the federation" is used in a number of declarations, in the sense of "basic unit of the federation." The declarations owed a good deal to the sovereignty declarations of the union republics, or at least to debates over the content of these declarations, which had begun only slightly earlier in 1990.

In addition to the concept of voluntarily joining in a federation, the sovereignty declarations of the former ASSRs share the following characteristics, in many particular variants and with a few exceptions:

- the declaration of sovereignty as the basis of the republic's future constitution;
- a new name for the republic (most have now rejected the designations "autonomous" and "socialist" in their official names, so they are no longer ASSRs);
- the right to secession and/or self-determination (with the distinction between these two concepts left unclear);
- the supremacy of republic laws over those of the USSR and (for the republics within Russia) those of the Russian Republic;
- the people as the source of political power, through a popularly elected legislature;
- the separation of powers;
- the right to make treaties and economic agreements with other governments;
- ownership and control by the republic of its natural resources;
- protection and promotion of the culture of the titular nationality;
- equal rights for all nationalities in the republic, including language rights and the right to preservation and development of their cultures;
- the recognized official languages;
- in some declarations, protection not just of the republic's citizens living outside the republic, but of all persons of the republic's titular ethnic group outside the republic.

By the summer of 1990, when the sovereignty declarations had begun to appear, Russia's newly formed Constitutional Commission had set to work to draft a new constitution. Among the basic problems which had to be resolved was the status of the republics: What rights, functions, and privileges should they enjoy beyond those of the other territorial units? Furthermore, should only the republics be designated as "subjects of the federation" in the sense explained above? If the oblasts and krais, which contain the bulk of the country's population and economic might, are not to be subjects of the federation, how can the resulting system be called federal?

The sequence of Russian constitutional drafts from 1990 to 1993 shows the stages of a dual contest: the struggle by the republics (former ASSRs) to secure a special status in the new constitutional order, and the efforts by the leaders of the economically stronger oblasts and krais to place their jurisdictions on an equal footing with the republics. The most important of the numerous draft constitutions were those formally submitted by the Constitutional Commission for discussion and possible adoption by the Russian Congress of People's Deputies. These include the drafts of November 1990, October 1991, and March 1992.[6] The three federal treaties signed in March 1992 were intended as the basis of the March 1992 draft constitution.

All the drafts state clearly that the bearer of the republic's sovereignty and the only source of its authority is its multinational people.[7] The "we the people" concept leaves no doubt that this is a federation and not a confederation. All the drafts treat all the different units of jurisdiction as components of the federation. The November 1990 draft follows the still-operative RSFSR Constitution in according special status and powers to the republics, with little improvement in the status of the remaining territorial subdivision. It includes the familiar provision, "The republics themselves determine their domestic policies and exercise legislative, executive and judicial power except for the powers assigned by this Constitution to the Federation." In the paragraphs apportioning functions between Moscow and the territorial units of the federation, the republics get a long, detailed list, which includes the right to make agreements with foreign governments. Of the oblasts, krais, and the remaining lesser units, the 1990 draft specifies only that they are "directly subordinate to the Russian Federation" and that they exercise "the right of self-government within the framework of the laws." The republics, oblasts, krais, and other territorial subdivisions are equal in their ability to exercise legislative initiative in the Russian parliament and to make agreements among themselves. There is also provision for the elevation of oblasts and the rest to the status of republics, also for any given ethnic group (the term *narod* is used in this case) to apply for republic status, provided that it is geographically concentrated in a given area.[8]

The failure of the 1990 draft prompted Oleg Rumiantsev and the working group of the Constitutional Commission to move in the direction of territorial federalism. There had been a lot of opposition to the first draft from provincial leaders, who in the majority of the oblasts and krais were of the old *nomenklatura* and opposed to Yeltsin's program of rapid privatization. The draft issued on October 24, 1991, in the expectation that the Fifth Russian Congress would ratify it, attempted to placate these leaders by reorganizing their jurisdictions into twenty *zemli* (lands) which would be the equivalent of the republics. While the republics would possess certain powers not given to the *zemli*, these were mainly symbolic. Debates and preliminary votes in the Russian parliament made it clear immediately that the *zemli* concept was unacceptable to a large majority. Republic leaders feared that the large *zemli* would erase their special status. Oblast leaders doubtless had the same kind of fears about lost positions and lost local control that so often bedevil efforts to merge local jurisdictions anywhere in the democratic world.

By the time of the constitutional draft of March 2, 1992, circumstances had changed. The republics were no longer asserting their right to the status of union republics in a Soviet Union which had disintegrated; furthermore, asserting the right to separate membership in the Commonwealth of Independent States did not seem important for the most part. The republics' other claims were still outstanding, however, including the claim of a number to independent foreign policies and the assertion of sweeping control over their resources and economies. Rumiantsev and the Constitutional Commission, while they knew that a strictly territorial federal system was out of the question, nevertheless seemed determined to make as few concrete concessions as possible to the republics. The March 1992 draft would have reduced the republics in most respects to the status of the krais and oblasts. There is a single list of exclusive federal powers and a single list of jointly exercised powers, which apply equally to the republics and the remaining territorial units. The status of the republics is given only symbolic elevation in language very reminiscent of the Soviet-era constitutions: "The republics possess full state powers on their territories, except for those powers which are assigned to the Russian Federation." This, however, is followed by a paragraph which specifies in somewhat different language the same arrangement for the oblasts (which include the cities of Moscow and St. Petersburg), krais, and autonomous oblasts. The powers of the okrugs (autonomous districts) are left to federal legislation.[9]

It is true that there are a few provisions of the March 1992 draft which set the republics apart somewhat. Rumiantsev points to the secession provisions of the draft whereby republics may secede from the Russian Federation if certain procedures are followed: the approval of two-thirds of all voters must be obtained in a referendum, and the Russian Supreme Soviet must approve the result by passing a law. (Note, however, that there are no secession provisions in the federal treaties that were signed at the end of that same month.) But even as concerns secession, the status of the republics differs only in detail from that of the other territorial units. The oblasts, krais, and autonomous oblasts are required to hold their own referenda to approve any change in the boundaries of the Russian Republic, and a second referendum must be held throughout the Russian Republic.[10]

Yeltsin had to move with particular care at this point, first of all by disarming the critics who since the fall of 1991 had been charging that a presidential dictatorship was in the making. Second, he had to assure the governments of the oblasts, republics, and other territorial-level subdivisions of a meaningful constitutional role. The three federal treaties signed in Moscow on March 31, 1992, were intended as the basis of a new constitution.[11] It was at least a temporary success for Yeltsin and the Constitutional Commission. Even if Tatarstan and Chechnia refused to sign—for the time being, at least—all the other republics and territorial jurisdictions did sign. Giving separate symbolic status to the republics while in practice putting them on the same level with the other jurisdictions was for the moment a successful compromise.

Why three treaties and not just one? One of the treaties was intended for the signatures of the then twenty-one republics, of which nineteen have signed at this writing; another was for the provinces (oblasts and krais) plus the cities of Moscow and St. Petersburg; the third was for the autonomous oblasts and okrugs; and the Russian Republic itself is a signatory to all three. The three texts differ only in minor details, and in general they leave the oblasts, krais, and lesser subdivisions on the same footing with the republics. And while the form of these agreements is that of treaties, the substance of them makes it clear that all these units of the system are the creatures of the Russian Federation rather than its creators. All three documents are signed not as treaties *among* the republics, oblasts, and the rest, but as treaties between their respective governments and the existing Russian Federation. All three preambles specify that the signatories (other than the Russian Republic itself) are republics, oblasts, and so on already within (*v sostave*) the federation.

In the treaty designed for the republics, the republics' sovereignty declarations are acknowledged in a general way in the preamble (also recognized is the Russian Republic's own sovereignty declaration). However, the treaties are clear about the supremacy of the federal constitution and federal laws; and, in the March 1992 draft constitution, there is a procedure for resolving conflicts of laws between the center and the republics.

The main purpose of the three federal treaties is to apportion functions or powers: the powers of the federal government, those exercised jointly, and those remaining to the units of the federation. In the three federal treaties and the March 1992 draft constitution, the first two categories are so comprehensive as to leave almost no powers exclusive to the republics. The residual-powers articles of all three federal treaties do acknowledge the right of all of Russia's republics and other territorial jurisdictions to carry on their own foreign relations, including international economic relations. But this is stated in somewhat conditional terms. The right to conclude treaties with foreign countries is not mentioned, although the republics and other territorial units are free to make agreements among themselves.[12] Foreign Minister Kozyrev reported in the fall of 1992 that a mechanism for coordinating the foreign relations of Russia's republics and oblasts was under discussion. But so far no concrete developments along this line have been reported.[13]

The treaties' provisions on ownership and use of natural resources set both the republics' position (in all sovereignty declarations) and Moscow's position side by side: natural resources are the property of the people of the republic, but questions of ownership and use will be determined by the laws of both Russia and the republics.[14]

The constitutional draft issued on November 11, 1992, distinguishes the republics from the other territorial units in regard to their form of government, though even here the differences appear slight. But regarding powers, the republics appear to be absolutely in the same boat with the oblasts, krais, and autonomous oblasts.[15] The draft was discussed at the Seventh Russian Congress, once again without result.

A portion of the battlefield of the "war of laws" lies in the process of drafting republic constitutions and territorial charters. The evolution of the republics' constitutions is a whole story by itself, and necessarily an unfinished story until the Russian Constitution is adopted, since the directive from Moscow to the republics is to wait for its final adoption. For our present purposes, it must be noted that all the main issues raised in the sovereignty declarations have reappeared in one form or another in the republics' draft constitutions: the supremacy of republic laws over those of the Russian Federation; the republics' absolute control over their economies and natural resources; the definition of citizenship; the right of the republics to conduct their own foreign relations and to make treaties with foreign governments; the right to join the Commonwealth of Independent States or other confederations; and the right of secession.[16]

Moscow and the Regions

The political transformations that have taken place in the Russian Republic's territorial subdivisions since 1989 add up to the adaptation of the existing local leadership to new circumstances, first of all to the weakening of the central administration and the end of the Communist Party's central institutions. The constitutional norms and administrative structures that now must hold Russia together by themselves have given way, according to a declaration by the Russian Constitutional Court, to a "legal nihilism."[17] In the former ASSRs, the adaptation has included compromises with local non-Russian nationalists and the exploitation of local nationalism even in republics where Russians are in the majority.

The republics' proclamations concerning autonomy and sovereignty, as well as statements apparently demanding the right to secede from the Russian Federation, must first be seen as bargaining positions. In fact, as a result of these many proclamations, the terms "sovereign" and "sovereignty" were emptied of any specific meaning: everybody was talking about "sovereignty," but few could agree what it meant in practice. By itself, this issue hardly mattered. From the summer of 1990, many of Russia's provinces and republics became centers of opposition to Yeltsin and the Moscow-centered democrats. Yeltsin was elected chairman of the Russian Supreme Soviet on May 29 of that year. The sovereignty declarations began with those of the North Ossetian Republic and the Karelian Republic, dated July 20 and August 25 respectively. It can hardly be said that the ethnic Ossetians and Karelians were taking the lead in asserting their claims to greater national autonomy, in view of the fact that both groups constitute just 10 percent of their own republics. The picture in such republics appears to be that of the local Russian (or mainly Russian) *nomenklatura* waving the flag of greater autonomy as one way of undermining Yeltsin's power.

Yeltsin himself must bear a degree of responsibility for the sovereignty declarations. The impetus for them was the series of analogous declarations by the union republics, which had begun in November 1988 with the Estonian declaration. Russia's own sovereignty declaration of June 12, 1990, adopted at the First Russian Congress, came at a point when only five other republics had declared their sovereignty (the Baltic republics, Azerbaijan, and Georgia). Nearly a year later, while Gorbachev was promoting his draft of the Union Treaty, the heads of all former autonomous republics—then sixteen in number—met with him in the Kremlin to insist that they too be signatories of the treaty. There was nothing illogical about this, they contended. The sovereignty proclaimed by the ASSRs differed in no way from the sovereignty of the fifteen union republics, including Russia. Therefore they should sign the Union Treaty on an equal footing.[18]

It is hardly surprising that Russia's former ASSRs, with their appetites whetted for an elevated status in the Soviet Union, should make increased demands on the Russian Republic as well. And there should be no surprise in the way in which a number of resource-rich oblasts, where ethnic rights are not a major issue, have tested the political waters with claims to special economic rights, political autonomy, an independent international role, and possibly even separation.

While the temperature around these issues was rising in the context of weakened Soviet power, the aftermath of the August coup attempt prompted Yeltsin to strengthen his government's jurisdiction over his oblasts and republics. He launched this effort on August 21, 1991, the day of the coup's defeat. Yeltsin's immediate goal was to establish central control over the governments of those provinces whose leaders had openly supported the coup attempt and to enforce his proscription of the Communist Party, in this case the party at the oblast and local levels. At the time, this was criticized in some quarters as an effort not just to take power away from these nests of coup sympathizers, but to establish direct presidential control of all local government and thereby to lay an important foundation for future dictatorial control of all government from top to bottom.

The legal basis for Yeltsin's authority in this case was a resolution of the Russian Supreme Soviet which empowers the president to dismiss the entire executive committee of any province or autonomous region that had refused to carry out Russian Republic laws or other directives. In place of the executive committee, the president could now appoint a head of administration. In addition, the president was given blanket powers of appointment and dismissal of these heads of administration, until such time as laws are passed defining the powers of local government (presumably under the new Russian Constitution, which, at this writing, has not been adopted). It is worthy of note that the president's power did not extend to the republics, the former ASSRs.[19]

Yeltsin immediately appointed heads of administration for thirteen oblasts, including some economically and politically important ones—Krasnoiarsk, Khabarovsk, Novosibirsk, and Volgograd, among others. More dismissals of heads of oblasts followed, in some cases by action of the Russian Supreme Soviet. Not unsurprisingly, the persons appointed were strong Yeltsin supporters. The extent of the new heads' powers was not clear at first. The deputy sent to Novosibirsk as the head of administration at first denied that he would wield executive powers, and explained his task as one of monitoring the observance of laws and official directives. But elsewhere, the new heads asserted and used their powers to dismiss and appoint officials and to use at least a suspensive veto on the actions of local soviets.[20]

The Russian president's powers vis-à-vis the republics were reinforced by a constitutional amendment adopted by the Russian Congress in early November 1991, which gave him the right to suspend acts of the republics' chief executives if they do not conform to the Russian Constitution and Russia's laws. In a related action, the congress passed a moratorium on referenda and elections in the republics.[21] Defiance in Tatarstan was the immediate problem; also the possibility that other republics might follow the Tatar example and adopt the pose of independent states willing to negotiate with the Russian Republic as equals.

Early in 1992, Yeltsin's heads of administration were joined by representatives of the Russian parliament. This was in part a move by Parliament Speaker Ruslan Khasbulatov to counter Yeltsin's growing power, and in part the result of a separate legislative oversight system which was much needed in its own right. It also gave parliament, whose majority was hostile to Yeltsin's economic reforms, a separate source of information on the economic, social, and political consequences of the Yeltsin–Gaidar version of economic "shock therapy."[22]

The federal treaties may only have whetted the appetite of oblasts and republics for more concessions, since demands for fresh concessions have increased rather than abated. Demands for more regional autonomy are by no means confined to the (presently) twenty-one nationality-based republics. It is almost equally strong in some of Russia's fifty-five oblasts, particularly those with promising economic resources and the possibility of developing foreign markets and attracting foreign investment.[23] In the majority of the oblasts, the political leaders and economic managers have been taking decisions increasingly into their own hands. From a distance, their behavior looks like a combination of power hunger and political defiance of Yeltsin and the center. But it must also be seen as the result of lack of material support from the center and from the rest of the country's economy. When enterprises and local economies must fend for themselves, it is hardly surprising that local leaders will resist any sort of interference from the center that might complicate their situation even further.

Movements for Autonomy

A comprehensive review of movements toward greater self-rule in Russia's regions would need a chapter or more to itself; each region has its own story to tell, its own combination of leaders, issues, and economic and political organizations. Even in the oblasts where there has been no particular impetus for more autonomy, the assumption of greater self-rule has been forced on local leaders by economic disorder and the growing ineffectiveness of those levers of central control that are still used by Moscow. Omitted in the following survey, in particular, are such important examples as Tiumen' Oblast, Khabarovsk Krai, and the Bashkortostan (formerly Bashkir) Republic. What follows is intended only as a representative list of cases, all of them representing unfinished stories.

Another word of caution: One reads everywhere that for the most part, Russia's regions are under the control of the old *nomenklatura*. Aside from the reality that the majority of today's regional administrators and managers held positions of responsibility before 1991, including posts in the Communist Party, this generalization says very little. To begin with, the old *nomenklatura* is not all old by any means, but also includes young and middle-aged executives. Second, while it is probably safe to say that a majority of Russia's old *nomenklatura* is critical of the Yeltsin administration and is inclined to support the Civic Union forces, today's territorial leaders and managers represent a wide spectrum of views. Furthermore, many of them are quite simply pragmatic rather than political or ideological in their basic outlook: they want to rescue their regions' economies by whatever route is open. Finally, this old *nomenklatura* includes most of the people in a given region who have practical management experience. Those who assert that the experienced executives are bureaucratic dead wood have little idea of the kind of initiative and management skills it has taken to keep a large state enterprise functioning (to take the most important kind of example), not just in the last few years but in past decades as well. Therefore, while the term "*nomenklatura*" is used in some of the following descriptions, it means quite simply the executives, whatever their views and aims, who also held leading regional positions—often the same positions—in the recent past.

Oblasts and Krais

Krasnoiarsk Krai

Krasnoiarsk Krai sprawls across the middle of Siberia and occupies 10 percent of the Russian Republic's territory. Its resources and industries, based primarily on nonferrous metals, chemicals, and timber, offer a real possibility for building an autonomous economic base and either defying Moscow or bargaining with it. Krasnoiarsk is also a straightforward example of an area in which the *nomenklatura* has had no difficulty remaining in control during the Yeltsin era. Moreover, Krasnoiarsk has offered fertile soil for Russian nationalist movements. Its local leaders and its population have been courted actively by the Russian National Assembly, the Industrial Union faction in the Russian parliament, and the militant Russian National Unity movement.[24]

In the light of this political reality, demands for more autonomy are understandable for two reasons: economic autonomy will enable the krai to continue as a bastion of opposition to the Yeltsin government, as necessary; and the profits of the large industries can be used—and are being used, actually—to support Russian nationalist movements. That is to say, the present drive for regional autonomy is simply an opportunistic one. The goal of the krai's leaders is not separation or even greater autonomy for its own sake, but progress toward a nationalist central leadership that will rebuild central authority, slow down the present headlong drive toward a market economy, and protect the state economic sector.

The Krasnoiarsk leadership was in the forefront of the more powerful territories demanding equal status with the republics. These demands continued even after the signing of the three federal treaties, since Krasnoiarsk and others have been complaining that Moscow is still treating them as second-class territories within the new federal relationship. In October 1992, for example, the Krasnoiarsk Krai Soviet issued an ultimatum to Yeltsin and the Russian parliament. At the center of the krai's concerns were economic rights, particularly the claim to control over its natural resources, and economic self-determination as distinct from political self-determination. Property questions remain unsettled: Which levels of government own what, and who has the right to dispose of this property? With this ultimatum came a warning that if the oblast did not gain sufficient resource control, at least equal to that of the republics, separatism in the form of a Enisei republic could become a serious factor to be reckoned with. The theme of Siberia as Moscow's long-standing colony has been prominent in official and public discussion. The issues include the export of raw materials with little compensation to the territory, the huge industrial installations built at Moscow's order with no consultation of local governments and populations, and prisoners released from the krai's many labor camps and settled in the area. Before the August 1991 coup, there was talk of a Siberian Soviet Federated Republic as part of the Soviet Union. A Russian autonomous region on the banks of the Enisei, or a Enisei republic, had also been proposed. While failure of the coup pulled the ground from under such ideas, the economic issues remained and can in turn raise the political issues all over again.[25]

Hardly was the ink dry on the three federal treaties than the Krasnoiarsk leaders were confronted with demands for rights and greater autonomy by two of their own subregions, namely the autonomous okrugs of Taimyr and Evenki. In both districts, the protests were powered primarily by claims for better economic treatment rather than by complaints of the small national minorities. Taimyr includes the polar mining city of Noril'sk and the mineral-rich lands around it. The Evenki Autonomous Okrug, though it is similarly rich in mineral resources, has a poorly developed economy and thus has much less to bargain with. But the situation only points to an illogical feature of the federal treaties: Krasnoiarsk Krai is a subject of the Russian Federation but contains within its borders two governments that are equally subjects of the same federation.[26]

Irkutsk Oblast

The postcoup demands put forth by a specially convened congress in Irkutsk included status as a full-fledged member of the Russian Federation and the oblast's right to adopt its own laws on a large variety of subjects. Interestingly, there were localities (such as the city of Angarsk) whose leaders accused the oblast leaders of trying to accumulate power for themselves at the expense of local governments and that threatened to secede from oblast jurisdiction if that happened.[27]

The "Siberian Republic"

Siberian complaints about being treated as a colony have been resounded loudly from early in the Gorbachev era up to the present: Moscow, European Russia, and the more industrialized Soviet republics were taking Siberia's natural-resource wealth, despoiling the environment in the process, and returning little to the Siberian population. Russia depends on Siberia, above all for its energy sources: 80 percent of its oil, 89 percent of its natural gas, and 63 percent of its coal. In the 1989 elections to the USSR Congress of People's Deputies, many Siberian candidates made this a major theme and floated the idea of an independent or quasi-independent Siberian republic as the solution. But once in Moscow, the deputies did not seriously advance this idea, so that outside of Siberia it received little public attention.

Yeltsin, himself from the Urals, was familiar with Siberian grievances. The "Siberian Agreement" was created by the working party of the Russian parliament in March 1991. The group met in Novosibirsk to find a way to bring Siberia's regional governments into the economic decision-making process. In June, Yeltsin, fresh from his victory as popularly elected president, traveled to Novosibirsk to put his blessing on the result. This was and remains an interregional agreement, not only for maximizing Siberia's voice in its own problems and destiny, but for reducing Moscow's interference in these decisions as well.[28]

As discussions began on the Siberian Agreement, there took place in Krasnoiarsk the First Congress of People's Deputies of the Siberian Territories. Some separatist voices were heard: "We can get along without Russia, but not Russia without us!" It was clear to all that the congress could be regarded as a provisional Siberian parliament, an idea emphasized by the white-and-green Siberian flag waving in front of the meeting hall. But for the most part the deputies sought solution for their regional problems within the framework of a stable Russian federal system. They pointed to the facts that the living standard in eastern Siberia is half that of European Russia, and that less than a quarter of the taxes collected in Krasnoiarsk are returned to it in any form.[29]

A number of national republics sent only observers rather than accredited delegates to this gathering; these included the Sakha, Buriat, Khakass, and Tuva republics. Their leaders feared (incorrectly, as it turned out) that separatism would prevail at the congress, and they had no wish to be associated with any independence movement. Perhaps they also feared a Siberian republic dominated by ethnic Russian leaders and managers. Another type of phenomenon was the Yamalo-Nenets Republic in the Siberian far north, a national area newly elevated to republic status. However, this elevation in status was actually the work of the local *nomenklatura*, mainly Russians, who sought jobs and control over the area.[30]

In fact, commentaries on both the Siberian Agreement and the congress repeatedly stress the dominant role of the "old *nomenklatura*." The principal aim of these officials is not an independent Siberia, but a Siberia sufficiently in charge of its own resources to enable the former party officials and economic managers to maintain their positions and protect their state enterprises, which are threatened by Yeltsin's market reforms. For them, the idea of Siberian independence is first of all a useful bogeyman.

Sakhalin

Business leaders and economists, Russian and foreign, are watching with interest the Fedorov experiment on the far eastern island of Sakhalin. At the end of the 1980s, Valentin Pavlovich Fedorov, head of a major Moscow economics institute, corresponding member of the (then) USSR Academy of Sciences, and holder of other distinguished economic research posts, moved to this ultraremote location, ran for head of the oblast government in the April 1990 elections, and won. Sakhalin, rich in fish, oil, coal, and timber, seemed to Fedorov a promising location for a Russian version of the Asian "little dragons" along the Pacific rim—Taiwan, Singapore, and Hong Kong.

While the Fedorov regime has generated its share of controversy, none will question the fact that some definite successes have resulted. During the first two years of Fedorov's tenure, 5,000 nonfarm businesses were established, particularly in the areas of food processing, fishing, retailing, and manufacturing. In addition, Fedorov won from Moscow the right to privatize Sakhalin's land, in a situation where land privatization everywhere else in Russia now appears delayed indefinitely. This produced 800 private farms by the beginning of 1992. Fedorov's formula resembles the economic "shock therapy" used in Poland and advocated by former Russian Prime Minister Gaidar. Businesses are to be as free from interference as possible, but may also receive substantial help from the government; and monopolies and mafias must be contained.[31] Critics of Fedorov's program point out that the prosperity of local businesses has not improved the lot of local consumers, who cannot afford market prices. If one looks at the overall results, Sakhalin has not been spared the ills that today beset the rest of the Russian economy, including inflation, falling output, and falling standards of living. The Sakhalin government's subsidies which prop up many businesses belie the assertion that market economy reforms are now paying off.

Fedorov himself took office in the April 1990 elections as a democrat and Yeltsin supporter, with the support of the local Democratic Russia organization. After the August 1991 coup he was among the heads of administration appointed by Yeltsin. But it was also during the postcoup months that Fedorov began to adopt a more and more nationalist orientation. He has stood firmly against any concessions to Japan on the issue of the contested southern Kuriles islands, and has roundly criticized Yeltsin for the latter's willingness even to entertain the notion of some sort of compromise arrangement. In his approach to economic reform, Fedorov has lately come to adopt a gradualist approach, and in 1992 he opposed the Gaidar program. He has done battle with Moscow over control of Sakhalin's extensive oil and gas deposits. For his stand on the Kuriles, and for his anti-Yeltsin alignment, he was elected in February 1992 to joint chairmanship of the conservative Russian National Assembly.

Thus, in spite of the unusual features of Fedorov's background, his rapid ascent to leadership on Sakhalin as a democrat, and his initial support of bold, swift market reforms, the picture of his leadership today does not differ greatly from that of a large number of those of other oblasts that today rely on the pre-1991 *nomenklatura* for their executive and management talent.[32]

The "Far Eastern Republic"

Here is a clear example of a separatist movement which today can be shrugged off as the posturing of political dilettantes, but which under changed circumstances might become serious. The original Far Eastern Republic (FER) had a life span of hardly more than two years, 1920–22. It was a product more of Lenin's diplomacy than of any sort of regional independence movement. In fact, it was a device for dealing with all the powers interested in the Russian Far East at a time when the Russian Civil War was winding down but the new Soviet regime was unrecognized by the powers that mattered most. Put more bluntly, it was a buffer state and a political front to help spare the new Soviet regime from further invasion, occupation, and subversion by the great powers. Its territory extended from Vladivostok and northern Sakhalin westward to the eastern shore of Lake Baikal. On November 14, 1922, following the exodus of the last occupying power, the Japanese, the republic's legislature adopted a resolution to dissolve the republic and join the new Soviet Russian state.

The Far Eastern Republican Party, which, according to reports, is mainly a youthful radical movement, has been pressing for the formation of an FER provisional government. It maintains that the dissolution of the FER was in fact unlawful occupation and annexation by Russia's Bolshevik regime. It has called on residents of the area to disregard Russian laws and not to serve in the CIS or Russian armed forces. Another organization has joined the independence drive, the North Pacific Forum. Its plans call for an extensive North Pacific federative republic, which among other things will have command of the Pacific Fleet plus the Far Eastern and Transbaikal military districts.[33]

Stavropol' Krai

In November 1992, the legislature of Stavropol' Krai adopted a resolution in support of the idea of making the territory a "self-governing zone." Particularly addressed in the resolution were economic regulation and taxation, including tax breaks to attract or keep industries, and the participation of foreign capital. In money terms, the main demand was a 50 percent reduction in the tax revenues that are transferred to the federal budget. This is justified, in the eyes of local leaders, in view of the fact that Moscow has now transferred the responsibility for meeting most social needs to the oblast level.[34]

St. Petersburg

In the fall of 1992, the St. Petersburg Council held a special session to consider its status under new federal arrangements. Deputies raised the question of whether St. Petersburg should have a lesser array of rights than Tatarstan or the other republics. There was debate over the concept of a "free city." Already St. Petersburg had moved ahead of federal legislation with its program for privatizing state housing, though Moscow then ended a possible confrontation by legalizing privatization throughout Russia.[35]

Republics

Yakutia/Sakha Republic

In its September 1990 Declaration of Sovereignty, the newly renamed Sakha Republic claimed exclusive property rights in its natural resources. While even at that early date the exclusive resource claim had become standard in the 1990 parade of sovereignty declarations, the party chiefs of Yakutia had a special resource in mind, for they were sitting atop enormous wealth in diamonds. Discovered only in the 1950s, Yakutia's diamonds constitute nearly all the diamond resources of the former Soviet Union. The stage was set not for a struggle over political separation, but quite simply for disposition of the profits.

By 1992, the republic had won the right to keep 20 percent of all minerals produced on its territory, including its diamonds. It may also keep 45 percent of the hard-currency earnings from foreign diamond sales, mainly to the De Beers diamond monopoly of South Africa. This is a noteworthy concession in view of the estimated annual $1.4 billion earned by Soviet (now Russian) diamonds. Yakutia today is covering two-thirds of its budget from these arrangements; formerly the republic's meager share of this income accounted for only 4 percent of its budget.

The entire diamond industry was recently placed under the control of a joint stock company, Diamonds-Russia-Sakha, in which the Russian and Yakutian governments hold equal shares. There had been quite a struggle between Yakutia's leaders and the Russian parliament over this arrangement. Moscow lawmakers were insistent on some degree of direct control, particularly after Yakutia had started making independent deals on the world's diamond markets. One lever in Moscow's hands is the fact that the diamond-cutting industry is located outside Yakutia.[36]

Tatarstan

The Tatar Republic's sovereignty declaration of August 30, 1990, differed from the other sovereignty declarations of Russia's ASSRs in one important respect: it made clear the republic's intention to be independent of the Russian Republic. The document states Tatarstan's willingness to sign the Union Treaty, but it makes no mention of Russia's proposed Federal Treaty, or of a future status as a subject of the Russian Federation. From that time to the present (early 1993), Tatarstan's radical stance has set it apart from all the other republics.

Three other developments confirmed the position taken in its sovereignty declaration: the republic's expressed wish to join the CIS, the referendum of March 21, 1992, and the Tatarstan leaders' refusal in the same month to sign the Russian Federal Treaty. Following the final collapse of the Soviet Union in December 1991, and in the midst of increasing pressure from the Russian government to sign the federal treaty, the Tatarstan parliament announced on February 21, 1992, that a referendum would be held to determine the future status of the republic. This was in direct defiance of the twelve-month moratorium on republic referendums adopted by the Russian Congress less than three months earlier. While President Mintimer Shaimiev denied that the referendum was about separatism and independence, it was widely perceived as paving the way for an ultimate decision on separation. There were criticisms that the referendum's wording was meant to obscure its real purpose, and thereby to garner additional votes for independence from those who supported greater autonomy for the republic but had strong doubts about separation.

More than 80 percent of the republic's population voted on March 21, and of these, 61 percent voted in favor. Of the entire voting-age population, barely more than 50 percent voted yes. The vote in favor was higher in the predominantly Tatar rural areas, while Kazan, the republic's capital, showed a slight majority opposed.[37]

Apart from the recent rumblings of separatism in the Chechen Republic, Tatarstan alone among Russia's republics has taken the route of separatism and defiance. Why Tatarstan? There is a pronounced background of historical factors, starting with the three centuries of Tatar dominance in Russia and their defeat by Ivan the Terrible in 1552. Add to this the proportion of Tatars in the former Soviet Union, where in the 1989 census they ranked sixth among the Soviet nationalities. This meant that the Tatars, recognized in the Soviet federal system only via their autonomous republic status within the RSFSR, outranked in numbers the titular nationalities of nine of the USSR's union republics. Against this circumstance, however, must be reckoned the facts that within the Tatar ASSR lived only slightly more than one-fourth of all Soviet Tatars and that in the present Tatarstan Republic, Tatars account for only 48 percent of the total population, while Russians make up 43 percent.

The Tatars' resentment over their low-level official status in the Soviet system goes back to the formation of the Soviet Union in the 1920s, when Tatar Bolshevik leaders first sought union republic status; then, when this demand was rejected, they sought enlarged powers for the autonomous republics. The issue of elevation to a union republic came up again with adoption of the 1936 Constitution, and it continued to arise during the post-Stalin era.

Tatarstan's status also involves a big economic issue, namely, the republic's oil production, which today constitutes more than one-fourth of total Russian production. While Moscow's nearly total control over the republic's industries was a situation typical of Russia's republics generally, it was and is viewed with particular resentment by a nation whose other grievances are so pronounced.[38]

During the remainder of 1992 the Tatar leadership prepared and then played its trump card in the "war of laws," the adoption in early November of the Tatarstan Constitution. More than the republic's refusal to sign the Federal Treaty, the adoption of its constitution can be interpreted as a formal legal break with the Russian Federation. The Kazan government now holds out the prospect of negotiating various bilateral agreements with Moscow, and there is even the prospect of its applying to join the CIS. As of this writing, a treaty between Kazan and Moscow appears to be close to completion. The new Tatarstan Constitution contains one interesting link between independent Tatarstan and Russia: Article 23 specifies that citizens of Tatarstan are also citizens of Russia. This is clearly a concession to the feelings and fears of the large ethnic Russian minority, as well as evidence of the possibility that many Tatars prefer dual citizenship.[39]

Conclusions

What can the U.S. government expect for the remainder of the 1990s concerning the ability of Russia to hold itself together? Will American businesses interested in Russian resources, investments, and trade be able to count on a reasonably stable political environment? On the basis of the examples cited in the preceding section, it can at least be said that there will be some turmoil and uncertainty in a number of economically and geographically important regions. In most of them, there are impulses in the direction of autonomy, with some voices calling for outright separation. Certain national republics may indeed claim their independence and enforce the claim against Moscow's resistance. On balance, however, the factors making for autonomy and possible separation are intertwined with the factors supporting Russia's territorial and administrative integrity.

Here is a summary of specific tendencies:

1. *Nationalism and separation.* Will the Tatarstan example serve to infect the other republics with the urge to separate? Neighboring Bashkortostan has been moving somewhat more cautiously in the direction of possible separation, but there are serious differences between its situation and that of Tatarstan. Meanwhile, the idea of a Bashkortostan–Tatarstan republic, as well as the larger idea of an Idel–Ural state resurrected from the time of the Russian Civil War, foundered on differences among the nationalities involved. More important, the factors that have pushed the Tatarstan independence drive are those which make the republic and the Tatar nation different from most of the other republics and nations within Russia's borders. Furthermore, Tatarstan's geographical situation—its territory landlocked and surrounded by the Russian Republic—will limit its political and economic freedom even as a sovereign independent state. There is also little indication that the ethnic struggles in the North Caucasus will spread elsewhere. There, the ancient hatreds, the territorial claims and counterclaims, and the problems left by Stalin's arbitrary republic borders are specific to the area. In this writer's experience, the overwhelming feeling elsewhere in the Russian Republic is that the strife in the North Caucasus should serve as a stern warning to reach amicable solutions to problems fueled by ethnic tension, boundary disputes, historic claims, resource disputes, and related factors.

2. *Regional economic realities.* Weakening central controls and a greatly weakened central budget have obliged the regions to fend for themselves. One might call this regional economic autonomy by default. To this is added elements of outright struggle in which most of the regional leadership has been opposing the Yeltsin leadership over the issue of economic reform. Specific areas of center-versus-region combat include control of property, licensing, bank control, local substitutes for the national currency, price regulation, and the need to fund local budgets locally.[40]

At the same time, there are long-term advantages for the regions in remaining in the Russian Federation. The country's monetary, banking, and transportation systems can be stabilized only at the center. Even if a number of Russia's regions become and remain economically strong, policies will still be needed to maintain balance among them and to ensure the continuity of a unified economic area.

3. *Political realities.* In most areas, power has remained in the hands of the *nomenklatura*, whose dominance of regional government typically points in two directions: the political opposition to the Yeltsin administration and the drive for greater command of the local economy. Both impel the regions in the direction of more autonomy. Where the leadership is predominantly Russian, however—

and this includes the leadership of some of the national republics, such as the Karelian and Komi republics—separation from Russia is not likely to be a goal. The leadership in Krasnoiarsk Krai and on Sakhalin, to cite just two examples, is thoroughly Russian nationalist. Whatever their complaints about Yeltsin's policies and Moscow's economic restrictions, the philosophical or ideological impulse of these regional leaders is not to cut Russia into autonomous pieces but to build it together again.

4. *"Little dragons" in Siberia and the Russian Far East?* The development of foreign trade, foreign investment, and joint enterprises in the resource-rich regions has begun and will continue to grow. It will be hampered by now-familiar weaknesses in the Russian economy, the problems with the ruble, inflation, inadequate infrastructure, and so forth. It will also be hampered in some areas by political contests among local political leaders and economic managers, as well as by those restrictions and controls which the central government is still able to impose. The fact that these problems are shared by the center and the regions will act as a brake on any movements for political separation. If one could imagine for the sake of argument that Sakhalin under Valentin Fedorov's leadership were moving in the direction of separation (which is certainly not the case), it is clear enough that for the present, in spite of all of Fedorov's economic initiatives, Sakhalin is not in a position to become a Russian Taiwan or Singapore. More likely, economic success would come at the price of extensive domination by foreign economic interests. In such a case, Central America and not Taiwan would be the model—hardly a desirable result.

5. *The demographic factor.* Ethnic Russians, who as of 1989 made up little over half the population of the entire Soviet Union, in that same year constituted 81.5 percent of the population of Russia. In only three of Russia's own national republics does the titular nationality account for more than 50 percent of the population; Russians are well distributed about their vast land. Furthermore, the migration into Russia of some of the 25 million Russians living in the other former Soviet republics will increase their proportion over time.[41]

The U.S. government and interested businesses, therefore, are unlikely to be dealing with an array of independent regions that have formally broken ties with Moscow. A demand to recognize a Tatarstan republic hardly seems a prospect at present. In the North Caucasus, on the other hand, any foreign oil companies that have an interest in operating in Groznyi's oil fields will most certainly have dealings with the upstart Chechen Republic. That, however, is a special case which is quite unlikely to be replicated in other parts of Russia. The prospects for a Far Eastern republic or a Siberian republic seem fairly remote. The leaders of those areas are loyal to Russia if not to the Yeltsin regime. At most, some of Siberia's leaders might use separatist movements and proclamations as they have on past occasions, as a handy club to shake in the direction of the Moscow government, as necessary.

Meanwhile, the environment for business, and for investment in particular, will be complex. For every major investment or other economic initiative, foreign businesses and (as necessary) government representatives will find themselves talking with different authorities who may well be working at cross purposes: ministers in Moscow, regional political leaders, and the managers of large enterprises. As well, whenever a large foreign corporation with a major investment tries to create its own economic environment and infrastructure, it is likely to face the charge of colonization from Russian nationalist groups.

6. *The "distraction factor."* It is almost certain that the government in Moscow, no matter who will be at the helm, will be distracted by continuing domestic crises and therefore less able to pursue a coherent foreign policy. The same is true of any government with large domestic problems such as the continuing recession that faces the Clinton administration. Because a good working relationship between Washington and Moscow is a highly desirable foreign policy goal for both countries, the Clinton administration would be well advised to refrain from doing anything that might exacerbate the tensions between Russia's regions and the central government. Certainly, the U.S. government ought to avoid the temptation—which will surely arise—to cut separate deals with regional governments. It should also restrain American firms from encouraging these same regional governments to defy or ignore the laws of the Russian Federation. To the extent that Washington is able to provide aid in the next several years, the rebuilding of infrastructure in Russia will be the best investment, with emphasis on monetary and banking systems, communications, and transportation.

Notes

1. See the list and details in Jean Radvanyi, "And What If Russia Breaks Up? Toward New Regional Divisions," *Post-Soviet Geography*, vol. 23, no. 2 (February 1992), pp. 69–77. See especially the table on p. 75. The Black Soil Regional Association is described in *Izvestiia*, January 14, 1993, p. 4.

2. Radvanyi, "What If," p. 71.

3. The texts of the declarations of sovereignty are contained in Institut teorii i istorii sotzializma TsK KPSS, *K soiuzu suverennykh narodov: Sbornik dokumentove KPSS, zakonodatel'nykh aktov, deklaratsii, obrashchenii i prezidentskikh ukazov, posviashchennykh probleme natsional'no gosudarstvennogo suvereniteta* (Moscow, 1991). This collection is cited hereafter as: *K soiuzu suverennykh narodov.*

4. R.R. Abdulatipov, L.F. Boltenkova, and Iu. F. Iarov, *Federalizm v istorii Rossii; kniga pervaia* (Moscow: Izdatel'stvo "Respublika," 1992), pp. 254–55, 355. See also Ann Sheehy, "Tatarstan and Bashkiria: Obstacles to Confederation," *RFE/RL Research Report*, vol. 1, no. 22 (May 29, 1992), p. 34.

5. Oleg Rumiantsev, "Tuva—respublika vsekh natsional'nostei," *Rossiiskaia gazeta*, October 1, 1992, p. 4.

6. The 1990 and 1992 texts are reproduced in *Argumenty i fakty*, 1990, no. 47 (November) and 1992, no. 12 (March); the 1991 text can be found in *Konstitutsionnyi vestnik*, 1991, no. 8 (November).

7. Article 1.2.(1) of the November 1990 draft and Article 1.(2) of the March 1992 draft.

8. See Article 1.9 and all of Section (*razdel*) 4 of this draft.

9. See Article 81 of the March 1992 draft and Section (*razdel*) 4 generally. The text is reproduced in *Argumenty i fakty*, 1992, no. 12 (March).

10. These provisions are in Article 74 (4) and Article 75(2).

11. The texts of these treaties are reproduced in *Etnopolis: Etnopoliticheskii vestnik Rossii*, 1992, no. 1, pp. 17–32.

12. This is Article III of all three federal treaties.

13. Olga Burkaleva, "Voprosy neprostye, obstanovka delovaia," *Rossiiskaia gazeta*, October 23, 1992, p. 1.

14. Ibid.

15. This draft is in *Konstitutsionnyi vestnik*, 1992, no. 13 (November).

16. See *Konstitutsionnyi vestnik*, 1992, no. 11 (April–May), p. 4663, for analyses of the draft constitutions of Tuva and Buriatia and for a review of the competence of the units of the Russian Federation in their relations with foreign governments.

17. "Konstitutsionnyi stroi pod ugrozoi," *Rossiiskaia gazeta*, June 27, 1992, p. 1.

18. G. Alimov in *Izvestiia*, May 13, 1991, pp. 1–2; trans. from *The Current Digest of the Soviet Press*, vol. 43, no. 19 (June 12, 1991), pp. 1–3.

19. *Vedomosti S''ezda narodnykh deputatov RSFSR i Verkhovnogo Soveta RSFSR*, no. 34: 1125, August 22, 1991.

20. See the articles in *The Current Digest*, vol. 43, no. 35 (October 2, 1991), pp. 21–22.

21. *Izvestiia*, October 30, November 1, and November 2, 1991. The Russian president's authority over acts of the republic presidents was incorporated in Article 121–28 of the present Russian Constitution. This provision was not included in any of the subsequent draft constitutions that have come to the author's attention.

22. Sergei Chugaev, "Parlament naznachaet komissarov v provintsiakh," *Izvestiia*, January 11, 1992, p. 2.

23. In addition to the twenty-one republics and fifty-five oblasts, the territorial subdivisons of the Russian Republic presently include ten autonomous districts (okrugs), one autonomous oblast (the Jewish Autonomous Oblast, known formerly as Birobijan), and the cities of Moscow and St. Petersburg, whose status is coequal with that of the oblasts.

24. See the account by Aleksei Tarasov in *Izvestiia*, December 3, 1992, p. 3.

25. A. Tarasov, "Budet li Eniseisskaia respublika?" *Izvestiia*, November 22, 1991.

26. Aleksei Tarasov, "Severnyi peredel," *Izvestiia*, September 3, 1992, p. 3.

27. V. Sbitnev, "S''ezd v 'Irkutskom gosudarstve,' " *Izvestiia*, November 18, 1991, p. 2.

28. Valerii Ivanitskii, "Troianskii kon' u vorot Sibiri," *Rossiiskaia gazeta*, June 12, 1992, p. 2.

29. Aleksei Tarasov, "Sibir' trebuet dekolonizatsii," *Izvestiia*, March 30, 1992, p. 2.

30. Valerii Iaroslavtsev, "Kak nam obustroit' Sibir'?" *Rossiiskaia gazeta*, April 2, 1992, p. 2.

31. See the account by Marshall I. Goldman, "Sakhalin: Russia's Big Success Story," *World Monitor*, December 1992, pp. 31–35.

32. Kathryn Brown, "Sakhalin's Valentin Fedorov Makes Nationalist Allies," *RFE/RL Research Report*, vol. 1, no. 38 (September 25, 1992), pp. 33–38.

33. Yelena Matveyeva, "A Pacific Nation with its Own Currency," *Moscow News*, October 11–18, 1992.

34. Lyudmila Leontyeva and Sergei Shelin, "Riot in the Province," *Moscow News*, November 29–December 6, 1992, p. 5.

35. Ibid.

36. Celestine Bohlen, "Poor Region in Russia Lays Claim to Its Diamonds," *The New York Times*, November 1, 1992.

37. Ann Sheehy, "Tatarstan Asserts Its Sovereignty," *RFE/RL Research Report*, vol. 1, no. 14 (April 3, 1992), p. 3.

38. Ibid., pp. 1–2.

39. Dmitrii Mikhailin, "Tatarstan vybral voinu konstitutsii?" *Rossiiskaia gazeta*, November 11, 1992, p. 2. See also a number of articles about the adoption of the Tatarstan Constitution in *The Current Digest*, vol. 44, no. 43 (November 25, 1992), pp. 15–16.

40. Andrei Neshchadin, "Russian Regions Oppose the Government on Economic Reforms," *Moscow News*, June 28–July 5, 1992, p. 9.

41. Galina Vitkovskaia, "Russians Coming to Russia," *Moscow News*, December 13–20, 1992, p. 8.

Comment

The American Vision of "What's Wrong With Russia" and How Cooperation Can Help

Nina Belyaeva

Need for a Common "Knowledge Zone"

Since the end of the Cold War, when both countries discovered that there is much less fear and much more curiosity about each other, it has become fashionable in the United States to be seen as an "expert on Russia." Many press people, business people, senators, and government consultants now compete to share their expertise, filled with excitement at the sight of a former enemy suddenly turned into a "younger brother" learning his first "capitalist lessons" from a former major political and military rival.

It is a learning process in itself to monitor the themes and subjects that Americans pick to treat and comment on in the mass media as well as in scholarly journals: from Gorbachev euphoria to the "Z" article; from studies on *glasnost'* and the independent media to analyses of legislation on economic reform and the dynamics of joint ventures; from discussions of the reasons for famine and civil war, to shock-therapy analyses and horror stories about mafias, prostitution, and total corruption.

For whatever reason, then, Russia has been and continues to be very popular with American analysts of every stripe. Sovietologists, economists, historians, political scientists, national security advisers, and human rights activists have quite literally developed libraries of newly published books, brochures, and special reports entirely devoted to exploring various aspects of *perestroika* in Russia and what this means for Russia's own future, for the future of U.S.-Russian relations, and in terms of the impact on the Third World and on the world at large.

I have seen and heard many predictions that once things get relatively settled in Russia (so that there is no immediate threat of a military coup), Americans will lose interest. Happily, this has not happened. My view is that U.S. interest in developments in Russia is not only growing, but deepening. This is a timely and necessary development: there is still much more for the West to learn about Russia and the important events and processes that are only now (in 1993) beginning to unfold.

Serious studies of Russian political development cannot now be pursued on the basis of historical knowledge and correct intuition. New studies must be based on specific data collection within measurable parameters and demonstrate facility with quantitative social science methods. The new conditions in Russia clearly lend themselves to the formulation of new explanatory social and political concepts. (For example, using modern political polling techniques tailored to the reality of Russia today to get at ideological preferences, combined with behaviorist theoretical concepts, also adapted to Russian political culture, to measure the likelihood of support for one or the other political party or bloc in new elections.)

Needless to say, these types of inquiries will require regular professional cooperation between interested American specialists and their Russian counterparts working through newly established social science research centers—similar to what would be called "independent think-tanks" in America. Such specialists will have made it their professional occupation to regularly monitor current sociopolitical trends, and they will have acquired, through experience, their own visions and concepts, as well as research techniques.

Today, many Western analysts conduct their studies without the benefit of this kind of research and information. Their knowledge of Russian history remains for many the primary source for their insights into current political developments in Russia. One of the most prevalent examples of this propensity is the argument that since the Russians have never had any enduring tradition of or experience with democratic governance, it is unreasonable to assume that they can learn and adopt it today. For sources of current information, many Western analysts draw on the Russian mass media; and as it is of course absolutely impossible for a Western researcher to absorb *all* the significant publications, the picture he or she gets is very often incomplete—but it helps to prove the author's views, whatever they may be. Furthermore, the concepts that many Western analysts use are frequently borrowed from the Cold War era—totalitarianism, bureaucracy, modernization from above—and are not always applicable during a time of rapid social transformation and massive political action.

It is my deep conviction that one of the reasons why so many skin-deep descriptions of developments in Russia persist among U.S. analysts lies in the lack of professional cooperation between American scholars of Russia and the independent think-tanks in Russia (numbering approximately ten in Moscow and perhaps two hundred in the whole country),[1] which really are the best sources for current information and analysis of what is actually happening in Russia's sociopolitical development today. It is these institutions that are engaged in an effort to build a comprehensive picture of the new and emerging social forces and their interactions in Russia today.

I would even go so far as to indicate the questions that must be considered in search of common ground for cooperation between Russia and the United States during this transitional period.

• What are the existing social trends that shift beliefs, form mass behavior, articulate social and political interests, and shape political forces and blocs?

• How do these existing trends affect and/or relate to political stability, economic development, and the creation of democratic institutions? Do these trends hurt or help the process of political development?

• Is there something in this process that demands to be governed, and, if so, how much and in which direction?

• What should those governmental measures be (political, economic, educational, legal)? What are the limits to these measures and who should implement them: the Russian leadership, foreign countries, the international community at large, or an informed and guided indigenous political movement?

Without addressing these questions and building solid partnerships between U.S. and Russian professionals, it is absolutely impossible to contemplate any serious cooperation between our two countries in solving practical problems.

To my mind, it is precisely because of this almost total absence of common ground in understanding what is happening and what needs to be done that researchers and politicians on both sides find themselves confused; as a result, much effort is lost or wasted, even if intentions to cooperate are very sincere. The best example here is the case of humanitarian aid distribution. The message was sent out (by Gorbachev? Yeltsin?) as a cry for help in order to ensure survival (of the people? of the regime? of the leadership?). The message received was taken very seriously, and the response was enthusiastic: Russia is hungry, let us feed her! Millions of dollars were allocated for Russia from the U.S. foreign aid budget and contracts with U.S. businesses and nongovernmental organizations (NGOs) for the distribution of aid were concluded—but most of those businesses and organizations had little or no experience or expertise vis-à-vis Russia, and priorities of needs (which products and where to deliver them) were never examined. Systems of distribution and networks for allocation were discovered or created much later than when they were needed, if at all.

It would be easy to calculate what a huge difference that aid could have made if it had been directly invested in new agricultural enterprises, which would have allowed Russia to produce the necessary agricultural commodities for many years to come. Instead, the aid was consumed—for the most part feeding bureaucratic distribution agencies or enriching the mafia on the black market.

This is why, when asked to comment on the three papers by my colleagues that address issues of Russian constitutionalism, right-wing parties, and regionalism and their effect on Russian-American relations—with a focus on possible cooperation between our countries for a better future—I wanted to start by underlining *the necessity for cooperation in knowledge-building*. This is the first and essential step on the road to expanded cooperation.

Because American scholars are engaged in shaping public opinion as well as governmental policies, what they think and write about Russia is of tremendous importance. Without common ground for understanding the *needs* and *means* of possible aid, investment, adoption of social and political models, training and learning, and so on, "cooperation" could turn into "the American way of rebuilding Russia for Russia's sake" and that might result in a reprise of the attempt at shock-therapy treatment for Russia's economy.

The reasons I have given for the necessity of Russian-American intellectual interaction in what is now called post-Soviet development studies in the countries of the former USSR, and my sense of frustration about its current status, will become more understandable as I comment on the papers presented by my colleagues.

Review of Scholarly Papers

My overall reaction to the foregoing essays is one of great hope and enthusiasm because I see in them signs of potential recognition, from the American side, of the necessity for closer intellectual cooperation. I trust the authors will appreciate my comments as a further effort to foster this common "knowledge zone" in Russian studies. The very fact that these American scholars were willing to be reviewed and criticized by a Russian colleague is itself a rare and significant event. I am honored to have been invited and hope that my participation will assist in the establishment of a pattern that both sides would benefit from.

To begin, there are several points common to the three articles. First, all of them note some light at the end of the tunnel in the processes they analyze. This marks a pleasant departure from the propensity of most American scholars to portray everything in Russia as going from bad to worse, with even more deterioration in the offing. I would not, however, call these pieces optimistic. (I generally dislike this term, but it is constantly being used in our field to describe a scholar or his or her work.) Rather, they strike me as solidly grounded, realistic, striving to be precise in detail. All three scholars focus on the "work in progress," whether they are looking at constitutionalism, a political party's image versus its real role, or the state of administrative-territorial disintegration.

Mr. Osborn, as he describes the connections between nationalistic demands and territorial claims, also recognizes that there is "little indication that the ethnic struggles in the North Caucasus will spread elsewhere." Mr. Barry, though aware of the weaknesses of the USSR Constitutional Supervision Committee, nevertheless believes that it set an important example, "frankly facing" some controversial issues and in a number of cases showing considerable courage. Mr. Petro, dealing with the most troublesome and worrying factor that threatens Russian democracy—nationalism (at least it is so viewed in the West)—is also prompted to draw the conclusion that "passionately anti-Western foreign policy rhetoric" should be understood as designed "largely for popular consumption" and does not bespeak a clearly defined and established foreign policy concept—so the phenomenon should not be seen as an immediate threat to stability and democratic change.

Thus each author analyzes his subject within the dynamic context of his field of interest in terms that leave one with a feeling that something better will eventually emerge because all natural social processes have their own logic of development—toward more balanced, more even, more stabilized environments —and even negative social processes operate within their own boundaries and limitations.

Second, what I particularly liked about all three papers is their attention to detail—the authors' willingness to explore the specifics of each individual case, be it a political movement, a region in Siberia, or a particular Constitutional Court decision. This love of detail is the only truly scientific method in social science. It allows the researcher to create a general picture out of tiny fragments—piecing together, for instance, the different motives for secession or bids for more sovereignty in each individual krai, oblast, or autonomous district to figure out that the general reason behind disintegration boils down to a struggle to assert control over natural resources that can earn a quick income. Such attention to individual cases is a good safeguard against oversimplification of the kind that still plagues the literature of Russian studies—especially, the genre in which theories and conclusions were formulated many years ago and today make use of particular examples just to validate old theories over and over again.

Third, all three essays occasionally struck me as too descriptive and even difficult to understand as region after region, party after party, decision after decision were described and explained. I do not think it is realistic to try to retell history—even one as exciting as what Russia is living through these days! Close scrutiny of individual cases should not be abandoned and important details should not be lost, but it does not make much sense to repeat all those details in every case, especially when the subject of each study is so broad. I would also recommend that the analytical sections should not be left for the tail end of the essay, where the conclusion usually figures. Much more interesting observations could be made within the text of the essays—comparing different cases with each other, tracing their connection to general trends, explaining offshoot tendencies, and delineating common rules and exceptions. Otherwise, this vast amount of collected material serves just to prove some generalization, summarized on the last page—and this is unfortunate because the material in each essay is extremely rich and could be organized to reveal the unifying thread between the different parts of the picture.

My final criticism of all three papers (and one I recognize as very personal) is that they all lack solutions. Perhaps this is where the difference lies between a 200-page book on the history of Russian nationalism and the essays we are now discussing. Still, it is not so much a matter of size, but of genre. In a history *book*, one is definitely expected to describe events and possibly indicate their importance at the time and now. In an *essay* or a report covering contemporary events, especially one dealing with "hot issues" that are having dramatic impacts in the present—that are "roiling" as we describe them—a researcher, to my mind, cannot avoid addressing the consequences, the likely outcome of existing trends; and where he or she sees particular danger, an author should at least venture an idea of what might be done to avoid or substantially reduce the negative effects. In my opinion, whatever claims academic researchers make for themselves or their work, nobody is exempt from the necessity to answer the famous "so what?" question.

What follows are my comments on the specific topics of the individual essays. I believe their themes were chosen exactly right in that they are equally important to the future of Russia and to U.S.-Russian understanding of what must be done here, including, of course, how cooperation can serve to make it happen.

Nationalism: Looking Toward Historic Roots Helps to Find Solutions

We begin with the theme suggested by Nicolai Petro, singling out the central issue of the threat of rising Russian nationalism—whether it poses a real threat to future stability and democratic development in Russia.

In fact, the author casts his net much wider. He addresses nationalism and its different variants—from traditional Slavophile patriotism to contemporary statism—as general issues of "conservative politics." These issues also reflect the importance of national identity to the Russian politics of our day and show the deep infiltration of the national idea into a very broad spectrum of contemporary political forces. Looking generally at the politics of the right, one can clearly see how the concepts of national history, historic mission, national specificities, and national pride become meaningful for the self-definition of many political forces which otherwise might advocate quite different ideas. For example, orthodox national communists, as represented by Nina Andreeva, will call for restoration of the dictatorship of the proletariat, of party-state ideology, of planned economy, and of bureaucratic order. On the other hand, the Russian Christian Democratic Movement, which is also included in the study as an example of metamorphosis away from National Bolshevism, advocates a free-market system, individual liberties, and multiparty pluralism.

Here we have the most controversial point in the approach adopted by Nicolai Petro: a dedicated effort to monitor the precise doses of nationalism and patriotism balloons his subject. These ideas can now be found in the prospectuses of a large number of political movements, especially as they evolved to reflect changing public attitudes—that is, as they discovered the appeals of "new patriotism" in the search for a new ideology. These new attitudes articulated in political programs and statements prompted Professor Petro to tackle virtually the entire spectrum of Russian politics—from the National Salvation Front to the Civic Union, from *Trudovaia Rossiia* to Aleksandr Rutskoi's People's Party of Free Russia. If all the above forces represent the politics of the right, what remains on the left? Only the "hard Westernizers" of Democratic Russia?

A further question must be raised in this connection, a very old question for those analyzing contemporary Russian politics: what are the criteria for distinguishing "left" from "right" and where does one draw the line between them? I get the impression that the author's approach is to see the right as reactionary or "calling to the past," in contrast with "progressive forces" that search for new solutions in the future. But the "new communists" like to argue that they want to build something completely new which was never properly implemented in Soviet history; and on the other side, future-oriented free-marketeers and defenders of private property, such as Viktor Aksiutchits or Nikolai Travkin, inject—in differing modes, but unambiguously—a national-patriotic flavor into their programs and rhetoric. This is why, to my mind, using "left" and "right" in political analysis is becoming increasingly confusing, unless the index is pegged to objective economic criteria applicable worldwide: "left" stands for more government involvement and control in the economic field, also meaning more social programs and social protection; "right" means less government, less protection, and more market mechanisms.

But this is not a perfect tool for analysis either, because our political forces have only *talked* about their economic programs so far; they have not had a chance to prove them in practice, and some are not even clear about their economic program. This is why I prefer not to use "left" or "right" definitions at all, unless first carefully defining what I mean by them. Returning to Petro's work, then, regardless of the problematic issue of "right" versus "left," he has provided a solid, factually based analysis of the *role of nationalism* in contemporary Russian politics.

"Violent Russian nationalism," the threat of its rise and spread, its potential transformation into fascism, the reestablishment of a totalitarian regime in Russia coupled with aggressiveness toward neighboring countries and the whole world—these are probably among the most popular scary themes of Western political doctrine in the nineties. From books by Richard Pipes to recent articles by Peter Reddaway, American Sovietology considers nationalism in Russia almost inevitable and, very possibly, as posing an imminent or even present danger. Russian history is often used only to derive negative examples, such as lack of democratic experience, all of which definitely adds up to a hopeless picture. That is how—willingly or unwillingly—the idea has been planted in American public opinion that Russian nationalism is a real threat, which could easily escalate into the feeling that Russia is still something to be afraid of. Needless to say, none of this promotes better understanding between the two countries.

Professor Petro approaches history in a different way, by examining nationalism's roots in social-philosophical debates and the ways by which its conceptions and practices have responded to society's demands, whether rightly or wrongly understood. A very important part of Professor Petro's study is the historical comparison between traditional Slavophile patriotism and national communism in the ways they served their contemporary societies: studying the roots lends both ideas some legitimacy. It simply means that something which grew through the centuries cannot be denied or completely rejected or militantly confronted as an absolute evil. If an ideology has developed for centuries, it must have been useful, appealing, and effective and, at the very least, represents something that cannot easily be expunged from the national culture as a mistake.

Understanding the phenomenon prompts a very different approach to how to deal with "the threat of Russian nationalism." The term "nationalism" often figures in political programs and speeches as a technique for establishing self-identity and not necessarily as a manifestation of hostility and aggression. But if every sign of Russian patriotism, Russian national pride, and Russian national identity is treated as "dangerous nationalism," it could finally provoke hostility and confrontation (for example, in the case of violation of the rights of ethnic Russians and Russian-speaking people outside the borders of the Russian Federation). Clearly, too, condemning and fighting against nationalism does not always help, and could even hurt because, in the absence of some other political identity, nationalism can assume the form of opposition to enforced Westernization. Keeping this in mind and being sensitive to these issues could be very helpful to future U.S.-Russian relations.

Another important idea—though it might sound quite paradoxical—is that if patriotically spiced forces represent the majority of the population of the country, they might contribute to stability much more than a devoted and forceful but unpopular minority that is backed by Western countries only because it shares the values and propagates the models operating in the West (a good example is the enduring Western support for Democratic Russia).

Generally speaking, I wholeheartedly agree with the author that the threat of Russian nationalism has been greatly exaggerated.

Federalism: Is Russia Falling Apart or Decentralizing Power?

Federalism is the second most important issue to be discussed by Western Sovietologists as a major threat to the country (some analysts consider it the paramount issue). The tenor and tone of these discussions differ markedly. According to the Western vision, what is happening amounts to a paralysis of central power, a rupture of horizontal connections, the collapse of the economic infrastructure, and political and legal anarchy.

Russian sources portray the issue of territorial sovereignty with deep irony, showing how the level of local ambition is directly related to the store of natural resources in the respective territory, and how local leaders, not seriously thinking of secession, are always quick to use this argument to bargain with the center for more economic rights—basically to let them consume or sell privately a larger share of the natural resources that happen to be located within their territory. I was glad to find much of this same attitude in the essay by Robert Osborn. He labors to avoid generalizations and strives to describe each of the autonomous republics, as well as large and small independent territories, with all the singularities of their political, economic, and cultural development.

First, some general comments on the issue of federalism, clarifying what about it is viewed differently inside Russia and abroad, and why.

What greatly worries the West is the idea that the center does not have any power to keep the country together, in which "keeping together" is understood very much in terms of what the USSR was prior to the eighties. A common example of the center's "powerlessness" is that when a business agreement to exploit some resources in, say, Irkutsk Oblast in Siberia is signed in Moscow, it is not necessarily fulfilled forthwith by the local soviet in Irkutsk. Further negotiations are required to clarify the details, or the whole agreement may in fact have to be rewritten to close the deal. This is described as a "disaster" due to the crippling lack of authority at the center because many of our foreign friends got used to solving all issues in Moscow through the central apparatus, forgetting that the same procedure would not be possible in their homeland, where decision making is decentralized and local authorities exercise a lot of power in governing their states, counties, cities, and towns. Why, then, is it so surprising in the case of Russia, where one of the primary tasks has always been to decentralize decision-making?

One may argue that in other countries it is very clearly stated which organ of which level of government has the authority to decide a particular type of issue. The mandate exists in writing so as to avoid confusion, and everyone from bureaucrat to citizen knows the applicable norms and follows them. To this argument we can only answer that Russia has not reached this level of development in terms of either legislation or legal culture and that other countries, including the United States, spent many decades to develop such effective systems as they now have. Given the expanse of territory, the complexity of problems, and the time frame of less than two years—how could we possibly expect any better?

It is important to emphasize how much impatience can hurt in cases like the above example: both parties could get frustrated, lose trust in each other, or act outside the law, thereby contributing to organized and nonorganized corruption. On the other hand, patience, education, necessary homework on the subject, and knowledge of existing legislation could be the means of creating the legal framework for the functioning of the local authorities. The fact of the matter is that defining the balance of powers between federal and local authorities is an ongoing process, although the essential division of powers has been spelled out in the three federal treaties which are now being tried and tested.

In short, there are substantial differences between Russian and American visions of Russian Federalism: the Americans want the *end result*, while we are still *in process*.

There is also much to say concerning the Western attitude generally and the American attitude in particular, toward the issue of recognition of various autonomous republics and other independent "sovereign" territories within Russia.

Several statements have already been made by politicians and scholars to the effect that there is enough reason to grant official recognition to certain autonomous republics of Russia because of American economic interests in those areas. The implication is that if American oil companies become interested in operating in the Groznyi area, the question of recognizing the Chechen Republic might show up on the U.S. State Department's agenda. Needless to say, the question of recognition and nonrecognition is a political more than a legal decision, and it will be made by the U.S. government whenever the latter considers the time ripe for such a move. My job, though, is to point out the need to consider this issue in all its complexity, taking into account all the consequences of U.S. recognition.

First, by recognizing the Chechen Republic, the United States would seriously offend Russia, which still considers Chechnia part of Russian territory. Hence, the decision must be made whether the Groznyi oil is more valuable than good relations with the Russian president. Second, no argument then comes to mind to refuse similar recognition to Tatarstan, Bashkortostan, the Yakut-Sakha Republic, and so on. At such a point, the question becomes whether the total disintegration of the Russian Federation benefits the United States and its security interests. Third, on the basis of law as set in the federal treaty, the large administrative territories, the krais and oblasts, have the same quantum of powers and opportunities—*the same quantum of sovereignty*. So, again, there is no reason why Krasnoiarsk Krai—which is about ten times larger than Tatarstan and also has constitutive documents, its own legislature, and all the rights that are granted to former autonomous republics—should be denied the right to be represented in the United Nations if the other republics of the Russian Federation are recognized as entitled to that status.

Finally, it is very important for our American friends to realize that just by raising these questions in public—by demanding the right to negotiate such issues directly with the regions and to skip over Moscow by developing trade and barter inside Russian territory in circumvention of the existing rules and procedures—they are provoking more separatism and furnishing the local authorities with even stronger arguments in their bargainings with the center.

Again, it is up to the U.S. government alone to decide whom it wants to support, but that ought to be done after a general policy has been elaborated. Otherwise, the process will slip out of control and then no choice will be left to be made.

Constitutionalism: Theoretical Models versus Practical Demands

Putting constitutional development last in the list of urgent issues to be discussed and resolved with an eye for Russia's stable democratic development might seem strange, given that I myself am a constitutional lawyer; the decision to do so is dictated not by lack of respect for the supreme law of the country, but by my profound conviction that the Constitution must finalize, summarize, and cap the process of legal reform in the period of transition rather than begin it. However, the theoretical scheme turns this around: first comes the Constitution, which lays the foundation of the country's political system, defines the division of powers, spells out the respective functions, secures citizen's rights, distributes the powers between the central and local authorities, and establishes an independent judiciary as supreme arbiter. So the foundations are now clear and safe and all further legislation rests on this footing.

This is an ideal. And America was extremely fortunate to come closer to that scheme than many other countries; fortunate that the founding fathers had the luxury to consciously plan and design on paper what the future country would be in terms of governance.

The social, political, and legal transformations which Russia is facing now are an outgrowth of the previous regime and call not only for rewriting specific normative acts, but for changing the whole legislative practice, creating new government institutions, nurturing new political parties and movements, and introducing a whole new political and legal culture. But all of this is happening within the frame of the old government structure, the old legislative mentality, old beliefs, and the hopes and habits of the population. We still have a lot of old problems to solve—getting child-care and the schools to work properly, getting the people's court decisions executed, getting the deputies just to attend the sessions. . . . And fresh problems are knocking on the door—relations between the president and the parliament, the status of parliamentary groups and factions, national sovereignties and violations of minority rights, market reform, new businessmen and the unemployed, free-market prices, enormous inflation, customs and borders cutting through the former union, civil wars in the neighboring republics, humanitarian aid, refugees, homelessness. . . . The catalog is endless, and the reason I mention these items is that this is all happening at the same time and we do not have the means to solve these new problems.

It is still a big mystery how the country has thus far managed not to collapse. My guess is that it is because the institutions do not behave rationally. Schools distribute humanitarian aid, state child-care organizes a cafeteria in the evening hours, KGB officers join private security services, and small businesses give money to charity without benefit of tax exemption. Everyone's preoccupation is to *survive*—personally, physically, or institutionally.

The struggle for life and *raison d'être* is waged not only at the community level; the same struggle for survival is waged among and within governing structures: the parliament wants to stay in power for at least another year, the president is trying to reestablish his image and influence after his defeat in the Seventh Congress, and the opposition is trying to exploit the weaknesses of both and form a new government. All this directly relates to the new Constitution.

The Constitution will make sense only when there is a public consensus to make it work. This can happen only when a balance of powers takes hold, at least on the general level. If neither the president nor the parliament observes the terms of the existing Constitution, what will induce them to follow the new one, if they disagree over every entry in its text?

If the alignment of the future power structure is not clear to the confronting forces, if the entire society is on the move, redefining itself—from new roles in material production to a new cultural identity—how can some distinguished commission sit around the table and coin the norms that everyone will suddenly find acceptable and worth following?

But Western experts are so excited at the prospect of participation in the drafting of a new Russian constitution! We have dozens of delegations crossing the borders in both directions to participate in these discussions, but none of this traffic has helped Russian society to come closer to a consensus. Probably, then, things should be done differently. And American specialists can greatly contribute to the practical process of political consensus-building instead of spending time endlessly rewriting some provision or other.

This is how I see the constitutional process in Russia for the near future: the parliament and the president *have to agree* on setting the day for new elections; elections should be held this year (1993) toward the end, so that the different parties have time to prepare and the parliament has time to pass a new law on elections and political parties that will place the electoral process on a solid legal base. Only a representative parliament can take the initiative and enjoy the legitimacy to design and vote on a new constitution. And if in this process we would need our Constitutional Court (and its chairman Valerii Zor'kin) to play an active role—I would rather sacrifice the court's theoretical purity from politics, which almost never exists in its fullest sense anyway (the first U.S. Supreme Court was very involved politically), in exchange for its crucial contribution to the survival of the principle of division of powers—and perhaps the survival of the democratic experiment as a whole.

I do not wish to suggest disrespect for the "normal theory" of separation of powers and mutual noninterference, without which we risk conflicts of interest and, ultimately, the destruction of the system of checks and balances. I think Professor Barry is absolutely correct when warning us of the danger that

Zor'kin's deeper involvement in the political debate in the guise of consultation and mediation could destroy the image of the Constitutional Court and justice generally. My only point is that as 1993 dawned, Russia faced much greater dangers. I just hope we manage to survive this ordeal and enter the stage of "normal" political development whereby all the good and wise theories will work and command respect.

Note

1. The Kennan Institute of Advanced Russian Studies of the Woodrow Wilson Center in Washington, D.C., has published a directory of such institutions.

C

REGIONAL ISSUES

5

Ukraine and Russian-American Relations

William C. Bodie

> Millions of Russians are convinced that, without Ukraine, it is impossible to
> speak not only of a great Russia, but of any kind of Russia at all.
> —L. Karpinsky, *Moscow News*[1]

> Russian democracy stops where Ukrainian independence begins.
> —Rukh cofounder Ivan Drach[2]

Introduction

While it is almost banal to assert that the end of the Soviet Union has under-mined the analytical basis of U.S. strategy, it is nevertheless useful to recount a few hitherto unimagined security scenarios facing America's first post–Cold War administration.[3] Less than four years after the first breach in the Berlin Wall, the United States faces not one hostile superpower, but a pro-Western regime in Moscow and fourteen other republics competing for economic assistance and even security guarantees. Rather than honing strategies to deter World War III, Washington now must contemplate the scarcely less alarming prospect of multiple—perhaps even subnational—controls on nuclear weapons in the four nuclear successor states to the USSR.[4] In place of a clear ideological challenge directed by communists against Western interests, U.S. policy-makers confront a dizzying array of inter- and intrarepublican conflicts fueled by incomprehensible enmities and historical ambitions.

Among the upheavals that accompanied the Soviet collapse, however, none is of greater significance than the establishment of an independent Republic of

The views expressed here are those of the author and do not reflect the official policy or position of the National Defense University, the Department of Defense, or the U.S. Government.

Ukraine and its relationship with postcommunist Russia. Combined, the two republics account for eighty percent of the population and seventy percent of the land in the former USSR. The economic ties between the two are extensive, albeit fractious, particularly in the energy and agricultural sectors.[5] Armed conflict between Russia and Ukraine could destroy Ukraine, cripple Russia's fragile democracy, and provoke a global crisis.[6] Cooperation, or at least detente, between the two is the *sine qua non* for stability and economic growth throughout Central and Eastern Europe.

During the Gorbachev years, most students of Soviet "nationalities" characterized Ukraine as a quiescent junior partner in Moscow's political conglomerate. According to Charles F. Furtado, Jr., and Andrea Chandler:

> [T]he western USSR was considered by many experts to be the strategic reserve of Soviet nationalities policy.
>
> If Central Asia was likely to be the "Achilles heel" of the Soviet Federation, then the Soviet west along with the Russian Republic would provide the center with a cushion of much-needed demographic, economic, and political stability. Viewed as the most politically integrated and culturally assimilated of all non-Russian republics, Ukraine, Byelorussia, and Moldavia were viewed as the last places likely to give birth to large-scale ethnic unrest.[7]

While the Western political community accepts the Russian Federation as a natural "successor" to the Soviet Union, few NATO capitals contemplated the arrival of a separate, sovereign Ukraine—a new state in the heart of Europe with a population equal to France's, an army larger than Germany's, and 176 intercontinental ballistic missiles on its soil.[8] Even the substantial Ukrainian diaspora population in North America was unprepared for the momentous events of August 1991 when, as Mark Beissinger puts it, "the Ukrainian declaration of independence on August 24 . . . dealt the final death-blow to the new Union treaty and the idea of a renewed federal Soviet state."[9]

Moreover, as Ukraine is the birthplace of Russian civilization, has 11 million citizens of Russian ethnicity, and hosts a fleet christened by Catherine the Great, many in the Russian Federation appear resistant to the notion of permanent Ukrainian statehood.[10] In discussions about the newly formed Commonwealth of Independent States (CIS) in February 1992, Henry Kissinger was told by a Russian legislator, "We would never have proposed the Commonwealth if we had thought it possible that Ukraine might actually become independent. I will never accept Kiev as a foreign city."[11] Few speeches are delivered on the floor of the Ukrainian parliament without an impassioned recitation of Russia's past predations and future designs on Kiev. If familiarity breeds contempt in the affairs of states, then the economic and cultural ties that bind Russia and Ukraine also engender numerous scenarios of conflict.

Therefore, as Washington forges new ties with Moscow, it will unavoidably become enmeshed in Ukrainian-Russian relations. No U.S. policy objectives toward Russia—nuclear disarmament, democratization, marketization, integration into Western institutions—can be accomplished without Kiev's active participation or passive concurrence. At the same time, as the United States begins to develop a multifaceted, nuanced diplomatic approach to the former republics of the USSR, especially Ukraine, it risks provoking Russia in an extremely sensitive region—the *blizhnee zarubezh'e*, or "near abroad," where even the most liberal Muscovite feels Russia has special rights.

In this chapter, we shall analyze Russian-Ukrainian ties since the August coup and some key issues that continue to divide Moscow and Kiev; assess the internal political forces that are driving policy; consider U.S. policy toward the dissolution of the USSR and its emerging position toward Ukraine; and offer some observations about Western policy options in the near future.

The Two Augusts

The major disputes between Russia and Ukraine—nuclear weapons, the status of the Crimean peninsula, ownership of the Black Sea Fleet, the division of Soviet properties and obligations, and CIS issues—are best understood in the context of the republics' radically divergent experiences in August 1991 and their conflicting visions of a post-Soviet community. An anticommunist revolution took place in Moscow, while in Kiev a separatist movement which had been coopted by local elites assumed power.[12] As *The Economist* put it, "With the downfall of the Soviet Union, Russia won radicalism (Boris Yeltsin is outreforming Mikhail Gorbachev); Ukraine won independence, a prize Ukrainians put before all else, including the removal of communism."[13]

In Moscow, even the most liberal reformers viewed Russia as the rightful *primus inter pares* of former Soviet republics and the recognized conductor of a new interrepublican concert. Meanwhile, the political establishment in Kiev acted as if national self-awakening—and *nomenklatura* self-preservation—required a heightening of differences with Moscow. Soon, many Ukrainian leaders had difficulty distinguishing between the Russia of Boris Yeltsin and the Soviet center which had extinguished Ukrainian independence in 1920 and terrorized its people for decades.

The Yeltsin government quickly moved to assure the world that, as the main legatee of Soviet treaty commitments and financial responsibilities, it would assume control of the major all-Union military forces and overseas holdings. Ukraine acted with equal alacrity to stake its claim on Soviet-era assets on its territory as well as a commensurate share of external properties. To ease its own geopolitical anxieties, Kiev made overtures to other ex-Soviet republics and the states of Eastern Europe in a diplomatic effort that Moscow saw as distinctly anti-Russian.[14]

Internally, Russian reformers were overwhelmed with tasks of decommunization, democratization, and marketization while shaping a postcommunist Russian constitutional order. At the same time, Ukraine sought to establish the trappings and suits of statehood without nurturing the civic culture and institutions of a functional democracy. All of this took place in an environment of severe industrial decline, a breakdown of preexisting state institutions (police, military, etc.), and several outbreaks of violence in and around the borders of Russia and Ukraine. Such an environment would vex the most patient of statesmen; for the leaders of Russia and Ukraine, it made normal political discourse almost impossible.

Arms and Independence

Although Ukraine declared state sovereignty in 1990, the notion of a fully independent Ukraine was chimerical to many Ukrainian politicians. Parliamentary Chairman Leonid Kravchuk was caught off guard by the arrest of Gorbachev and the creation of the Emergency Committee.[15] Kiev was quiet, and Kravchuk displayed little of Yeltsin's leadership qualities during the putsch, justifying his actions by noting that the state of emergency had not been announced in Ukraine (a curious statement considering Gorbachev was under arrest at the time on Ukrainian territory in the Crimea.)

Still, Kravchuk seized the opportunity to assume the mantle of Cossack leader Bohdan Khmelnitsky while Moscow and the rest of the world appeared paralyzed by the coup. He nationalized property, established a series of extraconstitutional advisory committees and ministries, removed his old party colleagues who supported the coup, and dispatched many leaders of the noncommunist opposition abroad as ambassadors.[16] He rode to victory in the December 1991 presidential election over two opponents by marketing himself successfully as the indispensable man who stood up to Moscow and delivered on the promise of full independence.

Kravchuk, a Communist Party ideologist who until 1990 was a harsh critic of the Rukh popular front and other proindependence forces, linked the birth of Ukrainian independence with his defiance of Moscow in the military field. Kravchuk claimed in an interview that the post–World War I Ukrainian republic failed due to the flaws of its leader, Pavlo Skoropadsky, who "made two cardinal mistakes. He entered into a political alliance with Russia and he did not create a Ukrainian army."[17] The new Ukrainian leadership would not make the same mistake, although it was helped considerably by the fact that, unlike in 1917, the new government in Moscow was not led by Bolsheviks.

In the fall of 1991, preceding the national referendum on independence, Kravchuk and his defense minister (Konstantin Morozov, an ethnic Russian and former Soviet Air Force general), quickly drew up plans to "activate" Soviet military assets, establish the legislative framework for the Ukrainian armed forces, and administer loyalty oaths to the estimated 1.2 million Soviet Army personnel in Ukraine.[18] These actions outraged Soviet holdovers such as Marshal Shaposhnikov, then busily drawing up plans for new general-purpose forces under a Moscow-based central command.

One of the reasons the General Staff counted on maintaining control of military units in Ukraine was the predominance of Russians in the services. Of the approximately 650,000 men and women serving in the Ukrainian armed forces today, roughly 35 percent are ethnic Russians.[19] Even with the introduction of loyalty oaths, which were taken by the vast majority of officers serving in Ukraine, some Ukrainians are concerned about the reliability of the officer corps. Many officers were said to make the pledge for economic reasons: "they are pledging loyalty to their flats," went the joke in Kiev.[20] Criticizing top Ukrainian officers, the chairman of the Ukrainian Officers Union[21] said, "Yesterday, they supported the Emergency State Committee and championed the indivisibility of the Soviet Union and its Armed Forces, but today they take a loyalty oath to Ukraine to get high appointments. . . . That's why we don't have an Army capable of defending the independence of Ukraine."[22]

In the end, the loyalty of Ukraine's armed forces will be linked to Kiev's economic performance as much as to its diplomacy toward Russia.[23] At present, Ukraine is succeeding on neither front; economic output in 1992 was dreadful,[24] and the disputes with Russia, while contained, are nevertheless unresolved. Time is another critical factor. If Ukraine avoids conflict with Russia for three to five years, it will have a chance to consolidate the loyalty and effectiveness of its armed forces. In the meantime, notes a NATO expert on the former Soviet military, "No one today can predict, should there be a clash of direct orders and the likelihood of battle, whether general purpose formations in the Ukraine would fight for Moscow or Kiev."[25]

Internal Stresses in Ukrainian Politics

For all the outward success the Ukrainian government has had at establishing state structures and armed forces, Kiev's state-building effort came at the expense of a fully representative republican government with the legitimacy to implement the socioeconomic reforms necessary for long-term stability. Kravchuk's determination to prop up state institutions primarily with his Soviet-era cronies has had two side effects—it delayed, if not prevented, the introduction of market and legal reforms, and it demonstrated to the populace that Ukraine's communist elite had changed its flag but not its political appetites. As of early 1993, Ukraine was operating under the Soviet Constitution, albeit one modified by measures enacted since the Ukrainian Declaration of Sovereignty in 1990. No concrete timetables have been set for parliamentary elections or constitutional revision. These delays have contributed to an erosion of elite consensus on many issues, prompting a growing alienation between parliament and the president and between Kiev and the other regions. On a more practical level, veterans of the now-outlawed party still dominate all key decision-making positions throughout the republic, and many of them will resist even modest political and economic reforms.[26]

Regarding macroeconomic policy, Kiev seems to have one firm conviction—Russia's 1992 experiment with "shock therapy" is a nonstarter. According to one Kravchuk adviser, "There has been no Gaidar here, and there won't be." Ukraine's leaders "view stability as so much more important than economic reform."[27] Even so, there is little hope for stability with an economy whose only growth figures can be found in inflation rate. Prime Minister Kuchma had barely moved into his office before he noted, "There isn't a single sector of the economy that isn't disastrous—agriculture, industry, the credit finance system, health, ecology."[28]

In the political sphere, Kravchuk continues to display the skills, as well as the flaws, of a career communist bureaucrat. He outmaneuvered democratic critics by forming an extraconstitutional advisory council, inviting leaders from *Rukh* and the New Ukraine movement to offer economic policy input. The move ruptured the opposition and spread the blame for economic misery to the non-communist reformers. At the same time, Kravchuk instituted a Soviet-style "prefect" system, appointing presidential plenipotentiaries to coordinate policy on the regional and local levels.[29]

Moreover, the president's autocratic tendencies became more pronounced. During an August 1992 meeting of the World Forum of Ukrainians in Kiev, Kravchuk threatened to expel foreigners, close down newspapers, and otherwise deal harshly with those he believed complicated the consolidation of Ukrainian independence. He summed up his position on dissenting voices:

> No matter what ideals guide a particular leader or party, if their activity threatens independence or the people, there can be neither justification nor forgiveness for this. Today the only criterion in ordering our priorities should be their conformity or nonconformity with the cause of building an independent Ukrainian power. It is the very idea of statehood that should unite everybody.[30]

An emerging academic view holds that Ukraine likely will develop into a limited democracy, plebiscitarian yet authoritarian, along the lines of Mexico or Turkey. Remarking on the lack of ethnic politics in Ukraine, Bohdan Harasymiw points out that

> there are as yet no political parties based primarily on ethnicity, because that would unravel whatever degree of national unity already exists. The bad news is that the growth of presidentialism indicates a very long-term transition to democracy, a transition that has characterized Mexico: a dominant presidential party; controlled participation on the corporatist rather than pluralist model; highly centralized government; an authoritarian tradition; and corruption.[31]

Unlike Mexico, however, Ukraine has the resources, population, and infrastructure necessary for the rapid creation of a modern industrialized economy. Also unlike Mexico, Ukraine has experienced seventy years of communism and lacks a stable, supportive northern neighbor.

The View from Moscow: *Bez Ukrainy,*
Net Rodiny [Without Ukraine, No Motherland]

> Should the intelligentsia's Ukrainian idea . . . strike the national soil and
> set it on fire . . . [it will lead] to a gigantic and unprecedented schism
> of the Russian nation that, I firmly believe, will result in a veritable
> disaster for the state and for the people.
>
> —Petr Struve, 1912[32]

Eighty years later, many of Struve's intellectual heirs in Moscow would echo his
sentiments. Despite the numerous gradations on the Russian political spectrum
today, one of the few issues on which the disparate forces agree is the need for
Russia to reassert itself as a great power, especially around its borders. And any
effort by Russia to articulate a "Eurasian Monroe Doctrine" restricting Kiev's
strategic maneuverability will likely provoke a fierce surge of nationalism in
Ukraine.

The "near abroad" issue is often overlooked by Western analysts, but in
Russia it is a conceptual framework adopted by liberals as well as neopatriots, or
derzhavniki as they prefer to call themselves.[33] The rights of Russians and the
interests of Russia in the near abroad have become central themes of conservative parliamentarians; indeed, the reassertion of state power on the periphery is
among the most popular causes in Russian politics.

In June 1992 Russian Foreign Minister Andrei Kozyrev wrote an article in
which he condemned the rising "party of war,"—those seeking to unify the
Russian people by adopting bellicose stands toward others in the old empire.[34]
Yeltsin later criticized Kozyrev, delivering an address October 1992 which re-
sembled a *derzhavnik* manifesto, replete with promises of a renewal of Russian
greatness. A major issue during the summer of 1992 was the possible establishment of a new ministry for Commonwealth affairs, a separate foreign office for
Ukraine and the other republics.[35] Yeltsin also convened a presidential security
council to coordinate foreign and defense policies, which many believed would
further diminish Kozyrev's influence even as he remained in office.[36]

Beyond these developments, Russian military leaders have assumed an assertive voice in foreign policy debates, even as they show signs of impatience with
civilian authorities. Figures such as General Staff Academy Chief Igor Rodionov
and Chief of the General Staff Mikhail Kolesnikov make pointed attacks on
policies and politicians with which or whom they disagree. Rodionov delivered a
paper at a General Staff Academy conference in May 1992 stating that "all
Commonwealth states are in the sphere of Russia's vitally important interests,"
that they should avoid alliances with the West, and that "for many centuries
Russia fought for an outlet to the Baltic and Black seas, since the impossibility of
a free outlet to them always ran counter to its national interests."[37]

The Russian military hierarchy is particularly concerned about the active or
retired military personnel among the 25 million Russians in the other republics.

The use of force in protecting their rights was included in a draft of the Russian defense doctrine published in May 1992. As James Sherr, a fellow at Sandhurst's Soviet Studies Research Center, describes it, "The new doctrine is striking for its disquieting, pre-Gorbachevian combination of defensive intent and aggressive mood."[38] While Western analysts highlight the draft's sections on nuclear weapons and the role of high technology in warfare, Ukrainian commentary has dwelled on the Army's arrogation of special interventional rights in Russia's "near abroad."

Evidence of disrespect toward Ukrainian sensitivities is not confined to nationalist deputies or officers, however. On August 24, 1991, on the same day Ukraine declared its independence, Boris Yeltsin's spokesman noted that Russia reserved the right to renegotiate its borders with other post-Soviet states. Yeltsin himself has been clear on Ukraine's reticent attitude toward the CIS: "If Ukraine refuses to participate in the union, we will be on opposite sides of the barricade."[39] In one of his first statements on the subject, Vice President Aleksandr Rutskoi stated, "The historical consciousness of Russia does not permit anyone mechanically to bring the borders of Russia in line with the Russian Federation."[40] While Ukrainians often exaggerate the importance of bellicose statements by minor politicians, Rutskoi's comments reflect a significant body of influential opinion in Russia today. Igor Torbakov puts it best with respect to the *derzhavniki* and Ukraine:

> Probably the most painful problem for Russian imperial nationalists is the emergence of an independent Ukraine and Belarus. The very fact that these states have gained a sovereign existence is regarded by Russian nationalists as a sheer anomaly. It is not so much geopolitics that matters here as the problem the emergence of these states has posed for Russian self-identification. For indeed, what is Russia without these two Slavic nations and without Kiev—the cradle of ancient East Slavic civilization and the center of Kievan Rus', claimed by Russian nationalists as the first "Russian state"?[41]

The government in Moscow did come to realize that Ukraine was determined to create its own armed forces by the end of 1991, and CIS Commander Shaposhnikov acknowledged that reality at the time of the Minsk summit.[42] Some Russian analysts went so far as to suggest that Ukraine held key advantages as a result of the withdrawals of the Soviet forces from Central Europe in 1989–91.[43] But it is nevertheless reasonable to assume that Russia's own internal political perturbations will prevent the emergence of a new understanding of Ukrainian perspectives.

Three Unresolved Wrangles

Beyond the persistent anxieties over their divorce, Ukraine and Russia continue to maneuver on three disputes which could spark the crisis both presidents seek to avoid: the continuing disagreement over how, or whether, Ukraine will divest itself of the Soviet-era nuclear weapons stationed on its territory; the Black Sea Fleet and Crimean autonomy; and the various approaches to an already violent conflict in the Trans-Dniester region of Moldova. While an optimist could point to constructive developments in each of these areas during 1992, a pessimist could claim with equal validity that they remain volatile situations whose outcomes Yeltsin or Kravchuk may be unable to control.

Nuclear Weapons

As far as the rest of the world was concerned, the dispute over Ukraine's nuclear status was by far the most important, if not the only, issue on the agenda.[44] Although Ukraine's oft repeated non-nuclear protestations have been vigorous, its actions have been ambiguous. On March 10, Ukraine suspended transfers of tactical nuclear weapons to Russia, citing Russia's unreliability as a negotiating partner and questions over whether the weapons were being destroyed. The Ukrainians subsequently resumed these transfers, but the incident highlighted anxieties about the sincerity of Kiev's commitment to denuclearization.[45]

At the same time, the CIS command disputed Ukraine's right to assume control of the strategic air bases in Ukraine, which contain forty-two long-range bombers, including twenty Tu-160 Blackjack bombers in Priluki.[46] During the summer and fall of 1992, Kiev continued its efforts to assume "administrative control" of strategic weapons sites in Ukraine, placing officers who swore loyalty to Ukraine in charge of launch sites. Kiev, along with Kazakhstan and Belarus, signed the Lisbon START protocols in April 1992, pledging full implementation of weapons reductions within seven years of ratification. The agreement has been criticized on the eve of the parliamentary ratification debate, with many deputies insisting on certain financial and security conditions which may require treaty renegotiation.

In the face of mounting international criticism, Kravchuk maintained that Kiev's non-nuclear intentions were both forthright and consistent, going back to Ukraine's Declaration of State Sovereignty adopted on July 16, 1990: "Ukraine will pursue a policy aimed at the total destruction of nuclear weapons and the components of their basing located on the territory of the Ukrainian state."[47] Ukraine is both annoyed over the Western concerns about nuclear weapons and cognizant of the value that that attention brings.[48] The Ukrainian foreign ministry in December 1992 noted that Kiev was not responsible for the deployment of the weapons on its soil and had taken the historically unprecedented step of renouncing claims to them. Still, "instead of real assistance in destroying ICBMs together with nuclear warheads, [Ukraine] receives only 'negative' impetuses to accede to NPT and to destroy nuclear weapons."[49]

As 1993 began and the United States and Russia signed the START II follow-on accords, the Ukrainian government remained confident that its parliament would ratify the START I and the Nuclear Non-Proliferation Treaty (NPT). Voices in parliament, however, were concerned about Western security guarantees, financial assistance, and Ukraine's participation in the disarmament process. Some even argued that Ukraine should retain the weapons as a deterrent to Russia, much as Britain or France retain their small forces.[50] At the very least, a significant bloc of Ukrainian lawmakers are dissatisfied with the vague assurances of diplomatic support for a denuclearized Ukraine.

Black Sea Fleet/Crimea

If nuclear weapons attracted the most attention in the world at large, other issues marred Ukrainian-Russian relations as well. According to Bohdan Harasymiw, "The issue of the Crimea continued to be politically relevant throughout 1992, while the other claims to autonomy subsided."[51] Russian agitation for Crimean autonomy was aggravated by the dispute over how to divide the Black Sea Fleet, which, though rusting, retains major symbolic value for Russia and Ukraine.[52]

The rhetorical conflict over the region escalated after the Russian parliament voted in January, by an overwhelming 166 to 13, to "look into the legality of Nikita Khrushchev's transfer of the Crimea to Ukrainian jurisdiction in 1954."[53] Following a mid-summer lull in the conflict due to the two Yeltsin–Kravchuk summits at Dagomys and Mukhalatka, the issue returned when the Russian Congress of People's Deputies voted in December to reevaluate the status of Sevastopol, the home port of the Black Sea Fleet. According to the Ukrainian foreign ministry, this action is "not one which will further the strengthening of Russian-Ukrainian ties or the improvement of their atmosphere."[54]

Some analysts feel that Russia, lacking sufficient warm-water ports, will continue to press Ukraine on this issue. As Paul Goble notes, "With the departure of the Baltic states and Ukraine, Russia's immediate warm-water, deep-port capability is reduced by nearly 80 percent. Given its need to export raw materials and to import finished goods, Russia will have to seek guaranteed access to the Baltic ports and through Ukraine."[55]

On the positive side (at least from Kiev's perspective), the CIS Black Sea Fleet commander, Igor Kasatonov, whose anti-Ukrainian statements were front-page news throughout Ukraine, was removed in late 1992. At their Crimean summit, Kravchuk and Yeltsin agreed to place the fleet under joint Russian-Ukrainian jurisdiction for three years.[56] For critics, however, the agreement merely postponed the difficult questions on the division of naval assets. The deal was greeted with skepticism and hostility in parliaments in both Ukraine and Russia. Given the tumult on the eastern littoral of the Black Sea, where Russia and Georgia are backing opposing forces in Abkhazia, it is unlikely that Moscow and Kiev will come to a mutual understanding about the use of Black Sea Fleet ships in the near future.

Moldova/Trans-Dniester

Another CIS hot spot is located on Ukraine's western borders, on the east bank of the Dniester River in Moldova. The tranquility of former Soviet Moldavia has been shattered by the armed skirmishes between the ethnic Romanian government in Chisinau and the Russian communists in the "Dniester Republic." As in Serbia, the Trans-Dniester communists have adopted a born-again nationalist, racist agenda, abetted by the Fourteenth Russian Army stationed in Tiraspol.

The conflict, on Ukraine's western border, has been exacerbated by the local Russian military commander, General Aleksandr Lebed.[57] Lebed has called the government in Chisinau illegitimate and has continued to make political addresses even after Russian Defense Minister Pavel Grachev banned such statements.[58] Lebed also defied President Yeltsin's statement that the Fourteenth Army would be pulled back to Russia, saying, "I do not believe such an order will come. . . . Russia is not completely ready for that."[59] And, in fact, the army has not been withdrawn, but rather is transforming itself into self-styled "Dniester Forces," taking advantage of the summer cease-fire and of Ukraine's tentative move toward supporting self-determination for the Dniester region. Kravchuk had previously insisted on the principle of inviolability of borders within the CIS, but shifted during the Dagomys summit with Yeltsin. This was not enough for General Lebed, who charged that "on orders from the Kiev leadership, Ukrainian special services have made repeated attempts to discredit the 14th Army."[60]

Ukrainians will have a great interest in the future of the Russian force on its western frontier. Any movement of Russian troops would take place through Ukrainian territory or airspace, and a potential refugee problem has forced Kiev to move regular army units to the border with Moldova. As Harasymiw points out, "Sovereignty is up for grabs on Ukraine's doorstep; armed conflict spilling over into Ukraine at this time would be a setback for democratization as it might reopen a whole series of secessionist and irredentist battles."[61] Moldovan leader Mircea Snegur has sided with Ukraine, saying Moldova "will not give up the Dniester to anyone, particularly not to those who also want to get the Crimea and also create here an outpost against Ukraine."[62]

The U.S. Approach to Imperial Dissolution

> Empires like to deal with empires—there is something neat about it. But to treat Ukraine as though it still belonged to the sphere of Russia was a mistake.
> —Roman Szporluk[63]

During the months leading to the coup, the United States fundamentally misread the dynamics of the coming Soviet collapse. Washington, interested primarily in Moscow's cooperation on arms reductions, German reunification, and Middle East negotiations, doggedly supported Mikhail Gorbachev's Union Treaty. Only three weeks before the August coup, President George Bush traveled to Kiev to deliver a speech decrying "suicidal nationalism" and warning Ukrainians not to consider the "false choice" between Gorbachev and the anti-Moscow leaders of independence within the republics.[64]

In the frenzied weeks following the failure of the putsch and the Ukrainian declaration of independence, the Bush administration seemed petrified, unable to articulate a position on the implosion of its superpower adversary. On September 5, Secretary of State James Baker made his first statement on the subject, in which he "carefully avoided spelling out the type of government the United States would like to see evolve," but hoped for the continuation of "some central authority with which the United States and its allies can work on military and diplomatic issues." He pointedly avoided mentioning Ukraine, or any other republic, with the exceptions of the Baltic states.[65]

As it became clear that there would be no reconstitution of central authority in Moscow under Gorbachev, the United States began to deal with the heretofore derided Boris Yeltsin. Ukraine, however, believed it was being overlooked in U.S. policy calculations. The only issues pressed by Undersecretary of State Reginald Bartholemew on his first visit to Ukraine, Belarus, and Kazakhstan were nuclear weapons transfers to Russia and republic accession to the Non-Proliferation Treaty. While the United States recognized Ukrainian independence in December 1991, Ukrainian leaders felt that, beyond nuclear issues, Washington was uninterested in Ukraine.[66] On the day Ukraine held its referendum on independence, Adrian Karatnycky notes:

> U.S. Ambassador to Gorbachev Robert Strauss was shown on Soviet television handing over $600 million in food credits to Ivan Silaev, the Soviet prime minister without portfolio, if you will. The legacy of this approach is that, as of December 25, we had a policy for a country that didn't exist and a close relationship with a leader who had no power. It also meant we had only two U.S. consular staff on the ground in Ukraine, covering a country of 52 million, and no one permanently based in Kazakhstan, Belarus, or the other emerging nation states.[67]

In February 1992, after the establishment of the CIS and the proliferation of serious Russian-Ukrainian tensions, Washington appeared unconcerned. According to Kissinger, "The United States has been remarkably slow in dealing with the new republics. . . . The rare visits of U.S. officials deal almost exclusively with the nuclear issue, an important but limited dialogue, since it will end when the nuclear weapons are removed."[68] In retrospect, it is clear that the unitary Western focus on nuclear weapons may have unexpectedly complicated relations between Ukraine and Russia.

By early spring 1992, after Ukraine had suspended its shipment of tactical nuclear weapons to Russia, U.S. policy shifted slightly. Led by the Defense Department, a high-level delegation visited Kiev in an "acknowledgement by

American officials that the way they had been handling Ukraine was not working."[69] Given that the democratic shortcomings of the Ukrainian government were already apparent, some argued that this backing and filling was unwise. According to *The Economist*, the West "blundered" in its policies toward Ukraine: "First they failed to spot that its independence was unstoppable and tried to discourage it. . . . Now they are overcompensating by being too nice to a Ukrainian government still stuffed with ex-Communists."[70]

One year later, the United States has beefed up its diplomatic presence in Kiev, and $175 million has been earmarked for Ukraine for implementation of START and NPT. The Ukrainian government remains extremely disappointed in the West's attitude, often blaming the Russian media for what they believe is a distorted image in the West. While U.S. relations with Boris Yeltsin's Russia are warmer, Ukraine feels frozen out. As Prime Minister Kuchma dryly noted, "We were always told, by our own Mikhail Gorbachev and by the politicians in Europe and America, that when we cease being an enemy they won't leave us in the lurch. Now we're left in the lurch waiting for a dictatorship that will be worse than the last one."[71]

Opportunities and Options

In order to prevent the coming dictatorship forecast by Kuchma, the United States must first realize the gravity of the situation. "Unfortunately," according to Kuchma, "there is already a conflict. Worse still, this is a conflict in which there can be no victors."[72] Any of the above-mentioned frictions, from nuclear control to civil unrest to military insubordination, could militarize Russian-Ukrainian relations. Second, if the United States does not become engaged in assisting both nations more directly, as opposed to investing hope in Commonwealth structures, that conflict is more likely. Third, even though ethnic tensions between average Ukrainians and Russians are virtually nonexistent, official relations between the two governments will remain cool at best for some time. Ukraine will continue to view Russia as the principal threat to its sovereignty or even survival in the next decade. As General Rodionov's 1992 speech suggests, Russia in turn will utilize its resources to prevent the extension of NATO or other Western security pacts to Ukraine.[73]

Three general positions toward Russian-Ukrainian relations have emerged in U.S. policy debates. To oversimplify somewhat, they may be labeled the "Russia-first" approach, the "Cold War II" scenario, and the "democratic engagement" strategy.

The Russia-first approach makes a "realist" argument; that is, as U.S. security can be jeopardized only by a hostile or insecure Russia, American policy must place the highest priority on developing solid relations with the largest and most powerful successor state.[74] In addition, a weak, fragmented Russia is by far a greater security problem than an isolated Ukraine. Another Russia-first position

is that Ukraine's ambivalence on START and NPT represents a dangerous proliferation precedent, and that strong pressures should be brought to bear on all
non-Russian nuclear republics.[75] Interestingly, a Russia-first doctrine would also
support the CIS as a means of creating a web of economic and security links
tying the republics to Russia.

The Russia-first approach would press for greater aid to Russia, even if
Yeltsin's reform measures stall. It would inevitably recognize Russia's special
role and influence in its contiguous regions, much as Washington considers the
western hemisphere a zone of U.S. vital interest. The United States would use its
influence to examine Russian complaints about treatment of Russians in the
Baltic states. Washington would support Russian demands for access to Black
Sea ports, and it would take a hands-off approach to the Moldovan-Dniester
conflict. To some degree the Russia-first approach was followed, albeit cautiously and without acknowledgment, by the Bush State Department.[76]

The Cold War II approach also stems from a realist perspective, but draws an
opposite set of policy prescriptions based on a divergent reading of the security
environment. This argument holds that Russian nationalist forces are ascendant,
that Moscow cannot become a full partner with the West,[77] and that Russia itself
may soon disintegrate into various regional fiefdoms. Moreover, in order to
prevent hostile coalitions, Paul Goble suggests, "Russia will necessarily pursue a
policy of *divide et impera* around its periphery" that will foster new conflicts in
Central Europe.[78] Therefore, the United States should build up the fragile democracies in Central and Eastern Europe to serve as a buffer between Russia and
the West, and perhaps to serve as developmental models for Moscow.

Such a policy would include drastically boosting aid to the nations on
Russia's periphery, including Ukraine and the Baltic states. It would encourage
cooperation between Ukraine and the new democracies in Central Europe, particularly Poland, Hungary, and the Czech Republic, for the purpose of eventual
integration into European economic institutions. Above all, this approach would
give serious thought to some form of security guarantee to Ukraine.[79]

Given the endurance of anti-American attitudes in Russian and Ukrainian
military circles, there are clear drawbacks to both of the above strategies. The
United States can be more active in supporting those forces in Ukraine who want
democracy as well as independence; in encouraging Russians who are state-
builders rather than empire-preservers; and in providing targeted aid and expertise in the construction of republican institutions and civilian enterprises. Such an
effort will be costly, and will require patience and determination; it also reflects
American values and promotes American interests in the long term.

The strategy of democratic engagement recognizes the need to respect, and
perhaps to contain, Russian power. It acknowledges that a democratic, non-
nuclear Ukraine could play an important role in preserving international peace. It
would take a much more activist role in helping to mediate current disputes. It
would offer membership in Western economic and security institutions, provided

those nations meet certain principles of democratic self-government such as civilian control over the military, transparency of government operations, rule of law, and guarantees of civil liberties. The best articulation of this strategy has come from Zalmay Khalilzad, whose "zone of peace" concept was introduced when he was with the Department of Defense.[80]

Western financial assistance in this approach would carefully target both countries, seeking to avoid the large state enterprises and to encourage the expansion of entrepreneurial businesses. Such assistance would also be linked to specific timetables for the introdûction of elections and constitutional reforms. Both republics require massive help for the process of defense conversion. While Western economists and arms controllers argue that the military- industrial base in Ukraine must be reduced, little has been offered for coping with the accompanying industrial decline, unemployment, and erosion of scientific and technological facilities.[81]

Other specifics of the democratic engagement agenda might include the following: The United States would press the Russian government to guarantee Ukrainian borders and to abjure any military aggression against Ukraine, conventional or nuclear. The United States would consider an offer to dismantle ICBMs and nuclear devices on bomber bases on Ukrainian soil, disassembling the missiles and purchasing the fissile materials. The Ukrainians argue vociferously that while they have no desire to host nuclear weapons, they lack the resources and facilities to dismantle the weapons and they mistrust Russian intentions. Such an initiative would test Ukrainian sincerity on that issue.

The United States would also offer a package of risk-reduction mechanisms and confidence-building measures with the republics, including upgrading warning capabilities and providing equipment for secure transport and disposal of nuclear materials.

The North Atlantic Cooperation Council, with an active if not leading U.S. role, should offer to convene a political summit on the future of the Moldovan and Trans-Dniester region, to determine future borders, political arrangements, and armed forces of the republic. If requested, a NATO peacekeeping force could be inserted to help monitor the results of the summit and to assist in the transport of troops and equipment from Moldova to Russia. If necessary, assistance would be provided for Ukraine to assist it to cope with voluntary population transfers or refugee resettlement.

Finally, the United States and Canada would launch a concerted effort to expand their contacts with defense officials in Russia and Ukraine. This initiative would include expanding defense attaché presence and military contacts, organizing officer exchanges, and composing curricula for military and civilian defense professionals. Such an effort would allow greater interaction among military officers in the region and would greatly expand the pool of qualified civilians involved in defense decisions in Ukraine and Russia.

Postscript

For a United States interested in the stable development of democratic institutions in the former USSR, neglect—benign or otherwise—is not an option. The new realities in the Slavic heartland of the former USSR demand an unusually high level of diplomatic dexterity. We must ensure that Western assistance to both countries does not injure relations between them.[82] We must assist the institutionalization of freedom—democracy—without promoting those who would direct populist sentiment toward increased tension between the two nations.[83] We must persist in calling for the denuclearization of Ukraine and for the disarmament of Russia and ask both to desist from destabilizing arms sales, without bolstering nationalist militants in each country. We must support the consolidation of Ukrainian independence without bruising Russian sensitivities about the loss of the former republics. And we must acknowledge the proper importance of our relationship with Moscow without slighting Ukrainian aspirations. It is a tall order. But it is and will be the truest test of American global leadership in the post–Cold War world.

Notes

1. *Moscow News*, no. 51, 1991, p. 8.
2. Quoted in Abraham Brumberg, "Not So Free At Last," *The New York Review of Books*, October 22, 1992, p. 60.
3. Even before the collapse of the USSR, some officials and analysts were predicting that the West would soon mourn the passing of the Cold War era's geopolitical stability. See, for example, John J. Mearsheimer, "Back to the Future: Instability in Europe After the Cold War," *International Security*, Summer 1990, pp. 5–56. Even Francis Fukuyama's notable 1989 essay, "The End of History?" waxed wistful about the unifying energy which propelled the West before the passing of Marxism-Leninism from the world scene. See *The National Interest*, Summer 1989, pp. 1–18.
4. In addition to the Russian Federation, strategic nuclear forces are currently located in Ukraine (176 ICBMs, 42 strategic bombers), Belarus (estimated 80 ICBMs), and Kazakhstan (104 ICBMs, 40 bombers). Ukraine hosts 1,656 long-range nuclear warheads, 1,240 of which are on multiple-warhead SS–24 and SS–19 missiles. See map insert, "Territory of the Former Soviet Union and Its Neighbours," in International Institute for Strategic Studies, *The Military Balance 1992–1993* (London: Brassey's, 1992). Moscow claims to retain full command and control over these forces, although Kazakhstan and Ukraine are seeking "administrative" control over these systems, and Ukraine asserts that it has a "technical veto" over nuclear launches from its territory.
5. According to former Russian Deputy Foreign Minister Fedor Shelov-Kovediaev, "Our fates are intertwined in the most astonishing way," listing the "financial problem (including mutual settlements, trade turnover, and the fate of the ruble supply after Ukraine switches to the grivnya)" as one of the major issues between the republics. See *Nezavisimaia gazeta*, July 30, 1992, pp. 1, 5. For other views of Ukrainian-Russian economic ties, see John Lloyd and Dmitry Volkov, "Russia cracks the whip over rouble zone," *The Financial Times*, July 31, 1992, p. 2; and Chrystia Freeland, "Kiev gripped in Russian stranglehold," *The Financial Times*, July 23, 1992, p. 5.

6. According to one U.S. government official, "Without overstating it, this is the place where the whole thing could come crashing down, and where we would have no choice but to get in the middle of it." Quoted in Thomas L. Friedman, "The U.S. Takes a Serious Look at Ukraine," *The New York Times*, April 19, 1992, sec. 4, p. 5.

7. Charles F. Furtado and Andrea Chandler, eds., *Perestroika in the Soviet Republics* (Boulder, CO: Westview Press, 1992), p. 215. Significant exceptions to this academic trend include Nadia Diuk and Adrian Karatnycky, *The Hidden Nations—The People Challenge the Soviet Union* (New York: William Morrow, 1990); Paul Goble, "Ethnic Politics in the USSR," *Problems of Communism*, July–August 1989, pp. 1–15; and Roman Szporluk, "Dilemmas of Russian Nationalism," *Problems of Communism*, July–August 1989, pp. 15–35.

8. Kiev's conventional capabilities are impressive as well, at least on paper: "Ukraine now has more tanks, armored vehicles, and combat aircraft than any other country in Europe after Russia. Even under the CFE cuts its entitlements for tanks and armored vehicles are Europe's third largest, and for artillery and aircraft the second largest." See David White, "The empire splits up," *The Financial Times*, December 22, 1992, p. 10.

9. Mark R. Beissinger, "The Deconstruction of the USSR and the Search for a Post-Soviet Community," *Problems of Communism*, November–December 1991, p. 29. Beissinger was among the few Western analysts who argued for a "selective dismemberment" of the USSR as a way for Mikhail Gorbachev to prevent the explosion that occurred in August 1991. Ukraine was not listed among those select republics. See Beissinger and Lubomyr Hajda, eds., *The Nationalities Factor in Soviet Politics and Society* (Boulder, CO: Westview Press, 1990), esp. chapter 13.

10. For historic Russian views on Ukraine and Kievan Rus', see Dmitrii Likhachev, *Reflections on Russia* (Boulder, CO: Westview Press, 1991), esp. "The Greatness of Kiev," pp. 62–76, and chapter 3, "The Baptism of Rus' and the State of Rus'," pp. 97–118; Roman Szporluk, "The National Question," in Timothy J. Colton and Robert Legvold, eds., *After the Soviet Union—From Empire to Nations* (New York and London: W.W. Norton, 1992), pp. 84–112; and Orest Subtelny, *Ukraine—A History* (Toronto: University of Toronto Press, 1988), esp. Part Three, "The Cossack Era."

11. Henry Kissinger, "The New Russian Question," *Newsweek*, February 19, 1992, p. 34.

12. For an excellent account of the August 1991 events in Ukraine, see Zenovia A. Sochor, "Putsch and Politics in Ukraine," paper delivered at the Twenty-fourth National Convention of the American Association for the Advancement of Slavic Studies, Phoenix, Arizona, November 20, 1992.

13. *The Economist*, February 1, 1992, p. 15. Months after the coup, one of the leaders of the Ukrainian opposition, Viacheslav Chornovil, noted, "If you look at a map of Ukraine to see how democratic it is, then three-quarters of the territory should be painted red or pink because, even today, it is under control of our sovereign Ukrainian communists." Quoted in Laurie Hays, "As He Builds a National Ukraine, Chief Becomes Thorn in Yeltsin's Side," *The Wall Street Journal*, March 17, 1992, p. 1.

14. Ukrainian diplomats assert that Kiev could serve as a conduit for democratic values in the East, thereby serving Western interests. Ukraine's relations with Poland are good, and according to Polish Labor Minister Jacek Kuron, "Without an independent Ukraine, there can be no truly independent Poland." Kiev's ties with Hungary, which could be sensitive due to the presence of Hungarians in the western provinces of Ukraine, are also solid. Ukrainian-Slovak relations, however, are problematic. Moscow has offered military support to Slovakia, and according to Jan Obrman, "Slovakia's relationship with Ukraine will also be influenced by the quality of contacts between Bratislava and Mos-

cow. In fact, Russia might well try to maintain a 'special relationship' with Slovakia in order to keep Ukrainian influence in Central Europe under control." See Jan Obrman, "Uncertain Prospects for Independent Slovakia," *RFE/RL Research Report*, December 11, 1992, p. 45.

15. On Kravchuk's maneuvering during those weeks, see David Marples, "Radicalization of the Political Spectrum in Ukraine," *Report on the USSR*, RFE-RL, August 30, 1991, pp. 30–33.

16. See Adrian Karatnycky, "The Ukrainian Factor," *Foreign Affairs*, Summer 1992, pp. 90–107; Taras Kuzio, *Ukraine—The Unfinished Revolution* (London: Institute for European Defense & Strategic Studies, 1992); Roman Solchanyk, "Russia and Ukraine: The Politics of Independence," *RFE/RL Research Report*, May 8, 1992, pp. 13–16.

17. Quoted in Chrystia Freeland, "Kiev Leader: From Apparatchik to Nationalist," *The Washington Post*, May 6, 1992, p. A16. Such analogies, widely shared by Ukrainian nationalists, somewhat simplify an incredibly complex tapestry of world war, revolution, and imperial breakup. See Subtelny, *Ukraine—A History*, esp. chapter 19, "The Ukrainian Revolution," pp. 355–79.

18. On the Ukrainian campaign to nationalize Soviet armed forces on its territory, see Bohdan M. Pyskir, "The Silent Coup: The Building of Ukraine's Military," *European Security*, Spring 1993.

19. The percentage of Russians serving in the Ukrainian officer corps is even higher. The Ukrainian Ministry of Defense reports that 53 percent of Ukrainian General Staff officers are Russian, as are 90 percent of general officers, 80 percent of air force officers, and over 50 percent of all officers. The ministry also estimates that 300,000 senior and warrant officers of Ukrainian origin serve outside Ukraine. See *Molod Ukrainy*, August 21, 1992.

20. One opinion poll indicated that most officers who swore loyalty did not take the oath seriously, and the Ukrainian enlisted ranks continue to suffer the same levels of desertion and draft evasion as the Soviet Army. The Ukrainian military has introduced a "social-psychological division" to cope with morale problems in the officer corps, although critics compare it to the Soviet system of military control. See *Political Review*, a publication of the Ukrainian Center for Independent Political Research, October 1992, pp. 82–83, on the success of the loyalty oaths.

21. The Ukrainian Officers Union (UOU) claims to have 50,000 members in an "independent association dedicated to the defense of Ukrainian officers' economic interests." Some argue that the UOU has become a military party or a shadow defense ministry, seeking to arrogate unto itself the responsibility for the appointment and promotion of officers. For more on the UOU, see *Political Review*, Ukrainian Center for Independent Political Research, Kiev, October 1992, pp. 85–86.

22. Col. Grigory Omelchenko, quoted in *Nezavisimost'*, March 20–26, 1992. He repeated that claim after the summer summits between Yeltsin and Kravchuk. See Vladimir Ruban, "Rozhdenie voennoi derzhavi," *Moskovskie novosti*, August 9, 1992, pp. 6–7. An independent Russian journalist writes about Ukrainian hopes to nationalize its officer corps and troops: "The threat that they will lose control of the troops is quite real. The army could quickly become completely independent and at the same time a fairly uncontrolled political force." See Pavel Felgengauer, *Nezavisimaia gazeta*, January 3, 1992, p. 1.

23. The case of Major General Valerii Kuznetsov is instructive in this regard. Kuznetsov, who had sworn loyalty to Ukraine, was removed as a senior Ukrainian commander after asserting that he would not fight against Russia. The Kuznetsov affair was trumpeted by both the UOU and Russian activists in Crimea, but his views are shared by many other officers in the Ukrainian armed forces. See the poll results in *Political Review*.

24. In a January 1993 speech to a joint session of parliamentary commissions, Prime Minister Leonid Kuchma listed the following statistics for 1992 in Ukraine: national income decreased by 14 percent; labor productivity declined by 15 percent; industrial output was down by 9 percent, consumer goods by 10.9 percent, foodstuffs 14.9 percent, meat by 18 percent, eggs by 19 percent, milk by 21 percent. See Victor Tkachuk, "Ukraine Assumes Responsibility for Union Debts," *Ukrainian News*, January 25, 1993, p. 3.

25. Christopher Donnelly, "Evolutionary Problems in the Former Soviet Armed Forces," *Survival*, Autumn 1992, p. 39.

26. See "Ukraine—Independent, but not yet free," *The Economist*, June 13, 1992, pp. 54–55.

27. Quoted in Margaret Shapiro, "Ukraine's Leaders Retreat from Reform," *The Washington Post*, October 24, 1992, p. A17. The autumn appointment of Leonid Kuchma, a 25-year veteran of the Soviet military industrial complex, as prime minister initially confirmed the fears of economic reformers in Ukraine, where inflation is running at 30 percent per month. Kuchma has introduced tentative reform measures, however, and some observers feel his approach may in the long run succeed where the Russian prime minister's shock-therapy plan failed. See "Man of Iron," *The Economist*, December 26, 1992/January 8, 1993, pp. 62–63.

28. Quoted in Serge Schmemann, "New Leader in a Lament for Ukraine," *The New York Times*, November 9, 1992, p. A9. The depression is particularly acute in the eastern mining and industrial oblasts, where many of Ukraine's 11 million Russians live. That Kiev is shifting military units to the region is illustrative of the social pressures which could explode should the economic gloom continue.

29. On the system of presidential prefects, see Roman Solchanyk, "Ukraine: Political Reform and Political Change," *RFE-RL Research Report*, May 22, 1992, p. 3.

30. Quoted in *Nezavisimaia gazeta*, August 25, 1992, p. 3, translated in Foreign Broadcast Information Service, "Daily Report—Central Eurasia," no. 92–167, August 27, 1992, p. 53. Hereafter referred to as FBIS.

31. Bohdan Harasymiw, "Transition to Democracy in Ukraine," paper delivered at the Twenty-fourth National Convention of the American Association for the Advancement of Slavic Studies, p. 22.

32. Petr Struve, "Obshcheruskaia kultura i ukrainski partikularizm," *Russkaia mysl'*, January 1912, p. 85, quoted in Subtelny, *Ukraine—A History*, p. 580.

33. On the *derzhavniki*, derived from the Russian word for "great power," see Leon Aron, "The Battle for the Soul of Russian Foreign Policy," *The American Enterprise*, November/December 1992, pp. 10–16; Walter Laqueur, "Foreign Policy Concepts of the Russian Right," *New Times*, 1992, no. 38, pp. 12–14; and Rolf H. W. Theen, "The Appeal of Autocracy and Empire: A Threat to Russian Democracy," *The World & I*, vol. 7, no. 9 (1992), pp. 583–609.

34. Kozyrev, who has been accused of poor management skills and is rumored to have lost influence with Boris Yeltsin, nevertheless continued to make spirited defenses of a liberal foreign policy platform with erudite articles and speeches, culminating in a dramatic mock-presentation before Western foreign ministers in December 1992, in which he played the role of a *derzhavnik*. See, for example, his "Transformation or Kafkaesque Metamorphosis: Russia's Democratic Foreign Policy and Its Priorities," *Nezavisimaia gazeta*, August 20, 1992, pp. 1, 4, and FBIS-SOV-*92–167*, August 27, 1992, pp. 19–25, in which Kozyrev defends his policies with references to Kafka, the Bible, Berdiaev, Solov'ev, and the League of Nations.

35. On the debate over the Ministry for Commonwealth Affairs, see Pavel Golub, "The Creation of a Separate Ministry for Commonwealth Affairs May Be a Political

Mistake," *Izvestiia*, July 24, 1992, p. 7. Translated in *Current Digest of the Post-Soviet Press*, vol. 44, no. 30, p. 1. Golub asks, "Are the authors of the idea of creating an independent Ministry for Commonwealth Affairs setting the task of adjusting Russia's foreign policy course in the direction of great power status and emphasizing its role as a mother country with respect to other CIS members?" The ministry idea faded during the fall, but its supporters in the Russian parliament continue to attack the Kozyrev foreign ministry relentlessly.

36. On the security council, see Suzanne Crow, "Russia Prepares to Take a Hard Line on 'Near Abroad,' " *RFE-RL Research Report*, August 14, 1992, pp. 21–24, and Stephen Foye, "Russian Army Marches Right," *Meeting Report*, Kennan Institute for Advanced Russian Studies, vol. 10, no. 1.

37. *Voennaia mysl'*, July 1992, pp. 6–14.

38. "Thus," writes Sherr, "not only military, but also political figures proceed from peculiarly Soviet notions of what 'independence' ought to mean." James Sherr, "Russian Orthodoxies—Little Change in Military Thinking," *The National Interest*, Winter 1992–93, pp. 41–49. On Russian defense doctrine, see Sergei Rogov, *The Debates on the Future Military Doctrine of Russia* (Alexandria, VA: Center for Naval Analyses, December 1992); James Holcomb, "Russian Military Doctrine—Structuring for the Worst Case," *Jane's Intelligence Review*, December 1992, pp. 531–34; Mary C. Fitzgerald, "Russia's New Military Doctrine," *RUSI Journal*, October 1992, pp. 40–48.

39. Ibid., p. 44.

40. Aleksandr Rutskoi, "V zaschituiu Rossii," *Pravda*, January 30, 1992. Boris Vasilev, a liberal writer, notes, "Russians have not developed into a nation. They never knew where the borders of their state were, and they still do not [know]." These are chilling words for many Ukrainians. See Vera Tolz, "Russia: Westernizers Continue to Challenge National Patriots," *RFE/RL Research Report*, December 11, 1992, p. 2.

41. Igor Torbakov, "The 'Statists' and the Ideology of Russian Imperial Nationalism," *RFE/RL Research Report*, December 11, 1992, p. 13.

42. See Stephen Foye, *Military/Security Notes*, RFE/RL Research Institute, November 24, 1992.

43. See Andrei Kortunov, "Strategic Relations Between the Former Soviet Republics," *Backgrounder* no. 892, The Heritage Foundation, April 17, 1992.

44. On Russian perspectives toward post-Soviet nuclear weapons issues, see Sergei Rogov et al., *Commonwealth Defense Arrangements and International Security*, a joint paper by the Institute of USA and Canada and the Center for Naval Analyses, 1992. See esp. "The Nuclear Dimension," pp. 17–26.

45. Some Ukrainian politicians trace the later disputes over strategic weapons to the flap over tactical weapons transfers. Parliamentarian Serhij Holowaty, recalling that Ukraine received no compensation for the tactical weapons transfer, said in an interview, "Ukraine has been so burned by Russia in financial and economic matters, that after a year of this we will not lightly give up any more assets." Serge Schmemann, "Ukraine Finds Nuclear Arms Bring a Measure of Respect," *The New York Times*, January 7, 1993, p. A12.

46. IISS, *Military Balance 1992–93*, p. 86. See also Serge Schmemann, "Friction Rises as Ukraine and Russia Clash over Ex-Soviet Armed Forces," *The New York Times*, March 3, 1992, p. 3.

47. Interview with Leonid Kravchuk in *Holos Ukrainy*, December 16, 1992; FBIS-SOV-92-245, December 21, 1992, pp. 52–54. On Kravchuk's attitudes toward Russia and nuclear weapons, see his interview in *Der Spiegel*, "Habt Keine Angst Vor Uns," February 3, 1992, pp. 155–63.

48. According to Serhij Holowaty, "Our deputies don't care where these things are

aimed. They know that they must get something for them." See Serge Schmemann, "Ukraine Finds Nuclear Arms Bring a Measure of Respect," *The New York Times*, January 7, 1993, p. A1.

49. Memorandum, Ministry of Foreign Affairs, Republic of Ukraine, December 15, 1992. Konstantin Grishchenko, head of the disarmament department of the foreign ministry, had indicated that among the "conditions" Ukraine might attach to START I ratification would be security guarantees from nuclear powers, up to $1.5 billion in foreign assistance, and a "clear cut" admission by Russia that the plutonium and uranium in the weapons deployed in Ukraine belong to Kiev. See *RFE/RL Daily Report*, no. 249, December 30, 1992, p. 1.

50. Mark Smith of the Royal United Services Institute in London noted, "It is largely a bargaining chip, but we can't be sure." Another British academic, recalling Deputy Prime Minister Ihor Yukhnovsky's proposal that Ukraine sell its fissile material "to the highest bidder," noted, "Why should they give it away, if they distrust the Russians?" See White, "The empire splits up," p. 10.

51. Bohdan Harasymiw, "Transition to Democracy in Ukraine," pp. 15–16.

52. See Celestine Bohlen, "In Russia–Ukraine Fight Over Navy, Crimea Lies at Heart of the Struggle," *The New York Times*, March 31, 1992, p. A6.

53. "A New Crimean War?" *The Economist*, February 1, 1992, p. 15. Shortly thereafter, Russian Vice President Aleksandr Rutskoi traveled to the Crimea and made several statements that incited the Ukrainians.

54. Sergei Tsikora, "No Time to End Dispute Over Crimea Before One Starts Over Sevastopol," *Izvestiia*, December 9, 1992, 1: FBIS-SOV–92–239, December 11, 1992, p. 24.

55. Paul Goble, "After the Soviet Union: The Parameters of Change," *The Harvard Journal of World Affairs*, Spring 1992, p. 56.

56. On the Yeltsin–Kravchuk summits, see John Lloyd, Chrystia Freeland, and Anthony Robinson, "History bears down on States of the Union," *The Financial Times*, August 19, 1992, p. 3.

57. For an excellent background on Ukrainian involvement in the region, see Bohdan Nahaylo, "Ukraine and Moldova: The View from Kiev," *RFE/RL Research Report*, May 1, 1992, pp. 39–45.

58. Grachev issued an executive order in July 1992 prohibiting political activities by military officers, noting that only the minister and deputy minister could issue statements on policy. According to Grachev, "Whoever cannot manage without politics, let him engage in it. But first he is obliged to discharge himself from the ranks of the Russian Armed Forces." See "Russian Federation Defense Ministry Press Center Reports," *Krasnaia zvezda*, September 1, 1992, p. 1; FBIS-SOV–92–170, September 1, 1992, p. 14.

59. Interview with Major General Aleksandr Lebed in *Sovetskaia Rossiia*, August 4, 1992, 1. FBIS-SOV–92–151, August 5, 1992, pp. 71–72.

60. Quoted in *RFE-RL Daily Report*, no. 1, January 4, 1993, p. 6.

61. Bohdan Harasymiw, "Transition to Democracy in Ukraine," p. 18.

62. Quoted in *RFE/RL Daily Report*, no. 95, May 19, 1992, p. 3.

63. Quoted in Friedman, "U.S. Takes a Serious Look at Ukraine."

64. After acknowledging that "the spirit of freedom thrives" in Ukraine, Bush added, "And yet freedom is not the same as independence. Americans will not support those who seek in order [sic] to replace a far-off tyranny with a local despotism." These words were hardly encouraging to his audience. *Rukh* cochairman Ivan Drach complained that Bush acted like a "messenger" who was "hypnotized by Gorbachev." See Francis X. Clines, "Bush, in Ukraine, Walks Fine Line on Sovereignty," *The New York Times*, August 2, 1991, p. A8.

65. Thomas L. Friedman, "U.S. Hoping Moscow Can Retain Control of Soviets' Nuclear Arms," *The New York Times*, September 5, 1992, pp. A1, A12.

66. For a contrasting policy, see Clyde H. Farnsworth, "Ukraine is Getting Canadian Credits," *The New York Times*, February 23, 1992, p. 14. Canada was the first country to recognize Ukraine after the December referendum, as well as the first Western country to provide a line of credit to Kiev in February 1992. At the same time, the United States delayed its own contributions to a stabilization fund administered by the IMF.

67. Adrian Karatnycky, "Minsk Meet," *The American Spectator*, February 1992, p. 33.

68. Kissinger continued, "Some Western leaders exhibit a subconscious impatience with the emergence of multiple sovereignties. At times they act as if they would prefer the old superstate, simply leavened by democratic ideals and market economies." Henry A. Kissinger, "The New Russian Question," *Newsweek*, February 10, 1992, pp. 34–35.

69. Friedman, "U.S. Takes a Serious Look at Ukraine."

70. "Message to Kiev," *The Economist*, February 8, 1992, p. 15.

71. Quoted in Serge Schmemann, "New Leader in a Lament for Ukraine," *The New York Times*, November 9, 1992, p. A9.

72. Quoted in Chrystia Freeland and John Lloyd, "Russia 'trying to paralyse Ukraine,' " *The Financial Times*, February 19, 1993, p. 2.

73. Although in early 1992 then-Lithuanian President Landsbergis and some Ukrainians discussed ideas of a Baltic-Black Sea security confederation, no real progress has been made beyond some vague bilateral cooperation agreements. See Andre Kortunov, "Strategic Relations Between the Former Soviet Republics," *Backgrounder*, The Heritage Foundation, no. 892, April 17, 1992, p. 6.

74. See Ted Hopf, "Managing Soviet Disintegration: A Demand for Behavioral Regimes," *International Security*, Summer 1992, pp. 44–75. Hopf focuses on Ukrainian intentions, writing, "A Ukrainian government that builds a 400,000-man army with protestations of good faith is one thing. A Ukrainian government that fields such an army while it simultaneously passes legislation barring Russians from educational and employment opportunities is quite another." He neglects to note that no such laws have been passed.

75. A bracing essay illustrating this point of view is Virginia I. Foran, "Ukrainian Holdout: The Real Problem With the Treaty," *The Washington Post*, January 3, 1993, p. C3. Foran writes, "Kiev must be made to understand that its intransigence threatens the collective security of the post–Cold War world. Ukraine should experience a tidal wave of diplomatic pressures from all governments that will benefit from the overall reduction of nuclear arms in the world." On Ukrainian concerns, she is less emphatic: beyond START and CFE, "the United States and Russia could reaffirm their pledges not to use nuclear weapons against a non-nuclear state. The United States could also suggest that Russia issue a declaration respecting Ukrainian borders."

76. Jim Hoagland describes two opposing camps—"Russia First" and "Russia Last"—which he associates with Richard Nixon and Zbigniew Brzezinski, respectively. See Jim Hoagland, "The Russia Debate: Nixon vs. Brzezinski," *The Washington Post*, March 26, 1992, p. A21. See also the recent writings of George Kennan, e.g., "For Russian Troops, a House to Go Home To," *The Washington Post*, November 8, 1992, p. C7. See also Hopf, "Managing Soviet Disintegration," and Francis Fukuyama, "Trapped in the Baltics," *The New York Times*, December 20, 1992, p. 23. Fukuyama and Kennan focus on the Baltic region, but their analyses derive from a conviction that non-Russian concerns must be subordinate to U.S.-Russian dialogue.

77. Evidence for this argument can be found in Sergei Stankevich's article, "A State in Search of Itself: Notes on Russian Foreign Policy," *Nezavisimaia gazeta*, March 28, 1992, later adapted in *The National Interest*, Summer 1992.

78. Goble, "After the Soviet Union," p. 56.

79. For an articulation of this point of view, see George Melloan, "Will State Ever Get Ukraine's Message," *The Wall Street Journal*, March 23, 1992, p. A11; Sherr, "Russian Orthodoxies"; Ian Brzezinski, "The Geopolitical Dimension, *The National Interest*, Spring 1992, pp. 48–52; V. Garber, "Ukraine is Key to Eastern European Stabilization," *Armed Forces Journal International*, February 1992, pp. 26–27; and Kuzio, *Ukraine—the Unfinished Revolution*.

80. Khalilzad delivered a speech in Ukraine in May outlining the goals of this general approach. See Zalmay Khalilzad, "Solving Ukraine's Nuclear Dilemma and More," *The Wall Street Journal*, December 30, 1992, p. 6, for proposed steps to include Ukraine in a new Western collective security arrangement in exchange for Kiev's rapid denuclearization. For a well-argued contrarian view on once and future collective security arrangements, see Richard K. Betts, "Systems for Peace or Causes of War? Collective Security, Arms Control, and the New Europe," *International Security*, Summer 1992, pp. 5–43.

81. In Ukraine, for example, the Mikolaev Shipyard on the Black Sea is lagging in a plan to shift from naval to commercial vessels, despite offers of help from the European Bank for Reconstruction and Development. According to Yuri Markov, the director of the shipyard, "This is what conversion means to us. Everything is lying dead." See Chrystia Freeland and Edward Balls, "Old ways dull the call to a new Ukraine," *The Financial Times*, January 5, 1993, p. 2.

82. Several Ukrainian officials have complained about Western aid packages to date in Central Europe and about NATO's focus on Russia. When General John Shalikashvili, Supreme Allied Commander in Europe, met with Kravchuk in November 1992, the latter complained, "Poland and Hungary get support and Ukraine goes unnoticed," adding, "We must find a formula to guarantee the security of the former states of the Soviet Union, Europe, and the world at large, not just the two superpowers." See "Military and Security Notes," *RFE/RL Research Report*, November 27, 1992, p. 55.

83. In Ukraine, for example, some of those most in favor of a nuclear arsenal have the most impeccable democratic, anticommunist credentials, such as Stepan Khmara of the Ukrainian Republican Party and some in *Rukh*. See George Kraus, "Ukrainian Opposition to a Nuclear Ukraine," *Notes on Russia & Central Eurasia*, Foreign Systems Research Center of Science Applications International Corporation, November 25, 1992, p. 1.

6

Central Asia and the New Russian-American Rapprochement

Martha Brill Olcott

The Collapse of the USSR

The collapse of the USSR caught both the U.S. and Soviet policy-making establishments by surprise and created new dilemmas for both sides. U.S.-Soviet relations had steadily improved during the Gorbachev years, and by the time of the USSR's dissolution, the two states had already developed a cooperative relationship that fell just short of alliance.

The demise of the USSR brought with it Gorbachev's dismissal and introduced not one but twelve new heads of state for the United States to deal with. Boris Yeltsin has repeatedly made the claim that Russia is the USSR's legal heir. In most issue areas, the international community has accepted Russia's premise, and certainly the post-USSR Bush–Baker policy was to see good relations with Russia as a key foreign policy goal. The newly appointed Clinton foreign policy team seems to have embraced this premise with even greater enthusiasm.

Now, though, whether U.S. leaders like it or not, they must deal with a plethora of newly independent states, and not just Moscow. Moreover, because of the desire to keep on good and ever improving relations with Yeltsin's Russia, U.S. policy-makers would ideally like to advance U.S. interests in these republics in a way that is not perceived as threatening to Russia.

The Russian leadership, too, has made its preferences clear. Boris Yeltsin and his foreign minister, Andrei Kozyrev, publicly leave no doubt that Russia believes it has special rights and privileges throughout the geopolitical space of the former USSR.[1] The message to U.S. policy-makers is clear; accept this or be

Support for the research summarized in this article was provided by the United States Institute of Peace.

prepared for a deterioration in the U.S.-Russian relationship.

Even without this, U.S. policy-makers were little prepared for developing separate foreign policies toward each of the newly independent states, or even for the various regional configurations of new states. The U.S. intelligence establishment's information base on each of the new states was scanty, and—except in regard to the Baltic republics—throughout the early years of *glasnost'* and *perestroika* U.S. policy-makers paid virtually no attention to what was going on in the Soviet republics, save in the area of human rights violations.

Not until 1990, when forced by events in Lithuania, were U.S. policy-makers willing to concede that the universe of Soviet foreign affairs extended beyond Moscow's Ring Road. Even then, so great was the concern of the Bush administration to ease the pressures on Gorbachev, that the U.S. political establishment downgraded its commitment to Baltic independence.[2] For more than forty years, the United States had refused to recognize Soviet rule over Latvia, Lithuania, and Estonia. In 1990 and 1991, however, the Bush administration refused to recognize the new Lithuanian, Latvian, and Estonian states prior to Gorbachev's own and the USSR's formal diplomatic recognition of their existence. Moreover, though there was some criticism of the Bush administration's stand in the U.S. government, this policy generally had bipartisan support.

We were even more cautious about championing the independence claims of other USSR nationalities. Not only did the U.S. government fail to support the nationalist aspirations of the politically important diaspora communities in the United States—the Armenians and Ukrainians for example—but President Bush used the occasion of his 1991 visit to Ukraine to chastise the Ukrainian people for undermining the process of democracy-building in the USSR with their nationalist zeal.[3]

Certainly, U.S. policy-makers gave no thought to the idea of independent states in Central Asia during this period. There was relatively great official interest in Kazakhstan, largely because of Chevron's plans to develop the Tengiz oil field. Kazakhstan's President Nursultan Nazarbaev was a vigorous defender of the idea of a renovated but preserved union,[4] so here too there was a confluence of interests with both the official U.S. and Soviet positions.

Coming to power in an anti-Communist Party putsch, Kyrgyzstan's President Askar Akaev also seemed an attractive figure to U.S. policy-makers, and he seems to have made a strong impression on Secretary of State James Baker during the latter's visit to Kyrgyzstan in 1991. But in Kyrgyzstan, too, there was a strong commitment to reforming, not destroying, the existing state structure.

In fact, nowhere in Central Asia was there official support for the formal dismantlement of the USSR, either among the official elite or among the opposition. Central Asia's leaders wanted to see change and wanted to gain control of their republics' own natural and man-made economic resources. But serious politicians in the region expected that Russia would hand over more than partial control; and immediately prior to the demise of the USSR, all were engaged in negotiations at both the presidential and ministerial levels over what degree of control they would receive.[5]

With the formal dissolution of the USSR, this situation changed. Turkmenistan, Uzbekistan, Kyrgyzstan, Kazakhstan, and Tajikistan received the formal appurtenances of a sovereign independent existence, ranging from the most critical—membership in the United Nations and other international bodies—to the more minor—state airlines and new stamps. These republics also formally took over control of their respective economies, and their leaders received sole responsibility for managing them.

This change in status created enormous problems for Central Asia's leaders, who received responsibilities far in excess of what they had anticipated or desired. To help solve these problems, they looked abroad—to Russia and, to a lesser degree, to the United States. For, as the Gorbachev regime had done before it, these new leaders also expected that the United States and, more generally, the international community would become sponsors and guarantors of the economic transformation brought on by the demise of the communist system.

The Central Asian View of the Problem

All the public statements of Central Asia's four presidents[6] championing their independence notwithstanding,[7] in most important ways the five republics continue to be at best quasi-autonomous appendages of Russia. Their economies are still almost inexorably tied to Russia, which also still serves as their primary international transportation and communication hub; Russia provides the source of their military manpower or defense; and, probably most important, Russia is the home of their formative intellectual and bureaucratic training.

Economically the republics are still fully dependent upon and largely controlled by Russia, which is the largest trading partner of each of the new Central Asian states. Trade is carried out through government-to-government purchase agreements as well as enterprise-to-enterprise transactions. As a result, the Russian government still exerts a great deal of direct control; and as the principal supplier of energy and, generally, of grain, it generally holds the upper hand in most commodity talks. Even more important, Russia is still the exclusive banking center of the former USSR. Only the three Baltic republics have managed to secede from the USSR's banking network, largely because they had their own gold reserves.

The national banks established in the remaining republics are still vulnerable to the edicts of the former USSR—now Russian—state bank. Moreover, until the Minsk summit, Boris Yeltsin and the Russian delegation opposed Nazarbaev's proposal to have this institution transformed into a CIS-wide banking system. That proposal was shelved at the Bishkek meeting of the CIS in October 1992.[8]

At the January 1993 Minsk meeting of CIS leaders, Yeltsin supported a revamped version of the Nazarbaev proposal, whereby Russia would get half the votes in a multinational bank that regulated financial affairs in the ruble zone.[9] However, the economic importance of this decision was undercut when Nazarbaev and Russian Prime Minister Viktor Chernomyrdin announced that they hoped to move the former republics to an energy-based pricing system for interrepublic trade.[10] As the single largest energy producer, Russia's domination was assured, especially as, with Kazakhstan, they had a clear lock on the market.

This means that even should the Central Asian republics create their own separate currencies—and all but Tajikistan have at one time or another claimed that they have the intention to do so—they will still have to suffer from a Russian-induced inflation. This inflation has oftentimes been magnified by distance, so that, for example, gasoline, high enough in Moscow, is twice as expensive in Kazakhstan and three times as high in Kyrgyzstan (which lacks any oil refineries). Alternatively, the decision to combat this inflation through a program of state subsidies has led Turkmenistan (which has the highest state subsidies) and, to a lesser extent, Uzbekistan, to institute and maintain strict border control to prevent the outflow of their cheaper consumer goods and foodstuffs.

All the Central Asian republics are running large budget deficits—nearly a third of the total budget on average—while simultaneously experiencing officially admitted drops of productivity of more than twenty percent.[11] In sparsely populated resource-rich republics like Turkmenistan, the leadership is willing to gamble that future profits will make up for current imbalances. In more heavily populated resource-rich republics like Kazakhstan, the bonuses delivered on signing mineral-extraction contracts with foreign firms are too small to provide much room for short-term financial maneuvering. Moreover, the major investment projects in the region, like Chevron's development of Tengiz, are set up to use initial profits to help recover initial cost, so that the immediate returns from even a major oil deposit like this one are not sufficient to fund economic recovery, let alone a major national economic development program.

The whole issue of foreign investment has been a very frustrating one from the point of view of the Central Asians. They expected far more assistance from the international lending community than has been forthcoming. To them, "lines of credit" means simply that—loans offered that will be spent as they see fit. To many Central Asian diplomats, the IMF appears to be a paternalistic organization, dictating terms to the borrower. Listening to their off-the-record complaints, it is clear that Central Asia's new financiers would be shocked by the terms generally offered by the average American savings-and-loan bank to a first-time home-buyer.

U.S. private-sector investment has been far less than the Central Asians expected, too, although only a portion of that disappointment could be said to be America's fault. A good percentage of Central Asian disappointment may be ascribed to their own inexperience with international market practices and their consequent tendencies to wildly overvalue what they wish to sell to the world, to undervalue what is coming in, or to suspect that they are being cheated. Their suspicions are heightened by the fact that sometimes they are, in fact, cheated, for American business firms (and American law firms) have gotten each of these republics to grant exclusivity in an area of its economy simply by being the first ones there. More common though, is the withdrawal of tender by American firms that fail to get the legal guarantees necessary to secure their investments.

Other problems arise from the general slowness with which these new nations have adopted the laws and institutions necessary to encourage business investment. In December 1992, the legislatures in both Kazakhstan and Kyrgyzstan— the countries regarded by the international community as the most capable in the area of international finance and business—failed to pass proposed enabling legislation designed to attract foreign investment. These types of laws are particularly necessary in the absence of a developed banking system and a convertible currency. None of these republics has passed the full packet of legislation necessary to establish a firm timetable for privatization, with the result that uncertainties over ownership of property are magnified.

The lack of laws and the proliferation of lines of authority have also encouraged corruption, which further discourages foreign investment. On a January 1993 evening's drive through downtown Alma-Ata, half a dozen new Mercedes sedans were spotted—most without license plates. In Tashkent, the government itself owns a dozen Mercedes and services them at the new Mercedes dealership. The cars are reportedly a gift from a mafia chieftain, and the service station is said to be a joint venture backed by mafia funds.

Official bribe-taking has become not only ubiquitous but also expensive. The going rate for the cooperation of a Kazakhstani minister, for example, is said to be one million U.S. dollars. In this case, the tale is of bribe accepted to queer a deal—Kazakhstan's contract with Chevron—so that neither honesty nor corruption can provide a guarantee of a foreign investor's success. Needless to say, these corrupt and murky working conditions threaten to attract investors who have little, if any, interest in helping these new nations to develop; and this raises the specter of a further cycle of dependency, poverty, and resentment of foreigners.

Other nations have fared somewhat better than the United States in establishing a commercial (and political) presence in Central Asia. U.S. business people sometimes privately complain of the competitive disadvantage at which the strict U.S. antibribery legislation leaves them. At the beginning of the period of Central Asian independence, Turkey attempted to position itself as the natural model for Central Asia and its bridge to the world. Many of the Turkish efforts have proven to be more air than action, however, perhaps because Turkish firms, just like American firms, have been reluctant to commit their own resources to effecting a policy which the Turkish government wants but has not funded.

In their turn, Central Asians who have dealt with the Turks often claim to have been disappointed. They find little to attract them in the ways in which

Turkish society has developed and find the Turks themselves quite distant cultur-
ally, and even linguistically. The widely supposed mutual comprehensibility of
Turkish and the Central Asian languages does not in practice seem to be true.

Iran presents another sort of developmental model, about which both Central
Asian leaders and most Central Asian citizens are understandably nervous. Although Iran has some commercial and cultural representation in the area, it has
not so far been large-scale outside of Turkmenistan and Tajikistan. Turkmenistan
is the only Central Asian state with which Iran shares a border, and Iran hopes to
become its largest foreign trade partner outside of Russia. Iran is helping to
develop its neighbor's oil, natural gas, cotton processing, and clothing industries,
and is willing to construct relations on a barter basis. Tajikistan is the only
Farsi-speaking nation in Central Asia. Though aid to this republic was increased
during the brief (May–December 1992) period of an Islamic-democratic coalition government, Iran provided humanitarian aid (foodstuffs, medicines, and
educational/cultural materials) to the Communist regimes which both preceded
and succeeded the short-lived noncommunist government.

For all of the talk of their commitment to secularism and their fear of Islamic
fundamentalism (and the implied threat of Iran), all the Central Asian states save
Kyrgyzstan have signed major economic agreements with the Islamic Republic
of Iran. The most recent, in early 1993, was signed between Iran and Uzbekistan
after Iran's Foreign Minister Ali Akbar Veliayati was warmly received in Tashkent by Uzbekistan's President Islam Karimov—the same Karimov who had
spent earlier months berating Iran for seeking to destabilize political conditions
in the region.[12] Another actor in the area is Pakistan, which has made some
incursions into Central Asia in the areas of trade and light industry. However, it
is not lost on Central Asians that in many important regards, such as literacy and
general levels of health-care, their societies are better served than is Pakistan's.

As for other foreign presences in Central Asia, there has been very direct
economic involvement by the countries of the Middle East. Saudis promised
large lines of foreign credit,[13] but are eager to link financial assistance to the
distribution of Korans and the construction of mosques. Saudi banks have been
offering credit in the area since 1989, and are most active in Kazakhstan.

The largest long-term Middle Eastern presence in the region is likely to be
through Omani participation in the pipeline by which Kazakhstan's oil will
eventually be shipped; the pipeline is a joint Omani-Kazakh-Russian production,
put together largely on Russian initiative. Indeed, most Arab commercial activity—and for that matter most Turkish activity as well—is still oriented toward
Russia. Israel too, has begun large-scale projects in Central Asia. Many of the
smaller Israeli projects involve the private capital of former residents of the
regions who are now Israeli citizens. The larger projects are generally Israeli
government initiatives, such as the Israeli participation in a jointly funded U.S.-
Israeli cooperative agriculture development program for Kyrgyzstan,
Kazakhstan, and possibly Uzbekistan. Israel is of interest to the Central Asians

because of its experience in nation-building. The leadership, though, is nervous about possible repercussions if that interest is expressed openly. That was seen in Kyrgyzstani President Askar Akaev's gaffes during his January 1993 visit to Israel, when he publicly championed the cause of Palestinian independence and then, to compensate, accepted Israel's suggestion that Kyrgyzstan open its embassy in Jerusalem instead of in Tel Aviv.[14]

Another foreign actor that seems likely to make significant inroads into Central Asia is China, which is already Kyrgyzstan's and Kazakhstan's largest non-CIS trading partner. Rapidly improving rail and road links between these republics and China are likely to lead to a rapid increase in China's share of Central Asia's market. Unlike prospective Western trade partners, the Chinese are eager to engage in complex barter deals and have no hesitation about flaunting international regulations prohibiting third-party transfers of technology. Low-cost (and low-quality) Chinese-made goods are already well represented in the bazaars of Central Asia, while considerable scrap aluminum and other metals have been shipped out.

The Central Asian leadership and population, especially those like the Kazakhs and Kyrgyz who are nearest the Chinese border, are nervous about this growing presence. There has been antipathy for the Chinese among the Turkic nomads since at least the sixteenth century; at the same time, however, the leadership of Central Asia is uniformly fascinated by the success of an economic model which is not only Asian but manages to combine the close social control of the familiar communist system with material comforts and pleasures—to say nothing of the chances for personal enrichment—which come from the capitalist system.

For their part, the Chinese are not concerned by the questions of political stability which disturb many foreign investors. Nor are they plagued by the transport difficulties which isolate these five virtually land-locked countries.[15] Kyrgyzstan, for example, has had no more than one airline flight in or out per week since mid-December 1992 because of local fuel shortages. Alma-Ata and Tashkent have limited direct international service, but an international traveler missing a connection to or from Istanbul or Frankfurt will wait three days for the next flight, seven days if en route to London. Service within the region is becoming quite unpredictable, with tariffs and routings changing regularly. Most international travel to and from Central Asia still moves through Moscow. Russia controls Central Asia in other important physical ways as well. Though parallel networks are slowly being introduced, Central Asian nations are still hooked to world telephone and telex networks through Moscow as well.

Bureaucratically, each of the countries is closely controlled by Russia: a large portion of the international business is conducted through Russian embassies and consulates. Of the five nations, only Kyrgyzstan and Kazakhstan have embassies in America (though an Uzbekistani representative is soon to arrive), and only the Kazakhs have a consular section, which opened in February 1993. Russia is still an agent for and not a partner with these states. In December 1992, Russia changed the procedures for issuing visas to all CIS countries, without informing their ambassadors.

Significantly, the USSR government and security communication networks also remain in place; perhaps more important, the leadership of the republics continue their past habits of conferring with one another on them. Central Asians still watch Moscow television and, to a great degree, read Moscow newspapers —although Uzbekistan's government refused to allow subscriptions to several of these in 1993 because they had been critical of Karimov's treatment of political opposition groups.[16]

Turning to Moscow is a very important part of the mindset of each of Central Asia's leaders. Each is Russian-speaking and educated primarily (and in some cases exclusively) in a Russian-language education system. The professional patterns and associations of all these men have been through Moscow. Most worked for two decades or more as senior administrators in the Moscow-commanded all-union bureaucracy. The only one who did not, Askar Akaev, lived most of his adult life in Russia and not in Kyrgyzstan.

More important, the Central Asian nations are coming to the reluctant recognition that Russia is also the only predictable ally any of them are likely to find in the region. Part of this is a concern over security relations. Any temptation to strike out on an independent foreign policy course on the part of Uzbekistan's Karimov government was stifled after the Tajikistan government began to crumble in April–May 1992, and Karimov's insecurities were heightened after President Nabiev was forced from office in September 1992.

Thus Russia still dominates regional security arrangements as much from local Central Asian pressure as it does to provide a security buffer for Russia. The Turkestan Military District of the Red Army was dissolved, and national armies were created in Kyrgyzstan, Kazakhstan, and Uzbekistan. But the command structure of these armies—considerable in the cases of Kazakhstan and Uzbekistan in particular—are drawn almost exclusively from the ranks of those serving in place. They in turn have been augmented by returning local nationals who were serving the Soviet Army outside of their home republics. All these armies are in formal alliance with the Russian Army,[17] and all plan to retain full integration of their military training institutions with those of the Russian armies. A joint Russian-Turkmen army was formed in Turkmenistan, and the Russian government recently announced plans to create a national army in Tajikistan on the basis of the irregular detachments that brought the Rahmonov government to power.[18]

Kazakhstan is the only one of the republics to have CIS strategic forces stationed on its territories, making it technically a nuclear power. The question of whether or not Kazakhstan actually controls its nuclear weapons is one of considerable controversy among specialists in the U.S. arms-control community. Certainly, the weapons are unlikely to be removed from the republic without

Nazarbaev's permission, but how critical his involvement would be in a decision as to whether or not to detonate these weapons is less clear.

Kazakhstan is also home to the former USSR space facility, Baikonur. The facility has become a jointly (Russian-Kazakh) managed all-CIS facility, and its territorial jurisdiction (Leninsk) has been given an independent legal status equal to that of Alma-Ata, with the base commander named as mayor. Nonetheless, there have been incidents of interethnic fighting at the base, and complaints by those serving there that the privileged standard of living they previously enjoyed has all but disappeared because Russia has ceased supplying the facility.[19]

The governments of Central Asia are well aware of the potential threats which Russia poses them, but they are equally aware of potential problems among one another and from within their own populations. Thus to the leadership, Russia appears to be the only guarantor of stability, of the perpetuation of their own rule, and of the existing borders in the region. This is always how it has been, and as leaders dealing with a constantly changing set of political and economic conditions, they seem to take comfort from leaving in place the physical and psychological dependency that Russia has traditionally provided.

Each of the Central Asian leaders believes in the need for greater regional cooperation—but each refuses to pursue this goal at the expense of his personal power or the potential prestige of his own republic. Central Asia's leaders have met on a regular basis since June 1990, when a regional cooperation accord was signed in Alma-Ata.[20] At the most recent meeting, in Tashkent in January 1993, they even agreed to establish a trade union in the region.[21] However, the Tashkent accords did not include concrete proposals for reducing the trade restrictions that are currently in place, and much of what was agreed there would be effectively annulled if the subsequent negotiations on establishing a "mini-OPEC" within the CIS that took place between Chernomyrdin and Nazarbaev come to fruition.

Russia's Concerns

Notwithstanding all the continued bilateral and multilateral cooperation that exists between the Central Asian states and Russia, Russia has largely disappointed Central Asian expectations. Indeed, the Central Asian leadership appears not wholly to have assimilated the implications of the Slavic republics' dissolution of the USSR.

At least one reason why Russian leaders were willing to accede to the breakup of the union was that Russia no longer wanted to bear the expense of Central Asia's immense social needs.

Not surprisingly, Russian indifference has continued since independence. For at least six months, for example, no vaccines of any sort, for humans or animals, have been shipped into Kyrgyzstan. In the cases at least of Tajikistan and Kyrgyzstan, republics which have almost no basis for an independent economy, the state budgets are still financed largely on money from Moscow; on at least one occasion (in summer 1992) large Russian loans were promised but not in fact delivered.[22] Similarly, only Russia's citizens can receive free treatment at Moscow's former all-USSR facilities, although republic facilities were never built precisely because of the existence of the Moscow ones. And increasingly, the supplying of finished goods is being moved to a cash-only basis, which has effectively meant a virtual commercial boycott of parts of Central Asia. This, despite the fact that Russian firms complain when non-Russian ones seek to offer similar terms of trade for the supplying of parts or unfinished goods.

For the time being, the shortfalls are being covered by promises and hope, but disillusionment is growing, with attendant rising hostility toward Russia. The general population and leaders alike have begun to complain with increasing frequency (but without attribution) that Russia wants to continue to extend the dependency relationships with the Central Asians which will make the republics cheap suppliers of raw materials and a handy captive market for Russian goods that can not compete on the larger world market. And even that bargain, disadvantageous though it is for the Central Asians, is not an entirely reliable one, because of the continuing disintegration of Russia itself, both economically and politically.

Russia, too, is dissatisfied with the new relationship, though still not as much as it was with the old one. In dealing with Central Asia, Russia has three primary concerns: to ensure secure borders, to secure the necessary raw and semifinished materials for its industries, and to ensure the well-being of the more than twelve million ethnic Russians living in these republics.

Although the central Russian press is filled with articles about the sad fate of their "stranded" conationals,[23] and although various Russian national groups in these republics are rumored to receive direct funding from Russia's own nationalist parties and movements, Russia's government has not yet intervened either directly or indirectly on behalf of this population. The citizenship of these ethnic Russians is ambiguous. They can choose to become citizens of Russia; but it is unclear how many will choose this option, even though the Central Asian republics currently recognize dual citizenship with other CIS states.

Central Asia's current leadership would prefer that the European population remain in place, as would Russia. Though local Russians feel besieged, and resent having to learn local languages and to respect local ways, the Central Asian leaders have all been pushing to modify the laws that regulate the role of the official (national) language in public life. Oftentimes, as in the case of Nazarbaev and the recent fight over the language provisions in Kazakhstan's new constitution,[24] these interdictions have left both the Russians and the local nationalists dissatisfied.

The U.S. View

Close ties with Russia are the oftentimes displeasing reality of the foreign policies of the Central Asian states. Drastically improved ties with the United States are

Central Asia's unfulfilled dream. All five states were proud to have the U.S. Embassy among the first to be opened in their new nations; and Uzbekistan, Tajikistan, and Turkmenistan were offended when they were left off Secretary of State James Baker's December 1991 list of the embassy-worthy. In Kyrgyzstan, desires for good ties to America were so strong that democratic activists floated a rumor that a U.S. air base would be opened there, in the hopes that U.S. and Kyrgyzstani officials would take up the project in earnest.[25]

For its part, the United States still does not know how to deal with the new Central Asian states, or even where to assign them in its bureaucratic hierarchies. Having been committed to the continued existence of the USSR long after it was amply clear that the Soviet Union was doomed, U.S. policy then continued by inertia to be committed to the idea of a substitute body, such as the CIS. When that body failed to crystallize, the United States became increasingly more comfortable in allowing Russia to serve as intermediary in those issue areas affecting the republics which did not require direct bilateral attention.

This has unquestionably been the case on the nuclear issue. Nuclear arms control negotiations are still overwhelmingly Russian-American affairs, although the Belarussian, Ukrainian, and Kazakhstani governments are as affected by their outcomes. Moreover, the West has assumed from the outset that only Russia should be allowed to remain a nuclear state. In part because of the nuclear question and the related problem of defense conversion, Russia has also been the focus of most of the U.S. relief efforts.

U.S. foreign policy has also pursued a double standard on the question of human rights. There has been a great deal of concern about the potential for violations of the human rights of ethnic Russian populations in the Baltic republics, and to a lesser extent those in Central Asia. But there is no international concern over the violated human rights of ethnic non-Russians "stranded" in Russia.

Similarly, where the return of Russian Orthodoxy to Russia is widely considered to be positive, the corresponding return to Central Asia's historical religious heritage—Islam—is held to be a threat. In general, American fears of increased Islamicization of Central Asia are so great that the United States is willing to downplay the repressive policies of Uzbekistan's Islam Karimov because he promises stability; and having recently recognized the "lawfulness" of Imamali Rahmonov's rule in Tajikistan, the U.S. government is at a loss as to how to deal publicly with his persecution of the opposition.

U.S. views on these questions have overlapped very nicely with Russia's own policy preferences in the region. This is not just coincidental. Taking advantage of its position as gatekeeper of information about the area, and making use of the general ignorance of Central Asia—which in large part was created by the isolation in which the Soviet Union kept the region—Russia has manipulated the issues of Islamic fundamentalism, political instability, and supposed Asian barbarism to create a climate of negative opinion about Central Asia.

Arguing in terms that often are overtly racist, Russian commentators and government officials alike have suggested that Central Asians are incapable of democratization, are too backward for development, and do not deserve Western investment, support, or encouragement. At the same time, Russia seeks to establish itself as interpreter and agent for Central Asia whenever possible, supplying the world with information about the region and channeling and controlling such investment and interest as may be attempting to reach the region.

It must be said that Russia has been almost entirely successful in this attempt. Russia's relationship with Central Asia—which by any standard is a postcolonial relationship between colonizer and colonized—has come to be viewed by the West through the eyes of the colonizer, not the colonized. World opinion and, even more so, most government policy, has put a priority upon assisting Russia, at the expense of its former colonies and to a degree that is unimaginable in the case, say, of Belgium and Zaire, or England and India. Because the rest of the world agrees with the priority of Russia's needs and requirements in Central Asia, rather than of the needs of the new nations themselves, it seems inevitable that Russia will be successful in establishing a new kind of colonial relationship with the Central Asian states. It will be one in which Russia will continue to extract the cheap raw materials it requires at even lower cost than that paid by the Soviet Union, which at least had made a token effort to provide some social services in return.

Realistically, there is probably not a great deal that the United States could do to counter Russia's continuing influence in Central Asia. For all its current economic and administrative distress, Russia remains a huge power with the military might to enforce its will over considerable distance. Unlike other decolonial situations of the recent past, Russia is contiguous with its former empire, and so retains a natural interest in its governments and affairs. In fact, the security relations that the Russian government has defined with each of the Central Asian states allow Russia to transcend the sovereignty of each one—and it has done it with the full cooperation of the local partner.

Even if it were to define a foreign policy for the Central Asian states that is separate from its policy toward Russia, the United States would face the same sort of delicate task that U.S. allies faced in trying to influence U.S. actions in Central and South America. Although the nations south of the United States were not formally its colonies, U.S. interests were so strongly defined—and defended—that effectively there was very little other nations could do to oppose them.

The fact that, in most cases, U.S. interests and those of the people of the Central and South American states did not coincide—and that conflicts were generally resolved in favor of U.S. interests—is probably also an indicator of what the future relationship between Central Asia and Russia is likely to be. During the Great Game of the nineteenth century, when England and Russia vied for influence in Central Asia, it may have been possible to imagine other futures for the region. Ever since Russia won that game, however, the priority of Russia's hegemony in the region has been unquestionable.

Notes

1. *Rossiiskaia gazeta,* December 3, 1992.

2. For details, see Martha Brill Olcott, "The Lithuanian Crisis," *Foreign Affairs,* vol. 69, no. 3 (Summer 1990), pp. 30–46.

3. For a discussion of U.S. policy in Ukraine during this period, see Adrian Karatnysky, "The Ukrainian Factor," *Foreign Affairs,* vol. 71, no. 3 (Summer 1992), pp. 90–107.

4. *Vremia* (television news program), December 10, 1991.

5. For details see Martha Brill Olcott, "Central Asian Independence," *Foreign Affairs,* vol. 71, no. 3 (Summer 1992), pp. 108–30.

6. Tajikistan's legislature abolished the post of president in December 1992.

7. Independence-day speeches are prime examples of this. For examples, see *Kazakhstanskaia pravda,* December 16, 1992; *Turkmenskaia iskra,* November 24, 1992; and *Pravda Vostoka,* September 2, 1992.

8. *Izvestiia,* October 12, 1992.

9. *Izvestiia,* January 24, 1993.

10. *Kazakhstanskaia pravda,* January 26, 1993.

11. For figures on Kyrgyzstan, see *Slovo Kyrgyzstana,* January 13, 1993.

12. *Izvestiia,* February 6, 1993.

13. *Komsomol'skaia pravda,* October 18, 1992.

14. *Literaturnaia gazeta,* February 11, 1993.

15. Kazakhstan and Turkmenistan have ports on the Caspian, but that too is a land-locked sea, although it does provide Kazakhstan with direct access to Iran.

16. *Izvestiia,* December 13, 1992.

17. *Rossiskaia gazeta,* June 1, 1992.

18. *Nezavisimaia gazeta,* February 7, 1993.

19. *Kazakhstanskaia pravda,* June 6, 1992.

20. *Kazakhstanskaia pravda,* June 8, 1990.

21. *Izvestiia,* January 6, 1993.

22. *Svobodnye gory,* August 6, 1992.

23. *Literaturnaia gazeta,* November 2, 1991.

24. *Kazakhstanskaia pravda,* December 13, 1992.

25. *Komsomol'skaia pravda,* August 13, 1992.

Comment

On "Ukraine and Russian-American Relations"

Leonid Rudnytzky and Oleg G. Pocheptsov

Dr. Bodie's essay is a lucid, trenchant analysis of a most complex subject. In a succinct yet comprehensive manner, the author manages to come to terms with most major factors underlying Russian-Ukrainian relations, to provide several insightful and penetrating critical remarks on recent U.S. policy toward Russia and Ukraine, and to suggest several specific points for future U.S. policy vis-à-vis these two countries.. Professor Bodie is quite correct when he asserts, at the beginning of his essay, that "Cooperation, or at least detente, between the two [Russia and Ukraine] is the *sine qua non* for stability and economic growth throughout Central and Eastern Europe." Thus, while we have no significant difference of opinion regarding his major theses, we do wish to offer some remarks on several minor points of contention and supplement his presentation by referring to a number of additional factors which we deem to be important in forging new U.S., Russian, and Ukrainian policies and in preserving peace in that part of the world.

To begin with, the policy of the United States, as well as the policy of other states, is often profoundly influenced by rhetoric and terminology. A good example here is the use of the term "Soviet nation," which was readily accepted by American leaders and applied indiscriminately to all the nationalities of the former Soviet Union. Another example is the term "ethnic," as in ethnic unrest, ethnic tensions, or ethnic conflict. While no one would deny the usefulness and validity of this term, its indiscriminate use often tends to minimize the profound national and cultural differences that exist now and existed during the days of the Soviet empire. The all-pervasive use of these and similar words and phrases by the political establishment of the United States and by the media served to fortify the mythic image of the Soviet Union as a single nation-state, which it never was. The Soviet Union, we submit, even in the days of starkest Russification, was always a multinational state, and recent historical events have made this point clear beyond any shadow of a doubt. Professor Bodie's use of such terms as "subnational" and the application of quotation marks to the term "nationalities" in reference to the peoples of the former Soviet Union are indications of "old thinking," the result of a Soviet terminological legacy which should be put behind us as quickly as possible. These, of course, are merely matters of terminology, but they are important inasmuch as their use often tended to obfuscate rather than clarify the issues.

On a more substantive level, we believe one can take issue with the author's statement that "the economic ties between the two [Russia and Ukraine] are extensive." To be sure, in the recent past they were extensive, especially as they were mandated by the division of labor that existed among the different Soviet republics. Today, however, these ties are unsystematic, feeble, and fragile. It is their actual breach in many spheres of the economy, especially on the state level, that accounts for the catastrophic fall of production in both countries, especially in Ukraine. Premier Leonid Kuchma of Ukraine constantly stresses the need to renew these economic ties and strengthen economic cooperation between Russia and Ukraine. This economic cooperation is closely tied to the problem of the division of Soviet assets and responsibilities vis-à-vis the Soviet debt, and no progress at all seems to have been made in this regard. The recent Russian-Ukrainian discussion of this problem, which was prompted by President Yeltsin's *ukaz* of February 8, 1993, concerning state ownership of Soviet assets outside the USSR and took place in Moscow during February 12–13, ended in complete failure, at least according to the official Ukrainian communiqué. During a briefing held for journalists on February 23, Ukrainian Deputy Foreign Minister Mykola Makarevych explained Ukraine's position on the question of assets of the former Soviet Union—the major bone of contention between the two countries insofar as their mutual economic relations are concerned. According to Makarevych, the government of Ukraine has sent a note to 160 countries stating that: Ukraine is one of the successor states to the Soviet Union; Ukraine does not recognize Russia's exclusive claim to the foreign assets of the former Soviet Union; and Ukraine does not recognize Russia as the sole successor to the Soviet Union. The note also requested that foreign countries not permit Russia to act in a unilateral fashion on matters relating to the assets of the former Soviet Union.

On the whole, Professor Bodie is correct in stressing that "Ukraine's communist elite has changed its flag but not its political appetites" and that "veterans of the now-outlawed [Communist] Party still dominate all key decision-making positions throughout the republic." But it would be wrong to assume that the proverbial leopard cannot change its spots, especially since many of the former communists were, even in the darkest days of the Brezhnev era, also Ukrainian patriots. Examples are plentiful: Dmytro Pavlychko (b. 1929), chairman of the parliament's foreign affairs committee; Ivan Drach (b. 1936), one of the leaders of Rukh; Oles' Honchar (b. 1918), the guiding intellect of democratic reforms in Ukraine; and Deputy Prime Minister Mykola Zhulynsky (b. 1940), to name but a few.

In addition, we differ somewhat with Dr. Bodie on his interpretation of President Leonid Kravchuk's activities. To be sure, here we have a bona fide former communist, but one who never lost his Ukrainian national identity. Dr. Bodie takes Kravchuk to task for the rather aloof attitude he displayed during the putsch in Moscow. To be sure, his speech in Kiev, made over Ukrainian radio on the day of the putsch, could be characterized as appeasing at worst or neutral at best, and yet at the time it produced a beneficial, calming effect on the Ukrainian populace, as many will attest. It may be that by distancing himself from the events in Moscow, Kravchuk managed to convey to his fellow Ukrainians a sense of separateness, which served as a stepping-stone toward the proclamation of Ukraine's independence on August 24, 1991. Also, the importance of his outburst during the August 1992 meeting of the World Forum of Ukrainians in Kiev, when he threatened to expel some foreigners from Ukraine, was rather exaggerated by the Ukrainian and Ukrainian émigré media. Kravchuk spoke in heat, just as President Bush did when he called his rivals "bozos" during the 1992 presidential campaign. It should be kept in mind that President Kravchuk is the first democratically elected president of Ukraine, having won a resounding majority of the popular vote during the referendum of December 1, 1991, which affirmed the proclamation of Ukraine's independence.

In this connection, it should be pointed out that the thesis mentioned by Dr. Bodie that "Ukraine likely will develop into a limited democracy, plebiscitarian yet authoritarian, along the lines of Mexico or Turkey," is rather dubious. Kravchuk is just as committed to democracy as Yeltsin is. The contrast between the two is much more in temperament and personality than in *Weltanschauung*. Both are former communists and both are patriots of their respective nations. Yeltsin is dynamic and flamboyant, a politician who thrives on crises, indeed one who often seeks confrontation. Kravchuk, on the other hand, is rather low-key and reserved, bent on avoiding conflict. His major achievement is the preservation of peace in a region which could easily have erupted into a Yugoslavia-like scenario. He prefers to proceed methodically, at a slow pace, working gradually to turn Ukraine into a nation of laws, as attested, among other things, by the fact that the process of writing a constitution for Ukraine, which includes experts from the Ukrainian diaspora and a number of foreign countries, has been taken very seriously. As a result, the constitution is progressing at a rather slow pace, matching, as it were, the tempo of his economic reforms. However, by February 20, 1993, work on a draft version was completed and, according to Volodymyr Lapynsky, head of the department of the Ministry of Foreign Affairs that deals with the Conference on Security and Cooperation in Europe, it has received a positive assessment from European Council officials and from the Venice Commission.

Professor Bodie might agree that the threat to Ukrainian democracy is more external than internal. The imperial ambitions of the Russian neopatriots or *derzhavniki* which have their roots in the messianic Russian doctrine—Moscow as the Third Rome—currently pose the greatest danger to the Ukrainian state. One of the delicate tasks of United States diplomacy is to neutralize the aspirations of Russian imperial nationalists. Kravchuk, it would appear, has done well in controlling the Ukrainians and preventing major provocation over such issues as the Crimea, the Black Sea Fleet, and nuclear weapons. Can Yeltsin do the same with the Russians? His recent diplomatic initiative suggesting that Russia should be granted special powers to stop "ethnic conflicts in the former Soviet Union" (as reported by *The New York Times* of March 1, 1993) does not bode well in this regard. Without the right kind of American diplomatic initiative, it will indeed be a difficult task to maintain peace in this region.

In this connection, it is worthwhile to stress another point made by Professor Bodie. He correctly states that "ethnic tensions between average Ukrainians and Russians are virtually nonexistent." This holds true both for Ukrainians living in Russia and for Russians living in Ukraine. Indeed, the majority of the Russian population of Ukraine voted for Ukraine's independence on December 1, 1991, and the Ukrainian government as well as the Rukh organization have taken great pains to accord equal treatment to all minorities and especially to the Russians. Both Russians and Ukrainians need to be reeducated regarding their relationship to one another so that, in the future, any tensions, such as those prevailing in some of the Baltic States, can be neutralized immediately. The Russians must work on eliminating an inbred imperial attitude, while the Ukrainians must shed their subservient (not to say servile) mentality and assume full responsibility for their own fate.

In developing a new policy toward Eastern Europe, the United States must accord equal treatment to all the countries involved. No longer can America afford a policy directed toward the center of the empire, for the empire no longer exists. Similarly, the United States cannot pursue a Russia-first policy, for the neglect of Ukraine and Belarus will prove costly in the long run. Nor can the United States forge a policy based on the existence of a Commonwealth of Independent States, for the CIS will not last. The United States must develop separate policies, one toward Russia and one toward Ukraine, that would encourage the building of democratic institutions in both countries. In addition to meaningful humanitarian assistance, these policies should contain appropriate measures to prevent the rise of a "Great Russian chauvinism" and offer guarantees for the peaceful development of an independent Ukraine. To do so, the American people and the American media must strive to learn more about the peoples of Russia and Ukraine, about their languages, their customs, their traditions, their national aspirations, and their religious beliefs.

There is a great religious revival currently afoot in Russia and Ukraine, and the church will play a prominent role in both countries. In Ukraine, the spiritual void created by the hegemony of Marxism-Leninism is being rapidly filled by a resurgent Ukrainian Christian awareness. The emergence of the Ukrainian Catholic Church (also known as Greek Catholic or Uniate) from the underground where it was driven in 1946 following its forcible incorporation by the Soviet regime into the Russian Orthodox Church, is a historical event of great magnitude. Also important is the reintroduction of the Ukrainian Autocephalous Orthodox Church (liquidated by Stalin in 1930) in Ukrainian life and the resulting gradual but inexorable removal of the Russian Orthodox Church from Ukrainian soil.

Tainted by association with the Soviet regime and often accused of being its willing tool in the liquidation of the two Ukrainian churches, the Russian Orthodox Church is struggling to stop the erosion of its power base in Ukraine. In the western part of the country it was forced to return more than 2,000 parishes, which it had taken from the Ukrainian Catholic Church after 1946, and in the eastern part of the country it has yielded considerable power and influence to the Ukrainian Autocephalous Orthodox Church. This already volatile religious situation is further complicated by the emergence of a sizable number of Protestant denominations, which find Ukraine a fertile soil for their evangelization, and by the breakdown of the traditional denominational division of the country: in the east, Orthodox; in the west, Catholic.

There is a distinct possibility that the Moscow Patriarchate, which, as in the past, maintains strong ties to the Russian government, will continue to nurture existing imperialist notions among the Russian people regarding Ukraine; thus, conflict among the churches is an important factor in future relations between Russia and Ukraine. The United States cannot ignore this religious component of the Russia–Ukraine equation.

_____ Comment

On "Central Asia and the New Russian-American Rapprochement"

Dilbar Turabekova

Martha Brill Olcott is a prolific writer whose work on Central Asia is well known and appreciated in that region. She is also currently engaged in a project on democracy in Central Asia. Finally, she has a well-earned reputation as a critic of U.S. policy toward Central Asia, a policy that I would describe as often tendentious and pro-Russian. To illustrate this point, I would like to mention Dr. Olcott's recent articles in which she offers a persuasive analysis of ethnic and political conflicts in Central Asia, including the civil war in Tajikistan.

Relations between Russia and Central Asia are one of the important aspects of the regional scene that she analyzes in her most recent works, such as her article "The Future of Central Asia" (*The Harriman Institute Forum*, October 1992), which deals with the lingering role of Russia and the important Russian influence on the economies of the Central Asian republics. Although these republics have gained nominal independence and have their own presidents, parliaments, and constitutions, they are faced with numerous problems. Thus, Uzbekistan has adopted its new constitution but continues to be economically dependent upon and controlled by Russia. That is so because the ruble remains the basis of regional currency, even though the Uzbek government promised to create a separate currency.

Being tied to the ruble, Uzbekistan has no choice but to suffer the inflation which is rampant in Russia and which has created economic and social problems. Prices are rising despite government subsidies on bread, butter, rice, cooking oil, sugar, and some other products. A kilo of meat or butter costs about 500 rubles, while the average monthly salary stands at about 5,000–6,000 rubles. Pensioners receive 3,000 rubles a month, forcing them to live mostly on bread and tea.

Uzbekistan is a multinational state with a total population of 20 million persons. Uzbeks comprise more than 14 million, or more than 70 percent, of all of its inhabitants. The Russian-speaking population, predominantly representatives of Slavic nationalities (mainly Russians), as well as well as Tatars, Jews, and others, constitute some 16 percent of the population. In addition, many other Central Asians reside in the republic.

In December 1992, the Constitution of the sovereign Republic of Uzbekistan was adopted by the republic's parliament. The Constitution proclaims the establishment of a humane, democratic, law-governed state as the republic's main task. December 8, the day of the adoption of the new Constitution, was proclaimed a national holiday. Drawing on its historical values, independent Uzbekistan has chosen the path of democracy and is working to develop a market-based economy. In its foreign policy, Uzbekistan stands for the principles of nonintervention in the internal affairs of other countries and for resolution of all disputes by peaceful means. Uzbekistan is doing everything in its power to ensure peace and stability in the countries closest to it.

Among the issues that I have mentioned earlier, there is also the nationality question. Among the social problems, the question of the ethnic Russian minority is one of the more troublesome. Some 10 million Russians who live in Central Asia do not speak the native languages and do not want to learn them. The adoption of laws on state languages by the independent republics has caused many Russian-speaking persons to emigrate to Russia. However, finding no support from the Russian government, some have returned to Central Asia. Hence, the problem of linguistic discrimination remains unsolved. This state of affairs is not acceptable to most Central Asians, including the Uzbeks. They feel that the Russians must recognize the Uzbek language as the official one and must therefore learn it if they wish to live in Uzbekistan. They must also respect local customs and local history.

The Central Asian republics, and particularly Uzbekistan, had great hopes for foreign investments from China, Turkey, the United Arab Emirates, Saudi Arabia, Malaysia, and other foreign countries, but progress has been very slow, due in part to Uzbek inexperience with world economic practices, the lack of laws, and so on. Moreover, the privatization of government property has not yet begun in Uzbekistan.

There is a Turkish political and commercial presence in Central Asia. Turkey has actually begun to offer assistance in the educational and certain other spheres, but the Uzbeks have been quite disappointed by the level of development of the Turkish society. Specifically, most of our students who went to study in Turkey did not find the level of education there up to their standards. The intellectual level of Turkish television programs is very low; the language is unclear. Uzbekistan must therefore look for other ways of solving this problem, and find contacts with more developed countries.

Saudi Arabia supports the publication and distribution of the Koran as well as the reconstruction of mosques in Uzbekistan. Recently, the construction of a new mosque was started in Tashkent. The sponsor of this construction is the Islamic Community of Saudi Arabia. This kind of support inspires the religious people, but it is not the kind of support that Central Asia requires today.

Uzbekistan believes that its closest neighbor, China, will help it. China is ready to do so, but we are not ready to accept this help. We do not have the legal framework to handle such assistance, including laws governing international investments and commerce. Good relations have been established between Uzbekistan and Malaysia. There is large-scale cooperation in the economic sphere and in the development of the banking system. An agreement on economic, scientific, and cultural cooperation has also been signed. Normal relations have been maintained with the Republic of Korea and with Indonesia as well. Finally, Uzbekistan has also established diplomatic relations with Egypt. Our peoples have centuries-old historical connections, based on shared appreciation of world civilization. Important bilateral agreements in the political, economic, and cultural areas were signed during our president's visit to Cairo. They represent a solid foundation for the development of cooperation between our countries.

Uzbekistan has its own state airline, Uzbekistan Havo Jullari, the largest in Central Asia. As of today, direct service has been established between Uzbekistan and Turkey, Pakistan, India, Great Britain, Kuwait, the United Arab Emirates, Saudi Arabia, China, Malaysia, and Germany. There are as yet no direct flights between the United States and Uzbekistan; their initiation depends on the reciprocal wishes of the two countries. I would like to believe that this question will be resolved in the near future, opening new opportunities for bilateral cooperation.

Uzbekistan is a member of the United Nations and has been recognized by more than 120 states. Approximately fifty of them have opened embassies in Tashkent. An Uzbek ambassador will soon arrive in the United States, and we hope that in future Uzbekistan and the United States will have good relations.

An American embassy has opened in Tashkent, but it appears to many Uzbeks that it pursues a pro-Russian policy. All visas are still issued through the American embassy in Moscow, and one must go there in order to obtain a visa. The embassy itself gives the impression that only Russian-speaking personnel are employed there, none of whom know Uzbek. Even the Peace Corps volunteers study more Russian than Uzbek during their training. It often appears that the Russian *diktat* remains in effect.

The republics of Central Asia are in a transitional period; market relations are being created and economic policy is being formulated. In my opinion, all the republics are eager to cooperate with Russia, but as equals, under equal conditions, and for their mutual benefit. Central Asia is tied to Russia politically and economically, and rupture of these ties would be very dangerous.

It is fair to say that all the republics are interested in all-around cooperation with Russia. For its part, the Russian government has signed a number of treaties with all the Asian republics. However, Russia does not want to bear the expense of Central Asia's immense social needs and has stopped the deliveries not only of fuel and wood but also of drugs and vaccines. The pharmacy warehouses and drug stores in Uzbekistan have an assortment of the necessary drugs, but these drugs have come from Georgia, Latvia, and Tatarstan, which have remained suppliers, as well as from Turkey, India, and Hungary. (The president of Uzbekistan has allocated $50 million for medicine, and most of the drugs have been purchased with that foreign currency.) Uzbekistan's ambassador to Russia, Yusuf Abdullayev, spoke about this in his speech on the occasion of the first anniversary of Uzbekistan's independence. He said that a treaty of economic cooperation between Russia and Uzbekistan for 1993 was being drafted and that he hoped that both sides, and especially Russia, would keep their word.

All the Central Asian states remain committed to the idea of a single ruble zone in the CIS. At the same time, as the presidential committee said, the unstable economic situation in Russia, including the shortage of cash, was forcing the republics to issue their own currencies. In Uzbekistan, we are expecting our own currency to be put into circulation later this year.

In conclusion, I would like to reiterate that Russia must continue to play a stabilizing role in Central Asia. It is the main link in the mutual security agreements that have been concluded among the Central Asian republics. Therefore, these agreements represent the might, the strength, and the prestige not only of Russia but of Central Asia as well.

Comment

Understanding Ukraine

Sergo A. Mikoyan

There can be no doubt concerning the significance of the relationship between Ukraine and Russia for the foreign policy of the United States. Dr. Bodie's essay is a comprehensive study of the problem, based upon essential documents, literature, and data. The author brought his work right up to date, using the latest information on such issues as nuclear armaments.

Still, the events and changes in public opinion develop very rapidly; they have raced ahead of some of the author's conclusions. And in some cases, this makes all the difference. For example, the assumption that the Russian Federation appears psychologically incapable of accepting the permanence of Ukrainian statehood was indeed true some time ago,[1] but such psychological difficulty to accept the idea was not restricted to Russia. If we look carefully at the results of the referendum in Ukraine in March 1991 concerning the future of the union, we see that 70.5 percent of the voters wanted the union to continue; and 80.16 percent confirmed their wish for Ukraine to be within the union on the basis of the Declaration of National Sovereignty of Ukraine.[2]

As we know, the putsch of August 19–21, 1991, changed much in the whole union, not only in Ukraine but in Russia as well. Only eight months after the March all-union referendum, the December referendum in Ukraine produced absolutely different results. Among various factors, the economic one was the most important: even the Russians living in Ukraine believed that the country would prosper as soon as it was free from ties with the rest of the union. Not only were the military "pledging loyalty to their flats" (a phrase cited by Dr. Bodie), but civilians believed that a Ukraine on its own would be much more prosperous than a Ukraine within the union. Such thinking was characteristic of people living in many republics of the former union. I remember talks with friends in Kiev, in Vilnius, in Uzbekistan, in Armenia, and in Georgia. Each of them thought it was also true of their case. All of them thought the main reason for the slow development of their economies to be the centralized distribution of their natural and productive resources.

Psychologically, this was quite understandable: the pressure of Moscow was humiliating and almost unbearable in many fields. The pressure was also stupid, since it depended on the capricious thinking of bureaucrats rather than on the established division of authority. In national issues, the Soviet dictatorship was much more than a nuisance; it was frustrating for most people in the republics, including some in the ruling elites.[3] It was totally counterproductive even from the point of view of the interests of the center itself.

Actually, the central apparatus did not always try to conceal its unwillingness to share economic decisions in serious matters with the local authorities. By so doing, the center got blamed for all sorts of difficulties, even though in reality the roots of many problems could be found elsewhere. The resources were centralized; however, the majority of the local populations thought only about the materials and goods which were *taken from the republics*, not about those which were *given to them*. No wonder the conviction that a republic was "robbed" by the center was so widespread.

I daresay that conviction was based in an illusion. And today's economic situation in Ukraine, after Russia only recently stopped delivering oil for nothing, shows this very clearly. But the illusion was quite understandable in the context of the Soviet government's domination. True, the regime took much from the republics. But nobody should forget that the republics received oil, gas, metals, cars, and assorted other goods almost free of charge. As a result, the least prosperous was the population of Russia itself, especially her central and northern parts. This fact just provided additional arguments for those who did not know why this was so. Of course, there was the Soviet empire. But it was in no case a Russian empire. The regime was not bothered by the fact that state prices for agricultural production in Russia proper were much lower than in other republics. The nonequivalent exchange favored those who were dominated by Moscow. Why such an anomaly? Again, the answer is that the totalitarian regime was neither national nor ethnic. It was exploiting *all* nationalities, *all* ethnic groups, but most of all Russians.

Moscow was ruled not by Russians but by Soviet power. A certain amount of attention to the economic interests of the republics was even considered necessary (I mean, of course, during the years after Stalin) as a sort of compensation for the absence of political autonomy. Where the Russians were concerned, they could not complain on that score anyway.

I had an opportunity to express this opinion in the press.[4] I pointed out that it was enough to look at the ethnic composition of the almighty Politburo (though for some years the name was changed to "presidium," nothing changed in its role) to see that, beginning with June 1957, the body was controlled by ethnic Ukrainians. The same was true of important departments of the Central Committee. Not by them only, of course. None of this is grounds for declaring the dictatorship a Ukrainian one—it was Soviet, Bolshevik, Communist—whichever name one prefers.

Professor Roman Szporluk from Harvard tried to argue with me, claiming, for instance, that Shelest and Chernenko were transferred to Moscow after Khrushchev's fall, and that Chervonenko allegedly never worked in Moscow.[5] Regrettably, however understandably, *The New York Times* decided not to continue the polemics, and I could not prove that I was right.[6] Perhaps Professor Szporluk was shocked by the expression "Ukrainian mafia," but it was widely used in Moscow in those years. It had nothing to do with the Ukrainian people—as the anti-Stalinist campaign never smacked of anti-Georgian feeling. People in the former Soviet Union were sufficiently well-educated to see the difference; this we must admit. Actually, the Politburo did not trust Muscovites, thinking that they were less tough, more "spoiled" by Western influence, by talks about democracy, and so on. I remember very well a meeting of the Central Committee, during which Andrei Kirilenko was cited as saying, "We shall teach Muscovites how to work!" Of course, he did not mean Suslov, always the evil genius of the regime, but rather those in the apparatus who really were more flexible toward the intelligentsia, not wanting to lose face in Moscow society.

Let us return to the reasons for the crucial changes in public opinion in Ukraine. First, extremist elements, mainly from the western provinces and then, unfortunately, "the political establishment in Kiev," as Dr. Bodie puts it correctly, "acted as if national self-awakening . . . required a heightening of differences with Moscow."[7] However, they found partners in Russia only among leaders of Zhirinovskii's stripe who were not taken seriously in Moscow. Solzhenitsyn also wrote against Ukrainian separation from Russia. But Russian public opinion was rapidly moving away from the old convictions that Ukrainians and Russians were so closely connected that they practically did not feel much difference between themselves, and that the secession of Ukraine was unimaginable. That was true in 1990, much less true in 1991, and untrue in 1992. There are no "future designs on Kiev," despite all the speeches in the Rada.

These developments did indeed proceed very fast. In August 1990, I had a talk about that with the well-known sociologist and political scientist Aleksandr Tsipko (an ethnic Ukrainian who grew up in left-bank Ukraine). He told me that the majority of Ukrainians never would follow those extremists from western Ukraine who hated everything Russian. And I believed him because a lot of people around me in Moscow, a lot of my good friends are ethnic Ukrainians, and I had met a lot of Russians in Kiev, Kharkov, Donetsk, and Odessa. Nobody drew any difference. Here was something special, not like the attitude toward Caucasians, or Central Asians, or Balts. Only Belarussians were on the same level of full psychological equality and even identity.

I do not at all mean that there were no reasons for feelings of humiliation among different ethnic groups in the USSR. On the contrary, there were a lot of reasons. The absolute power of the people in the Kremlin could not but create anti-Russian feelings, even though their control was no less harsh in the Russian areas of the USSR. People in Kostroma or Tula or Cheliabinsk were irritated by the command system just as much as they were in Kiev or Tallinn or Tbilisi. But they could not vent their indignation against "Russian domination," whereas the people in the republics often interpreted the Soviet dictatorship in national terms. Most of the dissidents lived in Russia; Andrei Sakharov was their leader. But dissidents in the republics almost inevitably were persecuted for "nationalist" activity.[8]

That kind of repression was combined with a steady diet of demagogy concerning the rights of all the nations in the union, mostly in the cultural sphere. "The federal structure appears still to be politically necessary to give ethnic minorities a sense that their cultural autonomy be preserved, even though economic and political direction are becoming increasingly centralized," wrote John N. Hazard.[9] The outstanding Ukrainian philosopher and cultural scholar Vadim Skuratovsky spoke of the "cultural revolution" in Ukraine as a product of the October Revolution: "Culture, however, started to develop 'in breadth.' Ukrainian intellectuals of the beginning of the century could only dream of today's circulation of books by Shevchenko, Kotliarevsky, other classics. . . . After the revolution we had the most intelligent government in Europe, which aspired to upgrade the socially oppressed 'small human being' above purely physical existence. But, as a result, 'citizens Sharikovs' took the offensive and seized the power."[10]

"Sharikovs" were an all-union phenomenon. Many of them actually became Communist Party activists and even leaders. In some of the republics, they were more royalist than the king himself.[11] As Vernon Aspaturian put it: "The elites of the various nationalities are forced to play two social roles, each responding to different pressures and constituencies, often pulling in opposite directions. Since the political constituency of the non-Russian Soviet official is in Moscow, though his natural constituency is his national republic, he is more likely to be responsive to the interests of Moscow than to those of his republic."[12] The situation was a constant irritant for every nationality, including the Ukrainians, despite their "privileged" position in comparison with the Baltic, Caucasian, and Central Asian nationalities. We can easily understand and share the indignation of Ukrainian patriots at the intimidation of their national aspirations as soon as they sounded dangerous to the "people in power." Repressions against many of them were shameful. But what could be expected from a government that enunciated the "Brezhnev doctrine" proclaiming "a limited sovereignty" even for the independent countries of Eastern Europe? The cynical leadership in the Kremlin was stupid, too, for it could not understand that "the suppression and intimidation of criticism does not eradicate it, but creates greater alienation and resentment."[13]

For all that, we can only wonder, together with Dr. Bodie, why "many Ukrainian leaders had difficulty distinguishing between the Russia of Boris Yeltsin and the Soviet 'center' which extinguished Ukrainian independence in 1920 and terrorized its people for decades."

Dr. Bodie analyzes the major disputes between Russia and Ukraine: nuclear weapons, the status of the Crimean peninsula, and ownership of the Black Sea Fleet. I do not agree with that list. First of all, nuclear weapons turned more into an American-Ukrainian problem than a problem for Russia. Russians were more angered by Kiev's call to the military to recast its loyalty, regarding it—rightly or not—as a provocative attempt to foment a quarrel with Russia. The nuclear weapons in Ukraine—since Yeltsin forgot to talk about their future in Belovezhskaia Pushch'a in December 1991—became an object of discussions, but the issue was more important from the point of view of the United States than of Russia. I am convinced that nobody, in either Russia or Ukraine, believes that nuclear weapons can ever be used by one against the other. That kind of nonsense may look useful for political gamesmanship, but it has no real value.

It is safe enough to say that even conventional war is not only improbable but impossible: there are too many Russians in the Ukrainian army and too many Ukrainians in the Russian army. Cultural ties, historical traditions, the absence of reasons serious enough to fight over, and the existence of reasons to continue contacts in all spheres of life—everything gives grounds for considering the present tensions temporary and passing. Here, I disagree with Dr. Bodie's belief in the probability of a near-term war between Russia and Ukraine. Such a conflict can erupt only if major efforts are intentionally exerted to this end.

Actually, nuclear weapons in Ukraine serve as a means to strengthen the country's bargaining position vis-à-vis the United States. The U.S. administration seems to understand this very well, as we can see from recent angry statements in Washington to that effect.[14] The administration evidently does not think that attempts to get more financial aid in exchange for signing START I constitute good diplomacy on Kiev's part. This became absolutely clear after Kazakhstan and Belarus ratified the treaty. Ukraine remained the only country of the former USSR not to ratify it. But failure to do so makes it difficult to hope that the terms of "a more ambitious second treaty that was signed by Russia and the United States" would be fulfilled.[15] It is certain that the new treaty signed by Bush and Yeltsin in Moscow eighteen days before Bush left the White House was a victory for American diplomacy. Hence, in order to save the victory and give it a long life, the United States needs the nuclear disarmament of Ukraine (promised by Kiev more than once) much more than Russia does.

Angry reaction in Washington to the absence of any hurry on the part of Ukraine to fulfill her promises and follow the example of Kazakhstan and Belarus prompted an article by the Ukrainian ambassador to the United States in *The New York Times*.[16] The ambassador repeated the argument already used in Kiev: "Kiev seeks a substitute [for nuclear weapons]: security assurances from the nuclear powers, primarily Russia and the U.S. We want a guarantee that the powers will never use nuclear weapons against Ukraine, never resort to conventional force or threat of force, will abstain from economic pressure in a controversy and respect our territorial integrity and the inviolability of borders. So far, the guarantees Moscow offers have not met our minimal demands." This attempt to toss the ball into the opponent's court is likewise interesting for its wording: Russia is again treated as a loser; the demands sound like an ultimatum to a defeated country. It is also an attempt to lump different matters into one package, to pressure Russia with American help. Of course, the borders the ambassador means are those of the Crimea. This is a clever diplomatic move.

But not all active Ukrainian superpatriots are diplomats. Certainly this cannot be said about O. Vitovich, a deputy in the L'vov City Council, who looks at the nuclear weapons in his country somewhat differently. Speaking before thousands of people on the central city square in the spring of 1991, he said:

> We need today a change of orientation. We are no longer satisfied by the slogan "Ukrainian *samostinaia* power." We dream of a superpower, we dream of supremacy of the Ukrainian nation. We dream of such a power that would be able to dictate conditions to the whole world. We dream of such a Ukrainian nation that would not be half a head, but three heads, ten heads taller than other nations. We understand that this struggle will be mortal: either the *moskaly* will defeat us or we will defeat them. There is no third option.[17]

Dr. Bodie pays ample attention to those Russians who expressed unwillingness to see Ukraine totally disconnected from Russia. But he did not find enough evidence for the trends Mr. Vitovich personifies.

The problem of the Black Sea Fleet is more of an emotional issue than a matter of serious political or military importance. The fleet is heir to the heroic history of the Russian fleet in the eighteenth and nineteenth centuries, built by Peter the Great, strengthened by admirals Ushakov, Makarov, and others, and glorified for the defense of Sebastopol during the Crimean War of 1852–55[18] and World War II. Its military importance was great in the past. But soon after World War II, only the North and Pacific fleets became really important for Russia because of their access to the open sea. That is why Ukrainian claims to the fleet and its base—Sebastopol—were very badly received by the Russian military and by people in general. This looked like an attempt to heap new humiliations on a nation already suffering from enough of them.

Some Ukrainian extremists challenged the military discipline of the fleet. The most dangerous moment came when a destroyer left its base and went to Odessa. This was a moment when the Russian side showed more common sense and responsibility.

And, again, for some of the Ukrainian leaders, the Black Sea Fleet is just an instrument to achieve several goals: to aggravate Ukrainian-Russian relations; to claim the city of Sebastopol, the chief port in the Crimea; and, eventually, to sell the ships of the fleet for hard currency. Dr. Bodie cites Kravchuk's words charging Pavlo Skoropadsky with committing two errors in the aftermath of

World War I: one of them was that "he entered into a political alliance with Russia. . . ." The conclusion was evidently reached by this very experienced politician that the new leadership had to cultivate animosity toward Russia. And we must admit that he succeeded, at least on the surface. The question of the Baltic Sea Fleet was masterfully manipulated; it became a vehicle for these ulterior purposes. I am afraid that Dr. Bodie fails to analyze the motivation of the Ukrainian president in this respect.

The section of the essay about internal stresses in Ukrainian politics strikes me as very interesting. But it would appear that the attitude of Kiev to economic reforms is more cautious than Yeltsin's. Nobody doubts the necessity to move toward a market economy. But how fast and making what kind of sacrifices? Kravchuk and Kuchma are more attentive to social questions than their colleagues in Moscow. I can only envy the Ukrainians that "there won't be a Gaidar" there. The idea of initiating the movement toward a market economy not by the medium of privatization of production and trade but by lifting price controls could occur only to a scholar lost in his books and totally blind to the real conditions in the country. Of course the reestablishment of ministries in Kiev looks disappointing. It is to be hoped that Kravchuk and Kuchma will institute privatization; or at least use the Chinese example, but without the Tiananmen experience.

Dr. Bodie's trust in Gaidar's "shock therapy" is not surprising: the Western media have too long simply refused to look at the matter objectively, avoiding the stereotypical dichotomy of planned economy–shock therapy. The real contradiction is much more complex. *The Economist* became, perhaps, the only Western periodical that expressed some doubt over whether the "shock" would bring "therapy." How can you stop inflation when production is falling and there are no investments? How can you decontrol prices if the old state enterprises exercise monopoly power in the country's economy and trade? Small traders under such conditions just play the same game of hiking prices in the absence of any of the usual economic correctives, such as those dictated by the interplay of demand and supply. The Ukrainian leaders cannot be faulted for their unwillingness to repeat Yeltsin's mistakes.

The essay draws attention to the fact that former Communist leaders still occupy leading positions in the Ukrainian government. This can be said about Russia too. Such a "strange" situation is not at all strange. The former Soviet leaders had long ago simply turned into the "people in power," as Elizabeth K. Valkenier of Columbia University has put it. They remain in power behind different ideological disguises and controversial political façades. Kravchuk is no exception. He is no better and no worse than Yeltsin (though perhaps smarter and more educated). Regrettably, much too often cynical politicians make good politicians.

In a section titled Opportunities and Options, Dr. Bodie elaborates on three "general positions" in U.S. policy debates in connection with Ukrainian-Russian relations. One can understand the roots and implications of their implementation. However, the author's evaluations require a few comments: Russian attention to Ukraine's potential military alliances is no less natural than would be U.S. attention to the alliances of Mexico or Canada. We know that even Central America and the Caribbean are considered as a sphere not unrelated to the interests of U.S. security. Sometimes even more distant areas were declared to fall within the same sphere. Why this kind of double standard?

Furthermore, Russian willingness to maintain economic or cultural links with Ukraine should not be read as "imperial thinking." Everyone who knows the degree of interdependence of the economic mechanisms of the two countries will readily admit that much of the decline of their economies can be explained by the sudden rupture of links between enterprises on opposite sides of the border, many of which are mutually dependent and complementary. There is even more objective necessity to maintain the links in this instance than for the countries of Western Europe to join the European Community.

The cultural aspect is also very easy to understand. And not only because millions and millions of people remain in countries of other ethnicities. It is highly improbable that the extremists in either Ukraine or Russia will be able to sunder the historical, religious, literary, musical, and other cultural ties between the two brotherly peoples. Neither is "the elder brother"; they are equals, and they are doomed to have close ties in many fields, irrespective of the activity of ultrapatriots, wherever they live.

The foreign policy of the United States should take these factors into account and not be misled by temporary differences, often instigated artificially and intentionally for unholy ends. The United States will be more realistic if its policies in Eastern Europe are not based on the premise of its global role as the superpower to which everything is permitted. Its global responsibility does exist, however. The burden of such responsibility means that Washington must avoid involvements in unpredictable situations which threaten to further destabilize areas plagued by a rash of conflicts. Its efforts at least should be so directed as to avoid any aggravation of the differences between Ukraine and Russia. Any irresponsible attempt to play "the Ukrainian card" or "the Russian card" against one or the other will be ruinous for U.S. influence in the region and harmful for security and peace in the huge area covered by the two states.

On that note, the approach which Dr. Bodie calls "the strategy of democratic engagement" is, in my opinion, the most correct one. Such democratic engagement should be multifaceted and pointed at all azimuths. Strobe Talbott is quite correct when he says that "the U.S., the West Europeans and the United Nations must use their own considerable influence with the newly independent states to protect the rights of the Russian minorities there. Otherwise, Russia may take matters into its own heavy hands."[19] The example of the Baltic states is instructive on that score. Does every republic need leaders like Brazauskas to come to power in order to stop discriminating against local Russians? And, again, why take revenge on the Russian people for the sins of the past regime?

Were not some of the leaders of the republics, now discriminating against Russians, themselves part of the Soviet regime?

Democracy may well be the only guide for the peoples of the former Soviet Union to help avoid unnecessary hostilities and disputes. However, democracy was not taught in the school of Soviet socialism. It was not taught in tsarist Russia either. The best thing the West can do for the newly independent states is to show what democracy is and to expect them to respect this brand of human society. To achieve such a goal, the West and the United States should treat democracy on its merits, excluding any kind of double standard or calculations as to what might or might not bring them advantages. This is indeed a difficult requirement, but it is the only one that can be counted upon to promote social, economic, and political progress in the area.

Notes

1. This point of view was also expressed by Strobe Talbott in *Time* magazine, December 7, 1993. But he is more cautious, saying that "*many* Russians have not yet been able to accept the idea that the 14 non-Russian republics of the USSR are today independent foreign countries." "Many" does not mean "majority." And I do not think that there are really many.

2. *Pravda Ukrainy*, March 21, 1991. Least favorable to such ideas was the population of the Ukrainian capital, Kiev, and of three western provinces: L'vov, Ivano-Frankovsk, and Ternopol'.

3. However, many of the local elites misused the dictatorial authority they were given in local affairs, and the corruption became widespread and almost unpunishable; those responsible were quite happy with such "division of authority."

4. "Stop Treating Russia Like a Loser," *The New York Times*, March 25, 1992.

5. See "Crimea Has Been Ukrainian Since 1954," *The New York Times*, April 15, 1992.

6. Who brought Shelest to Moscow—whether Khrushchev himself or those whom he had brought to Moscow—is not important; it only proves that the "Ukrainian mafia" did not disappear in 1964 together with its "founding father." True, Chernenko came from Siberia to work with Brezhnev in Moldavia. It is easy to understand the unwillingness on the part of Professor Szporluk to consider him a Ukrainian. So far as Chervonenko is concerned, he is of course better known for his notable contribution to the shameful and criminal intervention in Czechoslovakia (where he was the Soviet ambassador at the time of the "Prague Spring"). By the way, I am pushed by my opponent to recall that when it decided to crush the Czechoslovak democracy, of the eleven full members of the Politburo, only four were from Russia, but five from Ukraine and the other two from Latvia and Belarus. The latter was represented by Kirill Trofimovich Mazurov, who went to Prague under the code name of "Trofimov" to supervise the operations of the Soviet troops and of the KGB in the political sphere. But later on, after several years of work in Paris, Stepan Chervonenko came to Moscow to head a very important department, perhaps one of the most important and vile in the Central Committee, charged with deciding which Soviet citizens could be allowed to cross the iron curtain and which could not. Besides, the department controlled the behavior and often severely punished people working abroad: diplomats, journalists, trade representatives, engineers, laborers, fishermen, sailors, drivers, and even their wives and children. The department was closely connected

with the KGB. On a hot July day in 1987, I was sitting in the air-conditioned office of Chervonenko, who was interrogating me, consulting a thick volume of my dossier on his big desk. He asked whether I had had secret meetings with U.S. Ambassador A. Hartman and what for; why I had taken liberties to talk freely with (and entertain at home) foreigners, especially Americans and other "representatives of the NATO countries"; did I realize that my talks could be interpreted as anti-Soviet, and so on: a whole string of crimes which the KGB had collected as reasons not to let me cross the border for four years and to demand my ouster from the job of editor-in-chief (they almost succeeded; but the times were changing!). True, Chervonenko permitted me to go abroad with a delegation, but not before Anatolii Dobrynin, former ambassador to the United States and at that time a secretary of the Central Committee responsible for international affairs, talked with him about me and said that he "answered for me." So, I strongly doubt that Professor Szporluk can teach me who was who and what was what in Soviet politics.

7. There is little surprise in the fact that extremists adopted such a posture: historical experience shows that the easiest way to fan nationalistic feelings into chauvinistic passions is to have an enemy. Hitler used Jews, Khomeini used Americans, the Soviet regime used "imperialism," American ultraconservatives used "communism," Hamas of the Palestinians is using Jews again, and so on. Unfortunately, the search for an enemy seems to serve as a very convenient excuse for not thinking rationally and in a civilized way.

8. John N. Hazard points out: "Not only republican leaders, but ordinary individuals as well had their way blocked when they have wanted to exercise their right to free speech, guaranteed by the Constitution, to urge secession. . . . Arrest and prosecution of dissenters urging secession have indicated that the [criminal] code has indeed been implemented." *The Soviet System of Government* (Chicago: The University of Chicago Press, 1980), p. 107.

9. Ibid., p. 111. Actually, the cultural sphere was more favorable for the nations in the USSR than the economic or political one. Particularly positive were the 1920s, when great efforts were made for the development of different cultures, including the Ukrainian. In 1926, the party secretary of Ukraine, V. Zatonskii, made a special report "On the Results of Ukrainization." See I. Dolutskii, *Materialy k izucheniiu istorii SSSR* [Materials for the Study of the History of the USSR] (Moscow, 1989), p. 88.

10. *Dnipro* 1991, no. 2, p. 184. Sharikov is a figure in Mikhail Bulgakov's story "The Heart of a Dog," a symbol of a small, barely literate man, who unexpectedly realizes that he can dictate his will to more cultured and professionally superior people and thereby usurp their property and prestige.

11. I remember how amazed I was when a friend of mine, Doctor Tatiana Mikhailichenko, told me in Kiev how "vigilant" some Ukrainian representatives of the Kiev elite were: when a doctor appeared in the hospital dressed in a sweater with blue and yellow colors he was summoned to the director, who told him, "I give you 45 minutes to go home and change!"

12. Vernon Aspaturian, "The Non-Russian Nationalities," in Allen Kassof, ed., *Prospects for Soviet Society* (New York: Praeger, 1968), p. 173.

13. David Lane, *State and Politics* (New York: New York University Press, 1985), p. 277.

14. See *The Washington Post*, January 7, 1993. "A senior U.S. official said the Ukrainian delegation was told emphatically at the State Department that Washington would not engage in a bargaining process to persuade Ukraine's legislature to ratify its commitment to remove nuclear weapons from its soil. 'We're not going to bargain for their vote,' said the official, who asked not to be quoted by name. 'We're not going to bid up the price.' "

15. *The New York Times*, February 5, 1993. The article explains: "Ukraine's leaders have demanded more compensation for giving up expensive nuclear components in the

176 strategic missiles on its territory, rejected as insufficient an initial offer of $175 million from the United States."

16. *The New York Times*, February 11, 1993. Among other things, the ambassador points out that actually his country did not get a cent out of the promised $175 million. That must be true, but the discussion of "how much?" and "when?" will take place through diplomatic channels in Washington, not in Moscow.

17. *Rabochaia tribuna* (Moscow), March 5, 1993. Of course, this is very close to V. Zhirinovskii's pronouncements. But the Russian ultrachauvinist has lost all his support in the last couple of years. However, the extremists in western Ukraine are still listened to. Ivan Drach, the well-known poet and a leader of Rukh, said that there were no "nationalists" in Ukraine (ibid.).

18. Leo Tolstoy wrote his "Sebastopol stories" based upon his personal experience as an officer there. The stories are read by all schoolchildren in Russia.

19. *Time*, December 7, 1993, p. 35. "The dominant local nationalities now treat these Russians [25 millions] as second-class citizens or worse," says Strobe Talbott.

D

FUNCTIONAL ISSUES

7

Russian-American Cooperation in Policing Crime

George Ginsburgs

Legal themes figured prominently in past Soviet-American polemics. Washington continuously faulted the Soviet record in the field of human rights, especially with regard to emigration procedures, and criticized Moscow's failure to afford its citizens effective safeguards for substantiating even those civic liberties to which local law said they were entitled. In those days, very little in the Soviet-American picture remained unaffected by the political dispute. The sphere of civil law, normally immune from such controversy, was not spared as U.S. courts wrangled, for instance, over whether or not to let individuals living behind the "Iron Curtain" inherit from deceased relatives in the United States, who had named them beneficiaries under the terms of their wills. Whatever cooperation between the respective justice departments did occur involved petty matters; for example, judicial commissions from American courts addressed to Soviet courts which consisted of requests to interrogate as witnesses persons residing in the USSR whose testimony might be pertinent in a civil case pending in the United States. There were also instances of American courts approaching Soviet judicial organs with requests to record the testimony of experts at a court hearing. Traffic in the opposite direction—sparse at best—called for the procurement of similar routine services.[1]

Given the climate of hostility and mutual suspicion, no contacts of that sort were maintained in the province of criminal law, nor, indeed, were official liaisons here seriously considered throughout the era of superpower confrontation and ideological crusade. Rather, American spokesmen missed no opportunity to denounce the quality of Soviet criminal justice, and the notion of transacting business with a partner whose reputation was so besmirched seemed outrageous.

Thus, the recent changes in this precinct offer a convenient yardstick for gauging the success of the current bid to engineer a rapprochement between the two countries and are a good indication of each regime's revised perception of the other. Inasmuch as both parties have pragmatic reasons for promoting this rapport, their motives on this occasion can likewise shed light on what new phenomena in the objective environment have prompted them to seek to pool their resources in order to deal with pathological strains whose quarantining through concerted action is now seen as furthering a common interest.

* * *

Of course, political forces set the stage for the present phase of the Soviet (Russian)–American detente. Nevertheless, professions of commitment to the desirability of a fundamental reform of the Soviet legal system lay close to the heart of the glasnost'-cum-perestroika scenario and contributed to making its proponents attractive to the American administration. The contents of the proposed package struck a responsive chord in U.S. circles which tended to hear in Gorbachev's public pronouncements echoes of familiar tunes that made the Soviet leader sound like someone who shared our faith in the cardinal principles of the Western world's legal ethos. The attitude is understandable. After all, here was the Soviet Union's top leader enthusiastically endorsing the concept of the primacy of international law with twin goals in mind: (1) to convince the world that the Soviet hierarchy subscribed to the commandments tabulated in the universal bill of rights and, hence, was a worthy partner in the task of managing global affairs; (2) to prod the custodians of internal standards into complying with the superior norms designed to police behavior among states.

Two features distinguished Gorbachev's mode of conduct in these matters from that of his predecessors and thus enhanced his credibility abroad. First, the Soviet regime had always shopped in the international law market—mostly, perhaps, for the sake of appearance and out of ulterior political motives—but had done so in a clearly selective and discretionary manner. No sense of duty animated those operations, whereas now the notion being bandied about was that no self-respecting member of the international community could afford *not* to espouse the ensemble of "peremptory" rules associated with civilized culture as articulated in the "constitutional" documents of humankind and, to justify that status, in fact had to join the compact. A compulsory mood replaced the erstwhile voluntary style. Although views still differed as to what specific "purchases" might be expected of a candidate to the club in order to meet the criteria of eligibility, Soviet rhetoric drew a picture of a solid consensus within the local "liberal" constituency to the effect that a minimum investment in legal staples was deemed a *sine qua non*.

Second, during the Brezhnev dark ages ratification of an international charter did not guarantee that appropriate revisions would then be effected in the corresponding domestic law texts to create a uniform procedure whereby the norms crafted on an international scale served as a model for the home medium and thus compelled the latter to improve its performance accordingly. The Gorbachev people soon claimed that this schizophrenic affliction was being cured on their watch and, with the patient on the mend, assured all concerned of their determination to concentrate next on upgrading domestic law to the level of its international counterpart. Gorbachev himself assigned top priority to this job in signaling that "it was necessary that national legislation and administrative rules in the humanitarian sphere be brought into accordance with international obligations and standards everywhere."[2] Although the "humanitarian" aspect was singled out for attention on that occasion, the message had general import and plainly called for achieving congruence in quality between legal fare bearing a universal seal of approval and the analogous Soviet brand. Indeed, even if the "humanitarian" mission was under the spotlight, the stakes remained sufficiently high to earn prime foreign credit.

Gorbachev's words became a refrain, and spokesmen in his entourage seized every opportunity to make the same pitch. Both senior diplomatic personnel and academic analysts rushed to proclaim that one of the main attributes of a "law minded" state was "respect for international law, which implies full reflection of international legal obligations in internal legislation and compliance with them."[3] To quote a typical sample of this genre of pronouncement:

> By forming a state governed by law in our country, we are proceeding on the assumption that primacy in solving all problems must pertain to international obligations. We are keying our own domestic processes on the international obligations which have been adopted by us; they are functioning in the role of a unique kind of standards to which our domestic legislation has been catching up in the process of perestroika. We are attempting to bring our legislation and practice into line with international norms, to achieve a commensurate quality of the transformations taking place in our country in the political, cultural, economic, and other spheres with those of the world-level experience. Examples of this are furnished by our adoption of the obligations with regard to the Helsinki Concluding Act and those of the Vienna Agreements. All this is in our interests and the interests of the international community.[4]

The focus of the present study is emergent evidence that the province of criminal law and criminal procedure is not impervious to such "impregnation." These hallowed precincts, once immune to the virus of "imported" mores, have also succumbed. The debate in progress among Soviet (Russian) legal practitioners and scholars over the projected codes in these disciplines abounds with references to the need to comply with internationally recognized standards in drafting these key pieces of legislation.[5] Some radical versions being floated in this connection go so far as to espouse the value of natural law conceptions of human rights here (stripped of their metaphysical connotations) and embrace the

Universal Declaration's writ that the rights of the individual share a quality common to all mankind. Admittedly, an uphill battle lies ahead in striving to elevate Soviet criminal policy, and so, not surprisingly, action lags behind talk in this sector—which is not to say, of course, that no thaw has occurred. For instance, in January 1989, the Soviet Union joined the Standard Minimum Rules for the Treatment of Prisoners approved by the UN in 1955.[6] The domestic repertory in the penal field was expected to follow the example set by "this superb charter of humanitarian rules" and to match its more enlightened prescriptions for handling these cases.[7]

In the area of criminal procedure, the key issue was described as affording the courts much greater power in dealing with the fate of the individual. We were reminded that the Soviet Union had signed the International Covenant on Civil and Political Rights and the Final Act of the Vienna meeting which proclaims the right of every detainee to demand that the validity of the arrest be verified by a judicial instance. Local critics pointed out that "no such norms nor such practice exists in our country up till now." A lot had been written on the subject over the years, but "the cart still has not budged." Projects were elaborated recommending that

> the citizen have the right to contest in court an unlawful arrest, dismissal from the job, dispatch to a medical facility for performance of psychiatric tests. And in practice there are many unlawful refusals to file criminal charges. Under the terms of our draft, such a refusal—in essence, a denial of justice—can also be appealed to court, just as the unlawful dismissal of a case at the stage of preliminary investigation. Let the court control preliminary investigation not upon its conclusion, but during, when one can still correct errors. This will raise the role of the court as the principal organ in the criminal process.[8]

At long last, modest progress can be reported on this front as well. Thus, the Russian Republic's code of criminal procedure has recently been supplemented with a clause that sanctions relief by medium of judicial review of the legality of an arrest upon such application by the *de cujus*—tapping the historical precedent of how the writ of habeas corpus has operated elsewhere.

Add that, in a move flush with dramatic possibilities, the Soviet Union adhered to the Optional Protocol to the Covenant on Civil and Political Rights, which grants the UN Committee on Human Rights authority to examine complaints against states instigated by private persons or their representatives. The concept of letting Soviet citizens appeal to an international body against actions of their own government was nothing short of revolutionary, which explains the long delay in consummating the engagement. A variety of hurdles had to be surmounted and the explanations of what these entailed ranged from the rather tactful confession that "differences of opinion between Soviet government agencies so far have prevented our country from joining the protocol"[9] to tough talk about the accession "being blocked by the refusal of certain of our government departments to allow Soviet citizens to lodge with the UN

Human Rights Committee complaints against violations of their rights."[10]

In any event, thanks to the successful completion of the undertaking, a Soviet (Russian) citizen today can bid to have the committee evaluate the way he or she has been treated by the regime on the scale established by the Covenant and issue an opinion as to whether or not the latter's terms were observed on the disputed occasion. The committee's mandate extends to a broad array of criminal law and criminal procedure safeguards which the authors of the pact chose to assign to the human rights basket owing to the master role they play in protecting the individual's vital interests. True, the committee's findings are not legally obligatory for the offending party, but not many states are eager to incur adverse publicity by continuing to resort to methods to which so august an assembly of their fellows has officially objected. The Soviet brass fully realized the consequences it incurred by entering the arrangement, recognizing that the weight of public opinion has frequently induced states to introduce "changes into legislation, constitutions included," and confirming that the Soviet Union would be prepared to follow suit if presented with "convincing arguments" on the need to upgrade its score. As Shevardnadze reminded the UN General Assembly at its forty-third session, "international control in the domain of human rights is the imperative of our time."[11]

By hook or by crook, then, the Soviet (Russian) record in this sphere is henceforth bound to attract the kind of international scrutiny that will make it very difficult for the local authorities to pursue a course here that grossly deviates from the applicable norms to which the global community has lent its stamp of approval.[12]

* * *

A few signposts from the past will help measure the distance the Soviet Union traveled down this road in U.S. company. The treatment of skyjacking offenses offers a convenient starting point and the Brazinskas case can serve as a good example of how such traffic once fared in the Soviet-American lane.

On October 15, 1970, a Soviet civilian airliner on a domestic run from Batumi to Sukhumi with fifty-one persons aboard was hijacked by two passengers who killed the stewardess, Nadezhda Kurchenko, and seriously wounded the pilot and copilot, forcing them to fly to the Turkish port of Trebizond. Another passenger was also wounded during the incident. The air pirates were subsequently identified as Pranas Brazinskas-Koreivo and his son Algirdas, of Lithuanian origin. On landing, the hijackers requested political asylum; they were taken into custody and charged with carrying arms, inflicting injuries on three persons, armed assault, and homicide. The Soviet authorities immediately asked Turkey to extradite the pair and the Soviet media reported that they were wanted as "criminal murderers for trial in the Soviet Union."[13]

The law was invoked to justify the demand for the surrender of the offenders. The criminal act had been committed in Soviet airspace, on board a Soviet aircraft, and thus Soviet criminal jurisdiction clearly applied. As a member of the United Nations, Turkey was expected to abide by the decision of the Security Council of September 9, 1970, and the resolution adopted by the twenty-fourth session of the General Assembly calling for the implementation of necessary measures to prevent the seizure of civilian planes and punish the persons committing such acts. The return of the culprits to the country that owned the hijacked aircraft was said to be the proper procedure in these situations. Furthermore, it was claimed, the perpetrators were not eligible to receive asylum inasmuch as they had committed a common crime which violated the principles concerning guarantee of the safety of air traffic which the General Assembly and the Security Council had repeatedly espoused. Since the crime had occurred in Soviet territory and the victims were also Soviet citizens, the Soviet Union had a primary stake in trying the criminals. No special treaty was required to effect the transfer of the guilty persons: current practice favored waiving that precondition and the trend was to regard skyjackers as a modern breed of pirates whose rendition to the state most interested in punishing them was sanctioned without benefit of formal entente.[14]

Just two weeks later, a couple of young Soviet students succeeded in hijacking a small plane to Turkey. No one was hurt on this occasion. The hijackers asked for political asylum and expressed the wish to go to the United States. However, after spending a year in a Turkish refugee camp, with no prospect of emigrating to a third country, they were shipped home in December 1971 by agreement between the Soviet and Turkish authorities. The terms of the deal were not disclosed.[15]

Brazinskas *père et fils* were luckier. Turkey resisted Soviet demands for their extradition and, instead, tried them for manslaughter: the son was acquitted, the father received an eight-year prison term. He was released under a general amnesty in 1974 and the pair was placed in a refugee camp. In June 1976, according to press accounts, they left a camp for displaced persons in the central Turkish town of Yozgat, reportedly complaining that the father was sick and both were suffering from depression. They unsuccessfully sought political asylum at the United States Embassy in Ankara and finally surrendered to the police after five days on the run. Ford administration officials explained their refusal to comply with the fugitives' request for political asylum on grounds that the United States "could not appear to slacken in its opposition to international piracy," but admitted that the embassy staff in Ankara had sought prior assurances from the Turkish government that Turkish law would not permit the return of the Brazinskases to the Soviet Union before they were advised to turn themselves in.

A news story datelined Istanbul July 11, 1976, reported that the Brazinskases had been freed by the Turkish authorities after spending six years in custody and had left that same day for Rome; no reason was given for the decision to release the detainees. TASS criticized the procedure, which, it said, was "in sharp contradiction to the demands of the Soviet public for the extradition and exemplary punishment of the two."[16] Official diplomatic protests followed. On July 15, 1976, the Soviet ambassador to Turkey called on Prime Minister Demirel and made a statement setting forth his government's view that Turkey's handling of the matter militated "against the intensification of the struggle against hijacking of aircraft," that "the protection given the criminals" constituted "an unfriendly act towards the USSR," and that the wrong signal had been sent to others who might be inclined to take this route:

> The Turkish authorities handled the case so that the criminals got away with unjustifiably light punishment and were then given their freedom. What is more, they were allowed to leave Turkey for a country which, so the Turkish Foreign Ministry declared, would grant them asylum—and the criminals took advantage of this. . . .
> All that has happened with the Brazinskas virtually means that acts of international piracy in the air are being condoned. They have even found asylum, although what right of asylum can one speak about when it is a case of murderers, admitted to be criminals by a Turkish court as well?[17]

The affair and its immediate consequences cast an interesting light on the behavior of our chief protagonists. The Soviet regime which, until then, had maintained a studied aloofness to the phenomenon of skyjackings in the West was jolted by its own painful experience into joining international efforts to combat the problem. In short order, the USSR entered the International Civil Aviation Organization, supported a United Nations resolution against hijacking, and signed an anti-hijacking convention at The Hague. For the United States, the Brazinskas episode was a source of considerable embarrassment in that covert American intercession to ensure that the guilty parties would not be sent back "home"—allegedly because the seizure of the plane had been politically motivated—could not be squared with Washington's strident advocacy of closer international collaboration in suppressing offenses against the safety of civilian air traffic. Ironically, at about the same time, the United States was spearheading a drive to set up machinery for invoking collective sanctions against any country that failed to prosecute or extradite hijackers or aircraft saboteurs, including the automatic suspension of air service to the offending state, and disputing the Soviet charge that only the UN Security Council had the power to impose such penalties.[18]

The glaring inconsistencies that marked U.S. policy on this front may be attributed to pronounced anti-Soviet feelings in American political circles where hijacking was often perceived as a logical corollary to the Soviet stranglehold on the emigration process; moreover, there were strong pro-Baltic sympathies within the local constituency, and pressure was exerted by émigré organizations which hailed the Brazinskases as "freedom fighters" who had struck a worthy blow against the foreign occupants of their native land. Even so, the fact remains that the substance of the actions on this occasion did not match the tenor of the public rhetoric, and the discrepancy was bound to undercut the U.S. credibility.

The issue became a *cause célèbre* when the Brazinskas duo surfaced in the United States just a few months after leaving Turkey, ostensibly by deboarding an international flight during a stopover in New York and "getting lost in the crowd" in the airport. According to the Soviet press, no effort was made to locate the "illegal entrants" until their conduct attracted the attention of the immigration bureau. Detained by the police, the pair insisted that they had a right to political asylum. Meanwhile, the Soviet government reminded the competent American organs that it expected the extradition of the two "killers" and again warned that it would consider a decision to grant them sanctuary an "unfriendly act." All subsequent Soviet bids to secure the surrender of the wanted pair got nowhere.[19] True, at one point, the White House reportedly indicated that the Brazinskases had been denied political asylum in the United States "because they had committed a 'serious non-political crime,' and that they faced the prospect of deportation to Venezuela, from where they illegally entered the United States."[20] But there was never any mention that they might be returned to the Soviet Union, and even the talk about possible deportation to Venezuela soon turned out to be a red herring.

The American executive and administrative branches continued to stonewall Soviet inquiries on the subject of the Brazinskases' undisturbed sojourn in the United States despite having been officially denied political asylum. References to the provisions of the 1970 Hague convention which required the severe punishment of air pirates and to the UN resolution of November 25, 1970, calling for their extradition also proved to no avail. Soviet complaints fell on deaf ears notwithstanding valid claims that

> as a result of the maneuvers of the U.S. authorities conducted in the spirit of the cold war, an act which falls within the category of international terrorism had deliberately been reduced, in the case of the Brazinskas, to an insignificant breach of immigration legislation, the maximum penalty for which can be an order to leave the territory of the United States!
>
> It is appropriate to recall in this connection that the government of the United States has repeatedly made public statements about the necessity for a resolute struggle against international terrorism and has solemnly proclaimed that in that struggle it will strive for wider cooperation with all countries irrespective of their political system with the aim of preventing such acts and punishing those guilty.
>
> A legitimate question arises: How do these official statements square with the unseemly attitude taken up by the U.S. authorities in the Brazinskas case— an attitude which not only fails to promote the struggle against international terrorism but actually encourages terrorism?[21]

In a similar vein, Washington was accused of practicing a double standard when in August 1978, at a meeting in Bonn, the seven leading capitalist countries adopted a resolution declaring, inter alia, that if any country refused to extradite or prosecute a hijacker, the governments concerned would forthwith stop the flight of their aircraft to that country and would bar the aircraft of that country from landing on their territory. Grilled about the implications of that injunction for the future of the Brazinskas father and son, the State Department spokesman denied its applicability to the case and avoided answering the question of whether their extradition to the USSR might occur. According to the Soviet media, the gist of the message was that the Americans cared deeply about the seizure of their own planes, but were utterly indifferent when the planes and citizens of the Soviet Union and other socialist countries were the target of terrorist attacks. What it all boiled down to was that the seven Western powers intended "to appropriate the functions of an international policeman and be sole judges of air hijacking and the other acts of international terrorism," thus enabling them "to employ sanctions unilaterally at their own discretion and in their own interests."[22]

Over the years and despite every rebuff, the Soviets would still not quit the chase, using the Brazinskas example to flay the U.S. authorities for providing haven to international terrorists, filing official protests against the U.S. failure to hand the guilty parties over to Soviet justice, citing a growing body of international law norms designed to counter violence against innocent bystanders, and warning Washington (especially in the wake of the *Achille Lauro* incident) of the grave danger of drawing invidious distinctions between "good terrorists" and "bad terrorists."[23] Even as late as 1988, Soviet officials were still pushing Washington to live up to its international obligations in these matters and only the demise of the USSR finally put an end to the monologue.

Other instances of Soviet-American "coupling" in skyjacking incidents were less spectacular than the Brazinskas affair. In May 1989, Captain Aleksandr Zuev flew a MiG–29 to Turkey, where he requested political asylum in the United States. Moscow immediately posted a demand for the fugitive's return to face charges of attempted murder, hijacking, desertion, theft of firearms, and violation of international flight rules, claiming that Zuev had fed a cake laced with sedatives to fellow pilots at a base in the republic of Georgia, then attacked and overpowered a sentry, suffering a bullet wound in the arm, and had tried unsuccessfully to fire missiles at the planes on the ground that could have pursued him. As *The New York Times* reported at the time:

> In branding Captain Zuev a hijacker, the Soviet Union has implicitly raised the stakes. The Bush Administration has been promoting improved cooperation with Moscow on issues like terrorism and the environment, and therefore might find it more difficult to grant asylum to someone publicly described as a hijacker by the Soviet authorities.
>
> "This case is on the cutting edge of the change in East-West relations," one Bush Administration official said.
>
> Several American officials said that, barring any indications that the pilot has a criminal record, he would probably be granted asylum.

> Asylum requests can be made only when someone reaches American soil, so Captain Zuev cannot apply unless Turkey allows him to travel to the United States.[24]

Turkish Foreign Ministry spokesmen were quoted as saying that if Zuev was deemed a criminal, he would be tried in Turkey or returned to his country; if he was deemed a defector for political reasons, some charges could be dropped.

Soviet diplomatic quarters responded to the news that Zuev had sought political asylum in the United States by informing the American ambassador to the USSR that any decision to welcome Zuev in the United States would not only be legally and morally indefensible but would cause bewilderment in the Soviet Union and strike a discordant note in the prevailing positive tone of Soviet-American liaisons.[25]

According to an article published in the Soviet press shortly thereafter, a Turkish district procurator's office had filed charges against Captain Zuev for "violation of the passport regime and infringement of the state frontier." The question of granting the *de cujus* political asylum was scheduled to be considered in a different department of the local government apparatus: Zuev had previously expressed a wish to settle in Turkey, if the authorities did not object, or, in the contrary case, to seek asylum in the United States.[26]

Extradition to the Soviet Union was apparently not an avenue being seriously contemplated by the Turkish authorities, despite the fact that the Soviet leadership was now engaged in waging a vigorous international campaign for revision of the current legal norms pertaining to the treatment of air pirates. Instead of the existing procedure, which afforded the custodian state the option to try the criminal or extradite him, the Soviets were pressing for mandatory extradition of hijackers in all the international conventions on air safety, arguing that this was the most effective weapon against them.[27]

Later that same year, the name of the United States was invoked in another incident. A Chinese MiG–19 crossed into Soviet air space in the Soviet Far East and was compelled to land at a local airfield. The pilot allegedly claimed that his act was politically motivated and that he wanted to emigrate to the United States.[28] If precedent set in a reverse situation can be counted upon, the defector was probably tried in the Soviet Union and received a stiff sentence. Here we are extrapolating from the fate that befell a former Soviet pilot, Alimuradov, who hijacked a plane to China in 1985, was sentenced there to eight years in jail, then transferred to the Soviet Union and sentenced to an additional five years.[29]

* * *

The handling of war criminals has likewise fueled controversy. In the midst of World War II, the Soviet government issued a formal statement (October 14, 1942) to the effect that "it counted on all interested parties to extend each other mutual assistance in seeking out, surrendering, prosecuting, and meting out severe punishment to Hitlerites and their accomplices guilty of organizing, condoning and committing crimes on occupied territories."[30] The same theme was sounded by Stalin a little more than a year later (November 6, 1943). Reviewing the principal postwar goals of the United Nations alliance, he stressed the need "to take measures so that all fascist criminals guilty of the present war and the suffering of the peoples, no matter in what country they tried to hide, shall incur severe punishment and retribution for all the evil deeds they committed."[31] A duty to surrender war criminals was distilled, inter alia, from the tenor of various wartime declarations;[32] the corresponding articles in the armistice agreements with Italy, Romania, Bulgaria, Hungary, and Finland; the Four-Power declaration on the surrender of Germany of June 5, 1945; the UN General Assembly resolution of February 12, 1946; and the peace treaties with Italy, Romania, Hungary, Bulgaria, and Finland (1947).[33]

Relying on this material, Soviet spokesmen waged a concerted campaign to persuade the international community that international law mandates the rendition of war criminals as a universal proposition and that failure to do so constitutes a violation of a peremptory rule of international law which must be countered.[34] We were told, for instance, that "the Soviet Union and the countries of people's democracy struggle against the illegal practice of the countries of the Anglo-American bloc who shelter war criminals under the guise of procuring asylum," in breach of the international documents which they themselves had signed.[35] In this connection, Soviet sources recognized the validity of a major departure from the traditional policy of not surrendering one's own citizens in the imposition of a duty to surrender war criminals.[36] Moreover, the Soviet Union and the people's democracies were praised for "stubbornly struggling against providing shelter to war criminals because their punishment represents one of the paramount conditions for preventing the recurrence of aggression."[37]

However, others did not share those convictions, and no international consensus then existed that the law of nations currently required states to deliver "on demand" individuals suspected of having committed war crimes to their foreign accusers to stand trial in the country where the offenses were perpetrated, in the absence of specific extradition arrangements and on the strength alone of indications of general intent. Attitudes now seem to be gradually shifting in the direction first designated by Moscow, but initially the Soviet position met with skepticism and rejection in many quarters and the bid to portray its opinion as the true faith attracted few converts.

Such demurrers notwithstanding, Soviet analysts pressed forward with their case, arguing that the right of asylum was properly afforded to "fighters for freedom and progress evading persecution by reactionary governments," but that

> war criminals and the leading functionaries of fascism patently have nothing in common with the defenders of freedom and progress. One cannot use the

concept of political offender with respect to those for whom politics are but a convenient excuse for the satisfaction of racial hatred and predatory greed, to those who in bestial fashion exterminated millions of people (the death factories at Maidanek, Hartogenbosch, Auschwitz, etc.) and committed destruction and devastation utterly unprecedented in their brutality (Lidice, Novgorod, Smolensk, Kiev, etc.). Like ancient pirates, they can only be viewed as enemies of the human race.[38]

The premise logically leads to the conclusion that "the rendition of war criminals is considered a legal obligation of all states"[39] which, Soviet legal experts took care to underscore, operates on a *sui generis* footing:

the presence or absence of such bilateral treaties [i.e., prescribing rendition] has no bearing in deciding the questions of surrendering war criminals inasmuch as, with respect to these persons, imperative international law norms apply, qualifying their rendition to the interested state as a legal obligation of the state to which the demand for rendition is addressed.[40]

Testing what they preached, the Soviet authorities bombarded assorted Western countries with requests for the surrender of war criminals who had found local haven. These "legitimate demands" met with rebuff from, inter alia, the United States and Australia, who now copied the behavior of other "bourgeois regimes" that had opted earlier to slap a *de facto* embargo on such traffic with the Soviet Union.[41]

Interestingly enough, Soviet authors sounded more positive about the compulsory quality of the obligation to surrender war criminals when writing about members of the capitalist community than when referring to the corollary duties of the socialist constituents. Then, the tone suddenly turned tentative, as in the statement that "the Soviet Union admits the possibility of rendition of criminals on conditions of reciprocity, particularly war criminals and persons guilty of crimes against peace and humanity."[42] The mode verges on the discretionary and the insertion of the mutuality clause further weakens the original injunction, all of which stands in stark contrast with the harsh terms of the Soviet indictment of its Western opposites for not sticking to the strict letter of the law. Time lapse did not allay the antagonism and, while the Soviet style elsewhere tended to adapt to the niceties of the finale's less confrontational approach to East-West relations, the war crimes issue continued to generate intense irritation of the kind that, even as late as 1990, could still prompt the charge that:

The practice of granting asylum in capitalist countries is accompanied by numerous violations of generally accepted international legal norms. After World War II the United States, Great Britain, and several other capitalist powers opened their borders to Nazi war criminals, which is inconsistent with the goal of strengthening world peace and the purposes and principles of the United Nations.[43]

Despite the harsh tone of Moscow's public comments about Washington's policy of coddling war criminals,[44] working contacts were calmly pursued at the departmental level. Soviet sources claim that the relevant arrangements between the USSR Procurator's Office and American legal bodies originated in 1976, "when the U.S. side turned to us for assistance."[45] Marking a further rapprochement in this sector, in 1980 the USSR Ministry of Justice and the Office of Special Investigations (OSI) of the Immigration and Naturalization Service in the U.S. Department of Justice reached an entente to exchange witness affidavits and originals of documents on the question of the role of certain naturalized citizens of the United States in the commission of crimes on Soviet territory during the Second World War.[46] Over the years, a significant volume of such help was reportedly afforded by the USSR Procurator's Office, which

> collected and handed over to the special division [i.e., OSI] over 20,000 documents containing evidence against 144 persons suspected of Nazi crimes now in hiding in the United States. As many as 94 American lawyers (prosecuting attorneys, investigators and defense counsel) have come to the Soviet Union at various times to attend the examination of 189 witnesses in 28 cases.[47]

In 1983, for instance, "U.S. legal experts conducted investigations in Gomel and Cherkassy."[48] The following year, a two-man team traveled to Lithuania to gather evidence against Antanas Virkutis, a Lithuanian native living in Cicero, Illinois, accused of collaborating with the Nazis and presiding over a Lithuanian prison during the persecution, starvation, and execution of Jews, war prisoners, and other inmates.[49]

The American official heading the project characterized the operation as a success:

> [I]n 1980, when relations were speedily going to hell, United States and Soviet negotiators met in Moscow and quietly fashioned an agreement to document the extent of Nazi war crimes and to seek witnesses to testify in American judicial proceedings. That effort has proceeded, effectively and fairly and without propaganda, in the four years since.[50]

The Russians, in his estimate, had been "very cooperative":

> We've spent hundreds of hours there getting witness depositions. Imagine! We were importing American legal procedure into Russia. I spent a day explaining the rules of criminal procedure back to Magna Carta to the Procurator General of the USSR.[51]

A few examples will illustrate how the American side either was supplied with or foraged for the necessary materials. In April 1983, Juozas Kungys, of Clifton, New Jersey, was charged by the U.S. government with having participated in the massacre of 2,000 Jews in German-occupied Lithuania, illegally entering the United States, and obtaining citizenship by concealing information about his past. The five-count complaint against him was prepared by federal authorities who were aided in their investigation by Soviet officials in Lithuania.

At a 1984 hearing to deport John Demjanjuk, aka "Ivan the Terrible," to the Soviet Union (he had been born in Ukraine), the accused claimed to be under four death sentences in the Soviet Union and his lawyer contended that such persecution entitled his client to be granted asylum in the United States. However, the government submitted a memorandum from the Soviet Union that said that the *de cujus* had been convicted of no crimes there.

In March of that same year, Alexander Lehman, a former Nazi police officer accused of killing Ukrainian Jews during the war, consented to be deported to West Germany, after admitting the authenticity of a document provided by the Soviet authorities from Ukrainian archives showing his police employment.[52]

Engineering the return of wanted individuals to face Soviet justice presented a much tougher problem because daunting procedural hurdles had to be surmounted before a court decree might be issued ordering deportation or extradition. Success finally crowned the government's efforts in the case of Fedor Fedorenko, who was accused of having served as a guard in a Nazi death camp where 800,000 prisoners had been put to death. Fedorenko's U.S. citizenship was revoked in January 1981 on the grounds that it had been "illegally procured" because he had lied about his past upon entering the United States. In 1983, a U.S. immigration judge gave the government leave to deport Fedorenko to the Soviet Union, where he was born and where he had a wife and two children, but at the time it was uncertain whether the Soviet Union would accept him (deportees retain the right to choose the country of destination provided it agrees to accept them). Fedorenko opted for the Soviet Union and flew to Moscow in December 1984—the first suspected war criminal deported by the United States to the Soviet Union despite Soviet requests for the extradition of others. Indeed, Fedorenko was the first Nazi or Nazi collaborator ever deported from the United States[53] (by the end of 1986, the United States Justice Department had deported nine suspected war criminals to specified countries and had ordered five more to leave the United States).[54] In June 1986, a court in the Crimean city of Simferopol handed down the death sentence and in July 1987, TASS reported that Fedorenko had been executed.

The Fedorenko case was not really the best test since what was at stake here was deportation and not full-scale extradition proceedings. In fact, Fedorenko was deported not because of his wartime activities, but because he had concealed his Nazi service when he filled out his immigration application. The denouement was also quite atypical in that ultimately Fedorenko himself chose to go to the USSR.

The prosecution posted its next major victory when on April 20, 1987, Karl Linnas was escorted by American federal agents aboard a Czechoslovak airliner bound for the Soviet Union via Prague, the first suspected Nazi war criminal deported against his will to the USSR. According to a Soviet account published in 1985:

> the Soviet Union asked the United States three times to extradite Karl Linnas, former head of a concentration camp in Tartu. We submitted to the U.S. side incontrovertible proof of his involvement in the killing of more than 12,000 Soviet citizens. In 1962 a Soviet court sentenced him to death in absentia for his crimes. Nevertheless the request for the extradition was turned down.[55]

Linnas had in fact been stripped of his U.S. citizenship and ordered deported in 1981. After repeated efforts to find another country that would accept him failed, in the end there was no other choice than to send him to the Soviet Union, and Linnas was returned to his native Estonia.

Early statements from Moscow appeared to indicate that the Soviet regime intended to carry out the death sentence that the Estonian Supreme Court had imposed in 1962. In jail, Linnas was provided with a copy of the court's 1962 conviction (he had apparently been tried, convicted, and sentenced by a civilian tribunal) and told he had seven days to seek a pardon. He filed an appeal for pardon through a state-appointed Estonian lawyer, citing the passage of more than forty years since the actions at issue. His counsel ventured the opinion that "there would be no new proceedings since there had been such a great lapse in time," and reportedly the prisoner himself refused to cooperate in the investigation to determine whether he should be retried. The republic's judicial authorities decreed in June that no grounds existed to warrant a new trial. While waiting action on his appeal for a pardon, Linnas underwent surgery twice for various ailments and died on July 2, 1987, in a Leningrad hospital.

Data furnished by Soviet officials had played a crucial role in the OSI's successful prosecution of Linnas. At the 1981 trial, prosecutors were able to use videotaped interviews to prove that from 1941 to 1943 Linnas had been an officer in an Estonian partisan group that collaborated with the Germans and killed Jews and Communists. A three-judge panel of the U.S. Court of Appeals for the Second Circuit ruled in May 1986 that the evidence supported the government's allegations that Linnas had headed a death camp and personally participated in atrocities. As the Soviet press reported, much of the evidence consisted of Soviet-supplied documents and depositions of witnesses taken under Soviet supervision in Estonia by the Justice Department. After the *de cujus* was safely in Soviet hands, the tone of the official remarks about the quality of U.S. judicial proceedings in treating war criminals, until then highly skeptical, thawed visibly. Thus, TASS, quoting the procurator general's office, noted

> the objective attitude of the U.S. judicial authorities to the material in the Linnas case made available to the U.S. side by the Soviet Union.
> Soviet judicial bodies are prepared to maintain cooperation with U.S. justice authorities for the two countries were allies in the Second World War. The

decision of the U.S. authorities on the deportation of Karl Linnas demonstrates that they can be united in the just cause of bringing the war criminals to justice.[56]

Clearly, once the Gorbachev administration began dramatically improving the image of the Soviet regime abroad, some of the old barriers to doing business with the USSR were lowered. Soviet observers took heart from the fact that, following the Fedorenko and Linnas precedents, "the district court in Chicago . . . decided to deport the Nazi war criminal Liudas Kairys to the Soviet Union."[57] In 1987 the U.S. Supreme Court rejected an appeal by Conrad Schellong of Chicago, who faced deportation for concealing his role as a Nazi concentration camp guard (Schellong's lawyer had argued that the Soviet Union might be the only place that would offer to accept his client, since he had given up German citizenship at the time of his naturalization in the United States and could not count on permission to enter West Germany).[58] Then, we have the matter of Boleslavs Maikovskis, a former police chief in Latvia, who had been sentenced to death in the Soviet Union in 1965 and whom the U.S. had previously refused to extradite to the Soviet Union.[59] In the fall of 1988, the investigations office specializing in war-crimes cases won government sanction to deport Maikovskis to the Soviet Union, but the suspect managed to slip away to West Germany before he could be arrested.[60]

The quickened pace of the hunt for Nazi war criminals and their accomplices who had found refuge in the United States after World War II was reflected in numbers. In the spring of 1987, a Justice Department official figured that "more than a dozen foreign-born residents of the United States who had been accused by the Federal Government of lying about their involvement in Nazi war crimes could face deportation to the Soviet Union." About half of the twenty-seven people the government was then trying to oust from the country for lying to immigration officials about their Nazi pasts were accused of committing war crimes on territory currently controlled by the Soviet Union and so were eligible for shipment to that destination. In some cases, deportation orders had already been obtained. For instance, Kazys Palciauskas of Florida was in the midst of appealing an order deporting him to the Soviet Union. Government prosecution described Palciauskas as

> a former Mayor of Kaunas, the capital of Lithuania. The prosecutors say he lied to immigration officials when he entered the country in 1949, hiding the fact that he was Mayor from 1941 to 1942 by listing his job as office clerk in the meat and milk industry. As Mayor, the government said, . . . Palciauskas began a program to place all Jews in Kaunas in a central area, or ghetto.[61]

In virtually all such cases, the credibility of the information procured by Soviet law-enforcement agencies emerged as a hotly contested issue. American critics of Soviet-American rapprochement and spokesmen for exile organizations opposed these proceedings on grounds, inter alia, that they relied on evidence largely supplied by Communist regimes which, they contended, was "suspect," or "tainted," or "unreliable." They further charged that the government was lapping up phony evidence that had been fed to it by the Soviet bloc apparatus in order to smear those who had fought against Communist rule at home before fleeing to the West.[62]

In turn, the U.S. prosecutors insisted that their staff had painstakingly verified the authenticity of all evidence originating from the Soviet side; that in specific cases this evidence merely corroborated documented evidence from other sources; and that the courts were free to rule against admitting evidence about which there were doubts or relegate it to ancillary status and, indeed, sometimes did so. As the first director of the OSI explained:

> No document from the Soviet Union or from anyone else is presumed to be accurate. Every document is checked carefully. That can take the form of checking information against sources, of analysis such as ink and paper tests, handwriting analysis and other forensic techniques. . . .
> I don't even like the term "Soviet evidence." It's either evidence under American rules or it's no evidence at all. So we examine each document and each witness and reach our own conclusions. . . . We've never had a case where any fraudulent evidence has come from the Soviet Union.[63]

Not every U.S. court was persuaded. Thus, Edgar Laipenieks, a former Nazi security agent in Latvia, found guilty of the torture and killing of Soviet people, was ordered to be deported to Chile in 1983. However, at a subsequent hearing, the ninth district court of San Diego, California, "found no grounds for deportation" after refusing "to admit in evidence a videotape of the testimony of Soviet witnesses recorded in the Soviet Union by officials of the special investigations service."[64] John Demjanjuk, while fighting extradition to Israel, also filed an appeal with the U.S. Supreme Court designed to block his deportation to the Soviet Union, claiming that the Justice Department was using false documentary evidence forged by the Soviet Union in pursuing the case against him. In the end, he was extradited to Israel and put on trial there. Controversy continues to swirl around the authenticity of certain pieces of evidence central to the question of whether the accused was in fact the notorious "Ivan the Terrible"—in particular, a key identity card which, the defense has argued, was a KGB counterfeit.[65]

It should also be noted that in each instance of successful Soviet-American cooperation in this traffic, the medium deployed is deportation, and not extradition. Deportation works as an ad hoc device for ridding the host country of an undesirable "guest" by dumping the latter on another country consenting to admit the *de cujus*. By contrast, extradition calls for mutual trust between the parties in the quality of each other's performance in the administration of justice and, as a formal legal procedure, represents a superior form of collaboration by states for the purpose of effectively policing criminal phenomena. Even when relations between the USSR and the United States had warmed to a point where concerted deportation might have been possible, the political rapport never got close enough to allow resort to official extradition channels. Washington was always ready to dredge up the argument—specious, to my mind—that no valid extradition treaty linked the two countries, which putatively meant that this avenue remained blocked. In fact, the diplomatic repertory duly recognizes the practice of discretionary extradition as a normal exercise of the surrendering and receiving states' sovereign attributes. Thus, had there been the proper will, a suitable method could doubtless have been found. Nevertheless, to date, the U.S. side has been unyielding in its reluctance to assume or even appear to assume that kind of firm bilateral engagement with the USSR or its Russian heir.

As already noted, however, contacts flourished at other levels. In March 1988, the new director of OSI, Neal M. Sher, met with then first deputy procurator general of the USSR, Aleksandr Ia. Sukharev, to discuss aspects of Soviet-American cooperation in the exposure of Nazi atrocities.[66] That summer, the Soviet Union agreed to allow representatives of the U.S. Holocaust Memorial Council to see and copy Nazi documents, photographs, and other records of the Holocaust captured by Soviet troops at the end of World War II.[67] In the course of the trip, the delegation visited archives in Moscow, Lvov, Vilnius, and Riga, and was given fifty-seven documents from the Central State Archive of the USSR.[68]

In 1989, a multilateral conference was held in Washington, attended by representatives of the justice departments of the United States, Canada, and Australia, the Procuracy of the USSR, and the U.K. commission for the investigation of war crimes. A joint declaration was adopted in which the parties confirmed their commitment to assist each other in searching for, prosecuting, and punishing war criminals and their accomplices. A call was issued to step up activity toward that end and all concerned voiced their readiness to meet periodically on a multilateral as well as a bilateral basis in order to achieve these goals.[69] Finally, on October 19, 1989, U.S. Attorney-General Thornburgh and USSR Procurator General Sukharev signed a memorandum pledging the two countries to cooperate in the prosecution of Nazi war criminals. This put on a legal footing the existing policy of mutual assistance in tracking down, investigating, and trying individuals suspected of having committed or abetted the commission of Nazi war crimes during the Second World War.[70]

At this point, the Soviets had definitely won a seat on the board of directors and there was reason for fresh optimism that the task of punishing war criminals would be substantially advanced as a result of the unprecedented consensus that had been achieved by the major actors.

* * *

Additional positive developments were prompted by a growing awareness of the desirability of including the Soviet regime as a partner in policing criminal phenomena that spilled across state frontiers and posed a danger on an international scale. Some of the earliest initiatives advancing that idea were part of the Gorbachev leadership's effort to recast the image of the Soviet Union and thus gain admission to civilized company. In the summer of 1987, for instance, the USSR joined Bulgaria, Hungary, the GDR, Poland, Romania, and Czechoslovakia in addressing a letter to the UN Secretary General in which the respective governments collectively condemned international terrorism in all its guises, regardless of who committed the terrorist acts or the motives invoked by the perpetrators to justify their behavior. The letter called for effective cooperation of all states in combating terrorism, to be pursued on the basis of respect for the generally recognized principles and norms of international law and in strict accordance with the UN Charter provisions. Granted, national-liberation struggles and assistance to such movements were exempted from these strictures. Otherwise, however, the authors of the document urged a rapid deployment of common efforts to fight terrorism through bilateral as well as multilateral channels.[71]

Soon thereafter, in a bid to accent the Soviet Union's new enthusiasm for the concept of the primacy of international law, Moscow again noted the dire need to develop rules to enable the international community to deal successfully with the scourges of terrorism, drug addiction, and traffic in drugs and psychotropic substances. Foreign official circles—particularly in the United States—were now criticized for failing to appreciate the Soviet Union's constructive role in these matters and for insisting on portraying the USSR as a source of support for terrorist operations mounted by assorted clandestine groups.[72]

The call for collaborative exertions to contain drug addiction featured large in the Soviet Union's campaign to lift its diplomatic credit rating. Pledging his country's commitment to participate in concerted efforts to counter illegal business in drugs on the basis of standards and principles of international law, the head of the Foreign Ministry's International Law Directorate observed that

> the task of preventing and curbing drug addiction has become extremely acute in recent years, because the illegal trade in narcotics is undermining the economy of several countries and posing a direct threat to the political situation in some of them, while bringing billions of dollars in profits for the criminal syndicates.
>
> "It is perfectly obvious that the problem of fighting the drugs trade, which is closely connected with other varieties of organized crime, including the arms trade and terrorism, has grown into a political global problem that is impossible to resolve without broad international cooperation," he said.[73]

As further evidence of the seriousness of its intentions here, the Kremlin concluded intergovernmental agreements on cooperation and prompt interaction with Great Britain, the United States, France, and West Germany, and was drafting similar agreements with other countries.[74]

Thus, a central point on the agenda for "new thinking" and international law was the proposition that "the achievement of a safe world today cannot be imagined without resolving the problem of terrorism, trade in narcotics and organized crime."[75] Nothing could better illustrate the distance traveled by the Soviet regime from its previous policy positions in this sphere or the lengths to which the Gorbachev administration was prepared to go in order to demonstrate its good faith and establish its credentials.

Before long, the combination of Soviet self-advertisement and greater American receptivity to the message began producing tangible results in different fields of endeavor. The sample ranges from episodic affairs to rather elaborate arrangements requiring the pooling of resources for a considerable duration and on a sizable scale. For example, in Paris on January 8, 1989, Eduard Shevardnadze and George Shultz signed a memorandum of understanding on cooperation in combating illegal narcotics trafficking, the stage for which was set by an entente to that effect between Gorbachev and Reagan at their meeting in Washington in December 1987. The aide-mémoire, it was then reported,

> creates a legal basis for cooperation of law enforcement bodies of the two countries and envisages the exchange of information about suspects or persons known to engage in the illegal drug-trafficking via the territory of one of the two countries to the other or smuggling narcotics to the territory of the other country.
>
> Besides that, the memorandum envisages the possibility of a mutual use of the method of a controlled delivery or other such methods, exchange of information and experts dealing with narcotics contraband and methods of checking it.
>
> The memorandum creates the conditions for mutual information on cargoes of chemicals used for the synthesis of narcotics and also for the exchange of samples of narcotics and other dangerous substances.[76]

In April 1989, the media published accounts indicating that Soviet authorities had consented to meet with their U.S. counterparts to discuss cooperation between the competent agencies on the issues of terrorism, narcotics trafficking, and protection of the environment. Strong skepticism was voiced at the time on the American side about the rationale for cooperation against terrorism when the Soviets were still widely perceived as key players in state-sponsored terrorism, but exploratory talks on the subject were not ruled out.[77] That summer the United States and the Soviet Union revealed that they had just agreed to accept the mandatory jurisdiction of the International Court of Justice in disputes over seven treaties dealing with terrorism and drug trafficking. As reported in *The New York Times*:

> Under the accord, Washington and Moscow are to let the World Court adjudicate disputes over the interpretation of five treaties dealing with aircraft hijacking, sabotage and acts of terrorism and two other treaties relating to drug trafficking. Among other provisions, these treaties require the countries sign-

ing to extradite or put on trial accused terrorists and narcotics racketeers and to
seize drug smugglers' assets, officials say.

The agreement provides for disputes to be settled by a special chamber of
five judges chosen by the contesting sides from the 15 members of the full
court. The verdict would be final.

Under the accord, both parties may later add other treaties to the seven they
have agreed to place under World Court jurisdiction, as well as disputes arising in other specific areas of international law. But they expressly exclude
from the court's jurisdiction any disputes related to armed conflict or other
national security matters.[78]

The occasion marked the first step toward carrying out Gorbachev's 1987
proposal that the five permanent members of the UN Security Council agree to
let the court settle big-power disputes in clearly defined areas and then invite the
rest of the world to follow their example. Some months previously, Moscow had
unilaterally announced its decision to accept the court's jurisdiction in disputes
over the terms of six human rights conventions to which the USSR was a party.
In October 1989 the Soviets caused another stir by calling on UN member
nations to draft a "general instrument for the peaceful settlement of disputes"
that would bind countries to adjudicate quarrels and forgo the use of force.
Interestingly enough, the grand claim staked out in this case was that "the philosophy behind the Soviet Union's foreign policy is based on the need to ensure the
primacy of law in the policy and practice of states."[79]

At around the same time, a week-long unofficial symposium at the Rand
Corporation, sponsored by Search for Common Ground and *Literaturnaia gazeta*
in association with the Soviet Peace Committee, conducted a comprehensive
review of the phenomenon of international terrorism in order to pinpoint those
areas where it could be dealt with as a shared problem. The "task force" recommended: (1) a coordinated approach between Soviet and American intelligence
agencies; (2) cooperation to aid the release of hostages; (3) preventing "high-
tech" terrorism (including nuclear, chemical, and biological); (4) working together in the Middle East to prevent, limit, and punish acts of terrorism; (5)
strengthening national and international law; (6) sponsoring in 1990 a joint Soviet-American simulation for high-ranking officials of the two countries in which
they would work together in response to a simulated terrorist crisis.

Participating Soviet and American intelligence veterans agreed that their respective services should exchange information about terrorism and suggested
that neither country should supply nongovernmental groups with weapons useful
to terrorists, such as plastic explosives or surface-to-air missiles. With regard to
hostage incidents, it was thought desirable that cooperation be expanded to include the regular exchange of information on Soviet and American citizens held
against their will, in particular, in the Middle East and Southeast Asia, and that
the necessary machinery be deployed to facilitate continuing communication and
cooperation in resolving future hostage crises. Consensus was recorded concern-

ing the advisability of augmenting the capacity of the already established U.S.-Soviet nuclear crisis control centers both to counter terrorist threats to use other weapons of mass destruction and to exchange reports and monitor terrorists' potential to use such weapons.

Endorsement was also voiced for joint efforts to restrict the laundering of drug money, to exchange information on the production, smuggling, and distribution of narcotics in Latin America and Southwest Asia, and to explore the feasibility of providing material and technical assistance to countries on the front line in combating drug production—notably, Peru and Colombia. Because the activities of terrorist organizations crucially depend on freedom of movement across borders and access to funds, the United States and the USSR were now called upon to institute measures to restrict the movement and financial operations of terrorist factions. In the Middle East, exchange of information was deemed vital in contributing to both preventive and reactive actions against terrorists. In the legal domain, the participants favored an international convention to prevent deliberate targeting of civilians by terrorists and a U.S.-Soviet bilateral agreement on extradition and/or prosecution, along with a series of diplomatic steps in the United Nations and elsewhere to promote international cooperation among law-enforcement agencies and strengthen international law sanctions against terrorism.

The "private" nature of the meeting was considered a plus in that a crucial role was assigned to public opinion in the wholesale mobilization of resources to wage the fight against the common enemy. Nevertheless, the participation of a contingent of retired intelligence officials lent a special air to the occasion and certainly enhanced the chances that the opinions expressed would be duly conveyed to those in charge of making the real decisions. The advantages of this type of mutual aid in designated cases were evident to the Soviet side. Indeed, a former KGB department head noted that valid precedent already existed in these matters and presumably proved rewarding to the principal parties. According to him:

> The Americans have applied to us to investigate certain episodes, specifically those connected with Lebanon, and to give them a hand, through the appropriate countries, Syria and Iran included, in having hostages released. Through the trips of the leaders of our state to certain regions, the U.S. included, we passed on information to American secret services, on terrorist organizations, on individual terrorists and on mafia operating in this or that region. So we've got a good record of working together.[80]

Similar matters featured on the agenda of the visit by U.S. Attorney-General Thornburgh to Moscow on October 15–19, 1989. The ensuing discussions singled out the various legal questions in which both parties were interested and determined the basis for further exchange of experience and cooperation between the U.S. Department of Justice and the USSR Ministry of Justice as well as several other Soviet agencies. Inter alia, a key spot was reserved for the USSR Ministry of Internal Affairs and the USSR KGB in any bid to draw up plans for a concerted offensive against the drug trade, organized crime, and terrorism.[81]

Soviet-American consultations held in Moscow on November 30–December 1, 1989, on the subject of cooperation in the war against drug trafficking and drug addiction were attended by representatives of the respective foreign ministries and other competent agencies (including, at the Soviet end, the ministries of Internal Affairs and Public Health, the KGB, and the Chief Administration of State Customs Control). The parties confirmed their desire to cultivate contacts for purposes of curbing the drug trade. The track record of cooperation per the terms of the January 1989 memorandum was reviewed and possible new projects discussed within the frame of that entente. An agreement was drafted between the customs services for collaboration and closer coordination of policies against drug smuggling. Arrangements were proposed for the respective law-enforcement offices to expand their liaisons; consider methods for interdicting the leakage of chemical substances used in manufacturing illegal drugs; add aspects of medical treatment to the original bill of fare; and exchange delegations to observe the performance of the corresponding departments on site.[82]

Fresh progress on this front was reported in 1990. Thus, in January,

> TASS quoted KGB Chairman Vladimir Kriuchkov as saying there could be joint U.S.-Soviet action in the future in world "hot spots." TASS quoted Kriuchkov as saying that in such cases the KGB and the CIA might exchange intelligence information to devise and carry out joint action. According to TASS, Kriuchkov told *Moscow News* that such actions would require that the two countries have a joint interest in lowering tension in the "hot spots." Kriuchkov said the KGB will expand its contacts with the CIA and other foreign secret services this year. TASS quoted him as saying the contacts will be aimed mainly at blocking terrorism, narcotics trafficking, and smuggling.[83]

A few weeks later, the media chronicled the effective signature of the previously announced interdepartmental agreement which laid out the legal groundwork for a joint struggle against the spread and smuggling of drugs and called for the exchange of information and technical know-how, concerted operations, and so forth.[84] At the meeting of Baker and Shevardnadze in May 1990, a "packed dialogue" took place regarding the fight against international terrorism, the prevention of illegal trade in drugs, and so forth.[85] And, descending for a moment from the penthouse to the ground floor, a news story published in August 1991 described how American and Soviet police jointly patrolled the streets of Khabarovsk as part of an experimental program between the state of Alaska and the Khabarovsk authorities to learn about each other's techniques for preserving law and order. Prior to that, a group of police officials from Khabarovsk had toured the United States.[86]

The sudden collapse of the Soviet Union gave only brief pause to these diverse pursuits. When Presidents Bush and Yeltsin met at Camp David and issued their declaration on new relations (February 1, 1992), the commitment to counter terrorism, fight against the drug trade, and prevent the deterioration of the natural environment figured prominently on the slate of principles which the two heads of state endorsed.[87] In September 1992, the press indicated that CIA director Robert M. Gates was scheduled to visit Moscow in the fall to discuss potential cooperation with Russia's Foreign Intelligence Service. No details of the mission were revealed then, but after the trip the U.S. Embassy in Moscow released a statement indicating that Russia and the United States might pool intelligence services and naming as likely targets the proliferation of nuclear weapons, terrorism, drug smuggling, and organized crime.

The reference to nuclear proliferation and organized crime in this connection suggested that the feasibility of a broader-based cooperation than in the past stretched to cover addenda of growing mutual concern was now being contemplated.[88] In short, the succession from Gorbachev to Yeltsin and from the USSR to the Russian Federation did nothing to dampen either side's proclaimed enthusiasm for the prospect of mounting a joint assault on certain types of criminal entrepreneurship that threatened their own welfare and the stability of the world system which both powers wanted to preserve.

The picture would not be complete without a look at a parallel development on the multilateral scene where analogous cares were at stake, to wit, the Soviet regime's momentous decision, after years of virulent hostility to Interpol, to become a member of that organization. The move was bound to affect Soviet-American dealings in this venue as well by opening an extra channel of communication to complement the bilateral route followed so far. The ostensible reason behind the dramatic reversal of Moscow's attitude toward this consortium—about whose intentions it had hitherto always expressed the deepest suspicions, sometimes not without just cause[89]—was the realization under the stimulus of the so-called "new thinking" that

> there was a need also to be aware of certain new phenomena in the activity of the bourgeois police. Although the police in any class-divided society represents a political weapon of the ruling class, it nevertheless retains another function which in the past had rather unjustifiably been left in the shadows. The objective capability of the bourgeois police to defend designated positions in the interests of the entire community likewise presumes the necessity of letting oneself be guided not by narrow class, but by general national coordinates. The struggle against common crime is a task of all states, everywhere it has the same criminogenic dimension. . . .
>
> In our times, peaceful coexistence in an interdependent world is able to create political conditions for safeguarding the future. The common human significance of the problem of the fight against crime is obvious, and attention to and engineering of international cooperation are both politically and practically incontestable. The decisive factor in this matter is the revolutionary restructuring of our way of life and our mode of thought.

Witness to that is the readiness of the Soviet Union to engage in dialogue apropos international cooperation on problems of the struggle against crime with all countries on a footing of equality.[90]

According to early reports, business was booming. In the initial five-month period after Interpol approved the USSR's application for admission, the corresponding Soviet national bureau received around four hundred inquiries and notices and itself sent out two hundred "packets of data." The size of the traffic was attributed primarily to the fact that international crime bosses were attracted by the fresh opportunities generated by Soviet domestic reforms including the emergence of cooperatives on the world market, the establishment of joint enterprises, and the simplification of the procedure for entry into and exit from the USSR, as well as the limitless appetite of the home market for goods and services in perennial short supply. All this spelled a veritable explosion in the number and scope of economic crimes: illegal manufacturing and commercial practices, money "laundering," financial scams, tax evasion, computer fraud, contraband. Terrorism and organized crime constituted a separate item to which top priority was attached in dealings with colleagues abroad.[91]

Soviet-American contacts produced some tangible results. For example, the Soviet Union surrendered to the United States a certain Felix Kolbovskii, prompting the USSR Deputy Minister of Internal Affairs, Vasilii Trushin, to comment that:

> Instances of surrender of foreign criminals in our repertory have up to now been an extremely rare occurrence. However, judging by everything, the situation is noticeably changing. The question of Kolbovskii was decided in just a few days. Through Interpol channels, we were contacted with a request for his surrender only last week. We were remitted the necessary documents, including papers confirming that a warrant for the arrest of Felix Kolbovskii, citizen of the United States, had been issued, signed by the district judge of the city of St. Louis. Kolbovskii is accused of commercial fraud and misrepresentation.[92]

Armed with a permanent visa, the suspect had visited the Soviet Union regularly. His possession of the special entry permit, which few people were privileged to have, was explained by the fact that Kolbovskii headed a joint project in the USSR. His entrepreneurial activities on the local scene had already drawn the attention of the KGB, which had no difficulty pinpointing his whereabouts in Moscow. "After concerting with the USSR Procuracy, he was quickly arrested and handed over to officials in the U.S. embassy."

The story has a sequel:

> The festive mood was somewhat spoiled by a letter of thanks received from the U.S. embassy. Rather by its ending. Expressing their gratitude to the Soviet Interpol agents' contribution to the struggle against international crime, the diplomats said, nevertheless, that the U.S. authorities still could not guarantee

Soviets the extradition of requested Soviet citizens in the absence of a bilateral agreement.[93]

Notwithstanding the caveat, such favors have been returned. For instance, an inquiry was received from the United States concerning the identity of a certain Soviet citizen of Armenian origin who was being detained on charges of illegally entering the United States from Mexico. Officials in Moscow established that the man had logged four previous convictions in the USSR. Since he was in possession of a Soviet passport, the Americans shipped him back to the USSR.[94]

By local estimate, during its first six months of operation Interpol's national bureau in Moscow had processed about 1,800 inquiries—an average of three hundred per month or ten daily. The figure included both incoming and outgoing inquiries, Germany's share being the largest, followed by Austria, France, Britain, Finland, Sweden, the United States, and Poland, among others.[95] Reports for all of 1991 indicated that more than four thousand inquiries had been received by the bureau and as many had been dispatched to other countries. Incoming requests dealt with stolen cars, art theft, personal data (not necessarily of a criminal nature), drugs, forged documents, and counterfeit money. Locating relatives in the USSR was another service often provided.[96]

The transition from the USSR to the Russian Federation did not diminish Moscow's enthusiasm for the new partnership. The mass media continued to give Interpol high marks for its assistance in the battle against crime in Russia, crediting its help with bringing to light 217 thefts of motor vehicles, 149 economic crimes, 89 cases of currency counterfeiting and forgery of documents, 55 cases of illegal trade in drugs, and 52 thefts of cultural treasures and weapons.[97] For its part, the Russian bureau was praised for helping uncover many dangerous crimes of a transnational character: 10 killings, 71 thefts, 43 forgeries of documents, and 219 economic crimes. Using data furnished by Interpol, the bureau had confirmed the presence on Russian territory of 578 individuals suspected of having committed crimes and identified 28 missing persons.[98]

The Interpol "cachet" lent further impetus to the development of bilateral liaisons between Russian law-enforcement agencies and their counterparts abroad, especially vis-à-vis Austria, Belgium, Great Britain, Hungary, Germany, Poland, the United States, Turkey, Finland, Sweden, and Czechoslovakia. By mid-1992, close working relations had been established with the ministries of internal affairs of Germany, Hungary, Italy, Cyprus, Poland, France and other countries. Agreements on cooperation had been signed with the Ministry of Public Security of China and the ministries of internal affairs of Bulgaria, Mongolia, Czechoslovakia, and Finland. Such contacts with various branches of the justice apparatus in the United States were also said to be expanding satisfactorily.[99]

* * *

Assorted subjective and objective factors account for the genesis and subsequent development of this package of joint ventures.

1. A paramount consideration for the Soviet leadership in promoting this scheme was the quality of legitimization that accrued to the successor regime as a result of such association. Material signs of willingness to cooperate with the Soviet Union in the legal domain, especially the field of criminal justice, afforded proof that the reform team had won its spurs and was fit to be treated as an equal by the "elite" of international society. Here, American and Soviet views happened to coincide, in that Washington was eager to bolster what it perceived as a healthy trend toward a democratic ethos on the Soviet civic scene, and by bestowing upon the Gorbachev team that sort of accolade could enhance their stature at home and abroad and commensurately boost their political effectiveness, particularly in pursuing goals considered desirable on this side of the Atlantic.

2. Several of the documents intended to establish the shape of the fledgling Commonwealth of Independent States listed among the targets of the proposed consortium the need to operate a common legal space in order to ensure proper crime control within the territorial expanse of the former USSR. Russia likes to see itself as the cornerstone of that edifice. The Russian national central bureau, claiming to have assumed the persona of the national central bureau of Interpol in the USSR, has cooperated with the police services of the other countries of the CIS and the Baltic region (Lithuania has joined Interpol on its own), offered to represent their interests in the organization, and recommended that they assign liaison officers to the central headquarters or establish local branch offices.[100] At a meeting on April 24, 1992, in Alma-Ata, the ministries of internal affairs of eleven former union republics at the behest of their respective governments concluded an agreement on cooperation in the struggle against crime, and while many hurdles remain to be overcome before such collaboration can be pronounced a real success, all concur that the occasion marked a step in the right direction.[101]

Foreign recognition of Russia's role in these matters inevitably strengthened its premier status in the Commonwealth boardroom and gave it added authority in bidding to reknit close ties for purposes of collectively manning a viable defense perimeter in the face of increasing attacks by the enemies of law and order. Again, the United States shares the same concerns inasmuch as it wishes to stabilize the situation in this part of the world and prevent its slide into possible anarchy and prefers to deal through a main office rather than a dozen or more outposts. To the extent that Russia alone seems capable of presiding over this type of corporate enterprise, the decision to highlight its international reputation makes good sense as a way of improving its standing in the national league. The prospect of this vast geopolitical region splintering into so many competing fiefdoms that the criminal element would always be able to find sanctuary in some enclave whose chieftain wanted to flaunt his sovereign independence vis-à-vis his neighbors, is indeed chilling. Even a loose and imperfect association striving to exert a modicum of control over access to such immunity might offer relief from the kind of pain that "tribal" egotism is otherwise sure to inflict on all the parties engaged in this perverse game of one-upmanship.

3. On a more practical note, bitter experience has already demonstrated to the Soviet leadership, and its Russian heir, that certain brands of crime can be curbed only when the affected parties agree to act in unison to contain the infection. The phenomenon of air piracy may be cited as an example. From 1974 to 1990, seventy attempts to seize and hijack Soviet aircraft were recorded: fifty-eight were cut short, but in twelve cases the offenders did manage to divert the planes abroad. During that same period, ninety-five criminals were arrested and fourteen terrorists killed on board.[102] Violence by hijackers in the air and on the ground caused the death of 120 persons and the wounding of more than 200.[103] In just a one-month stretch in the summer of 1990, ten Aeroflot planes flying domestic schedules within the Soviet Union were hijacked and half the culprits made it successfully out of the country.[104]

Faced with a rash of incidents that threatened their own safety, the "host" countries began in 1990 to take a tougher attitude toward these uninvited "guests" and either filed criminal charges against them or, in a radical departure from past precedent when the normal tendency was to look at these people as political refugees, now opted to return them to the home authorities.[105] The growing reluctance to shield such "fugitives" from the Soviet Union and the bid to enlist the deterrent power of a jail sentence, whether pronounced by their courts or by those of the USSR in case of eventual rendition, did not immediately halt the epidemic. In 1990–91, thirty-seven attempts to hijack planes were reported; in twenty-seven instances, the would-be hijackers were disarmed. Seven perpetrators were returned to the USSR; one was sentenced in Sweden; and Pakistan was still investigating the so-called "Yakut hijacking" committed by a bandit group.[106] The wave crested then and the realization that the "joyride" was likely to lead to an unpleasant denouement seems to have discouraged further resort to this escape route.

International cooperation doubtless proved its value here. The Soviet regime could not but be pleased that the safety of its air traffic was rescued and, even if the need to rely on outsiders to achieve these results hurt its pride, the lessons of increased global interdependence whose writ did not exempt the USSR were not lost on Moscow. The realization applies to other areas as well. Soviet spokesmen expressed worry about the emergent alliance between terrorists of every stripe and traders in drugs and weapons. Around four hundred terrorist organizations and extremist factions were estimated to be operating on Soviet soil by mid-1991. Illegal armed detachments reportedly numbered thirty thousand men. In 1990–91 alone, there were two hundred explosions in which fifty people were killed and one hundred thirty wounded.[107]

The United States, too, has a major stake in protecting the lives of Americans in the Soviet successor states, including the expanding community of business-men, investors, and field personnel hunting for economic opportunities in the postcommunist marketplace. Contributing to making this environment more se-cure for American nationals means, inter alia, lending technical assistance to local law-enforcement agencies in order to upgrade the quality of their profes-sional performance. Crimes against foreigners are on the rise on the premises of the late USSR and the prognosis is that the trend will not only continue, but get worse. In a recent well-publicized episode of abduction of an Australian couple and demand for ransom from the victims' American relatives, the FBI literally walked its Russian counterpart through the procedures for dealing with kidnap-pers until the extortionists were captured and their hostages released un-harmed.[108] Like episodes will certainly occur and the pooling of police resources may indeed represent the best line of defense against such outrages.

4. Warranted fears were also expressed in Western Europe and North Amer-ica that the former Soviet lands might become a prime corridor for drug traffic. Soviet sources insisted that the USSR was never an arena for international drug operations, but did concede that the volume of cross-border drug smuggling and transit had recently posted a sizable jump. In addition to the traditional countries of origin—Hungary and Afghanistan—new suppliers had entered the picture, namely, North Korea, Romania, Vietnam, and Iran. Polish, German, and Aus-trian drug barons were reportedly pushing to forge a "Soviet Connection."[109] Of course, the territory of the former USSR is itself rich in the raw materials of drug production. While a powerful central apparatus existed, an effective war was waged against the harvesting and processing of these ingredients and those ef-forts had been stepped up once glasnost' revealed the true dimensions of the problem. In early 1990, for instance, the head of the USSR Ministry of Internal Affairs antidrug administration, Aleksandr Kotliarov, told the newspaper *Sovet-skaia Rossiia* that Moscow was currently setting up an interagency body to coordinate the fight against drug trafficking.

> Kotliarov said this step was needed, otherwise the Soviet Union might soon become one of the world's main drug exporters. According to Genrikh Khmel', an official of the Main Administration for State Customs Control of the USSR Council of Ministers, foreign drug dealers are already trying to establish themselves inside the Soviet Union, and Moscow is grateful for the cooperation it is receiving from other governments in combating this develop-ment. On February 22, Soviet Deputy Foreign Minister Viktor Komplektov said drugs were entering the USSR from Afghanistan and Pakistan.[110]

However, since the demise of the USSR the local and national antidrug agen-cies have had to go their separate ways and trust to their own devices and, as a consequence, their ability to restrain the flow has been quite limited.[111] Today, nobody disputes that East and West share an interest in fighting together against narcotics trafficking and organized crime, particularly when the East European hinterland's potential as a pipeline for pumping drugs from the Far East and Latin America into Western Europe and beyond is so obvious. Some working contacts have in fact been established here, albeit on a small scale. Thus:

> In return for training and equipment, East European police have been able to furnish the West with dossiers on local criminals who have taken advantage of new freedoms to expand their activities into Western Europe and the United States.
> The Russian police have been particularly helpful in providing U.S. agents with information on ethnic Russian gangs involved in drug smuggling and racketeering in New York and Los Angeles.[112]

As the USSR's fabric continues to unravel, much more must be done if hopes to stem the toxic tide by means of concerted East-West action are to weather the travails of an increasingly fragmented political map spanning a huge region, large segments of which are fast descending into utter chaos.

5. Nor should one forget that the dramatic events on the Soviet (Russian) civic scene have had a noticeable impact abroad as well, including the culture of the criminal community and its American offshoot. As *The New York Times* has reported:

> Exploiting the relaxation of travel restrictions in the former Soviet Union, émigré criminals in the United States have begun importing con artists, extortionists and hired murderers who carry out contract crimes for small sums of money and then disappear back home. . . .
> The intercontinental criminal traffic is the most striking way in which a small but violent underworld of émigré criminals has evolved to take advantage of the breakup of the Soviet Union. And although no one can know the extent of the crime, law-enforcement officials in New York and Los Angeles say they are starting to see evidence of such joint ventures in crime. . . .
> The traffic is two-way. The émigrés have also responded to the demise of travel restrictions and the hunger for free enterprise by returning to do business, and run swindles, in their former homelands. . . .[113]

The competent departments on both sides of the ocean have sought to adjust to this mobility by exchanging services designed to help block escape routes. Fleeing to the former Soviet lands or to Eastern Europe is not a foolproof refuge from the law since the very same collapse of communism that opened the door to these criminal liaisons also eliminated the barriers that once prevented law-enforcement cooperation. In one case, for instance, the Russian government reportedly sent a representative to the United States to seek help in prosecuting an émigré charged with defrauding the city of Sochi out of 10.2 million rubles in a business deal. It is hard to tell whether this is a typical sample of the kind of contacts that are being established in this sphere, but mutual aid of this sort is bound to become a staple feature of Russian-American relations if the trend toward further rapprochement between the two countries proceeds at its present pace. Gradually, of course, such practice will cease being treated as a piece of exotica and convert from an ad hoc to an institutional footing to ensure that the mechanism intended to benefit both parties will function in a smooth and efficient manner.

6. In the debit column, the record suggests that the rapport recently achieved in the matter of tracking down war criminals and bringing them to justice may now be seriously jeopardized by the downfall of the Soviet system. None of the successor regimes, in my opinion, has a comparable interest in prosecuting its own people implicated in mass atrocities during the Second World War. Indeed, many of the new states are currently prey to the kind of rabid anticommunist and anti-Semitic sentiments that impart to Nazi collaborators and members of the nationalist lunatic fringe the cachet of folk heroes whose behavior, even if admittedly a trifle "unorthodox," is retrospectively excused by the fact that they pursued the supreme goal of liberating their native land. In the Baltic states, Ukraine, and Belarus, history is being rewritten in that mode. Russia has more important preoccupations, and the rest of the former USSR does not really care about those issues. Ironically, just as the United States was poised to drop its objections to cooperating with the Soviet authorities in this sector, the Soviet partner went out of business and the whole operation may well lapse by default.

Notes

1. See G. Ginsburgs, *The Soviet Union and International Cooperation in Legal Matters*, Part 2: Civil Law, Dordrecht/Boston/London 1992, pp. 33–35.

2. M. Gorbachev, *Realities and Guarantees for a Secure World*, Moscow 1987, p. 13.

3. A. Adamishin, "Legal, Humanitarian and Consular Aspects of International Security." *International Affairs*, 1988, no. 10, p. 47. In similar vein, V.M. Vasev, head of the department for work with embassies of the Ministry of Foreign Affairs of Russia, in calling for a highly professional diplomatic service and discussing the manner of achieving those goals, lists among the entries on his agenda under the "functions" heading the "preparation of proposals for perfecting Russian legislation with an eye to its correspondence to the international law obligations of Russia." *Diplomaticheskii vestnik*, 1992, no. 1, pp. 30–33, at 31.

4. Interview with V.F. Petrovskii, *JPRS-UIA–89–017*, November 13, 1989, p. 4.

5. Cf., S. Pomorski, "Communists and Their Criminal Law Revisited," *Law and Social Inquiry*, 1989, no. 3, pp. 581–601. Note, for instance, the order of the USSR President of May 21, 1991, entitled "On measures to bring Soviet legislation in accord with the obligations of the USSR stemming from documents of the All-European process," which, inter alia, instructed the USSR Ministry of Foreign Affairs to prepare within two weeks proposals for the removal of reservations relating to the Convention against Torture and Other Cruel, Inhuman or Degrading Treatment or Punishment. In that connection, the ministry was also directed to submit to the USSR Supreme Soviet materials that would allow in the course of preparing the drafts of the Bases of criminal legislation and criminal procedure of the USSR and union republics to take into account the international obligations of the USSR concerning the prohibition of torture and other cruel, inhuman, or degrading treatment or punishment. Simultaneously, a recommendation was issued to the USSR Procuracy and the USSR Supreme Court, acting in concert with the USSR Minis-

tries of Justice and Foreign Affairs, to prepare and submit to the USSR Supreme Soviet within two months a bill calling for the punishment of persons guilty of inflicting torture and other cruel, inhuman or degrading treatment. *Ved. SSSR*, 1991, no. 22, Art. 648.

6. A. Zagorsky, Yu. Kashlev, "The Human Dimension of Politics," *International Affairs*, 1990, no. 3, p. 65.

7. Interview with A. Iakovlev, in *Literaturnaia gazeta*, February 1, 1989, p. 10.

8. V. Savitskii, "Pervoosnova—chelovek i ego prava," *Obshchestvennye nauki*, 1990, no. 1, pp. 8–9.

9. "The Foreign Policy and Diplomatic Activity of the USSR (April 1985–October 1989)," *International Affairs*, 1990, no. 1, p. 43.

10. Zagorsky, Kashlev, *op. cit.*, note 6, p. 65.

11. "International Control? Can Soviet people appeal to international organizations in case their rights are infringed upon?" *New Times*, 1989, no. 4, pp. 19–30; Adamishin, *op. cit.*, note 3, p. 47. See, too, the discussion by A.V. Reznik, "Formirovanie evropeiskogo pravovogo prostranstva (nekotorye problemy)," *Sovetskii zhurnal mezhdunarodnogo prava*, 1991, no. 1, pp. 45–49, of the concept of appeal to supranational judicial instances in the context of the European continent, especially within the emergent institutional framework of the Conference on Security and Cooperation in Europe.

12. For a good review of the process of elaboration of an array of international norms and recommendations enunciating standards intended to govern state practice in the fields of criminal law, criminal procedure, and penitentiary law, see E.G. Liakhov, "Razrabotka i osushchestvlenie mezhdunarodnykh norm i standartov v oblasti ugolovnoi iustitsii," *Sovetskii zhurnal mezhdunarodnogo prava*, 1991, no. 1, pp. 64–74. The author is somewhat critical of the current record on the grounds, inter alia, that many of the so-called "codes" and "digests of principles" prescribe desiderata that do not take realistic account of the existing level of state culture in these matters and all too often express the civic ethos of particular states at the expense of others with a different value system.

13. *New York Times*, October 16, 1970, pp. 1, 8, 9; October 17, 1970, p. 2.

14. E.g., V. Chkhikvadze *et al.*, "Etogo trebuiut i sovest, i pravo," *Pravda*, October 25, 1970; M. Lazarev, Iu. Kolosov, "Vopreki mezhdunarodnomu pravu," *Izvestiia*, October 24, 1970.

15. *New York Times*, September 16, 1972, p. 2.

16. *Ibid.*, June 28, 1976, p. 19; July 1, 1976, p. 13; July 11, 1976, p. 7; July 12, 1976, p. A2; November 23, 1983, p. A8.

17. *Soviet News*, 1976, no. 5842, p. 272; *New Times*, 1976, no. 30, p. 2.

18. *New York Times*, January 4, 1973, p. 74C. The Brazinskases were tried in absentia by the Supreme Court of the Georgian SSR. The elder Brazinskas was sentenced to death; the younger—to 10 years' imprisonment, out of consideration that "he committed the crime when he was underage," i.e., 19. N. Bazhenov, "No forgiveness for terrorists," *New Times*, 1987, no. 34, pp. 22–23.

19. Cf., *Pravda*, September 19, 1976; *New York Times*, September 19, 1976, p. 7, and April 17, 1977, p. 41; *Soviet News*, 1977, no. 5878, p. 138, no. 5580, p. 151, no. 5903, p. 368, and no. 5904, p. 376; *Izvestiia*, October 23, 1977.

20. *New York Times*, May 14, 1977, p. 3.

21. *Soviet News*, 1978, no. 5921, p. 83.

22. *Ibid.*, 1978, no. 5940, p. 270, and no. 5942, p. 288.

23. *Izvestiia*, December 18, 1979, and February 13, 1981; *Pravda*, February 12, 1981; B. Bannov, "Kak v Amerike zashchishchaiut vozdushnykh piratov," *Chelovek i zakon*, 1981, no. 9, pp. 91–96; *Soviet News*, 1985, no. 6296, p. 372; *New Times*, 1987, no. 34, pp. 22–23; *Vestnik Ministerstva Inostrannykh Del SSSR*, 1987, no. 1, p. 49, and 1988, no. 12, pp. 60, 61.

24. *New York Times*, May 28, 1989, p. 12. Back in 1976, a Soviet pilot flew his MiG–25 to Japan. While there was a flap over the delay in the return of the plane to the Soviet Union, the pilot's status caused less controversy because the defection had entailed no use of violence. The pilot promptly found asylum in the United States. The political atmosphere at the time, plus the absence of the usual attributes of a hijacking where the life and health of others are jeopardized in the process, distinguishes the handling of the Belenkov and Zuev cases.

25. *Vestnik*, note 23 above, 1989, no. 11, p. 63.

26. *Pravda*, June 22, 1990.

27. See, *Soviet Weekly*, August 2, 1990, p. 7.

28. *Izvestiia*, August 27, 1990.

29. *Literaturnaia gazeta*, July 18, 1990, p. 9; G. Lomanov, "Terrorist na bortu," *Pravitel'stvennyi vestnik*, 1990, no. 28, p. 12.

30. *Vneshniaia politika Sovetskogo Soiuza v period Otechestvennoi voiny*, Moscow 1944, Vol. 1, pp. 276–77.

31. I.V. Stalin, *O Velikoi Otechestvennoi voine Sovetskogo Soiuza*, Moscow 1950, p. 125.

32. Declaration on the punishment for crimes committed in the course of the war of January 13, 1942, signed by Czechoslovakia, Poland, Yugoslavia, Norway, Greece, Belgium, Luxembourg and the Free French; the Declaration on the responsibility of the Hitlerites for the atrocities committed by them, published by the Moscow Conference of Three Ministers of October 30, 1943. See, O.E. Polents, *Mezhdunarodnoe pravo* (E.A. Korovin ed.), Moscow 1951, pp. 254–55, and V.I. Lisovskii, *ibid.*, pp. 548–50. *Vneshniaia politika . . .*, note 30, pp. 363–64.

33. Polents, *op. cit.*, note 32, p. 255. See, too, N.A. Bazhenov, "Nerushimost printsipov Niurnberga i sotrudnichestvo gosudarstv v presledovanii natsistskikh voennykh prestupnikov," *Uroki Niurnberga*, Materialy Mezhdunarodnoi konferentsii, Moscow, November 11–13, 1986 (Doklady uchastnikov konferentsii), Moscow 1988, vol. 3, pp. 11–20; R.M. Valeev, "Niurnbergskie printsipy i voprosy vydachi lits, sovershivshikh prestupleniia protiv chelovechestva," *ibid.*, Moscow 1986, vol. 1, pp. 149–67.

34. The gist of the Soviet position here is that "rendition is an indispensable instrument both for the trial of already unmasked war criminals and for their detection. However, for the rendition of war criminals there must be set conditions substantially different from those which constitute the institution of rendition of criminals in the context of normal relations between states. The guarantees which are absolutely indispensable in normal conditions of peacetime and normal relations between states cannot be applied in respect to persons who have eternally covered themselves with shame through crimes the cruelty of which does not lend itself to description." N.N. Polianskii, *Mezhdunarodnoe pravosudie i prestupniki voiny*, Moscow 1945, p. 106. In legal terms, this translates into the postulate that: "The duty to surrender persons who committed crimes against humanity exists independently of the existence between states of conventions and bilateral treaties on rendition. This reflects one of the particularities of the application of the institution of rendition to the given category of crimes." Valeev, *op. cit.*, note 33, p. 157. See, too, Gy. Haraszti, "The Right of Asylum," *Acta Juridica* (Budapest), 1960, fasc. 3–4, pp. 372–73.

35. Polents, *op. cit.*, note 32, pp. 251, 253, 254. Likewise, P.S. Romashkin, *Prestupleniia protiv mira i chelovechestva*, Moscow 1967, pp. 256–57.

36. See, A.Ia. Vyshinskii, *Voprosy mezhdunarodnogo prava i mezhdunarodnoi politiki*, Moscow 1949, p. 370. In the same vein, Valeev, *op. cit.*, note 33, p. 157: "To persons who committed crimes against humanity likewise do not extend the principles of non-rendition of one's own citizens and political offenders."

37. Polents, *op. cit.*, note 32, p. 255. Bear in mind that on July 29, 1943, the Soviet government had already taken the initiative of instructing the Soviet envoys to Turkey and Sweden to furnish the latter with the text of the notes in which it called on the neutral countries to refuse sanctuary to war criminals and let it be known that the Soviet government would consider the granting of asylum, assistance, and succor to such persons as a violation of the principles for which the United Nations were fighting. *Vneshniaia politika* . . . , note 30, p. 348.

38. I.P. Trainin, V.E. Grabar, N.N. Polianskii, A.N. Trainin, V.N. Durdenevskii, D.B. Levin, "Ugolovnaia otvetstvennost prestupnikov voiny," *Sotsialisticheskaia zakonnost'*, 1945, no. 6, p. 10. In similar vein, N.T. Samartseva, *Mezhdunarodnoe pravo* (D.B. Levin, G.P. Kaliuzhnaia eds.), Moscow 1964, pp. 168–69; F.I. Kozhevnikov, *Kurs mezhdunarodnogo prava* (F.I. Kozhevnikov ed.), 3rd ed., Moscow 1972, p. 381.

39. Samartseva, *op. cit.*, note 38, p. 211. Likewise, N.T. Blatova, *Mezhdunarodnoe pravo* (L.A. Modzhorian, N.T. Blatova eds.), Moscow 1970, p. 277: "War criminals are not entitled to the right of asylum . . .—that is a universally recognized rule of contemporary international law."

40. Samartseva, *op. cit.*, note 38, p. 212.

41. Cf. F.I. Kozhevnikov, V.A. Romanov, *Kurs mezhdunarodnogo prava* (F.I. Kozhevnikov ed.), 2nd ed., Moscow 1966, p. 633. Also D.B. Levin, G.I. Tunkin, *Mezhdunarodnoe pravo* (G.I. Tunkin ed.), Moscow 1974, pp. 572–73; A.A. Urban, *Bez sroka davnosti (O natsistskikh voennykh prestupnikakh i ikh pokroviteliakh)*, Moscow, Izd. "Znanie," seriia "Mezhdunarodnaia," 9/1989. As recently as 1987, for example, the Ukrainian News Agency (RATAU) issued a statement in Kiev in connection with the International Day in Memory of Victims of Fascism, marked that year on September 13, which noted, inter alia, that the "people of the Ukraine adopted appeals to the governments of the United States, Canada, Britain, Australia, West Germany and Costa Rica asking them to extradite Nazi butchers staying in those countries to the Soviet Union." *Soviet News*, 1987, no. 6392, p. 333.

42. Samartseva, *op. cit.*, note 38, p. 172. Blatova, *op. cit.*, note 39, p. 279, reproduces the statement with the substitution of "socialist countries" for "the Soviet Union."

43. *International Law*, Moscow 1990, p. 216. Heavy reliance is placed in this connection on the Universal Declaration of Human Rights (1948) and the 1967 General Assembly Declaration on territorial asylum, which calls for denying asylum to "persons concerning whom there are serious reasons to believe that they have committed crimes against peace, war crimes or crimes against humanity."

44. For a typical sample, see M. Rogov, "Ukryvatel'stvo natsistskikh voennykh prestupnikov—politika SShA," *Sotsialisticheskaia zakonnost'*, 1985, no. 5, pp. 21–24. The author, identified as member of the collegium of the USSR Procurator's Office, after reviewing the American track record in these matters, concludes that "the obvious indifference of the U.S. authorities toward unmasking and punishing Nazi war criminals leaves no doubt on all counts" (p. 24).

45. "War Criminals Must Be Brought to Book," *New Times*, 1985, no. 35, p. 19. Lev Bezymensky's interview with Natalia Kolesnikova of the USSR Procurator's Office.

46. A.K. and B.A. Martynenko, "K voprosu o posledstviiakh ispolzovaniia natsistskikh voennykh prestupnikov pravitel'stvennymi organami SShA v poslevoennoi politiki antikommunizma," *Voprosy novoi i noveishei istorii* (Kiev), 1990, vyp. 36, p. 38.

47. "War Criminals . . . ," note 45, p. 19. The interviewee critically notes (p. 20): "According to available information, of the 144 persons evidence against whom had been submitted to the special investigation division only 10 have been deprived of U.S. citizenship. Seven have died without having been called to account. Thus, it is quite clear that the U.S. authorities are not interested in exposing and punishing nazi war criminals."

48. L. Bezymensky, "Absolution for War Criminals? No!" *New Times*, 1984, no. 6, p. 11.

49. Stuart Taylor Jr., "The Hunt for Nazis Shifts into 'High Gear,' " *New York Times*, September 23, 1984, p. E3.

50. Allan A. Ryan Jr., "Chernenko Deserves to Be at Normandy," *New York Times*, June 5, 1984, p. A27. According to U.S. Attorney General Benjamin R. Civiletti, a commitment to that effect had been extracted by him from Lev Smirnov, chairman of the Soviet Supreme Court, on October 11, 1979, in Washington. Smirnov promised that his government would do "whatever the United States felt was necessary to locate, investigate and deport proven participants in the Nazi atrocities." At the time, Civiletti mentioned the cases of Serhij Kowalczuk of Philadelphia, a Ukrainian policeman who allegedly commanded a squad that massacred 5,000 Jews, and Ivan Demjanjuk of Cleveland, "who allegedly ran the diesel engines in Treblinka which gassed hundreds of thousands of Jews." *New York Times*, November 8, 1979, p. B19. In connection with the 1980 agreement, "Soviet prosecutors have expressed willingness to permit Soviet witnesses to testify in American courts against former Nazi collaborators, providing the witnesses are healthy enough to travel and are willing to go. . . . The Russians had also agreed to allow lawyers to take testimony and cross-examine witnesses in the Soviet Union, and to videotape the proceedings for use in actions aimed at stripping the alleged collaborators of their American citizenship and possibly deporting them." *New York Times*, February 6, 1980, p. A4.

51. "No Minor Cases for U.S. Nazi-Hunter," *New York Times*, July 16, 1983, p. 4. For more on the OSI and its first director, A.A. Ryan Jr., see David O'Reilly, "He labels U.S. a refuge of Nazis," *Philadelphia Inquirer*, April 16, 1985, pp. 1-D, 10-D.

52. *New York Times*, April 6, 1983, p. B2; January 17, 1984, p. A16; March 1, 1984, p. A19.

53. A woman from Queens, Hermine Braunsteiner Ryan, was denaturalized in 1971 for selecting prisoners to be slain at the Maidanek death camp near Lublin, Poland. She was extradited to West Germany in 1973. In Bonn, she was convicted of murder and sentenced to life imprisonment.

54. *New York Times*, February 25, 1983, p. A15; December 23, 1984, p. 12; June 20, 1986, p. A2; July 28, 1987, p. A3.

55. "War Criminals . . . ," note 45, p. 20.

56. *New York Times*, May 9, 1986, p. B5; December 2, 1986, p. B4; March 6, 1987, p. A32; March 16, 1987, p. D11; April 2, 1987, pp. B1, B8; April 6, 1987, p. B6; April 7, 1987, p. B2; April 21, 1987, pp. A1, A25; April 22, 1987, p. A12; April 24, 1987, p. A6; May 14, 1987, p. A8; June 4, 1987, p. A17; July 3, 1987, P. A2.

57. Bazhenov, *op. cit.*, note 18, p. 23.

58. *New York Times*, April 7, 1987, p. B2; April 24, 1987, p. A6. The head of the OSI then indicated that the United States had a request pending with the West German government to send Schellong there. The Soviet Union had apparently expressed no interest so far.

59. "War Criminals . . . ," note 45, p. 20.

60. *New York Times*, September 19, 1985, p. B14; April 24, 1987, p. A6; October 15, 1988, p. 4; October 30, 1988, p. 9.

61. *Ibid.*, April 24, 1987, p. A6.

62. E.g., K.B. Noble, "Lobbying the Office that Hunts Nazi Suspects," *New York Times*, March 3, 1987, p. A20.

63. "The U.S. Was a Haven for Nazi War Criminals," *New York Times*, April 26, 1987, p. 2E. Interview with Allan A. Ryan Jr.

64. "War Criminals . . . ," note 45, p. 20.

65. *New York Times*, November 22, 1985, p. A20; February 25, 1986, p. A24; July 28,

1987, p. A3; July 6, 1992, p. A9. For a rare Soviet comment on the Demjanjuk case, see B. Piliatskin, "Kamen skorbi, simvol pamiati," *Izvestiia*, April 18, 1992.

66. *Vestnik*, note 23, 1988, no. 7, p. 57.
67. RL 371/88 (August 19, 1998), p. 11.
68. *Vestnik*, note 23, 1988, no. 18, p. 18.
69. A. Liutyi, "Krug suzhaetsia," *Pravda*, March 1, 1989.
70. *Sotsialisticheskaia zakonnost'*, 1990, no. 1, p. 69. See, too, Ph. Shenon, "East Berlin Opens Nazi Files to U.S.," *New York Times*, May 20, 1990, p. 15.
71. *Vestnik*, note 23, 1988, no. 10, pp. 18–19.
72. *Ibid.*, 1989, no. 1, pp. 55–56; 1989, no. 9, p. 38.
73. *Soviet News*, 1989, no. 6492, p. 303.
74. B. Mikhailov, in *Chelovek i zakon*, 1991, no. 2, pp. 56–60, at 58, adds Canada and Italy and also notes that interdepartmental agreements are being signed to "concretize" the mechanism of interstate cooperation here.
75. *Vestnik*, note 23, 1990, no. 4, pp. 41–47, at 45.
76. *Soviet News*, 1989, no. 6457, p. 5.
77. *New York Times*, April 7, 1989, p. A6.
78. *Ibid.*, August 7, 1989, p. A5.
79. *Ibid.*, October 8, 1989, p. 4. *American Journal of International Law*, 1989, no. 2, p. 457.
80. "Professionals talking shop, KGB and CIA: a joint answer to terrorism?" *New Times*, 1989, no. 43, pp. 34–35. Interview by G. Sidorova of Lieutenant-General Fedor Shcherbak (Ret.). See, too, *Report on the USSR*, 1989, no. 40, p. 35, and A. Shalnev, "Protiv terrorizma—vmeste," *Izvestiia*, October 3, 1989.
81. Cf., *Sotsialisticheskaia zakonnost'*, 1990, no. 1, p. 69; and *Chelovek i zakon*, 1990, no. 1, pp. 77–80.
82. *Vestnik*, note 23, 1989, no. 24, pp. 76–77; "Protiv narkotikov—soobshcha," *Izvestiia*, December 3, 1989.
83. *Report on the USSR*, 1990, no. 2, p. 33.
84. A. Blinov, "SSSR—SShA: Vmeste protiv narkotikov," *Izvestiia*, February 2, 1990.
85. Press conference by E.A. Shevardnadze and J. Baker, *Izvestiia*, May 20, 1990.
86. *Pravda*, August 6, 1991.
87. *Diplomaticheskii vestnik*, 1992, no. 4–5, p. 12.
88. *New York Times*, September 10, 1992, p. A10, and October 19, 1992, p. A6; *International Herald Tribune*, October 19, 1992, p. 2. However, in an OpEd piece, Nancy Lubin, "Central Asia's Drug Bazaar," *New York Times*, November 16, 1992, paints a much bleaker picture of the situation as regards U.S.-Russian cooperation. "Congressional sources have advised that, as of last summer, no one in the State Department's Bureau of International Narcotics Matters was assigned full time to the former Soviet Union, let alone Central Asia, and that agreements involving cooperation in fighting drug trafficking had focused on Russia and the western republics and been largely devoid of substance."
89. Alan Riding, "Interpol Regrets Shady Past, Vows Better Future," *New York Times*, February 22, 1990, p. A4. The piece correctly notes, for instance, that there were "certain truths about its submission to the Nazi authorities during World War II and its later refusal to pursue war criminals that Interpol preferred to camouflage behind the rule that it must avoid all involvement in politics."
90. Ia.M. Belson, *Interpol v borbe s ugolovnoi prestupnostiu*, Moscow 1989, pp. 236–37. For official contacts preceding the Soviet entry into Interpol, see Iu. Kovalenko, "Vstupaem v 'Interpol'," *Izvestiia*, December 27, 1989; A. Urvantsev, "Vstupim v Interpol?" *Pravda*, March 2, 1990; *Soviet News*, 1990, no. 6516, p. 81. Also, *Pravitel'stvennyi*

vestnik, 1990, no. 16, p. 3, on the resolution of the USSR Council of Ministers concerning the USSR's entry into Interpol, and interview with V.V. Bakatin, USSR Minister of Internal Affairs, on the occasion of the USSR's admission to Interpol at the 59th session of its General Assembly, Ottawa, Canada, September–October 1990, *Pravda*, October 7, 1990.

91. "Mech Interpola," *Pravda*, February 16, 1991

92. *Izvestiia*, March 13, 1991.

93. *Ibid.*

94. *Ibid.* See also: V. Kiselyov, "The gentlemen from Interpol live in a computerized paradise south-east of Moscow but catch criminals with bare hands," *Moscow News*, 1991, no. 31, p. 15; A. Liutyi, "Ostap Bender pozavidoval by," *Pravda*, April 6, 1991. The fact that the Soviet Union had signed only a handful of extradition treaties in its lifetime was now perceived as a major handicap to the pursuit of cooperation with foreign states in policing crime. See, in particular, Kiselyov, *op. cit.*, note 94, and A. Krivopalov, "Nashi syshchiki na rodine Sh. Kholmsa," *Izvestiia*, April 9, 1991. For an analysis of the Soviet track record here, see G. Ginsburgs, "The USSR and the Socialist Model of Cooperation in Criminal Matters," *Review of Socialist Law*, 1991, no. 3, pp. 199–278, and "Extradition in the USSR's Treaties on Legal Assistance with Non-'Socialist' States," *Canadian Yearbook of International Law 1991*, Vancouver, B.C., 1992, pp. 92–141.

95. Kiselyov, *op. cit.*, note 94.

96. S. Iakovlev, talk with Lieutenant-General B. Ignatov, head of the Bureau, *Pravitel'stvennyi vestnik*, 1992, no. 5, p. 6.

97. *Rossiiskie vesti*, July 16, 1992.

98. V. Rudnev, "Interpol zagovoril po-russki," *Izvestiia*, August 19, 1992.

99. *Ibid.*; A. Semeniaka, "Esli nado, Interpol pomozhet," *Pravda*, July 16, 1992. The latter source notes that in 1991 working contacts had been established with the criminal police services of thirty-five countries and that in 1992 that number had climbed to sixty (out of the 158 members of Interpol).

100. Iakovlev, *loc. cit.*, note 96.

101. Semeniaka, *loc. cit.*, note 99. In Iakovlev's conversation with Ignatov, the interviewee points out that the wider the gap between the successor states and the more numerous the barriers erected at the border, the easier it is for criminals to escape punishment. In fact, there have been cases where malefactors successfully eluded justice on the territory of former union republics, now independent states. Semeniaka, too, notes that law-enforcement personnel have encountered difficulties in resolving questions of criminal prosecution, rendition of criminals, and transfer of convicted persons. According to him, an urgent need existed to adopt at the interstate level a convention or bilateral treaties on legal assistance in civil, family, and criminal cases as well as other treaty documents pertaining to legal matters. Bilateral agreements have now been signed between the MVD of Russia and the MVDs of nearly all the republics of the former USSR for the financing and maintenance of a newly established interstate informational data bank for operational-informational, investigatory, and crime accounting. The importance of the project was said to be indisputable: in 1992 alone, such accounting brought to light every fifth crime in Russia. *Rossiiskaia gazeta*, November 17, 1992, p. 1.

102. See Lomanov, *loc. cit.*, note 29; G. Bocharov, "Hijacking: koshmar v nebe," *Literaturnaia gazeta*, July 18, 1990, p. 9.

103. V. Zaikin, "Kak borotsia s vozdushnym terrorizmom," *Izvestiia*, July 4, 1990.

104. Peter Conradi, Tom Rhodes, "Sky pirates jolt airport security," *The European*, July 20–22, 1990, p. 5.

105. Cf., RL 300/88 (July 8, 1998), p. 2; "Opiat ugon samoleta," *Pravda*, July 9, 1990; Bill Keller, "Hijacker Sent Back to Moscow, with a Message," *New York Times*,

July 18, 1990, p. A8; "Vnimanie: vozdushnyi terrorizm," *Izvestiia*, July 15, 1990; *Soviet Weekly*, August 2, 1990, p. 7, and K. Ivanov, "Facing the trial of air terrorism," *ibid.*, August 23, 1990, p. 14.

106. "KGB protiv terroristov," *Pravitel'stvennyi vestnik*, 1991, no. 30, p. 11.

107. "Skolko u nas terroristov," *Izvestiia*, June 7, 1991; A. Vasil'ev, "Terrorizm ne znaet granits," *Pravda*, June 7, 1991.

108. M. Wines, "F.B.I. and Russian Agency Thwart a Kidnapping," *New York Times*, January 18, 1992, pp. 1, 4.

109. D. Leonidov, "Soviet solutions for drugs trade without frontiers," *Soviet Weekly*, February 28, 1991, p. 4; Mikhailov, *op. cit.*, note 74, pp. 59–60.

110. *Report on the USSR*, 1990, no. 9, pp. 34–35, citing UPI, Reuters, February 22.

111. See "Drug trade picking up in Central Asia," *China Daily*, July 20, 1992, p. 1. Attempts are now being made to overcome this compartmentalization, at home as well as abroad. Thus, according to G. Ovcharenko, "Rossiia na igle," *Pravda*, October 3, 1992, an agreement has been initialed between the MVDs of the Commonwealth countries that would make it more difficult for criminals to find sanctuary in "their national homes." Meanwhile, the Russian MVD, together with the main administration of customs control of Russia, made plans for three large regional working sessions with foreign law-enforcement organizations in order to discuss methods of combating illegal trade in drugs. The first took place in Novosibirsk in November 1992 and was attended by special services from Kazakhstan and the Central Asian Republics, as well as Japan, China, South Korea, and other Far Eastern states. The second is scheduled to take place in St. Petersburg, with the participation of representatives of special services from Great Britain, the Scandinavian countries, Baltic and European states, and the United States. A summing-up session was planned for Krasnodar in mid-December to which specialists from India, Turkey, Afghanistan, Iran, and the southern republics of the former USSR would be invited. V. Romanchin, "Rossiia mozhet stat poligonom dlia otmyvaniia zarubezhnykh narkodollarov," *Rossiiskie vesti*, November 28, 1992, p. 2, and *Rossiiskaia gazeta*, November 24, 1992, p. 8.

112. J. Stalk, "Europe's Police Cast the Net Ever Wider," *International Herald Tribune*, September 9, 1992, p. 6. Also, B. James, "Is the EC Opening Its Doors to Crime?" *ibid.*, October 5, 1992, pp. 1, 4.

113. A. Mitchell, "Russian Emigrés Importing Thugs to Commit Contract Crimes in U.S.," *New York Times*, April 11, 1992, pp. 1, 28. See, too, *ibid.*, June 4, 1989, pp. 1, 38.

8

The New Nuclear Equation

David T. Twining

The demise of the Soviet Union and the emergence in its place of fifteen new independent states demands a reexamination of the issue of nuclear weaponry. Indeed, nuclear weapons represent a combination of technology, psychology, and strategy that has influenced more events, marshaled more people, and consumed more resources than any single weapons program in human history. The United States emerged as the world's sole nuclear power in the closing days of World War II, but this did not negate the herculean efforts of the Soviet Union to compete with its rival in the development of strategic weaponry. Today, the Cold War is over, but the thousands of nuclear weapons in both the United States and the former Soviet Union constitute a grim inheritance of that historic era.

This essay is an account of the development, multiplication, and perfection of a unique type of weapon by two competing political systems. These weapons cast a distinctive pall over forty-five years of often acrimonious relations and were the focus of conflicts which brought the world close to war on at least one occasion. The passing of the Soviet Union now requires a fresh look at nuclear weaponry, its utility in both war and peace, and the effect it has had on the human condition since mankind has created the very means to destroy all living things.

This weaponscentric reexamination reveals a complete reversal of earlier patterns of distrust and rivalry. Today, more than at any other time in history, the lethal capabilities of nuclear weapons have driven both great powers from a position of competition to one of cooperation. Russia—the former Soviet Union's principal weapons state—now finds itself working *with* the United States to reduce nuclear weapons and their means of delivery. At the same time,

The views expressed in this paper are those of the author and do not necessarily reflect the official policy or position of the Department of the Army, Department of Defense, or the U.S. Government.

both countries are trying to mitigate environmental damage and economic dislocations connected with their vast nuclear weapons programs.

The juxtaposition of Russia and the United States from postures of hostility to cooperation leaves the weapons themselves unchanged. Both countries acknowledge the weapons' inherent dangers as well as their declining military utility; both countries are working together to achieve a yet-to-be-defined posture of minimum deterrence. Indeed, these weapons have locked the United States and Russia in a Faustian embrace. Weapons which for so long represented mutual alienation during the Cold War will for the foreseeable future perpetuate a cooperative relationship based upon the imperatives of safe custody, environmental repair, and nonproliferation.

This is a story of parallel military-industrial establishments within two very different political systems, grinding away to produce weapons of mass destruction while strategists conceived methods for their use and nonuse. It is a story of epic proportions and the legacy of forty-five years of distrust and angst, with the consequence that Russia and the United States must now seek solutions to the many dilemmas raised by the very weapons both still embrace.

From the Attack on Japan

American scientists working at Los Alamos, New Mexico, under the leadership of Robert Oppenheimer and General Leslie Groves developed two atomic devices, with uranium processed at Oak Ridge and Hanford, to use against Japan. One was dropped on Hiroshima on August 6, 1945, and the other on Nagasaki on August 9. The resulting firestorms caused 340,000 deaths within five years—a figure far beyond early estimates, which nearly double the number of initial casualties—due to prolonged radiation sickness and burns.[1] Within five weeks of the weapons' detonation, Jacob Viner, a University of Chicago economist, articulated the concept that came to be known as nuclear deterrence, arguing that the possession of atomic bombs by two countries will create a condition that is largely psychological; this deterrent effect would aid peacekeeping, given the enormous cost to the side which uses such weapons first. Leo Szilard, a scientist who condemned the weapons' use against Japan, spoke of an "armed peace,"[2] while Viner astutely perceived the bombs' long-term impact:

> [T]he bomb will exert a certain subtle influence; it will be present at every diplomatic conference in the consciousness of the participants and will exert its effect. Then, sooner or later, Russia will also have the bomb, and then a new equilibrium will establish itself.[3]

Foundations of the Nuclear State

This subtle influence was anticipated by General George Marshall, who suggested in early 1945 that two Russian scientists be invited to witness the Trinity test. His proposal was quietly rejected,[4] and until President Harry S. Truman told Joseph Stalin of the weapons' existence on July 24, 1945, at Potsdam, neither the United States nor the USSR could fully appreciate that they would forever alter international relations.

Stalin, in fact, knew of the agreement of June 19, 1942, between Washington and London to develop the atomic bomb. He also learned of the Trinity test and had the benefit of U.S. weapons design data which Klaus Fuchs sent to Moscow from 1942 to 1949, shortening the Soviet nuclear quest by at least two years.[5] Nevertheless, Truman's supposed revelation at Potsdam motivated Stalin to send a message to Lavrentii Beria ordering that work on the atomic weapon should be accelerated.[6]

Beria, then head of the NKVD (the secret police), oversaw the Soviet nuclear weapons program. Beria's choice was no accident: he controlled the vast gulag network and had established scientific laboratories within selected prison camps. This made available nearly unlimited amounts of manpower, both scientific and manual, while the entire operation could be kept secret. The eventual U.S. decision to develop a thermonuclear or hydrogen device from the original fission design led Stalin to accelerate a crash program to do the same.[7]

In time, the Ministry of Medium Machine Building and the Committee on the Peaceful Uses of Atomic Energy were created in the USSR to exploit nuclear technologies. By June 1948, Andrei Sakharov had started working on thermonuclear weapons, and in March 1950 he moved to a secret city now known as Arzamas–16. This city, built in early 1946 by prisoners who were then sentenced to internal exile in Siberia, was the basis of Stalin's nuclear weapons program. With the help of captured German scientists, Soviet specialists succeeded in exploding an atomic device on August 29, 1949, with a thermonuclear explosion following in 1953.[8]

These early developments in the Soviet Union and in the United States led to the establishment of parallel institutions for designing and producing nuclear weapons. The United States developed a nuclear weapons infrastructure totaling some sixteen major installations ranging from specialized laboratories to nuclear waste facilities. By 1989, this complex represented an investment of $100 billion and was considered "one of the more potentially dangerous industrial operations in the world" by the General Accounting Office, an arm of the U.S. Congress.[9] Because most of the nuclear facilities were built in the 1940s and 1950s and are nearing the end of their operational life, it is estimated that more than $160 billion is required for their modernization and for environmental restoration.[10]

For the Soviet Union, Arzamas–16 was the first of a host of closed secret cities integral to the Soviet nuclear weapons program. Arzamas–16 was located some seventy kilometers from the real city of that name in the Volga region, and the Soviet Union's first atomic and thermonuclear devices were designed and built there. Starting with air-dropped bombs, three generations of series-produced nuclear weapons emerged from Arzamas–16. Andrei Sakharov's residence in Building No. 8 has been commemorated with a plaque. And in early 1992, Boris Yeltsin designated Arzamas–16 the Russian Federal Nuclear Center.[11]

Soviet nuclear weapons were also designed and manufactured in another secret city in the Urals, Chelyabinsk–70, with weapons-grade plutonium produced in nearby Chelyabinsk–65, as well as in Krasnoiarsk–26 and Tomsk–7 in Siberia. Weapons were tested in Novaya Zemlya in the far north and Semipalatinsk in Kazakhstan. Given the extent of scientific talent and other resources it dedicated to this task, it is little wonder that the USSR was able to produce the weapons necessary for a completely new form of warfare.

The entire Soviet nuclear program owed its origins to Stalin, who took the first steps to break the U.S. nuclear monopoly and achieve eventual strategic parity.[12] His death on March 5, 1953, led to a political interregnum, but it did not stop Soviet nuclear developments. Indeed, Moscow's detonation of a hydrogen bomb in August of that year was followed by an increase in heavy bomber production in an effort to catch up with the United States. No event shocked the United States in recent times as much as the Soviet Union's achievements in space, starting with the launching of Sputnik on October 4, 1957, after the testing of the world's first truly intercontinental ballistic missile earlier that year. Coincident with these developments was the convening of special seminars around the USSR to discern the changes that would be brought about in warfare by the introduction of nuclear weapons delivered by long-range missiles.[13] A series of documents called the "special collection" which described these changes was passed to the West by Colonel Oleg Penkovsky of the GRU, the Soviet military intelligence arm. They detailed the essence of a new strategy which emphasized the war-fighting capabilities of nuclear weapons.[14] This "revolution in military affairs" was represented by the nuclear weapon, the ballistic missile, and computer-driven guidance systems, or cybernetics. The Soviet Strategic Rocket Forces were established in 1959, and eventually an unclassified primer on the new era was released in 1962; *Military Strategy*, edited by Marshal V.D. Sokolovskii, codified the new reality.[15]

For the Soviet Union, "the basic, determining method of waging war is not the attack of the Ground Forces, as it was earlier, but the delivery of mass nuclear rocket strikes."[16] Indeed,

> the revolution in military affairs is an accomplished fact. It led to basic quantitative and qualitative changes in the military-technological base of the Armed Forces and in its structure. It marked a revolution in the methods of waging war, a revolution in the theory of military art and actual combat training of the troops.[17]

The United States, it would appear, was also aware of the strategic implications of nuclear weaponry. NSC–68, formulated two months before the outbreak of the Korean War in June 1950, depicted the USSR in stark terms. The United

States was building more atomic devices, and eventually the strategy of massive assured destruction was formally adopted as a result of President Eisenhower's "New Look" in defense policy. Nuclear weapons were seen as a relatively inexpensive way to defend national interests. Allegations of a U.S.-Soviet bomber gap and, later, a missile gap, were fueled by ongoing Soviet achievements, including their success at putting the first man in space in April 1961.

President Kennedy's strategy of flexible response, designed to provide a range of nuclear and non-nuclear responses to aggression, brought with it the implied threat of escalation and, in the end, of total war. The Cuban missile crisis of October 1962 made this clear, and in its wake both countries came to see their nuclear capabilities differently—as a means toward an "armed peace." Until that seminal event, the risk of nuclear war had not been fully appreciated.

The October 1962 crisis was precipitated by Khrushchev's desire to confront the Americans with a *fait accompli*, the presence of Soviet medium-range nuclear missiles just ninety miles from U.S. soil. The General Staff's "Plan Anadyr" also included a large-scale movement of rocket, antiaircraft, motorized rifle, and air force units to the island, making of it an "unsinkable aircraft carrier." An announcement to this effect was planned for November 25–26, when Khrushchev would be in Cuba.[18] After thirteen crisis-ridden days, a compromise defused the situation, yet the world has not forgotten this incident of more than thirty years ago, when both countries directly confronted the possibility of nuclear war.

The Arms Control Era

The end of the Cuban missile crisis brought with it increased interest by Moscow in arms-control negotiations. This included the "hot line" agreement of June 20, 1963, and the Limited Test Ban Treaty of August 5, 1963, considered turning points in U.S.-Soviet relations. This first detente was an achievement of great statesmanship given the recent crisis which had so threatened mankind.[19] During this period, the emphasis shifted from manned bombers to ballistic missiles as both countries pursued aggressive space and missile programs.

With the development of multiple independently targetable reentry vehicles (MIRVs) in the early 1970s, U.S.-Soviet competition in missile warheads began, leading to a vast proliferation of nuclear weapons.[20] By early 1970, the 1968 Nuclear Non-Proliferation Treaty entered into force, and it was followed by the 1971 agreement on Measures to Reduce the Risk of Outbreak of Nuclear War. In 1972 SALT I was signed; it included the first antiballistic missile (ABM) treaty and an interim agreement to limit nuclear strategic offensive weapons. The Threshold Test Ban Treaty was signed in 1974, and the Peaceful Nuclear Explosions Treaty was concluded in 1976. This "second detente" produced many advances in superpower cooperation until 1979, when SALT II languished without U.S. ratification, largely due to Moscow's invasion of Afghanistan.

By this time, both the United States and the Soviet Union recognized the inherent advantages of using nuclear weapons more selectively. In the United States, this recognition became part of the concept of "damage limitation," by which attack options were devised to permit escalation control, bargaining, and war termination. The strategy of flexible response held sway in the United States until the Soviet Union achieved nuclear parity, around the time President Nixon entered office in 1969. President Nixon adopted a policy of nuclear sufficiency: the U.S. capability would not be inferior to the Soviet Union's. This eventually yielded to a policy of essential equivalence under President Carter, who pledged that the United States would maintain deterrence by targeting a variety of Soviet military and nonmilitary installations. Presidents Reagan and Bush, for their part, adopted a countervailing strategy which held that the United States would prevail against any Soviet attack.

Implicit throughout was the threat of "assured destruction," defined by Secretary of Defense McNamara as the "ability to inflict at all times and under all foreseeable conditions an unacceptable degree of damage upon any single aggressor—even after absorbing a surprise attack."[21] This was the defining parameter of the U.S.-Soviet strategic relationship as embodied in the ABM Treaty: that as a pledge against launching a nuclear attack on its similarly armed opponent, each country's population would remain undefended.

Soviet military doctrine in the late 1960s began to acknowledge that wars could be entirely non-nuclear in character. The emphases, however, were on war-fighting and damage limitation by the employment of extensive preemptive strikes against military, or counterforce, targets. This concern with war-fighting was the essence of the concept of "deterrence by denial," which denied an adversary any possibility of victory should deterrence fail. Unlike U.S. theoreticians, Soviet strategists were skeptical about limiting nuclear strikes and instead advocated vigorous preemption to control damage and deny victory to an opponent.[22]

These competing concepts required the development of launch and nuclear capabilities for their execution. To exploit the targeting advantages now made possible by the MIRV, the United States deployed the Minuteman III ICBM and the silo-based MX missile, while the USSR developed the SS–17, the SS–18 (the world's largest and most lethal ICBM), the SS–19, the rail-mobile SS–24, and the road-mobile SS–25. The U.S. deployed the Trident or *Ohio* class ballistic missile submarines with the C–4 and C–5 missile, while the USSR deployed the Delta II, III, and IV, and the Typhoon, with SS-N–17, –18, –20, and –23 missiles.

Nuclear-armed cruise missiles further complemented each side's arsenal, while Moscow had the only deployed antiballistic missile (ABM) defense system. Nuclear weapons were becoming more complex, and road- and rail-basing modes showed considerable promise. President Reagan's 1983 Strategic Defense Initiative (SDI) sought to protect populations from this proliferating nuclear armada, but it was seen by Soviet strategists as a U.S. effort to achieve a first-strike capability. U.S. stealth technologies threatened to further destabilize the ongoing competition.

This proliferation of weaponry did not take place in a political vacuum. The Reagan defense buildup in the early 1980s was followed by Mikhail Gorbachev's ascension to power in March 1985. From the beginning, it was clear that Gorbachev sought significant arms reductions as a major curative for Moscow's increasingly strained economy. The catastrophic nature of the Chernobyl incident—the world's most serious nuclear power plant accident—on April 26, 1986, injected a new urgency and relevance for pursuing nuclear arms agreements.

Amidst this new reality, the 1987 Intermediate-Range Nuclear Forces (INF) agreement was concluded, which for the first time eliminated a complete class of missiles. Next, the Treaty on Conventional Armed Forces in Europe (CFE Treaty) was signed in November 1990, followed by the Strategic Arms Reduction Treaty (START I) in July 1991. Both agreements went far beyond the reductions and verification regimens that had been adopted thus far, but both were unavoidably complicated by the demise of the Soviet Union on December 25, 1991.

START I, now ratified by Russia and the United States, would bring nuclear warheads down from more than 10,000 for each side to 8,556 for the United States and 6,163 for Russia by the year 2000, with throw-weight differences accounting for the numerical disparity. In January 1992, President George Bush's State of the Union address proposed deeper cuts of strategic nuclear weapons, lowering the U.S. arsenal to 4,700 strategic warheads and bombs and the former USSR's to 4,400.

In a February 1992 visit to Washington, Boris Yeltsin offered further reductions, and during a return summit in June, figures of 3,000 weapons for Russia and 3,500 for the United States were codified in a verbal understanding which later formed the essence of START II. This framework agreement was signed by both leaders in January 1993, and it is the most significant strategic arms reduction treaty ever concluded. When ratified, inventories of nuclear bombs and warheads will be cut by two-thirds, and all land-based missiles with multiple warheads will be eliminated by the year 2000.

Critical to this process was cooperation by all four of the new nuclear states of the former Soviet Union—Russia, Ukraine, Belarus, and Kazakhstan—to abide by the limits previously agreed upon. While the Commonwealth of Independent States foundational documents acknowledged Russia as the principal nuclear successor to the Soviet Union, further talks were required to bring all four newly independent states into compliance with the CFE Treaty and START I.

In Lisbon on May 23, 1992, Kazakhstan, Ukraine, and Belarus agreed to yield all nuclear weapons to Russia by the year 2000 and to abide by the provisions of the Nuclear Non-Proliferation Treaty as non-weapons states. The Lisbon agreement meant that ratification of START I by all five parties could proceed.[23] Furthermore, in compliance with the Alma-Ata accord, all tactical nuclear weapons in the three new post-Soviet states were turned over to Russia for dismantling by late May 1992.[24] Finally, the last of the eight new states in the European zone covered by the CFE Treaty—originally signed by members of NATO and the Warsaw Pact—joined twenty-one other signatories to complete the treaty's ratification on October 30, 1992. The treaty entered into force on November 9, 1992. It mandates a 30 percent reduction in major items of conventional weaponry.[25]

Thus, after twelve months of unprecedented cooperation, the United States and Russia, as the Soviet Union's primary successor state and eventual sole nuclear trustee, stand at the precipice of truly historic and significant reductions in nuclear weaponry. Belarus, Kazakhstan, and Ukraine have declared their intention to become non-nuclear states. By mid-1993, only Ukraine has not ratified START I, which it expects to do once certain security guarantees and financial arrangements are in place.

To assist in the denuclearization of the former Soviet Union, the U.S. Congress passed legislation to commit $400 million for fiscal year 1992 and the same amount for fiscal year 1993. Called the Nunn–Lugar funds after the congressional proponents, this money is to pay primarily for dismantling nuclear weapons in the former USSR. Included are provisions for assisting Russia by building a storage facility for fissile material and furnishing 10,000 fissile material storage containers, 450 Kevlar blankets to protect weapons containers from gunfire, and 1,000 protective clothing items and other equipment for use in a possible accident. Similar assistance is to be rendered the other three nuclear states.[26] Additional monies have also been provided to support post-Soviet defense conversion, nuclear power plant safety, and controls of nuclear exports.[27] Further, a twenty-year agreement with Russia authorizes the United States to buy at least 500 tons of highly enriched uranium from dismantled weapons for use in diluted form as nuclear reactor fuel.[28]

The Dance of the Immortals

The irony of the present era finds the United States and Russia as the world's primary nuclear custodians. The two countries that had taken such far-reaching steps to oppose one another as an arms race, a space race, and global competition extending to the Third World now find themselves tied to the very weapon by which each once sought refuge from the other.

The United States spent $11 trillion opposing the Soviet Union during forty-five years of Cold War rivalry. Massive resources were mobilized and consumed by both countries to further develop the weapon which had helped to end the war against Japan on such conclusive terms. From that fateful day on July 24, 1945, when President Truman told Stalin of the new weapon of such devastating lethal-ity, both countries were tied to it by a Gordian knot. It stood totem-like through crises and detentes, through the bankruptcy of the Soviet Union and the implosion of communism, as a reminder of our mortality.

As Stephen E. Ambrose has observed, "From Potsdam on, the bomb was the constant factor in the American approach to the Soviet Union."[29] As the Soviet Union's principal successor state, Russia will inherit this mantle. A single weapon has long overshadowed the foreign and defense policies of two great nations. This preoccupation with the nuclear weapon and its associated technologies has brought more than 137 nations to agree to abide by international controls to preclude the weaponizing of nuclear fission.[30]

Circumstances beyond the weapons' "dark brooding presence"[31] have now made it possible for Russian and American political leaders to agree to limit its numbers, carefully yet quickly, to those required to deter each other, along with present, near, and future nuclear powers. Future reductions from START II limits are now likely. This development is an advance in both the annals of arms control and of common sense. As Robert L. O'Connell has observed,

> the possibility of nuclear disaster and the knowledge that these weapons are part and parcel of the political order raise grave contradictions to common sense which are not easily dismissed by official protestations that weapons are there to defend us.[32]

Could there have been a different conclusion to this story? Yes, if either side had acted with abandon or recklessness. The fear of surprise attack combined with the constant readiness of strategic nuclear forces could have transformed an incident into a broader conflagration.[33] Or, the use of force—either when the United States had a nuclear monopoly or later, when the USSR reached parity—by either side seeking to press an advantage in some evolving crisis could have ended similarly.

It took a convergence of interests after forty-five years to bring us to this point. Both sides exhibited a caution regarding nuclear weapons which bought precious time—time for other motive forces of change to take effect. That this was done without one nuclear weapon being fired in anger is a tribute to both Moscow and Washington. Now, that same expertise and dedication may be used for the antithesis of past policies: working together to reduce mutual arsenals and to constrain others, which presents the best hope for long-term peace.

Plans for Russia to be the sole nuclear custodian of the USSR's fifteen sovereign states will create a new duopoly of nuclear trusteeship, with U.S. and Russian specialists retaining the guardianship of a limited number of weapons necessary to maintain a stable minimum deterrence. Instead of planning scenarios, attack drills, and nuclear alerts in opposition to each other, the former enemies recognize the imperative of jointly preventing the further proliferation of the technologies and materials of nuclear weaponry.

It is the prospect of this new union to preserve a limited nuclear deterrent that forms the dance of the immortals. There is near unanimity that the threat posed by these weapons has brought the United States and Russia together in a trusteeship without end. This new purpose is now unfolding, as denuclearization of the former Soviet Union proceeds, eventually leaving Russia and the United States to insure that the remaining weapons are protected and never used.

This parametric shift in thinking, the rededication of former enemies to a new common task, requires a reorientation by both countries in terms of their foreign and defense policies. It also poses clear risks: that renegade scientists, groups, or nations may sell nuclear weapons, or exploit in some way the universal fear of nuclear disaster, or develop new conventional weapons technologies that can produce nuclear-like effects, or devise advanced weapons based on new physical principles. In Russia, with its agenda of pressing issues, much remains to be done to institutionalize democracy and the rule of law, a quest which communism itself unwittingly nurtured, while in the United States, the danger is one of neglect, as domestic priorities focus attention inward.

These risks require that the U.S.-Russian trusteeship be accomplished with the utmost care. The same dedication and determination which drove Moscow and Washington to summon their national wealth for purposes of war now require an equal dedication to preserve the nuclear peace. The Faustian embrace may have no end, but it should lead to other cooperative ventures involving problems no less challenging: ethnic and racial disharmony, human degradation and despair, and the staggering neglect of the unique attributes each person brings to the world. If such problems are addressed cooperatively, then the years of Russian-American hostility would have been worthwhile, despite the enormous mutual costs and sacrifice.

This undertaking in nuclear cooperation will not be the end of history in an ideological sense nor the end of war as a tool of statecraft,[34] but from this essential step may flow halcyon visions of a world transformed.

Implications for the Future of
U.S.-Russian Relations

The conclusion of START II has committed both Washington and Moscow to take additional steps to prevent the proliferation of nuclear weapons and weapons-associated technologies. Upon ratification, this treaty will result in two smaller, more stable, and more manageable nuclear forces. For Russia, the new treaty eliminates the heavy SS–18, termed a "dangerous magnet inviting a preemptive nuclear strike" by Deputy Defense Minister Andrei Kokoshin.[35] From Washington's perspective, it will reduce the twenty bases and 850 multiple warhead missiles that have constituted the United States' major strategic threat.[36]

The conclusion of START II also advances the imperative of resolving the CIS's awkward command-and-control configuration. Because the CIS strategic arsenal has been the responsibility of an army without a state, questions of nuclear stability and control in the former Soviet Union have been raised. According to Marshal Evgenii Shaposhnikov, "Regrettably, the reality today is that the missile troops on the territory of Belarus, Kazakhstan, and Ukraine are still without any state affiliation."[37] This situation has also threatened the weapons' security and readiness, a problem attributed to the difficulty in getting spare parts for the arsenal.[38]

Efforts by Marshal Shaposhnikov to vest the commander of Russia's strategic forces with overall responsibility for the CIS strategic forces have thus far been opposed by Ukraine, which fears that such an arrangement could seriously threaten its own security interests. The resulting conundrum has placed Shaposhnikov in the situation of controlling what are essentially Russian strategic forces in the name of the CIS, but subject to the command of Russia's president, Boris Yeltsin.

Attempts to clarify this situation were made at the Minsk summit of CIS states on January 22, 1993. On the day before its opening, Russian Defense Minister Pavel Grachev declared that all nuclear troops were subordinate to him, and that "the nuclear weapons belong to Russia in accordance with the Lisbon agreement."[39] CIS political leaders were unable to agree to a formula for control that was satisfactory to Kiev, which has continued to insist that it has the ability to block a nuclear launch but not to initiate one.[40] While Russian assertiveness on this issue may further alienate Ukraine, the CIS command system is artificial at best, and professionals such as Shaposhnikov find it unsatisfactory.

It is clear that Ukraine is central to the nuclear nonproliferation issue and to the ultimate success of START I and START II in the new states of the former Soviet Union. For Kiev, the 176 missiles and 30 strategic bombers totaling 1,656 warheads[41] on its soil are considered bargaining chips of major proportions. According to Serhiy Holovaty, a member of Ukraine's parliamentary foreign affairs commission, "Our deputies don't care where these things are aimed, they know that they must get something for them."[42] While the United States has offered $175 million to pay the costs of their dismantlement, Ukrainian authorities cite the figure of $1.5 billion as a more reasonable sum.[43] Ukraine also believes it is due compensation from Russia for the fissile materials contained in the tactical warheads it already handed over to Russia prior to the deadline of July 1, 1992. Kiev may also want to use the warheads now in Ukraine as fuel for its nuclear power plants.[44]

Perhaps more significantly, Ukraine insists upon receiving security guarantees from current nuclear powers to ensure that it remains secure once it is nuclear-free. Washington provided such a written pledge in early January, and the United Kingdom is also discussing a security guarantee for Kiev.[45] In direct negotiations with President Leonid Kravchuk on January 15, 1993, Boris Yeltsin offered to guarantee Ukraine's security from conventional and nuclear attack.[46] While negotiations have considerable distance to go before Kiev ratifies the Lisbon protocol, this dialogue is the necessary prerequisite to satisfying Ukraine's demands for international security guarantees, compensation, and the provision of fuel for its nuclear power reactors. Beyond this, both the United States and Russia are well aware that "alone among the non-Russian republics, Ukraine possesses enough skilled scientists to become a nuclear power in its own right."[47]

Once Ukraine's concerns are placated, Washington and Moscow can focus on the next level of nuclear nonproliferation: the growing legion of nuclear and near-nuclear states. Evgenii Primakov, head of Russia's Foreign Intelligence Service, announced on January 28, 1993, that sixteen countries—not counting the three Western powers, China, and the four new states of the former Soviet Union —either possessed or were close to possessing nuclear weapons.[48] This fact should give the original nuclear powers constituting the United Nations Security Council little satisfaction that the nuclear "genie" has been satisfactorily contained.

Both Washington and Moscow must acknowledge the need to intensify their efforts to stem the spread, threatened use, accidental use, or use in combat of nuclear weapons. As Thomas L. Friedman has observed, "As the world has become a safer place on the Moscow–Washington highway, it has become an increasingly dangerous place on many of the side roads, supposedly policed by the non-proliferation treaty."[49] This concern is the next priority for both countries once they begin the lengthy process of implementing START I and START II.

Both Washington and Moscow also face the moral imperative of cleaning up nuclear waste and, now that most will no longer be required, weapons manufacturing facilities. This enormous task represents a bill now coming due, as the debris of the Cold War is harming public health in both countries, as well as the health of citizens of neighboring states. Along with halting the proliferation of weapons, this is another cause eliciting mutual cooperation between the two former enemies.

As long as Moscow and Washington continue to maintain residual deterrent forces well into the future, nuclear warheads will have to be maintained, tested, and periodically replaced. This maintenance function could be accomplished jointly in a manner that gives neither side undue advantage. Cooperation in this area would minimize even further the need for duplicate facilities, and this would result in far less contamination of the air, soil, and water. It would also greatly reduce the need for underground nuclear testing required to validate the weapons' reliability and credibility, and it would provide the maximum reassurance that each party is abiding by relevant arms control agreements.

Finally, there is the urgent requirement to protect the remaining nuclear arsenals in both Russia and the United States in such a manner that they represent the most secure, stable deterrent to nuclear attack that can be devised. The nuclear risk-reduction centers in Moscow and Washington should be jointly staffed so that openness and visibility of both arsenals may be monitored on a continuous basis. Over time, this could result in the interpenetration of U.S. and Russian attack-warning centers and launch control facilities, providing further confidence to the populations of the globe's two largest nuclear weapons states that their deterrent forces are stable, secure, and responsibly maintained.

By the time the START II nuclear weapons reductions are complete, the United States and Russia may be jointly engaged in preserving their remaining arsenals to ensure their readiness to repel an attack by any renegade foolish enough to perceive some gain from such an act. To make an attack even less attractive, a single deterrent force, jointly staffed and requiring the consent of both heads of state before a launch order may be given, would even further affirm the principle of nonproliferation and the imperative of nuclear nonuse.

This is not meant to imply that deterrence in the current era can only be nuclear, or that the delivery means are ballistic missiles alone. Conventional forces and advanced conventional munitions serve to deter regional threats, though their psychological impact does not have the same deterrent effect.[50] For Russia and the United States, however, cooperation on a host of global and regional security issues becomes much more likely once the core obstacle to improved long-term relations—the status of their respective nuclear weapons—is resolved.

Russia and the United States each possess distinct cultures, histories, languages, and peoples, and both have domestic problems to resolve. Despite a growing partnership in nuclear matters, they will remain separate, sovereign nations with separate national armies to protect their respective national interests. The possibility of nuclear war, however—a fear which both Washington and Moscow confronted in their own ways during the years of the Cold War—is no longer a bilateral concern as many nations, large and small, have now acquired this collateral of superpower status. While antiballistic missile technologies hold some promise, nuclear weapons themselves remain the ultimate deterrent to nuclear use.

Bernard Brodie's admonition of 1959 still pertains: "A great nation which has forsworn preventive war *must* devote much of its military energies to cutting down drastically the advantage that the enemy can derive from hitting first by surprise attack."[51] Given the likelihood of additional strategic nuclear reductions beyond START II, as well as possible collaboration in weapons fabrication, testing, warning, and control, there is no reason both nuclear partners cannot contribute to one force to perform this necessary function together.

While the view may appear as yet obscure, this glimpse of a world largely safe from nuclear attack should encourage leaders in Russia and the United States to see the range of possible cooperative ventures which the essential step of START II and its follow-on agreements make possible. From this present perspective, the very weapon which separated these two great nations during years of Cold War hostility can now unite them in a stewardship without end. Weapons have brought little good to human affairs in the course of history, but nuclear weapons represent a catalytic force which holds the potential for transforming contemporary Russian-American relations in ways as yet unimaginable.

Notes

1. Richard Rhodes, *The Making of the Atomic Bomb* (New York: Simon and Schuster, 1986), pp. 734–41.

2. Ibid., p. 753.

3. Ibid., pp. 753–54.

4. Ibid., p. 646.

5. Ibid., pp. 690, 770; "Program Shows Closed Nuclear City of Arzamas–16," Moscow Ostankino First Program Network, 2030 GMT, November 19, 1992, in FBIS-SOV–92–227, November 24, 1992, pp. 3–4.

6. Dmitri Volkogonov, *Stalin: Triumph and Tragedy*, ed. and trans. by Harold Shukman (New York: Grove Weidenfeld, 1991), p. 498.

7. Ibid., pp. 334; 532–33.

8. Andrei Sakharov, *Memoirs*, trans. by Richard Lourie (New York: Alfred A. Knopf, 1990), pp. 99–114.

9. Statement of Keith O. Fultz, Director, Energy Issues, Resources, Community, and Economic Development Division, Before the Subcommittee on Energy and Power, Committee on Energy and Commerce, U.S. House of Representatives (Washington, DC: U.S. General Accounting Office, February 22, 1989), p. 3.

10. "DOE Management: Impediments to Environmental Restoration Management Contracting," United States General Accounting Office Report to the Chairman, Subcommittee on Oversight and Investigations, Committee on Energy and Commerce, House of Representatives, no. GAO/RCED–92–244 (Washington, DC: General Accounting Office, 1992), p. 2. Hanford, which produced weapons-grade plutonium until 1987 and is spread over 560 square miles in southeastern Washington State, alone could cost up to $100 billion for extensive earth removal and environmental restoration. Ibid., p. 3.

11. Mikhail Rebrov, "Three Generations of Bombs: Only Now Can We Talk About the City Where They Were Born," *Krasnaia zvezda*, October 27, 1992, p. 2.

12. Volkogonov, *Stalin*, p. 533.

13. Harriet Fast Scott and William F. Scott, *The Armed Forces of the USSR*, 2d ed. (Boulder, CO: Westview Press, 1981), pp. 39–41.

14. Ibid., 48–49; Jerrold L. Schecter and Peter S. Deriabin, *The Spy Who Saved the World: How a Soviet Colonel Changed the Course of the Cold War* (New York: Charles Scribner's Sons, 1992), p. 247.

15. Scott and Scott, *The Armed Forces*, pp. 74–77.

16. N.A. Sbitov, "The Revolution in Military Affairs and Its Results," in *The Nuclear Revolution in Soviet Military Affairs*, trans. and ed. by William R. Kintner and Harriet Fast Scott (Norman, OK: The University of Oklahoma Press, 1968), p. 28.

17. Ibid., p. 27.

18. Gennady Vasilev, " 'A Hedgehog in the Americans' Pants': Thirty Years Since the Caribbean Crisis," *Moscow News*, October 18–25, 1992, p. 12. Among the 45,000 officers and men comprising the group of forces planned for Cuba was a motorized infantry regiment commanded by Colonel Dmitry Yazov.

19. Alan Neidle, "Nuclear Test Bans: History and Future Prospects," in *U.S.-Soviet Security Cooperation: Achievements, Failures, Lessons*, ed. by Alexander L. George, Philip J. Farley, and Alexander Dallin (New York: Oxford University Press, 1988), pp. 178–79.

20. Arms Control Association, *Arms Control and National Security: An Introduction* (Washington, DC: The Arms Control Association, 1989), p. 25.

21. Peter C. Hughes and M.R. Edwards, "Nuclear War in Soviet Military Thinking: The Implications for U.S. Security," in *Journal of Social and Political Affairs* 1 (April 1976), p. 114.

22. Gary L. Guertner, "Offensive Nuclear Forces, Strategic Defense and Arms Control," in *Star Wars and European Defence—Implications for Europe: Perceptions and Assessments*, ed. by Hans Gunter Brauch (London: Macmillan, 1987), pp. 27–28.

23. Barbara Crossette, "4 Ex-Soviet States and U.S. in Accord on 1991 Arms Pact," *The New York Times*, May 24, 1992, p. A1.

24. Dunbar Lockwood, "U.S. Completes Announced Tactical Nuclear Withdrawal," *Arms Control Today*, July/August 1992, p. 27. The United States announced the withdrawal of all ground-launched and sea-launched nuclear weapons from worldwide bases on July 2, 1992, and promised the withdrawal of one-half of all air-launched weapons.

25. "Department Statements: Entry Into Force of the CFE Treaty," *U.S. Department of State Dispatch*, November 16, 1992, p. 835.

26. "Plans for U.S. Aid for Russian Warhead Dismantlement Detailed," *Arms Control Today*, July/August 1992, p. 27.

27. "Focus on the Emerging Democracies," *U.S. Department of State Dispatch*, vol. 3 (October 26, 1992), p. 791.

28. "News Briefs: U.S. to Buy Uranium from Russian Bombs," *Arms Control Today*, September 1992, p. 34.

29. Stephen E. Ambrose, *Rise to Globalism: American Foreign Policy Since 1938*, 6th rev. ed. (New York: Penguin, 1991), p. 69.

30. David Fischer, *Stopping the Spread of Nuclear Weapons: The Past and the Prospects* (New York: Routledge, 1992), pp. 324–27.

31. Robert L. O'Connell, *Of Arms and Men: A History of War, Weapons, and Aggression* (New York: Oxford University Press, 1989), p. 305.

32. Ibid.

33. See David T. Twining, *Strategic Surprise in the Age of Glasnost* (New Brunswick, NJ: Transaction, 1992).

34. See Francis Fukuyama, "The End of History," *National Interest*, Summer 1989, pp. 3–18, and John Mueller, *Retreat from Doomsday: The Obsolescence of Major War* (New York: Basic Books, 1989).

35. Doug Clarke, "Russian Defense Ministry: START–2 Serves Russian Interests," *RFE/RL Daily Report*, no. 3 (E-mail), January 7, 1993, p. 3.

36. Celestine Bohlen, "Ukraine, Stumbling Block at End of Nuclear Race," *The New York Times*, January 1, 1993, p. A10.

37. "Status of Nuclear Weapons Outside Russia Should Be Determined Before START II Treaty Is Ratified, Marshal Yevgeniy Shaposhnikov Believes," *Izvestiia*, January 12, 1993, p. 2; in FBIS-SOV–93–007, January 12, 1993, p. 1.

38. Ibid., and "Sees 'Trend Toward Upsetting Nuclear Security,'" Moscow INTER-FAX, 1148 GMT, December 21, 1992; in FBIS-SOV–92–245, December 21, 1992, p. 1.

39. "Vesti" newscast, Moscow Russian Television Network, 1700 GMT, January 21, 1993; in FBIS-SOV–93–013, January 22, 1993, p. 10.

40. V. Vozianov and A. Trotsenko, "The Ukrainian Leadership's Concept of Nuclear Weapons," Moscow *Rossiiskie vesti*, December 24, 1992, p. 2; in FBIS-SOV–92–248, December 24, 1992, p. 25.

41. Vladimir Tyurkin, "Commentary: Nuclear Button Against a Backdrop of a Bronze Bell," Moscow *Rossiiskaia gazeta*, January 21, 1993, p. 7; in FBIS-SOV–93–014, January 25, 1993, p. 1.

42. Serge Schmemann, "Ukraine Finds Nuclear Arms Bring a Measure of Respect," *The New York Times*, January 7, 1993, p. A1.

43. Chrystyna Lapychak, "Ukraine Gains US Guarantee Needed for START Support," *The Christian Science Monitor*, January 12, 1993, p. 1.

44. Doug Clarke, "Ukraine Wants to Use Warheads for Fuel," *RFL/RL Daily Report*, no. 6 (E-mail), January 12, 1993, p. 7.

45. Lapychak, "Ukraine Gains US Guarantee," p. 1.

46. Steven Erlanger, "Yeltsin Offers Guarantees if Kiev Backs Arms Pact," *The New York Times*, January 16, 1993, p. A3.

47. "Ukraine: Heels Dug In," *The Economist*, January 9, 1993, p. 46.

48. Doug Clarke, "Russian Intelligence Reveals Proliferation 'Black List,' " *RFE/RL Daily Report*, no. 19, (E-mail), January 29, 1993, p. 2.

49. Thomas L. Friedman, "Arms Control After Start II: A New Level of Instability," *The New York Times*, January 10, 1993, p. E1.

50. Bruce B.G. Clarke, "The Strategic Setting," in *Maneuver Warfare Anthology*, ed. by Richard D. Hooker, Jr. (Novato, CA: Presidio Press, 1993), pp. 8–9.

51. Bernard Brodie, *Strategy in the Missile Age* (Princeton, NJ: Princeton University Press, 1965), p. 394.

Comment

The Context of Russian-American Cooperation in the Fight Against Crime

Igor Ivanovich Lukashuk

The entire course of history demonstrates that the only acceptable form of existence and development of civilized society is democracy. This applies to both national and international society. Only under conditions of democracy is it possible to guarantee human rights and freedoms, the comprehensive development of the individual's personality, and, consequently, the flourishing of society as a whole. In international relations, democracy is the indispensable precondition for secure peace, cooperation on a footing of equality, and a just legal order.

Appreciation by the states of these cardinal principles finds expression in the growing number of international political and legal acts. The idea of democracy is expressed in the UN Charter, incarnated in the fundamental principle of democracy from which derive all the charter's other principles. The pacts and conventions on human rights have tremendous significance for the consolidation of democracy within states and in international relations.

An important new step in the development of democracy was recorded as a result of the adoption within the framework of the Conference on Security and Cooperation in Europe of the 1990 Paris Charter for a New Europe.[1] The participating states recognized democracy as the only system of government acceptable to them and committed themselves to strengthening it. They further declared that "they would cooperate and afford each other assistance with the aim of making democratic gains irreversible."

As a general principle of international relations, cooperation and mutual support in defending democracy is a totally new phenomenon. Its solidification is dictated by the fact that only such an approach can create safe guarantees for democracy. Democracy is a universal human value, on which hinges the fate of civilization. At the same time, one should not ignore the dangers posed by abuse of democracy, as in the case of organized crime, which takes advantage of democracy. Organized crime is the price we pay for the protection of individual rights from infringement by the government. However, one must also not forget that in an antidemocratic, totalitarian state, the authorities themselves constitute a criminal organization that tramples on human rights and freedoms.

We know that organized crime amounts to a serious problem in American society where it enjoys tremendous opportunities. Suffice it to say that the drug mafia alone earns more than 30 billion dollars annually in the United States. It has even been alleged that Ronald Reagan's 1980 presidential campaign fund received 200,000 dollars in contributions from such sources.[2]

However, organized crime represents an incalculably greater danger to a budding democracy. Where democracy has not yet gained strength, mafia structures can assume such proportions that democratic development will be imperiled. Something of the sort can be observed in the states that emerged on the territory of the former USSR, particularly in Russia. The disorganization of the state mechanism, including its law-enforcement organs, and its unpreparedness to function in conditions of democracy have made the ground fertile for the growth of all types of crime. A particular danger is posed by mafia organizations which, controlling enormous resources, suborn government officials. Today, corruption has infected many of Russia's state organs, at the center and locally, including the organs of law enforcement.

Organized crime in the former Soviet republics spills over national borders, creating an international danger as well. Mafiosi from these republics have entered into agreements with large criminal clans to divide up spheres of influence. In the fall of 1992, a secret meeting of the bosses of the Italian mafia with representatives of the criminal world of the former Soviet republics took place in Prague. An understanding was reached to coordinate operations. In particular, the Italians were to teach their Russian colleagues how to launder dirty money, while the latter assumed responsibility for securing the safety of transit and dissemination of drugs here.

The president, the parliament, and the government of Russia are taking definite steps designed to strengthen the fight against crime. More money is being allocated for the reorganization and maintenance of law-enforcement agencies, and parliament is considering various anticrime laws, including the draft of a special law on corruption. One has the feeling, though, that the authorities still have not properly grasped the magnitude of the danger which the orgy of crime poses to the social, economic, and political life of the community. Public opinion polls reveal that an ever growing number of those interviewed place the problem of crime at the head of the list of domestic issues. For the sake of solving it, people are ready to shoulder not only economic but also political sacrifices, casting a shadow on hopes for the consolidation of a democratic order in Russia.

It would appear that this is precisely one of those instances envisaged by the Paris Charter which requires states to cooperate and afford each other support in safeguarding democracy. Clearly, economic aid could play a decisive role. I believe that a democracy of indigents is altogether impossible. The primary job consists of underpinning democracy with a safe economic foundation. However, other types of aid are also of considerable significance—special assistance in fighting against crime through the transfer of expertise and technology as well as mutually beneficial cooperative arrangements.

Cooperation with Russia in the fight against crime is in the interest of the United States. One must not forget that organized crime is international in character; it does not stop at state frontiers, but uses them to its own advantage. That is why the fight against crime requires increasingly active cooperation between states, and this is becoming an element of foreign policy.

Governments of different countries are exerting considerable efforts to develop cooperative measures in the fight against crime: special international organs and organizations are being established, bilateral and multilateral treaties are being concluded. However, one gets the impression that the international ties are developing even more vigorously in the world of organized crime. In 1991, the head of Italy's financial security, General L. Ramponi, served notice that the mafia understood the new opportunities opening up in the countries of the former Soviet bloc faster than governments did.

* * *

All that has been said so far attests to the reality of the problem which Professor Ginsburgs addresses in his essay. Of considerable significance, too, is the fact that the author has studied these issues long and very successfully, as his publications attest.[3]

His essay here is devoted in the main to the interaction of the United States and Russia, and not to Russia itself, but this does not make it less interesting. In the first place, primary attention here is given not to technical legal details, but to the role of cooperation in the fight against crime within the general system of relations between the two countries. This problem has become even more important and complex in light of the changes that have occurred on the territory of the former USSR, for like any phenomenon, it refracts the unity of past, present, and future. Knowledge of the past is an indispensable precondition to understanding the present and to setting the paths to the future. Professor Ginsburgs pays considerable attention to setting these paths.

Note is taken of the fact that legal questions always featured quite prominently in Soviet-American politics. Unlike their role in U.S. relations with other countries, legal questions in Soviet-American relations were among the main objects of political struggle. Constructive interaction of the organs of justice of the two states, even in civil matters, was virtually nil; in the criminal-law sphere, in my opinion, it was the American side that essentially rejected the possibility of interaction with the "evil empire." In this connection, let me observe that under the conditions of the Cold War, the leading role in regulating Soviet-American relations fell not to the norms of international law, but to singular political norms, the rules of the Cold War game.

In this light, I would like to draw attention to a thought that strikes me as one of the essay's more valuable observations. Ginsburgs correctly writes that the changes occurring in the field of cooperation in the fight against crime can serve as a yardstick for gauging the successes of rapprochement between the two countries and as a reliable index to each regime's changing perception of the other. He draws attention to the fact that the attitude of the Brezhnev leadership toward international law was not sincere. There is some truth to that. But one must not forget that during this same period much was done to reflect the prescriptions of international law in the legislation of the USSR and the consciousness of its population. It was precisely the 1977 "Brezhnev" Constitution of the USSR that solidified the fundamental principles of international law as principles of the state's foreign policy.

This played a role in the matter of solidly implanting international law principles in the states that were formed as a result of the collapse of the USSR. In one of its first acts, the Declaration on State Sovereignty of 1990, Russia proclaimed "its commitment to the universally recognized principles and norms of international law."[4] It is most significant that the present leadership of Russia underscores the unity of democracy, legality, and morality in internal and foreign policy, and the priority of human rights. Addressing the UN Security Council session in February 1992, President Yeltsin spoke of the unity of the principles of internal and foreign policy which feature "the paramountcy of democracy, human rights and freedoms, legality and morality."[5]

International law, then, exerts a growing influence on the legal system that is taking shape in Russia. The current Constitution incorporates a clause stating that "universally recognized international norms pertaining to human rights have precedence over the laws of the Russian Federation and directly engender rights and duties of citizens of the Russian Federation" (Art. 32). Thus there are constitutional guarantees of internationally recognized human rights in the legal system of Russia. It is precisely the human being who is the subject here, and not only "citizens of the Russian Federation," if the Constitution is interpreted literally. International law mandates respect for human rights independently of an individual's citizenship and, according to the Constitution of Russia, foreigners and stateless persons enjoy the same rights and freedoms as the citizens of Russia (Art. 37).

The objective observer cannot help noticing the growing influence of international norms, standards, and practice on the legislation and other normative acts of Russia. As an example, one can point to the serious influence that the documents of the Conference on Security and Cooperation in Europe have had on the criminal and criminal-procedure law of Russia.

Obvious transformations are taking place in the character of interaction between the legal system of Russia and the rest of the world. The legal system of the country traditionally remained closed, introverted. Resort to the norms of international law was virtually monopolized by the central organs of executive power. The role of the organs of justice in these matters was insignificant. Nowadays, even such sensitive areas as criminal and criminal-procedure law, as well as the practice of law-enforcement organs, have become open to foreign influence. There is much more active cooperation in the international fight against crime, as the example of contacts through Interpol channels bears witness. Generally speaking, Russia's legal system today is no less prepared for international cooperation in the fight against crime than the legal system of the United States; where Russia lags behind is in the experience in such cooperation on the part of her law-enforcement agencies.

When in the past there was talk of interaction with the USSR in the fight against crime, the position of the United States was primarily determined by politics, and not law. It is enough to recall the case of the Brazinskases, who, contrary to a whole array of conventions, found sanctuary in the United States at a time when the U.S. administration was demanding that other governments step up the fight against air terrorism. By the same token, the U.S. government failed to fulfill its duties with respect to the prosecution and surrender of war criminals.

For Russia and the United States, as well as for their interaction in the sphere of justice, major significance attaches to the fight against crime within the republics of the former USSR. Thus far, the old ties inherited from the USSR still operate in this sector. However, there is an imperative need to lay new legal foundations promptly. International legal treaties between republics can play a decisive role here. For instance, one of the first decisions of the interparliamentary assembly of the Commonwealth of Independent States was the decision to prepare a draft of a convention on measures of coordination of the fight against organized crime.[6]

At the first meeting of the heads of the supreme courts of the CIS countries, in the fall of 1992, the participants displayed a common impulse toward business-like cooperation in coordinating the work of the courts, with the aim of insuring the protection of the rights and legitimate interests of citizens according to the universally recognized principles and norms of international law. Agreements were signed on cooperation in the sphere of justice, which also called for consultative meetings of the chairmen of the supreme courts of the CIS countries. The participants also addressed an appeal to the heads of state recommending a multilateral convention on the procurement of legal assistance and on legal relations concerning civil and criminal matters.[7] All this is but a sample of first steps which point the way toward the future.

* * *

Comparing Professor Ginsburgs's thoughts with mine, I was quite surprised to note how much they resemble each other. Such pronounced coincidence in the views of an American and a Russian jurist is symptomatic of the fact that today the paths toward development of Russian-American cooperation in the fight against crime is not barred by obstacles that are a matter of principle. True, this does not mean that the path is strewn with roses, although indeed it has its share of thorns. Both sides face a great deal of work.

A standard treaty of legal assistance could lay a general foundation for cooperation in the field under consideration. It seems to us that the government of Russia is ready for this. Such a step calls for greater effort from the U.S. government, but the significance of cooperation with Russia justifies the expenditure of such efforts. In this connection, let me recall that the USSR concluded its first agreement on legal assistance with the United States back in 1935. To be sure, it was rather circumscribed in content and was effected by an exchange of notes, but even so it was an agreement on legal assistance between two very different powers.

Besides a treaty on legal assistance defining the general legal regime of interaction in the domain of justice, more concrete agreements between law-enforcement departments, including the Russian Ministry of Security and the American FBI, will also be required. Such agreements could play an important role if they had real content, which is a question not simply of law, but of politics, in that it depends on the general state of Russian-American relations.

In this connection, let me point out that in the new laws of Russia concerning law-enforcement organs, the enumeration of the legal bases for their activity includes international treaties—for instance the 1992 Law on the Procuracy of the Russian Federation (Art. 3) and the Law on Security (Art. 6). It would be more correct in such cases to speak not of international treaties but of international law as a whole, inasmuch as customary norms can also have significance in this context. However, it is an old tradition of the lawmakers of the USSR, and now of Russia, to consider international law to be represented only by treaties.

Further development of Russian-U.S. cooperation in the fight against crime will require harmonizing legislation with its practical implementation. U.S. criminal and criminal-procedure law contains definite specifics in matters directly connected with such cooperation. Occasionally, this specific quality diverges not only from the national laws of other countries, but also from international law. To illustrate this, one can look at the question of the extraterritorial effect of criminal law. The majority of states adhere to the traditional territorial doctrine in this matter: the jurisdiction of a state is in principle circumscribed by the boundaries of its territory.[8] This doctrine was also reflected in the legislation of the USSR, and now a corresponding formula features in the draft of Russia's new legislation. According to this formula, foreign citizens can be held to account under the criminal laws of Russia for crimes committed abroad only in instances sanctioned by international treaties. All attempts by this writer to demonstrate to those who are drafting the laws that such a formula is partly obsolete met with no understanding.

Many countries have ventured to expand the scope of extraterritorial operation of their criminal law. On the whole, this tendency coincides with the proposition enunciated as early as 1927 by the Permanent Court of International Justice in the famous decision in the Lotus case. In particular: "Although it is true that in all systems of law the principle of the territorial nature of criminal law is paramount, it is equally true that the effect of all or nearly all these systems of law extends beyond the territorial limits of the states adopting them and that different states do so by different means. That is why the territoriality of criminal law does not constitute an absolute principle of international law and in no sense corresponds to territorial sovereignty."[9] This concept prompted widespread opposition from jurists, including several judges of the Permanent Court. However, the subsequent development of criminal legislation and practice in many countries attests to the tendency to expand the territorial effect of criminal law. This tendency stems from the need to defend the interests of the state and its citizens in circumstances of intense international intercourse, as well as from the expansion of international cooperation in the fight against crime.

The U.S. legislation has proceeded beyond what has been accepted by the legislation and practice of other states and international law. The 1986 Omnibus Diplomatic Security and Antiterrorism Act stretched the criminal jurisdiction of the United States to encompass murder and attempted murder, as well as the infliction of or the attempt to inflict serious injury on American citizens regardless of where and by whom these acts were committed.[10]

More than once and in violation of the sovereignty of other states, U.S. law-enforcement agents have seized in other countries individuals suspected of having committed crimes against American citizens. Let us recall the cases of the Lebanese F. Yunus or the Mexican A. Machain. In hearing the latter's case, the U.S. Supreme Court recognized that the "respondent and his amici may be correct that respondent's abduction was 'shocking' and that it may be in violation of general international law principles."[11] Nevertheless, the Supreme Court rejected the reasoning of the U.S. Court of Appeals for the Ninth Circuit that the court lacked jurisdiction to try the defendant. Thus, the Supreme Court confirmed that in contemporary circumstances the old Ker–Frisbie doctrine remained in force, upholding the view that "the power of a court to try a person for a crime is not impaired by the fact that he has been brought within the court's jurisdiction by reason of a 'forcible abduction.' "[12]

Special attention is due the case of General Noriega, which raises the question of the possibility of extending the criminal jurisdiction of a foreign state over a person occupying one of the highest posts in his country where he had committed a crime not connected with the performance of his official functions. It seems to us that armed intrusion into Panama with the aim of capturing Noriega cannot be recognized as lawful from the point of view of either international law or U.S. law. This affair offers an especially graphic example of how much damage can be inflicted on international legality by resorting to state force for extraterritorial exercise of criminal jurisdiction.

A serious defect in the U.S. conception of extraterritorial criminal jurisdiction lies in its unilateral character. While asserting jurisdiction within the sovereign sphere of other states, the United States does not recognize that they have analogous rights vis-à-vis the United States—an approach that clearly runs counter to the principle of the sovereign equality of states. One can, of course, understand the desire of the U.S. government to guarantee the safety of its citizens abroad. But real results can be obtained here through cooperation with other states, and not by unilateral action. It seems to us that the development of international cooperation in the fight against crime will take the edge off this problem, but at the same time it will require a more precise international-law solution of the problem of extraterritorial criminal jurisdiction.

* * *

International cooperation in the fight against crime today assumes new parameters. This concerns the aims, the content, and the form of cooperation. In the past, and not infrequently in our own times, such cooperation was understood very narrowly as the interaction of the law-enforcement organs of various states in taking into custody and punishing offenders. However, in actual fact the sphere of cooperation also encompasses crime prevention, the suppression and punishment of criminal acts, and the reeducation of prisoners. In conditions of growing interdependence among states, each has an interest in lowering the level of crime in other countries, which has important significance for the fight against crime both domestically and internationally.

International crime constantly expands into new spheres, including those which affect the vital interests of the state. Today, we are talking not only about such dangerous crimes as terrorism, drug trade, and laundering of money acquired by illegal means, but also about contraband trade in weapons, including weapons of mass destruction, their components and related expertise, and professional military mercenaries. Organized crime on this level is capable of posing a danger to the security of a state. All this calls for a new level of international cooperation in the fight against crime and, in particular, a new organization on the national as well as the international scale.

The history of cooperation in the fight against crime knows various forms. It is noteworthy that a permanent acting international organ for such cooperation was founded as early as 1872—the International Criminal and Penitentiary Commission, whose functions were assumed by the United Nations in 1950. At present, there exists within the UN system and outside of it a significant number of governmental and nongovernmental international organizations which deal with the fight against crime. The importance attributed to the problem is already attested to by the fact that the UN General Assembly at each of its sessions hears reports on crime. Even so, when one familiarizes oneself with the activity of all these organizations, one comes to the obvious conclusion that this activity is inadequately coordinated. This point is also noted by jurists who specialize in studying the problem of international cooperation in the fight against crime.[13]

The existing international organizations are in the main occupied with discussing, analyzing, and elaborating recommendations. All this is useful and in itself even indispensable. But it seems to us that the time has come to take a new step and create a permanently acting international organization charged not only with analytical and advisory but also operational functions. Such a need is further confirmed by Interpol's track record in both its positive and its negative dimensions. As a first step toward the indicated goal, the powers of Interpol could be expanded.

It strikes us as advisable to consider, too, the question of establishing an international court within the frame of the proposed organization. As is known, the existence of such a court is in principle sanctioned by a number of universal conventions dedicated to the fight with international crimes, starting with the 1948 convention on the Prevention and Punishment of the Crime of Genocide (Art. VI). Remember, too, that as early as 1937 a convention on the establishment of an international criminal court, under the auspices of the League of Nations, was opened for signature; however, it did not obtain the number of ratifications needed in order to enter into force. Today, an international criminal court could well turn out to be the optimal organ for hearing not only cases regarding such crimes as genocide and apartheid, but also cases such as that of the Libyans suspected of blowing up the Pan Am flight over Lockerbie, Scotland, in 1988.

Noting these points, I wish to record that Russian-American cooperation in the fight against crime represents a larger tendency of global proportions. Its effectiveness depends to a considerable extent on the effectiveness of the overall system of Russian-U.S. relations. While it is not unique in this regard, this fact cannot be ignored in setting the goals, principles, and forms of cooperation between Russia and the United States.

In closing, I want to underscore the fact that, en route to cooperation between the two powers in the fight against crime, important but still only beginning steps have been. A very hard road lies ahead; the necessary experience is lacking to surmount some of the hurdles. Considerable efforts will be required. Despite this, neither of the participants can, for the sake of national and international interests, afford to drop out.

Notes

1. *Izvestiia*, November 22, 1990.

2. *Rossiiskaia gazeta*, December 25, 1992.

3. Among the latest publications, see: G. Ginsburgs, "Russian-American cooperation in the fight against crime," *Mezhdunarodnaia zhizn'* (Moscow) 1993, no. 2; G. Ginsburgs, "Extradition in the USSR's Treaties on Legal Assistance with Non-'Socialist' States," *The Canadian Yearbook of International Law*, vol. 29 (1991).

4. *Argumenty i fakty,* 1990, no. 24.

5. *Rossiiskaia gazeta,* February 3, 1992.

6. The importance of this decision was stressed by the Assembly thereafter as well. See, for example, "Kommiunike o vtorom plenarnom zasedanii Mezhparlamentskoi assemblei." *Rossiiskaia gazeta,* January 4, 1993.

7. *Femida* (Minsk), 1992, no. 38, p. 7. The draft text of the designated convention on legal assistance was prepared by the Institute of Legislation and Comparative Legal Studies attached to the Supreme Soviet of the Russian Federation and published in *Moskovskii zhurnal mezhdunarodnogo prava,* 1992, no. 4.

8. For the corresponding practice of the Federal Republic of Germany, see *Fontes Juris Gentium,* ser. A, sect. II (Berlin, 1979), vol. 6, pp. 22ff. See, too, S. Dando, "Basic Concepts in and Temporal and Territorial Limits on the Applicability of the Penal Law of Japan," *New York Law School Journal of International and Comparative Law,* vol. 9 (1988).

9. Permanent Court of International Justice, 1927, ser. A, no. 10, p. 20.

10. Omnibus Diplomatic Security and Antiterrorism Act of 1986, Public Law, 99–399 (H.R. 4551), Washington, D.C., August 27, 1986, Para. 2331.

11. 60 U.S.L.W. 4523, U.S. June 15, 1992, no. 91–712, p. 4527.

12. 60 U.S.L.W., p. 4525.

13. S.V. Borodin, E.G. Liakhov, *Mezhdunarodnoe sotrudnichestvo v bor'be s ugolovnoi prestupnostiu* (Moscow, 1983), pp. 86ff.

E

FOREIGN POLICY

9

Germany as a Factor in U.S.-Russian Relations: An Essay on a Growing "Invisible" Challenge

Yaroslav Bilinsky

The point of this essay is that in the intermediate future—in the next five, ten, or fifteen years—the growing rapprochement between Germany and Russia may undermine and replace the American predominance in Europe. There is still time for the United States to seize the initiative and create a balance of power in Europe that would allow America to play the role of a balancer: effectively keeping the NATO structure could constrain a revisionist or plainly expansionist new Russia and, discreetly, also limit the freedom of maneuver of a more self-assertive Germany. Barring a strong American initiative now—which should be supported for at least a decade (an anathema to the U.S. Congress and possibly even to the administration, who prefer to think in two-, four-, or, at best, six-year terms)—I see a new power constellation emerging in Europe based on a strong continental axis stretching from Bonn to Moscow. A united Germany can no longer be taken for granted as a member of the Western alliance. Being a strong power in the center of Europe, Germany can expand its political and economic influence both west and east. As I see it, the tendency in Germany is increasingly to look east.

A preliminary version of this essay was presented as a paper at the round table on Moscow's Foreign Policy in the Post–Cold War Period (Professor Alvin Z. Rubinstein, chairman), at the National Convention of the American Association for the Advancement of Slavic Studies (AAASS), Phoenix, Arizona, November 19–22, 1992. In obtaining some major sources I was greatly aided by Mrs. Helga M. Schmid, Press Secretary for the Embassy of the Federal Republic in Washington, DC, and by Mr. Hans-Joachim Lehmann, of Vellmar, Germany. I would like to cordially thank the chairman and fellow members of the round table and my German consultants. I am responsible for any remaining imperfections in the text.

But does this not fly in the face of much contemporary evidence? At the end of 1992, what could the Russians offer the Germans except trouble—unpaid bills coupled with requests for further economic assistance? Was former Chancellor Helmut Schmidt not right when he sarcastically referred to Brezhnev's Soviet Union as an Upper Volta with missiles? And now, on U.S. initiative, are not most of those missiles supposed to be dismantled? Is the United States still not the strongest military and economic power? Furthermore, are there not several signs of political and economic malaise in Germany itself, with the country turning inward and Chancellor Kohl being attacked from the left and the right? On the other hand, is not Germany firmly anchored in a new Europe, which, beginning in January 1993, is becoming a reality before our eyes? Yes, those objections hold for the immediate future; and no, because they will become unimportant a decade hence, unless the United States quickly rediscovers Europe as it did once, under President Harry S. Truman. In the 1990s as it was in the 1940s, Germany remains the key to the European continent, an indispensable partner in both collaborating with and containing Russia.

The single event which is bound to influence German-Russian relations for decades has been the reunification of Germany. After inquiring about the Soviet Russian role in this miracle of 1989–90, I propose to address some unfinished military business, the trade and aid relations between those two countries, and the question of ethnic Germans in the former Soviet Union, which is sometimes referred to as "the little German question" (touching in this connection on the Ukrainian issue). At the end, I will also briefly refer to some major articles and speeches by German scholars as well as ranking German politicians, and will conclude by teasing out some implications for U.S. foreign policy vis-à-vis new —or old?—Russia.

First, an excursion into history: Why and when did Mikhail S. Gorbachev decide to open the way to German reunification? One of Gorbachev's closest political and diplomatic advisers was Foreign Minister Eduard A. Shevardnadze. But Shevardnadze's memoirs in this area are, on balance, disappointing. He does talk about the emotional and mental reservations that the Soviet elite, including himself, had against strengthening their World War II enemy, he mentions the unnaturalness of the division of Germany from the viewpoint of the German people, and he also throws in a concrete teaser:

> "When did you realize that reunification of Germany was inevitable?" Hans-Dietrich Genscher [the German Foreign Minister] asked me. We were talking at my home in Moscow, after my resignation. Since I was no longer bound by any official or political strictures, and since agreements had already been ratified, I could be very frank.
> "As far back as 1986. In a conversation with one of our top Germany specialists, I suggested that this issue would surface very soon. I said that in the near future the German question would define Europe. When a people has been divided for almost half a century, it is a nationality question, a question of the unity of a

nation refusing to be divided by the walls of ideology, weapons, and concrete."[1]

Shevardnadze is as eloquent as ever in asserting generalities and the very soul of discretion in not mentioning a more precise date of the conversation, nor the name of his interlocutor. Much more revealing on the emotional and intellectual blocks against tearing down the Berlin Wall and dissolving the German Democratic Republic (GDR) were Iurii P. Davydov, of the USA–Canada Institute, and Lieutenant-Colonel Dmitrii V. Trenin, who wrote in the German equivalent of *Foreign Affairs*:

> The boundary which ran through Germany and the Wall which bisected Berlin had acquired an enormous significance: They marked the boundary between the two world systems, between two economic blocs, two military alliances, two lifestyles, etc. In the mid-1980s it had become unimaginable that the boundary could be moved in either direction—except by war, which, too, had become unthinkable. Such ideas as that by [West German President] Richard Freiherr von Weizsäcker that "the German question should be kept open as long as the Brandenburg Gate is being kept locked" were being dismissed as wishful thought, if not something more sinister.[2]

In a very important article in *The Washington Post* of November 15, 1992, Michael Dobbs has shown on the basis of secret Communist Party Politburo and Soviet government documents that the Brezhnev regime could not bring itself to abandon the floundering Afghan Communists after the latter had declared themselves true Leninists and their country an addition to the Socialist camp.[3] Gorbachev, of course, stanched the "bloody wound of Afghanistan" by leaving the country. But even Gorbachev must have had serious blocks against abandoning a bridgehead of Socialism in the middle of Europe, and the native land of Marx and Engels as well.

To make a long story short, I am convinced that Gorbachev had decided that he had bigger fish to fry in West Germany: West Germany would help him economically in carrying out *perestroika*, would help him run the common European house. By opening the way to reunification, Gorbachev would fulfill the frequently declared supreme goal of West German foreign policy. He also hoped to use a united Germany to help pull Germany eastward, away from its alliance with the United States, which in the mid-1980s appeared less difficult than prying Germany out of a growing European union. The reunited Germans would surely help the "new-thinking" Soviet Union to reach the Atlantic Ocean in a figurative but politically significant sense. A later German source mentions that, as a quid pro quo for German unification, Genscher promised Gorbachev to gain entry into the institutions of the European Community.[5] In short, I believe that, whenever it was finally made, Gorbachev's decision to leapfrog the small and relatively poor East European states in order to woo Germany was sound in principle, even though it went against traditional Soviet thinking that the territorial expansion of Socialist states was proof that the future belonged to the USSR.

When did Gorbachev make the first decision to begin to explore the process of German reunification? I estimate that it was already in late December 1987, when Gorbachev received with unusual courtesies the conservative Bavarian Minister President Franz Josef Strauss.[6] Strauss had been very helpful in obtaining major economic credits for the Soviet Union, but his visit was a semiofficial one and carried less protocol weight than the state visits by German Federal President von Weizsäcker in July 1987 and by Chancellor Kohl in October 1988. From a later interview with Shevardnadze, it is clear that before the crucial Politburo decision of November 13, 1986, to gradually withdraw from Afghanistan —which was ultimately accomplished by February 15, 1989—Gorbachev could not seriously entertain the idea of a withdrawal from any Socialist domain.[7] From a Soviet expert on East Germany, Viacheslav Dashichev, we know that in November 1987 there was a meeting of the Scientific Advisory Council of the USSR Ministry of Foreign Affairs, which he chaired. At that meeting he discussed several options for solving the "German question," including a confederation of the two German states and outright reunification. At that meeting, admittedly, Dashichev was supported only by Iurii P. Davydov, who in his 1990 article in *Europa Archiv* claimed somewhat disingenuously that there had been no diplomatic position papers on the German question lying around in drawers in Moscow.[8] We know from the German press that in Gorbachev's meeting with Strauss in late December 1987—that is, a month after the meeting at the USSR Foreign Ministry—Gorbachev briefly mentioned to Strauss, who brought up the matter of German reunification, that while the division of Germany had for a long time been embodied in international agreements, it was West Germany itself that had rejected Stalin's reunification and neutralization offer of March 1952.[9]

I believe that in the closing days of December 1987 Gorbachev was deliberately raising the possibility of a new Soviet initiative on the German question, at a high price, because he saw that by that time the Germans were ready to explore such a Soviet diplomatic offensive. At the beginning of December 1987, at the Washington summit meeting between Gorbachev and President Reagan, the INF Treaty was signed. Constituting, as it did, a flip-flop on the deployment of Pershing 2s, it was far from popular with the former NATO military command and with some German general staff officers. Nor could Chancellor Kohl understand why he had literally staked his political life on the installation of those American missiles in Germany four years earlier if all of them—admittedly together with the Soviet countermissiles, the SS 20s—were to be all scrapped beginning in 1988. As I read the situation in December 1987, Strauss, Kohl, and others in Germany were disappointed with President Reagan and looking for an approach from Gorbachev, who held that famous German card.[10]

It is true that, beginning with 1988, President Reagan and his successor,

George Bush, started a "damage-control" operation in Bonn. Despite the announced candidacy of a Norwegian (who ultimately withdrew), a very able West German minister of defense, Dr. Manfred Wörner, was elected secretary-general of NATO, to assume office July 1, 1988. The election of a German to this post was unprecedented in NATO's history. (In October 1992 I was told that visiting Russian generals were so impressed with Dr. Wörner that they remarked among themselves that he was worth ten Russian generals. A German citizen, a leftist, was far less impressed and opined: "If that's so, they should take him with them! Good riddance!") Speaking in Mainz in May 1989, President Bush anointed the West Germans as "partners in leadership."[11]

To return to the chronology of Gorbachev's decisions: as late as a meeting of the International Department of the CPSU Central Committee toward the end of 1988, there was no consensus on how to proceed on the German question. Dashichev was not supported by anyone, and the head of the department, Valentin Falin, demonstratively left the room.[12] But Dashichev had the ear of Gorbachev. In early 1989, the decision was made to allow the East European states substantial internal autonomy, which would soon lead to the election of the first noncommunist government in Poland. Dashichev claims that Gorbachev accepted his memorandum of April 18, 1989, which was very critical of the Honecker regime.

In the literature, which is very ably summarized by Robert Gerald Livingston,[13] the predominant opinion is that Gorbachev soon lost control over the implementation of his decision to favor German reunification, which decision was publicly announced during his trip to West Germany in June 1989. Many authors stress a number of points: the unexpectedly rapid collapse of East Germany in October–November 1989; that Gorbachev practically wrote off East German Prime Minister Modrow when he announced before receiving him that "no one ever cast doubt on the unification of the Germans" [sic]; that he promised Kohl and Genscher, who visited him in Moscow February 10 and 11, 1990, "that the Soviet Union will respect the decision of Germans to determine the time and way of reunification"; that in early February 1990 he allowed the West Germans to swallow up East Germany in a politically finessed currency reform; his setback in the East German elections of March 18, 1990; and the even more obvious setback of having to allow for the membership of a united Germany in NATO (albeit modified by the Genscher formula that no NATO forces would be stationed in eastern Germany while there were still Soviet troops in that area and that NATO units could not hold maneuvers in the former DDR). This is all true, as is the view most forcefully put forward by Shevardnadze that the use of Soviet military force against the numerous demonstrators in October 1989 was *essentially* a nonoption: besides being the death warrant for *perestroika* in the USSR and any Western economic support for it, such an option was fraught with the danger of military confrontation with the Western allies.[14]

There is a possible minority opinion, articulated by Claus Gennrich of the

Frankfurter Allgemeine Zeitung, that Gorbachev did play a decisive role in preventing a bloodbath and thereby delaying the reunification. In Gennrich's words:

> Kohl will not forget that in the night of November 9–10, 1989 [the Berlin Wall had been opened during the day of November 9—Y.B.], against the desire of the KGB and of important [Soviet] military officers, Gorbachev prevented violence against the Germans. A message reached the Chancellor. . . . [as relayed via Bonn] that Gorbachev was asking whether it was true that unrest had broken out in East Germany and East Berlin. Immediately, Kohl had an answer sent to Gorbachev that this was nothing to worry about: the Germans were simply celebrating. *Gorbachev trusted Kohl more than he did his generals.*[15]

Gennrich's point, that the personal rapport between Kohl and Gorbachev was well established, is valid. I think, however, that not too much should be made of this episode: the time was late, the Germans were indeed celebrating the fall of the Berlin Wall, and it would have been very awkward for Soviet troops to clamp down by force that night.

A microanalysis of the events in Germany would probably show that if there had been any realistic chance to stop the disintegration of East Germany, it was in the first half of October 1989, not on November 10. Hence, Gorbachev's formal enquiry of Kohl that night sounds almost perfunctory. It almost required the evasively conciliatory response that Kohl gave. But Gorbachev may also have been guided by the same excessive self-confidence he displayed at the September 1989 Central Committee plenary session on nationality relations. Thus, Gorbachev still believed that he could fine-tune the engine in the East German car, but in fact the entire car was falling apart at all the welds. While admitting all this, however, I would still argue that, in principle, Gorbachev's decision to advance German reunification, taken probably in December 1987, was a sound one.

Equally sound was the decision of the Bush administration in the fall of that year to support Chancellor Kohl's reunification efforts, to the point of encouraging him to press his demands against the reservations expressed in France and notably in Prime Minister Thatcher's Great Britain. As explained by Nicol C. Rae, the U.S. government followed a pronounced pro-Bonn policy for two reasons:

> First, a German reunification on Western conditions and within the framework of NATO was seen by Washington as a significant strategic victory over the Soviet Union. Secondly, the Bush Administration believed that in the long run a reunited Germany would enable the United States to reduce their expensive and controversial military obligations in Western Europe—an especially important consideration at a time of record economic deficits. All in all . . . the Bush Administration considered a powerful united Germany in a more integrated Europe as a strategic advantage and a stabilizing factor in the international system.[16]

In 1989–90, of course, very few people could foresee the breakup of the Soviet Union in the latter half of 1991.

German reunification accomplished, what are the ties that continue to bind the new Germany to the former Soviet Union? In particular, which of those ties might in the long run be converted into pillars of a German-Russian condominium? The unfinished military business does not appear to be a good building stone for a lasting relationship. On closer inspection, however, we see not only that CIS—probably, Russian—troops will be stationed in former East Germany until August 31, 1994, but that a smooth disentanglement of the Russian postoccupation regime will contribute much good will toward more stable political relations.

As of September 30, 1992, of the original 337,800 ex-Soviet troops that had been stationed in ex–East Germany, 202,170, or 59.9 percent, have been withdrawn; likewise 107,218 of the original 208,400 civilian employees and dependents (51.5 percent), according to data from the German Ministry of Defense. The original withdrawal agreement runs until the end of 1994, and the German authorities appeared to be satisfied that the withdrawal would continue according to plan.[17] Unlike agreements with the Balts, which have run into withdrawal delays, the German treaty package of September 12, 1990, sweetened the deal with a grant of 12 billion German Marks (DM) and an interest-free loan of DM 3 billion, or a total of DM 15 billion, part of which (DM 7.8 billion) is to be spent for building lodging space for the repatriated ex-Soviet soldiers in Russia, Ukraine, and Belarus. Because the final settlement treaty was a solemn six-power treaty and, above all, because of the economic and political interests involved, I do not expect any serious trouble, provided that Yeltsin stays in power as an effective president and that the new Russian military will act rationally and not mistake Germany for Lithuania. During his December 1992 summit meeting with Yeltsin in Moscow, Chancellor Kohl very prudently chose to accelerate the process of CIS military withdrawal. For an additional DM 550 million, the troops and their dependents are to leave the so-called new federal states (ex-GDR) by August 31, 1994, or four months earlier than had been agreed upon in September 1990.[18] Even with the best of intentions on both sides, the continued presence of weakened and demoralized ex-Soviet units on German soil is an anomaly that should be ended, the sooner the better.

Looking a little further ahead on the issue of the military: reunified Germany has a contractual obligation to scale its united military forces down to 370,000 men and not to develop any weapons of mass destruction, notably nuclear weapons. I estimate that at the end of 1991 there were approximately two million former Soviet troops in Russia and about 500,000 in Ukraine. Moreover, of the 27,600 nuclear warheads in the entire former Soviet Union, at that time Russia had a total of 19,000; 7,449 of the balance of 10,271 were deployed on ICBMs.[19] One does not have to be Mearsheimer[20] to realize that this does not leave Germany in a very comfortable position, unless the Russians drastically reduce their nuclear arsenal and/or unless the United States maintains its nuclear strength to defend Europe.

But in the latter half of the 1980s the American nuclear umbrella, as seen from Bonn, started leaking dangerously and some American policy-makers in the 1990s are thinking of drastically shrinking that already diminished umbrella, going beyond the figures advocated by former President Bush to possibly as few as 500 nuclear warheads each for the United States and Russia. Admittedly, such a drastic reduction is what the Germans aptly call the "melody of the future," or *Zukunftsmusik.* The START II treaty, which was negotiated between President Bush and a weakened President Yeltsin merely calls for a reduction to 3,000–3,500 warheads each, by the year 2003.[21]

Furthermore, a well-known Munich columnist, Josef Joffe, reassured his American readers in 1989 that because of the "legacies of World War II and . . . the European order installed thereafter," West Germany could not fully exercise "its outstanding assets . . . [of] economic potential and geographic position." He added: "With the 'Iron Curtain' in place, West German economic prowess could not buy political influence in *the East—a traditional outlet for German energies. . . .* Surely, Bonn has the resources to build a first-class nuclear deterrent; it cannot do so by dint of imposed renunciation and political good sense"[22] (emphasis added). That was written before the reunification, however, and before the Balkan crisis of 1992–93.

The unstable military situation in Europe of 1993 is likely to grow even worse—with or without further debacle in former Yugoslavia, which in turn could be a prelude for a more extended Balkan war or even a major war in the former USSR. Given this instability, one need not be an absolute contrarian to realize that staying nuclear-free is a luxury that the new Germany will not be able to afford in the long run. To put it bluntly, if I were a German in Bonn or Berlin, I would seriously think of a good *force de frappe* right now. This might provoke an outcry in Paris and an even louder outcry in London, not to speak of bad feelings in Warsaw and Prague. But will Russia and the United States come together to effectively enforce the denuclearization of Germany in ten or twenty years? I doubt it.

Another point concerns the major economic ties between Germany and Russia. In a major article on German unification and the economic interests of the Soviet Union, Dr. Heinrich Vogel, the long-time director of the Federal Institute for East European and International Studies in Cologne, points out that German economics is anchored in the West. He writes: "The sense of reality and profit calculations of German businessmen are oriented toward the world market. *From this perspective it becomes clear that the future of the German economy does not lie in the East. In the foreseeable future, the share* [of the East] *in German foreign trade cannot exceed ten percent*"[23] (emphasis added). This is indeed so, and an excellent article in the *Harvard Business Review* for March–April 1992 documents the achievements of German firms in the world market.[24] Nonetheless, Dr. Vogel says that the world market has for a long time included Eastern Europe and that the division into West and East has long been obsolete. I also recall that in several conversations with the author between late 1982 and 1985, Dr. Vogel approvingly mentioned the "continental drift," or the separation between the United States and Europe. I would say that that foreign trade between West Germany and the Soviet Union was respectable, and that between East Germany and the Soviet Union was quite substantial in terms of quantity and, above all, quality.

To be more specific, let us look at some statistics in foreign trade in 1987, the last detailed figures available to me for both West and East Germany. In that year, West German imports from the USSR amounted to only $4 billion or 1.8 percent of all its imports, and German exports to the USSR made up only $4.4 billion or 1.5 percent of the total.[25] But in East Germany in 1987, the trade relationship was dramatically different. The Soviet Union was the GDR's foremost trading partner by far, with a yearly turnover of 68.5 billion "Valuta Marks" (VM) or 42.2 percent of the total. (East Germany's next largest trade partner that year was Czechoslovakia, with a turnover of 14.3 billion VM, or 8.8 percent of the total.)[26] In that year, the GDR exported to the Soviet Union VM 2.1 billion of agricultural implements and tractors, VM 1.4 billion of cutting lathes, and VM 1.2 billion of forklifts and similar equipment; and it imported from the Soviet Union 3.9 out of 7.2 million metric tons of coal, 17.1 out of a total of 20 billion cubic meters of natural gas, as well as VM 1.2 billion worth of electrical and electronic goods.[27] Small wonder that on meeting with President Yeltsin in Moscow in December 1992, Chancellor Kohl pleaded that Russia renew its former close trade relations with the former German Democratic Republic. It would help the stability of both Russia and Germany.[28] Similarly, according to an editorial in the business-oriented *Frankfurter Allgemeine Zeitung*, the only aid to Russia that made commercial sense was one linked to the restoration of the former East Germany's ties to the markets of today's CIS.[29]

The Russians have grown used to German quality goods, and the East Germans in particular know the old Soviet markets, so that, once former East Germany is rebuilt, it will look east to Russia to sell its machinery, optics, and so forth. Furthermore, as they say in Russia, it is not a coincidence that in 1991 it was German firms, not American firms, that had the largest number of joint ventures in the USSR: 351, compared with 343 for the Americans, although admittedly, the American ventures were somewhat better capitalized.[30]

As far as German economic aid to Russia is concerned, there is some dispute about the exact meaning of the DM 75 billion (or about $52.2 billion) which is frequently cited as the total amount of aid that has been extended to the former USSR by united Germany since the end of 1989. What is beyond dispute is that the German share in aid commitments (from September 1990 to February 1992) was relatively much larger than the U.S. share ($43.7 billion compared with $4.4 billion). This is exacerbated by the perception in some quarters in Washington that the U.S. aid that trickles into the former Soviet republics has been administered badly. The second largest donor to the former USSR, by the way, is not the United States, but Italy, with $5.7 billion in commitments. However, the aid commitments of both Japan ($2.4 billion) and France ($2.1 billion) are lower than U.S. commitments.[31]

Disaggregated, the German aid is roughly as follows. First, there is the grant of DM 12 billion (or $8.4 billion) that is really a payment for the withdrawal of former Soviet troops from the former GDR. (A German consultant who read this paper pointed out correctly that the grant of DM 12 billion has not only been in the German national interest, but has also been a constructive contribution to European security.) Because that payment is technically a grant, some sources add to that figure the German humanitarian aid in the winter of 1991–92. That humanitarian aid consisted of more than 12,200 tons of relief supplies furnished by private German charity organizations and $1.9 billion worth of relief goods provided since the end of 1989 by the West German government.[32] About $1 billion remains still not fully accounted for in the German-supplied subtotal of $11.4 billion for grants, including humanitarian and technical assistance. Other German sources add the DM 3 billion loan to the DM 12 billion grant, both of which were issued in connection with the *troop withdrawal* (DM 15 billion out of a total of DM 75 billion). Another politically motivated subtotal is DM 1 billion for the resettlement of Soviet Germans to Germany.[33] There appears to be a legitimate economic investment by Germany of $2.4 billion for increasing the production of natural gas and the mining of ore. German official sources also stress that on April 26, 1992, Chancellor Kohl persuaded the G7 nations to commit $24 billion in financial assistance to the former USSR, of which the German share was $4.5 billion.[34]

A critic might say that of the total figure of $52.2 billion in Germany's aid commitments, more than half ($33.7 billion) is somewhat debatable, particularly the $10.7 billion (DM 17.6 billion) in transfer rubles that the ex-USSR owes to the ex-GDR. This, incidentally, was recognized at the December 1992 Kohl–Yeltsin summit when payments on those sums—both interest and principal —were suspended until 2000.[35] Also, fully $23 billion of those $33.7 billion are state credit and export guarantees, which will be payable only if Russia defaults on its debt to private German suppliers. Such defaults are very likely, however, and the German government already budgeted DM 3 billion for guarantee payments in 1993 and DM 4 billion for such payments in 1994.[36] Furthermore, it was also revealed at the December 1992 Moscow summit that in the course of 1992, Germany had guaranteed another DM 5 billion for exports, thus raising the total German aid commitments to at least about DM 80 billion at the end of 1992, and possibly more in view of yet another commitment of DM 1 billion in restitution payments to victims of Nazi wartime terror in Russia, Ukraine, and Belarus.[37]

To summarize this highly involved business of aid, we stress that ultimately the German totals must be disaggregated into political debts, "accounting conventions" (the East German credit in transfer rubles), as well as real past and probable future payments. But at the same time, we must also recognize that, to the Russians, Germany comes out looking much better when she is compared with the United States, Japan, or France. In international relations it is those broad international comparisons that are decisive, not the economic fine print.

Let us now turn to the problem of the so-called Volga Germans. As many as two million citizens of the former Soviet Union who are of German extraction live scattered in Kazakhstan, Uzbekistan, the North Caucasus, and Ukraine. Many of them—or their parents—had been deported from the Volga Autonomous German Republic. Since 1987, about 150,000 of these Germans claiming to have relatives in Germany have left annually from the Soviet Union, and as many as 500,000 applications for emigration were still pending in early 1992. Chancellor Kohl would prefer to stem the heavy flow of immigrants and asylum-seekers to Germany. President Yeltsin promised during his November 1991 visit to Germany to restore an autonomous German territorial unit in the Volga area, but by February 1992, he in effect temporarily withdrew that promise. By the time of the Kohl–Yeltsin summit in Moscow, in December 1992, however, resolution of the issue of the restoration of the Volga German Autonomous Republic appeared to be on a fast track again. Given the inevitability of some disputes over economic aid and also about reparations for victims of Nazism, the Volga German question is perhaps a needless irritant in Russian-German relations.[38]

President Yeltsin's initial mishandling of the Volga German issue gave President Leonid M. Kravchuk, of newly independent Ukraine, an opportunity to approach the German government in a genuinely helpful way. Ukraine was formally recognized by Germany December 26, 1991.[39] During the following year, some policy differences emerged between these two countries over the repayment of the former Soviet debt (Ukraine initially preferred to pay her share directly, but the Germans successfully insisted on a central payment agency in Moscow). Further, so long as Germany remains denuclearized, it cannot but view with some misgivings the delay, at the time of this writing, in January 1993, by the Ukrainian Supreme Council (parliament) of its ratification of START I and of the surrender of its nuclear missiles to Russia.[40] However, by following up with concrete measures the offer that he made shortly before his first state visit to Germany on February 3–4, 1992, to resettle as many ethnic Germans on good Ukrainian lands as possible, President Kravchuk has caught the attention of the German media and of German political circles.

Ironically, perhaps, most of the ethnic Germans now living in the CIS want to emigrate to Germany rather than settle in a new Volga German autonomous republic or the southern steppes of Ukraine. But the government of united Germany—which has spent $100 billion annually to restore the former East German economy and quite substantial amounts on political asylum-seekers

—would prefer that, at least for the time being, ethnic Germans stay in the CIS. The German government is also willing to pay aid to those states such as Ukraine and Russia that create better living and cultural conditions for their fellow nationals. The Ukrainians would probably have invited German settlers anyway, to restore an injustice committed in World War II and to preempt the colonization of their underpopulated southern provinces by Russian peasants, but both Yeltsin and Kohl accelerated the good-faith Ukrainian offer.[41] In general, German policy vis-à-vis Russia can now be a little bit more flexible thanks to the as yet minor but not insignificant "Ukrainian card."

Most important is perhaps the overall shift in the weight of Germany in international relations. This shift is rendered particularly acute by the expected changes in the German chancellorship within the next few years, possibly even before the scheduled 1994 parliamentary election. In this regard, I would like to cite an editorial in the *Frankfurter Allgemeine Zeitung*, not only because it is so prudent, but because it is my understanding that it was a group of publicists allied to that newspaper who were the brain trust behind a small minority in the German Christian Democratic Union and Christian Socialist Union who took the issue of German reunification seriously already in the mid-1980s. On October 14, 1992, Johann Georg Reissmueller wrote:

> The government of Kohl/Kinkel has good reasons to [watch its step and] be considerate in dealing with Russia [*mit Russland pfleglich umzugehen*]. The Moscow state may not be a world power today; but it will reacquire that rank before long. In any case, Russia is a great power, whose word in Europe still carries weight.[42]

At the same time, there is growing criticism of the United States. For instance, a German scholar, Professor Dr. Gregor Schöllgen of Erlangen University, writes:

> The concerns over the new power of Germany that have been raised in the American media coincide with the situation of internal weakness in the U.S., to a certain extent are even caused by this. . . . The enemy and the challenger of the last half-century has disappeared. The United States now finds itself in a phase of psychological insecurity within and—so it would appear—of weakness without.[43]

Another German scholar, Professor Wolfgang Seiffert, justly criticizes the excessive German and U.S. preoccupation with European stability, which was exploded in 1989. But he goes, perhaps, a little far:

> Though united Germany [of 1990] is smaller than Germany within the boundaries of 1937 . . . we have to confirm the fact that reunited Germany is a European great power which, in the political and economic sense, is better equipped than all the former German states in their initial periods. Despite its

limitation to 370,000 men, Germany will be the strongest European power in NATO after the U.S.[44]

Please note this:

> Germany will confront the weaker or poorer European countries in Western and Eastern Europe as they had been confronted in the past by the Bismarck Reich of 1871, the Weimar Republic of 1919, or the Third Reich of 1933.[45]

Professor Seiffert also emphasizes that, although it is embedded militarily in NATO and economically in the European Community, "*this reunified Germany returns to its Central European position and into world politics*"[46] (emphasis in original). Seiffert is emphatic that without Gorbachev, German unification would have been impossible.[47] This, in my view, is historically correct. But it can also be easily expanded into an argument for continued German-Russian cooperation, although that is not explicit in Seiffert's article.

German scholars apart, what about the views of Chancellor Kohl's heirs apparent, Wolfgang Schäuble and Volker Rühe? Wolfgang Schäuble, the former minister of the interior, who successfully overcame a 1990 assassination attempt, is considered the favorite to succeed Chancellor Kohl. Born in Freiburg, in southwestern Germany, Schäuble is dedicated to the cause of European unity. He would continue trying to firmly anchor Germany in Western Europe.[48]

But Schäuble's rival for Kohl's succession, Volker Rühe, at present German defense minister, appears to have different views on foreign policy. Born in the Lüneburger Heide in northern Germany, Rühe gave a major foreign policy address at the annual meeting of the German foreign policy society (Deutsche Gesellschaft für Auswärtige Politik) in the summer of 1992. I found some disturbing notes in Minister Rühe's address. On its surface, there is a seemingly balanced juxtaposition of the "interests of Germany" with the democratic "values" which link Germany with the United States. There is a factually correct statement that the first generation of German politicians, scholars, journalists, and soldiers who have been intimately involved in the cultivation of German-American relations are passing away.[49] Although the explicit text is factually and politically correct, there is a strongly implicit critique of this openly pro-American political generation, of which Chancellor Kohl is a part, who are now passing from the scene.[50]

Above all, sandwiched between the politically and diplomatically correct tributes to Germany's trans-Atlantic relationship there are some very positive, ambitious references to future Russian-German cooperation. In Rühe's words:

> The trans-Atlantic community and the firm anchoring of Germany in the Western alliance constitute for Germany also the basis for our relations with Russia. We need [Russia] as a partner for the establishment of a European peace order, and for that reason we must not exclude [*ausklammern*] Russia from the Euro-

pean process of unity, even though there is no [immediate?—Y.B.] prospect for an integration of Russia into the European Community as is the case for the Central European democracies. *With no other land has Russia cultivated as varied relations as with Germany, or developed political, cultural and economic ties that have long traditions.* It is true that the history of the two states has known both light and dark periods. *In Germany, there exists both public opinion and sentiment* [Denken und Fühlen] *that is moving in direction of the East, as well as the readiness to cooperate with Russia.* Not least for the reason that the cooperation and the linkage [of Russia] in a coalescing Europe is a political, economic, cultural and strategic requirement [*geboten ist*, which is not an absolute must, but a must nonetheless—Y.B.]. [Emphases added.][51]

Admittedly, Rühe follows up this ringing endorsement of Russo-German cooperation with a cautionary note not to forget Germany's integration into the North American and West European system of democratic values [*Wertegemeinschaft*] that has served Germany well in the past. It seems to me, however, that, as in a sandwich, it is the meat that counts, especially when the surrounding bread is admittedly thin. Rühe may still become Chancellor Kohl's successor.

Let us take a brief excursion into political symbolism. On the seventieth anniversary of the 1922 Treaty of Rapallo between Germany and the USSR, Michael Stürmer passionately asserted that there would be no return to a special, exclusive relationship between Germany and Russia. The historic Rapallo Treaty had been made inevitable by the U.S. withdrawal from European politics after World War I and by the subsequent rapprochement of Germany and Soviet Russia, who had been intentionally *déclassés* and isolated by their European rivals. According to Stürmer, "For German-Russian cooperation there are a thousand reasons. For a German-Russian special relationship there are only counterreasons." He added for good measure that Russia had not yet reached the bottom of the abyss of her catastrophes. It was incumbent on German diplomacy to pull Russia into the European systems so as to share the costs of her recovery.[52] I was most intrigued, however, when at the conclusion of their December 1992 summit meeting in Moscow, President Yeltsin gave Chancellor Kohl a gift from the archives of the Soviet Foreign Ministry: original files that had belonged to the German Catholic *Zentrum* political leader and former Reich Chancellor Wirth—the very same statesman who had signed the 1922 Treaty of Rapallo on behalf of the German Weimar Republic.[53] Was Yeltsin simply acting the gracious host toward a fellow-Catholic chancellor or was he giving Kohl a diplomatic message?

Finally, what should the policy of the United States be in view of the German-Russian factor? In Europe, the United States is increasingly faced with a more self-assertive Germany. At the same time, Russian foreign policy is also becoming more self-assertive, nay, revisionist. There was the curious non-speech by Russian Foreign Minister Andrei Kozyrev at the CSCE meeting at Stockholm on

December 14, 1992, in which he castigated the "military presence of NATO and the WEU in the Baltic states and in other areas of the former Soviet Union" and solemnly promised that in its struggle the present government of rump-Yugoslavia could rely on the support of Great Russia against international sanctions.[54] Also disturbing is the increasing preoccupation of Russian foreign policy with the fate of the 25 million ethnic Russians in the so-called near abroad of the former USSR, which Professor Henry R. Huttenbach, of the City College of New York, who was invited to a three-day conference in St. Petersburg, November 27–29, 1992, organized by the Committee of Nationalities of the Russian Supreme Soviet, bluntly called the "Sudeten syndrome."[55]

Not only are both Germany and Russia becoming more self-assertive, which was perhaps inevitable, they are doing so in tandem. A thoughtful article in *The Economist* notes that in "the middle distance, sanguine Germans will see in German-Russian relations a new dawn." First, there is no longer a military threat to Germany from the east. Second, post-Communist Russia beckons as a "vast potential consumer market and a huge mineral-rich continent hungry for German engineers." *The Economist* continues: "The third reason for Germany's eastern hopes is harder to define, but no less real. *Germans and Russians share a feeling that, as Europe's world-sized powers, they have a special relationship*" (emphasis added).[56]

It would seem to me that the more or less implicit vision of some Americans to fulfill the prophecy of Tocqueville and set up a global American-Russian condominium has turned out to be a dream shattered by Gorbachev's farsighted policy to build a common European home with Russia and Germany as joint landlords. In practical terms, it would have been imperative that, for as long as possible, Americans stayed in Europe in large force: diplomatic, economic, and military. But in mid-January 1993, Washington rumors have it that the withdrawal of the 150,000 U.S. troops and their dependents who still remain in Germany will be speeded up—to make room for hundreds of thousands of political asylum-seekers.[57] How noble! But also what a tragi-comic end to almost fifty years of the United States' controlling presence in the center of Europe. And to European stability.

Notes

1. Eduard Shevardnadze, *The Future Belongs to Freedom* (New York: The Free Press, 1992), p. 131 (in the chapter titled "From Ottawa to Arkhiz: The Road to German Reunification").

2. Jurij P. Dawydow and Dmitrij W. Trenin, "Die Haltung der Sowjetunion gegenüber der Deutschen Frage" [The position of the USSR toward the German Question], *Europa Archiv*, vol. 45, no. 8 (April 25, 1990), p. 252.

3. Michael Dobbs, "Soviet Memos Trace Kremlin's March to War," *The Washington Post*, November 15, 1992, p. A1.

4. Dobbs, "Dramatic Politburo Meeting [November 13, 1986] Led to End of War," *The Washington Post*, November 16, 1992, p. A1.

5. Claus Gennrich, "Persönliches und Geschichtliches verknüpft Kohl und Gorbatschow und die Interessen Deutschlands und der Sowjetunion" [Tie-in between personal and historical relations: Kohl and Gorbachev and the interests of Germany and the USSR], *Frankfurter Allgemeine Zeitung [FAZ]*, August 20, 1991, p. 10. This is an important, retrospective article in the foremost German conservative newspaper, written on the eve of the August putsch.

6. Bernhard Küppers, "Der Gast kostet den Triumph aus" [The guest savors his triumph], *Süddeutsche Zeitung [SZ]* (Munich), December 30, 1987, p. 3. On December 28, 1987, Strauss, an avid flyer, had been allowed to pilot his own plane onto the Moscow airfield by himself, without the customary Soviet navigator; he had been invited to visit by the USSR Foreign Trade Commission, although, according to the customary Soviet protocol, as a Bavarian *state* official, not a German *federal* official, Strauss rated only an invitation from a Soviet *republic*. I have dealt with this in my unpublished conference paper, "Decoupling Through Nuclear Disarmament: Gorbachev's Diplomatic Offensive Against West Germany."

7. Dobbs, "Dramatic Politburo Meeting . . . ," *The Washington Post*, November 16, 1992, p. A16. Shevardnadze told Dobbs in 1992: "Everything else flowed from that [decision]."

8. On Davydov's claim, see Dawydow and Trenin, "Die Haltung der Sowjetunion. . . ," *Europa Archiv*, vol. 45, no. 8 (April 25, 1990), p. 253. The Dashichev interview was published as: " 'Dann erhebt sich das Volk': SPIEGEL-Gespräch mit dem Moskauer Politologen Wjatscheslaw Daschitschew über die Krise in der Sowjetunion" ('Then the People Will Rise': SPIEGEL-Interview with the Moscow political scientist Viacheslav Dashichev about the crisis in the Soviet Union), *Spiegel*, vol. 45, no. 4 (January 21, 1991), p. 137.

9. Küppers, "Nach dem Gespräch mit Gorbatschow—Strauss: Moskau widerspricht nicht mehr dem Begriff 'Einheit der deutschen Nation' " (After the talk with Gorbachev—Strauss: Moscow does no longer reject the concept of the 'unity of the German nation'), *SZ*, December 30, 1987, p. 1.

10. Bilinsky, "Decoupling Through Nuclear Disarmament."

11. Elizabeth Pond, "Germany in the New Europe," *Foreign Affairs*, vol. 71, no. 2 (Spring 1992), p. 115.

12. " 'Dann erhebt sich . . . ,' " *Spiegel*, vol. 45, no. 4 (January 21, 1991), pp. 139–40.

13. Robert Gerald Livingston, "Relinquishment of East Germany," in Richard F. Staar, ed., *East-Central Europe and the USSR* (New York: St. Martin's Press, 1991), pp. 83–101; besides Livingstone, there are very useful detailed accounts by Elizabeth Pond, "A Wall Destroyed: The Dynamics of German Reunification in the GDR," *International Security*, vol. 15, no. 2 (Fall 1990), pp. 35–66; and by Walter Schütze, the secretary general of the Comité d'étude des relations franco-allemandes (CERFA) in Paris, "De la 'note Staline' à la conférence '2 + 4'. La reunification allemande en perspective" (From "Stalin's Note" to the "2 + 4" conference: German reunification in perspective), in a special issue on German unification, disarmament, and the new European order of *Politique étrangere* (Foreign policy), 1991, no. 1, pp. 21–39.

14. Shevardnadze, *The Future Belongs to Freedom*, p. 118.

15. Gennrich, "Persönliches und Geschichtliches verknüpft. . . ," *FAZ*, August 20, 1991, p. 10; emphasis added.

16. Nicol C. Rae, "Die amerikanische und britische Reaktion auf die Wiedervereinigung Deutschlands" (The American and British reactions to German reunification), *Zeitschrift für Politik: Organ der Hochschule für Politik München* (Journal of Politics; Organ of the Munich Advanced School for Political Science), vol. 39, no. 1 (March 1992), p. 35.

17. See on this also the long article by Karl Feldmeyer, "Die halbe Armee ist weg: Der Abzug der russischen Truppen aus Deutschland verläuft vereinbarungsgemäss" (Half of the army has gone: The withdrawal of the Russian troops from Germany proceeds according to the agreements), *FAZ*, August 29, 1992.

18. "Kohl: Die deutsch-russischen Beziehungen von ungelösten Problemen entlastet . . . " (Kohl: German-Russian relations unburdened of unsolved problems), *FAZ*, December 17, 1992, pp. 1–2. Also, "Kohl und Jelzin unterzeichnen Grundsatzerklärung: Bonn stundet Moskau Schulden bis zum Jahr 2000: Sonderzahlung für früheren Truppen- abzug vereinbart . . . " (Kohl and Yeltsin sign a declaration of principles: Bonn suspends payments on Moscow's debts until 2000: Special payment for earlier troop withdrawal), *SZ*, December 17, 1992, p. 1.

19. Data on the number of troops in the Russian Federation are surprisingly hard to find. For instance, when on May 7, 1992, President Yeltsin decreed the establishment of Russian armed forces, no figures were given on their eventual size. Nor are such figures to be found in a French article, which does give details on missiles. See Jean-Christoph Romer, "Une armée russe: quelle armée?" (A Russian army: What army?), *Politique étrangere* (Foreign policy), 1992, no. 1 (special issue on the future of Russia), p. 71. Nor is there a figure in the otherwise informative contribution by Signe Landgren, "Post- Soviet threats to security," in SIPRI (Stockholm International Peace Research Institute) *Yearbook 1992: World Armaments and Disarmament* (New York: Oxford University Press, 1992). In despair, I have used the International Institute for Strategic Studies, *The Military Balance 1991–1992* (London: Brassey's, 1991), as follows: From a grand total of 3,400,000 for Soviet armed forces (p. 36), I have deducted 500,000 for forces stationed in Ukraine (source: CIS Deputy Defense Minister Col. Gen. Boris Piankov's interview in *Krasnaia zvezda*, December 24, 1991, as cited in Douglas L. Clarke, "The Battle for the Black Sea Fleet," RFE/RL Research Institute (Munich), *RFE/RL Research Report*, vol. 1, no. 5 (January 31, 1992), p. 54); have further deducted 373,000 troops belonging to the Soviet western and northern groups of forces, mostly stationed in former East Germany; 280,000 strategic rocket forces; 69,000 troops in the Baltic Military District (MD), 101,000 troops from the Belarus MD, and 127,000 in the Transcaucasian MD, which gave me a total of 1,950,000 (*The Military Balance 1991–1992*, p. 234). That total does not take into the account the troops stationed in the Central Asian republics, which troops are formally still subordinate to the CIS. It is a conservative estimate in that the Russian Federation in 1991 included the majority of the 280,000 strategic rocket forces. Ironically, with the withdrawal of former Soviet troops from East Germany, Czechoslovakia, Hung- ary, and Poland, the totals in both the Russian Federation and Ukraine increased a year later, at the end of 1992. For instance, in late 1992, the Ukrainian total was put at 700,000 troops, to be reduced to 450,000 by 1995 (see "1992: A Look Back: The task of nation- building," *The Ukrainian Weekly* [*Svoboda*] (Jersey City, NJ), vol. 40, no. 52 [December 27, 1992], p. 8).

20. In mid-1990, John J. Mearsheimer, of the University of Chicago published his provocative article "Back to the Future: Instability in Europe After the Cold War," *Inter- national Security*, vol. 15, no. 1 (Summer 1990), pp. 5–56, in which he advocated a "well-managed" nuclear proliferation in Europe (p. 37) or, more specifically, being pre- pared for West Germany developing nuclear weapons "as the best way to deter a Soviet conventional attack into Central Europe" (p. 36). See also the subsequent discussion by Stanley Hoffmann, Robert O. Keohane, and John J. Mearsheimer, "Back to the Future, Part II: International Relations Theory and Post–Cold War Europe," *International Secu- rity*, vol. 15, no. 2 (Fall 1990), pp. 191–99; and Bruce M. Russett, Thomas Risse-Kappen, and John J. Mearsheimer, "Back to the Future III: Realism and the Realities of European Security," *International Security*, vol. 15, no. 3 (Winter 1990/91), pp. 216–22.

21. See the thoughtful critical appraisal by Thomas L. Friedman, "Knocking at the Nuclear Clubhouse Door: Beyond Start II: A New Level of Instability," *The New York Times*, January 10, 1993, sec. 4, pp. 1 and 3. Also, Steven Erlanger, "Concessions on Arms Pact Made by U.S.," *The New York Times*, January 3, 1993, sec. 1, p. 8.

22. Josef Joffe, "The Revisionists: Moscow, Bonn, and the European Balance," *The National Interest*, no. 17 (Fall 1989), p. 50.

23. Heinrich Vogel, "Die Vereinigung Deutschlands und die Wirtschaftsinteressen der Sowjetunion" (The unification of Germany and the economic interests of the USSR), *Europa Archiv*, vol. 45, no. 13–14 (July 25, 1990), p. 414.

24. Hermann Simon, "Lessons from Germany's Midsize Giants," *Harvard Business Review*, March–April 1992, pp. 115–25.

25. United Nations, Department of International Economic and Social Affairs, Statistical Office: *1989 International Trade Statistics Yearbook* (New York: United Nations, 1991), vol. I (trade by country), p. 328.

26. Deutsche Demokratische Republik, Staatliche Zentralverwaltung für Statistik (GDR, Central Statistical Administration), *Statistisches Jahrbuch 1988* (1988 Statistical Yearbook) (Berlin: Staatsverlag der DDR, 1988), p. 242. Percentages calculated by author.

27. Ibid., pp. 259 and 245.

28. "Erster Moskau-Besuch Kohls nach Auflösung der UdSSR: Jelzin sichert Fortsetzung des Reformkurses zu" [Kohl's first visit to Moscow after the dissolution of USSR: Yeltsin ensures the continuation of the reform course], *SZ*, December 16, 1992, p. 1.

29. Werner Adam, "Neues Russland, alte Fragen" [New Russia, old questions], *FAZ*, December 17, 1992.

30. *USSR Facts and Figures Annual* (Gulf Breeze, FL: Academic International Press, 1992), vol. 17, p. 338.

31. The DM75 billion figure appears, for instance, in the September 30, 1992 address to the German American Business Council by H.E. Immo Stabreit, ambassador of the Federal Republic of Germany, "Germany, European Unification and Transatlantic Partnership," in the German Information Center, New York, *Statements and Speeches*, vol. 15, no. 15, p. 3. For comparison with other Western donors, see "Germany tops list of aid for CIS republics," in the Embassy of the Federal Republic of Germany, Washington, DC, press release, March 5, 1992, p. 1. The original source is European Community Commission, press release March 5, 1992, supplied by Mrs. Helga M. Schmid, Press Secretary, German Embassy in Washington. The quotation on U.S. aid is from Hobart Rowen, "US Has Bungled Aid to the Old Soviet Bloc," *The Washington Post*, January 17, 1993, p. H1.

32. See German Information Center, New York, *Focus on . . .*: "German Support for the Transition to Democracy and Market Economy in the Former Soviet Union," June 1992: A Position Paper of the German Embassy, Washington, DC, pp. 1–2; courtesy of Mrs. Schmid.

33. Communication from Germany, based on information supplied by an official in the German Ministry of Economics. It should, of course, be remembered that in December 1992 Germany committed another DM550 million to an accelerated troop withdrawal.

34. "German Support for the Transition to Democracy. . . ," pp. 2–3.

35. For an explanation of how that debt originated under "partly dubious circumstances" see Gerhard Hennemann, "Moskaus grösster Gläubiger: Bund bürgt für Forderungen in Höhe von 36 Milliarden" (Moscow's largest creditor: the Federal state guarantees claims totalling DM36 billion), *SZ*, December 17, 1992, p. 8; and on page 4 of the same issue, the editorial "Nichts zu holen in Moskau" (Nothing to be gotten in Moscow).

36. "Pläne für neue Schuldenentlastung Russlands . . ." (Plans for a new alleviation of Russia's debt), *FAZ*, October 31, 1992; similarly, Klaus Broichhausen, "Ein Fass ohne Boden: Bürgen für das GUS Geschäft" (A bottomless barrel: Export guarantees for CIS business), *FAZ*, December 9, 1992.

37. Hennemann, "Moskaus grösster Gläubiger. . .," *SZ*, December 17, 1992, 8; "Kohl: die deutsch russischen Beziehungen. . .," *FAZ*, December 17, 1992. I am deliberately imprecise on the total because the old DM75 billion figure refers to *June* 1992.

38. Anthony Heyman, "Refugees and citizens: the case of the Volga Germans," *The World Today*, vol. 48, no. 3 (March 1992), pp. 41–43; and "Auf Wiedersehen, Kazakhstan," *The Economist*, March 7, 1992, p. 52 (box). Also, Bilinsky's private conversation with a German official.

39. Information supplied by Mrs. Helga M. Schmid, Press Secretary, German Embassy in Washington.

40. For an excellent summary of Ukrainian thinking see Serge Schmemann, "Ukraine Finds Nuclear Arms Bring a Measure of Respect," *The New York Times*, January 7, 1993, pp. A1 and A12.

41. For details, see *Die Welt*, February 3–6, 1992, especially Manfred Rowold, Moscow, "Ukraine weckt Hoffnung bei den Deutschen: Der Rechtsanspruch an die Wolgarepublik aber bleibt" [Ukraine awakens hope among Germans: but the legal claim to (the restoration of) the Volga republic remains], *Die Welt*, February 6, p. 5. See also interesting follow-up by Yury Guly, "Ukraine Accepts First 500 Resettled Germans," *Izvestiia*, November 3, 1992, p. 1 and *Current Digest of the Post-Soviet Press*, vol. 44, no. 44, p. 26.

42. "Unser Nachbar Russland" (Our neighbor Russia), *FAZ*, October 14, 1992.

43. Gregor Schöllgen, "Deutschlands neue Lage: Die USA, die Bundesrepublik Deutschland und die Zukunft des westlichen Bündnisses" [Germany's new position: The USA, the Federal Republic of Germany and the future of the Western alliance), *Europa Archiv*, vol. 47, no. 5 (March 10, 1992), p. 125.

44. Wolfgang Seiffert, "Auswirkungen der deutschen Vereinigung auf Osteuropa" [The effects of German unification on Eastern Europe], *Zeitschrift für Politik*, vol. 39, no. 1 (March 1992), p. 37f.

45. Ibid., p. 42, for both quotations.

46. Ibid.

47. Ibid., p. 43.

48. See, for instance, his old article "Europa ohne Grenzen—eine sichere Gemeinschaft" [Europe without boundaries: A safe community], *Europa Archiv*, vol. 45, no. 6 (March 25, 1990), pp. 203–12. I, for one, am rather skeptical about the prospects for a comprehensive European union, as opposed to a simple free trade area. Here I would side with Josef Joffe's brilliantly cynical column "After the Geldkrieg," *The New York Times*, September 20, 1992, p. E17.

49. See "Vortrag von Volker Rühe (MdB), Bundesminister der Verteidigung: Sicherheitspolitik im Wandel; Die Zukunft der Bundeswehr in einem veränderten Europa" [Lecture by Volker Rühe, Member of Bundestag, Minister of Defense: The change in security policy; The future of the German armed forces in a changed Europe], *Europa Archiv*, vol. 47, no. 15–16 (August 25, 1992), pp. 467–68.

50. Ibid., p. 468.

51. Ibid.

52. Michael Stürmer, "Kein Wiedersehen in Rapallo" [No rendezvous in Rapallo], *FAZ*, April 16, 1992, editorial page.

53. "Kohl: Die deutsch russischen Beziehungen. . .," *FAZ*, December 17, 1992, p. 1.

54. Bernt Conrad, Stockholm, "Tumulte bei der KSZE: Moskau schockt Westen"

(Tumulteous scenes at the CSCE: Moscow shocks the West), *Die Welt*, December 15, 1992, p. 1.

55. Henry R. Huttenbach, "The Sudeten Syndrome: The Emergence of a Post-Soviet Principle for Russian Expansionism," in Association for the Study of Nationalities (Eurasia and Eastern Europe), *Analysis of Current Events*, vol. 4, no. 3 (December 1992), 3 pages. Huttenbach cited the following statement by the Foreign Affairs Committee of the Russian Supreme Soviet: "Russian foreign policy must be based on a doctrine that proclaims the entire geopolitical space of the former Union a sphere of vital interest . . . Russia must secure . . . the role of political and military guarantor of stability on all the territory of the former USSR."

56. "Germany and Russia: The trouble with Kohl and Yeltsin," *The Economist*, December 12, 1992, p. 56.

57. "Movers and takers," in "Washington Whispers," *US News and World Report*, vol. 114, no. 2 (January 18, 1993), p. 26.

10

Russia, America, and Northeast Asia After the Cold War

Rajan Menon

What Moshe Lewin has called the "Gorbachev phenomenon" unleashed a revolution.[1] The term "revolution" is appropriate: despite the failure of *perestroika*, Gorbachev's policies rearranged the international landscape, albeit not always in ways that he intended. (The destruction of the USSR and socialism in Eastern Europe was not on his agenda; nor was German unification.) For scholars and policy-makers, this transformation, which compressed epochal upheaval into a short span of time, has been exciting—but confusing as well. The familiar, seemingly immutable geopolitical assumptions that guided analysis and diplomacy during the bipolar Cold War era are no longer useful. While this holds true for every part of the world, it is particularly evident with regard to Northeast Asia, the focus of this essay. I define Northeast Asia here to include the Russian Far East, China, Japan, South Korea, North Korea, Mongolia, and Taiwan. The United States, though not geographically part of the region, is also included by virtue of its naval presence in the North Pacific and its defense commitments to and military deployments in Japan and South Korea. My purpose is to examine, in a manner that elucidates the implications for the United States, Russian policy in Northeast Asia and the effect on regional security of the Soviet Union's collapse and the end the Cold War.

The Obsolescence of the Old Framework

The components of the traditional analytical framework for understanding the dynamics of security in Northeast Asia were remarkably durable and lent a considerable degree of assurance to analyses: certain basic patterns and alignments could be taken as given. In essence, they were the product of the long shadow cast by Soviet military might. This took the form of substantial conventional and nuclear forces arrayed east of the Ural mountains, plus the ability of the Soviet Pacific Fleet—the largest of Moscow's four fleets—to disrupt Pacific sea lines of communication (SLOCs), to counter the U.S. Seventh Fleet, and, in the event of war, to attack U.S. forces in Japan and South Korea. In an operational-technical sense, Moscow still has this capability, despite the reduction of some 120,000 ground forces east from its Far East since 1985 and the sharp decrease in the Pacific Fleet's out-of-area operations.[2] Yet, in a Clausewitzian sense, these forces-in-being must be looked at differently. It is not very meaningful to spin scenarios based on their *capabilities*; the *political* context in which they exist has changed, as have Moscow's goals and priorities.

The fall of the USSR and the Communist Party of the Soviet Union (CPSU), the end of the Cold War, the fundamental changes in Russo-Chinese relations, the end of Moscow's strategic alliance with North Korea and Vietnam, and Russia's economic crisis together create a new context. War along the Russo-Chinese border, for instance, is not a serious possibility now. Nor are analyses based on the U.S. Maritime Strategy, the Pacific Fleet's threat to SLOCs and U.S. forces in Japan and South Korea, or Soviet-supported aggression by North Korea likely to illuminate the future. While this was true even before the formal collapse of the USSR in 1991, it is particularly true now. [3] This does not mean that the sources of conflict in Northeast Asia have been eliminated; it does mean that they flow out of new strategic conditions.

An alternative framework for understanding Northeast Asian security must incorporate the interactive consequences of several new problems. The first is the uncertain future of Russia. While a reversion to totalitarianism featuring a renaissance by the CPSU is essentially impossible, a mutation of Russia's struggling democracy into a hypernationalist authoritarianism is not. Such a denouement will not mean that Russia will merely use the forces-in-being to pick up where the Soviet Union left off; the end of the CPSU and the overwhelming economic constraints on any future Russian government will limit considerably its ability to maintain current military force levels—let alone add to them—as well as its ability to project military power far beyond its borders. The possibility of a turn to the right in Russia has important implications for the United States and the states of Northeast Asia. As the U.S. government seeks to cope with its domestic economic problems and to take advantage of the end of the Cold War by reducing its global military presence, it must decide how deeply American forces in the Far East can be cut, given that the Soviet threat has ended while the future of Russia, which still disposes of vast military assets, remains unclear. A reduced U.S. presence will be necessary for economic reasons. But a total American withdrawal may well spur an accelerated and potentially unsettling Chinese and Japanese build-up—in response to the emergence of authoritarian rule in Russia—that could alarm South Korea and Southeast Asia.

In addition to deciding what its future force levels in Northeast Asia must be, the United States must also, together with Japan and South Korea, develop a coordinated economic and technical assistance program for Russia. The goal of such an effort would be to prevent Russia's perilous transition out of the Soviet-era command economy from undermining its embryonic democratic institutions. In other words, Washington must orchestrate a security policy that looks beyond traditional military instruments, containment, and balance-of-power principles.

A second problem concerns the U.S.-Japanese security relationship. Essentially, it was cemented and sustained by the Cold War conception of the Soviet threat outlined above. With that environment having changed irrevocably, both countries need to develop a new rationale for the security treaty: What threats is it now meant to avert? What should the division of labor now be, given the more benign environment and the economic limitations that constrain not only Washington but, with the bursting of the "bubble economy," Tokyo as well? There needs to be a refurbished basis for U.S.-Japanese strategic concord that can survive rising neomercantilist economic discord.[4] Friction over trade balances and sharing the defense burden could infect the security relationship, leading to an independent and expanded Japanese military profile. Or U.S. pressure on Japan to do more to contribute to regional security may be driven by Washington's desire to economize to such an extent that the consequences for Northeast Asia of a militarily more powerful Japan are glossed over. Changes in Japanese defense policy may stem from U.S. pressure on Tokyo to assume a larger burden in regional security; or an erosion of the U.S.-Japanese partnership as a result of spiraling frictions over economic matters could lead Tokyo to consider a more independent defense strategy. Whatever the cause, a major change in Japan's military posture will inevitably generate reactions from Russia, China, and South Korea—each has long been wary of greater Japanese military power and has unresolved territorial disputes with Japan, to boot—and increase tensions in Northeast Asia. Thus the United States still finds itself balancing the Northeast Asian security equation; what is now less clear is who precisely is to be balanced.

A third problem is the place of China in Northeast Asian security. Its traditional role in the strategic triangle composed of Washington, Moscow, and Beijing has been bypassed by the march of history; China can no longer exert leverage against the United States or Russia by playing on their rivalry. Indeed, some have gone so far to suggest that, with both the USSR and the Cold War at an end, China's importance for the United States has declined dramatically, leaving open the possibility that disagreements over human rights, trade, and Beijing's export of nuclear technology and arms will no longer be cushioned by the overriding imperative of containing Soviet power.[5] At the same time, while the United States remains important to China for trade and investment, the end of the Soviet Union means that Washington is less critical for Chinese security. Indeed, Chinese conservatives wary of the growth of private enterprise, market economics, and human rights campaigns from abroad may believe that Washington has displaced Moscow as the more consequential long-term threat. A fractious U.S.-Chinese relationship could lead Beijing to adopt a truculent, nationalistic posture, and with increasing Chinese economic and military power, this could make for instability and anxiety in Northeast Asia.

The Chinese economy has grown by about 9 percent a year since 1978 and, if present trends continue, will have grown eightfold by 2002.[6] Moreover, its military might is now being fortified with arms purchased from Russia. (Such transactions between erstwhile enemies symbolize the extent of change in the post–Cold War world.) Thus China is a power on the ascendant; and while a more assertive Chinese policy in Northeast Asia is not inevitable, neither can it be ruled out. It is particularly apt to develop in the context of tension with the United States, unrest in Tibet, Inner Mongolia, and Xinjiang, and the Communist Party's inability to maintain its hegemony amidst the far-reaching changes in China's economy and society that have been set in motion by Deng Xiaoping's economic reforms.[7] A militarily more powerful and bellicose China would be disquieting for Japan, Vietnam, and most of the states of ASEAN, against whom Beijing has territorial claims in the East China and South China Seas. Were a change in China's posture to occur amidst reductions in the U.S. military presence in the western Pacific and a weakened, inward-looking Russia, the anxieties of these states would only increase.

A fourth problem in post–Cold War Northeast Asia is the new situation on the Korean peninsula. On the one hand, the momentum of events runs against the revisionist power, North Korea. One of its principal patrons, the Soviet Union, not only ceased to exist but, a year before its demise, established diplomatic relations with South Korea and embarked on a concerted effort to increase economic relations with Seoul. Russia under Yeltsin has continued to expand economic and political ties, leaving little doubt about which of the two Korean states it considers a more lucrative and consequential partner. China, North Korea's other major patron, also established diplomatic ties with South Korea (in 1992), and its economic ties with Seoul have also grown—indeed, they overshadow Russia's. North Korea has thus been robbed of its most important sources of economic, political, and military backing. All of this would suggest that the North Korean government is apt to be restrained and cautious. On the other hand, North Korea's isolation, its economic crisis, and its consequent sense of vulnerability coincide with the likelihood before long of a controversial transition of power from Kim Il-Sung to his son, Kim Jong-Il. A compelling argument could be made that these conditions portend upheaval in North Korea and thereby the danger of instability on the militarized Korean peninsula. The locus of the problem of maintaining equilibrium has shifted. It is now less a matter of maintaining stability between the two Korean states by using balance-of-power techniques to avert war; instead, the challenge will be to contain the fallout from disorder within North Korea. Both are difficult undertakings, but the former has been prepared for and thought about far more thoroughly than the latter.

China: Ascendancy or Upheaval?

The Gorbachev revolution and the subsequent collapse of the USSR improved vastly the external dimension of Chinese security, while complicating the internal dimension. In essence, Gorbachev's policies removed China's vulnerability to Moscow's superior military might and strategy of encirclement. After Gorbachev's December 1988 announcement in the United Nations that Soviet forces would unilaterally be reduced by 500,000, Soviet spokesmen clarified that 120,000 of that number would come from the troops arrayed against China, with the remaining Far Eastern units to be progressively reconfigured into a defensive mode. In late 1989, negotiations began on reducing Chinese and Soviet forces along the border, and during Chinese Prime Minister Li Peng's visit to Moscow in April 1990, an agreement on governing principles was signed. By the time the Soviet Union collapsed, five rounds of talks on achieving such reductions had been conducted.

In a much more pointed move, Moscow announced in 1987 that a phased reduction of troops in Mongolia would be initiated with the goal of eliminating the deployment entirely by 1992. The formations in Mongolia had been kept at a higher level of readiness than other Soviet troops along the border, and the Chinese had viewed them as the spearhead of any Soviet attack on Beijing. The reduced conventional threat from the north was complemented by the 1987 INF Treaty under which the USSR agreed to eliminate its intermediate-range nuclear missiles from Europe and Asia, thus accepting the concept of a "global zero."

Moscow's conventional and nuclear advantages continued to be decisive in all areas except raw manpower. But the important point was that the changes in Soviet military policy were supplemented by political ones as well. This changed the overall context in which Beijing viewed the residual Soviet advantage. Thus the USSR agreed under the Geneva Accords of April 1988 to withdraw its combat forces from Afghanistan by May 1989 and cajoled Vietnam into removing its troops from Cambodia by the end of 1989. High-level political contacts took place to alter the adversarial character of Sino-Soviet relations, the most important of which were the visits of Eduard Shevardnadze and Gorbachev to Beijing in 1989 and of Li Peng and Chinese Communist Party General Secretary Jiang Zemin to Moscow in 1990 and 1991 respectively. In 1987, talks on resolving the border dispute—earlier efforts having been derailed by the Soviet invasion of Afghanistan—had also resumed. By 1990, Soviet officials stated that "nine-tenths" of the differences had been resolved. These military and political transformations in Sino-Soviet relations were supplemented by a significant growth in trade—especially along the border—and agreements providing for thousands of Chinese workers to be employed in construction projects in Siberia and the Soviet Far East.

In essence, these were the changes that had occurred in relations between Moscow and Beijing by the time the Soviet Union fell apart and Boris Yeltsin became the president of an independent Russia. They transformed the bilateral relationship from hostility to rapprochement and cooperation; *People's Daily's* characterization of Jiang Zemin's visit to Moscow as having "ended the past and opened the future" can only be understood against their background.[8]

It is virtually certain that continuity will be the hallmark of Yeltsin's China policy. There is abundant evidence that justifies this conclusion. While the ideological basis for polemics between Moscow and Beijing was basically removed during the Gorbachev years—in fact, party-to-party ties were reestablished during the 1989 Deng–Gorbachev summit—the end of Communist Party rule in Russia and the reforms in China under Deng Xiaoping since 1979 render schismatic doctrinal disputes about "revisionism," "social imperialism," and "hegemonism" irrelevant. China's record in human rights and Beijing's use of force to suppress future Tiananmen-like challenges may well be criticized by Russians, given the birth of civil society and a free press in Russia. But there is little reason to believe that democratic interest groups will have the potency in Russia to make human rights the sort of problem it has been in China's relations with the United States. Nor will Russia's parliament, a conservative body populated by former communists and representatives of the *nomenklatura*, exhibit much ardor for compelling the executive to link economic and military contacts with China to Beijing's tolerance for dissent. Disputes over Taiwan will not be the irritants that they have been in Sino-U.S. relations, either. Russia has expanded economic ties with Taiwan, but it has taken care to characterize these and other transactions as unofficial and to stipulate that it regards Beijing as the sole legitimate government of a China that includes Taiwan.[9]

Russia's interest in building upon the Gorbachev legacy is clear from Yeltsin's (abbreviated) visit to Beijing in December 1992 and from the continued growth of military and economic cooperation. In 1992, Yeltsin's government completed the withdrawal of troops from Mongolia, which Gorbachev had initiated in 1987. Negotiations on force reductions along the border, also begun under Gorbachev, have continued as well. At the eighth round of talks in December 1992, both sides agreed that their troops would be pulled back one hundred kilometers from the border. Offensive weapons (tanks, strike aircraft, artillery, and tactical nuclear weapons) are also to be reduced in the resulting two-hundred-kilometer zone.[10] This arrangement entails greater complications for Russian than it does for China in at least two respects. China's defense perimeter is already more than one hundred kilometers from the border, whereas Russia's is not. Second, although the cuts will occur over a seven-year period, they are bound to aggravate the problems Russia already faces in finding employment and housing for military personnel returning from Eastern Europe and the Baltic states. Steps to reduce forces along the border have been accompanied by progress in settling the border dispute. In February 1992, a treaty on the eastern (or Russian-Chinese) segment of the Sino-Soviet border was ratified by the Russian and Chinese legislatures, although some issues (primarily concerning the ownership of some of the islands in the Amur and Ussuri rivers) remain to be settled.

Russia under Yeltsin has also begun to build up Chinese military power. The foundation for arms sales to China was laid by negotiations held in the Gorbachev years. But the move from talk to action has occurred under Yeltsin, with the impetus provided by the rapprochement between the two countries and Russia's shortage of hard currency. China has received Sukhoi–27s and will also acquire Sukhoi–31s, T–72 tanks, S–300 surface-to-air missiles, and technology to improve the accuracy of its surface-to-surface and air-to-air missiles. Additional arms sales are certain. Russia is desperate for hard currency, and weaponry is one of the few commodities in which it has a comparative advantage. With some $40 billion in hard-currency reserves, China could emerge as Russia's most important customer, particularly as the alteration of bilateral political relations removes Russian inhibitions about building up Chinese military might. And the Chinese will find few other suppliers able and willing to provide a comparable volume of equipment. They will also find it easier to integrate Soviet-era weapons into a force structure that is built around armaments of Soviet design.

Russian arms sales to China will undoubtedly make the other states of Northeast Asia uneasy, particularly because they are taking place at a time when the U.S. military presence in East Asia is being reduced—a trend certain to continue given the travails of the U.S. economy, the end of the Cold War, and the advent of a Democratic administration. Indeed, Japan has already expressed its concerns over this matter to Russia, but Russia's need for cash and the specter of politically destabilizing layoffs in its defense industry proved decisive for the Yeltsin government.[11] Japan's uneasiness over the Russian-aided expansion of Chinese military capacity will be a consequence not only of a reduced U.S. presence in East Asia, but also of the still unresolved Sino-Japanese dispute over the Senkaku (Diaoyutai) islands.

Vietnam, which is more exposed to Chinese power after the end of the Moscow-Hanoi alliance, is also embroiled in a dispute with China over the Paracel (Xisha) and Spratly (Nansha) islands. In February 1992, China's legislature adopted "The Law of the People's Republic of China on Its Territorial Waters and Their Contiguous Areas," which, in a nutshell, laid formal claim to the Senkaku, Paracel, and Spratly islands and proclaimed the right to repel foreign incursions.[12] China has already used force—in 1988 and 1992—to realize its claims against Hanoi and has proceeded to grant contracts to foreign firms for oil exploration in offshore areas where its sovereignty is disputed by Vietnam.[13] Military acquisitions from Russia will increase China's capacity to use force to back up its territorial claims. An inward-looking, economically troubled, politically unstable Russia and an America in retrenchment could well increase China's propensity to do so, and the offshore oil wealth of the islands could combine with increased dependence on imported oil to give it the motivation. This worries officials not only in Japan and Vietnam, but also in Brunei, Indonesia, Malaysia, and the Philippines.

Russian sales of arms that can increase China's ability to project air and naval power overseas will particularly increase regional apprehension. This is evident from reactions to news that the Chinese government has decided in principle to acquire aircraft carriers and is also seeking aerial refueling technology.[14] The expansion of China's limited capacity to project power will, of course, be a costly, protracted undertaking. But East Asian concerns about this have also been fueled by unconfirmed reports about contacts between Chinese and Ukrainian officials to discuss the possible sale to China of the unfinished *Variag* aircraft-carrying cruiser and talks between Russia and China over the sale of the aircraft carriers *Minsk* and *Novorossiisk*.[15]

Yeltsin has also continued an economic policy toward China that had been set by the Gorbachev trajectory. Under Gorbachev, Sino-Soviet trade—which had plummeted after the early 1960s and amounted to a mere $370 million or so in 1984—rose from $1.2 billion to $6 billion from 1985 to 1991.[16] While the latter figure is small in comparison with China's trade with the U.S., Japan, and Taiwan, the pace of growth is significant, and Yeltsin has sought to further expand Russo-Chinese economic ties. Russia's nuclear industry is to construct a nuclear power plant in China—two have already been built with Western assistance—and help to improve safety mechanisms. In addition to efforts initiated by the Chinese and Russian central governments, local officials have tried to expand trade and create joint enterprises. These efforts have succeeded in providing food and consumer goods for Russia's Far East and business opportunities for Chinese firms in Heilongjiang and Jilin provinces.[17]

While new areas of cooperation will emerge, the scope for bilateral cooperation will hinge on Russia's progress in achieving economic integration with the Asia-Pacific economy. This will require continuing Gorbachev's effort to gain admittance to the Asian Development Bank, the Pacific Economic Cooperation Council (PECC), and the Asia-Pacific Economic Cooperation (APEC) mechanism. It will also be furthered by Russian participation in multilateral schemes involving China, such as the Tiumen River Area Development Program, which envisages an investment of $30 billion to combine "Russian and Mongolian natural resources, Chinese and North Korean surplus labour, and South Korean and Japanese capital and technology."[18]

The importance of regional cooperation for the future of economic relations between China and Russia stems from the inherent limits of a purely bilateral approach. Ultimately, the two countries do not have much to offer each other; indeed, they are competitors for foreign investment and technology. While trade across the border will continue, the systemic, as distinct from local-regional, significance of Russo-Chinese economic ties will be limited if the approach remains bilateral. Neither is the best partner to provide the other with what it really needs: capital, technology, and export-driven industries. Both are apt to look for these needs to Taiwan, South Korea, and Japan. With China becoming more and more oriented to hard-currency trade, and less and less to barter,

Russia's indebtedness and shortage of hard currency, together with China's inability to extend sizable loans, constitute additional obstacles.

Yet multilateralism is no panacea, for Russia must overcome many obstacles before it can integrate itself into the East Asian economy. In contrast to China, its progress toward an economy based on private enterprise and market forces has been limited and is fraught with uncertainty. China's seaboard, its most developed region, offers investors enticing incentives, a fairly well-developed infrastructure, and a stable environment; Russia's Far East, the country's economic backwater, does not. Its lack of economic allure is compounded by political uncertainties. Separatist sentiments in Yakutia and visions of a Far Eastern republic add to the sense that the government in Moscow is beset by centrifugal forces. Despite steps such as the opening of Vladivostok to foreign investment in 1992 and the plans to set up special economic zones (SEZs) along the Chinese model, the Far East remains in Russian thinking an underpopulated, vulnerable expanse to be defended. A more complex conception that transcends matters of security and geopolitics and focuses on economic interdependence has been slow to evolve.[19] Thus the prospect of Russo-Chinese economic ties being energized by Russia's economic integration into the Asian Pacific economy is not bright.

My discussion so far suggests that the Soviet collapse and the rise of an independent Russia has been a net plus for the *external* dimension of China's security. But a different conclusion emerges if one considers the *internal* dimension of Chinese security. The demise of the USSR represented the unraveling of a multinational, totalitarian system—a system, that is, with some basic similarities to China's. Gorbachev's reforms cascaded into revolution, undermining the Communist Party's monopoly of power. This occurred at a time when the direction of China's own political economy had become open to doubt: reform and evolution, or change begetting cataclysm? China's leaders are divided on the basic direction of national development. On the one hand, there is the reasoning of Deng Xiaoping, who believes that, in a global environment where political legitimacy, national power, and economic performance are more closely intertwined than ever before, the Communist Party can maintain its authority only if it can deliver the goods economically. On the other side is the critique of this logic by Deng's nemesis and the rallying point for the conservative opposition, Chen Yun.[20] Chen asks (in what is, in effect, an application of the Marxist model of the interrelationship between base and superstructure) how the political monopoly of a Marxist-Leninist party committed to socialism can be preserved when since 1979 it has systematically promoted private enterprise, foreign investment, market forces, and cultural-intellectual openness vis-à-vis the outside world. This is a fundamentally important question, particularly because the state sector in China accounts for a sharply decreasing share of employment, exports, national income, and tax revenues.[21] Based on the outcome of the October 1992 Fourteenth Congress of the Chinese Communist party, this debate has been settled, for the time being, in favor of the reform coalition headed by Deng. But

the year leading up to the Congress provided ample evidence of the tussle between reformers and conservatives, and the passing of the eighty-eight-year-old
Deng could renew the struggle over China's future, particularly in the context of
political instability and economic difficulties.[22]

There are, of course, major differences between the circumstances in China
and the USSR. China's economic performance and the success of its reforms are
in sharp contrast to the Soviet and Russian experience. While both the USSR/
Russia and China are multinational societies, the non-Han peoples make up only
8 percent of China's population, while non-Russians constituted nearly half the
population of the USSR. Russia also has no counterpart to Taiwan and Hong
Kong to aid its economic transition. Yet for China's leaders, the spectacle of the
USSR's slide from reform into a revolution that ended the Communist Party's
grip on power was not comforting. Chinese conservatives in particular looked
hopefully at the August 1991 coup against Gorbachev; and China's extension to
the USSR of a $370 million loan in March 1991 may have been an effort to
bolster the crumbling edifice of Soviet socialism.[23]

The rejuvenation of nationalism in the former Soviet Union and its environs is
a particularly sensitive problem for China's leaders. The role of nationalism in
the fall of the USSR and its continuing challenge to the integrity of the Russian
Federation are apparent and need no elaboration here. But a post–Cold War
Eurasian context in which nationalism has become the main currency of politics
creates an inhospitable environment for multinational China, particularly as the
uneven benefits of its post-1979 economic reforms may increase the sense of
relative deprivation among minorities in Tibet, Xinjiang, and Inner Mongolia.

The implications for China's Xinjiang-Uigur Autonomous Region of the
emergence of independent, predominantly Turkic Moslem states in former
Soviet Central Asia are particularly important. Turmoil among the Muslim
Kazakhs, Kyrgyz, Tajiks, and Uigurs (who are the largest group, with a population of 6.8 million) of Xinjiang has the inherent potential to turn irredentist now
that the Kazakhs, Kyrgyz, Tajiks, and Uigurs across the border in Central Asia
live in independent states. The possibility of upheaval in Xinjiang already concerns Chinese leaders. There was an armed rebellion in that region in 1990, and
there continue to be intermittent reports of tension between Uigurs and Han
Chinese and of weapons-smuggling from neighboring Pakistan and Afghanistan.[24] Reports of a "Uigurstan Liberation Front" operating in Alma-Ata
(Kazakhstan's capital) and a meeting of a "For a Free Uigurstan" party in Bishkek (Kyrgyzstan's capital) can only add to Beijing's concerns.[25] Chinese leaders
undoubtedly fear that the rise of rabid nationalism in Central Asia could seep
into Xinjiang, or that the mere existence of independent predominantly Turkic
Muslim states across the border could strengthen nationalist sentiments in Xinjiang; they have said as much.[26]

The changes in Mongolia following the Gorbachev revolution could also
affect China's stability. On the one hand, Mongolia is no longer a client state of

Moscow; under the leadership of a restructured, reformist Communist Party, it is a fledgling democracy groping toward private enterprise. On the other hand, Mongolian nationalism is now a pronounced feature of the country's policies, a trend that could foster irredentism in Chinese Inner Mongolia.

Overall, the resurgence of nationalism in Eurasia, particularly among non-Russians in the Russian Federation, could stimulate separatism not just in Xinjiang and Mongolia, but also in Tibet.[27] Russia and China are apt to view any such trend as a common challenge. Neither stands to gain from heightened nationalism among minorities. Nationalism among its Moslem peoples poses the danger of the Russian Federation's Balkanization, while nationalism in Central Asia could aggravate tensions between Central Asians and the Russian diaspora of some eight million. For China, Turkic nationalism in Central Asia could portend instability in Xinjiang and increase strife between Chinese Moslems and Han Chinese. Since a Mongolian diaspora exists not only in Inner Mongolia, but also in the Russian autonomous republic of Buryatia, both Moscow and Beijing will look askance at the strengthening of Mongolian nationalism.

If, in the past, the USSR and China sought to exploit each other's vulnerabilities as states composed of different nationalities, both will now regard nationalism as a common scourge. This became apparent in a November 1992 meeting between Russian Foreign Minister Andrei Kozyrev and his Chinese counterpart, Qian Qichen. Kozyrev noted that Central Asia should "remain a CIS sphere and not a sphere of extremist forces and, in particular, of Islamic fundamentalism. And in this, I think, we can count on mutual understanding from our great neighbor." In response, Qian observed that Russia and China "have common interests in preserving stability in the Central Asian region" and that in expanding its economic relations with Central Asia, China would take into account the region's close links with Russia.[28]

The internal dynamics of Russia and China and the new relationship between Moscow and Beijing pose a number of challenges for the planning of U.S. policy in Northeast Asia. The policies of Gorbachev and Yeltsin have reduced sharply the danger of conflict between Northeast Asia's two giants, and this makes for a more stable environment. Yet the equation now features an economically and militarily more powerful China—a trend underscored by Russia's weakened, unstable state and its preoccupation with domestic problems. A key question to be addressed, therefore, is the extent to which China is now the entity to be balanced. A resurgent China in a region from which the United States disengages, for its own important and understandable reasons, could increase the sense of vulnerability in Japan and Southeast Asia. This raises the question of what the future basis for America's relationship with China should be. If the containment of Soviet power no longer offers a rationale, does this imply that the relationship transforms from one based on strategic partnership to one based on rivalry and containment? Now that the shared interest in checking Soviet power is over, will the traditional frictions between Washington and Beijing over trade and human rights be magnified to an extent that rivalry and conflict displace cooperation and strategic convergence?

This is a particularly important question for the Clinton administration, for the Democrats have in recent years advocated tougher policies toward China on disputes over trade and human rights. The old strategic rationale for U.S. policy toward China no longer exists; yet the prospect for instability in China is apt to focus U.S. attention on Beijing's treatment of dissent, opposition, and rebellion by minority nationalities. A policy of using sanctions to influence Beijing's reactions to such domestic challenges could have undesirable consequences: It could affect the balance of forces between reformers and conservatives at a time of political transition in China. It could also stimulate resentful Chinese nationalism, particularly if the leadership, sensing the declining appeal of Marxist ideology, seeks legitimacy by presenting itself as the source of resistance to foreign pressure. Neither outcome—the ascendancy of conservatives or the emergence of nationalism—would contribute to stability in Northeast Asia.

Japan: Defining Security in a Post–Cold War World

Yeltsin's policy toward Japan must also be seen against the background of the Gorbachev legacy. Gorbachev's Japan policy had three principal goals. One was to enlist Japanese investment and technology to supplement his efforts to reform and modernize the Soviet economy. He sought not only increased trade and investment from Japan, but also support for Soviet admittance into the PECC, APEC, and the Asian Development Bank. Gorbachev was well aware that, for these benefits to be realized, the entrenched perception in Japan of the USSR as its primary military threat had to be altered. A number of Soviet moves were partly aimed at changing this prevailing Japanese attitude: the withdrawal from Afghanistan; the signing of the INF Treaty; the pressure applied on Vietnam to withdraw from Cambodia; the force reductions in the Far East; and the proposals for regional economic cooperation and confidence-building measures (CBMs) unveiled at Vladivostok (1986) and Krasnoiarsk (1988). Thus a second Gorbachev objective was to transform the political context of Soviet-Japanese relations by breaking the Cold War mold in which they were formed. A third goal, again connected with the first, was to break the logjam in the dispute over the Northern Territories. Gorbachev and his advisers publicly rejected Tokyo's insistence that Soviet-Japanese cooperation on economic and security issues had to be preceded by a resolution of the dispute over the Kunashiri, Etorofu, Habomais, and Shikotan islands. But they were well aware that, at the very least, the Northern Territories problem set severe limits on how far the pattern of Soviet-Japanese relations could be changed.

It is clear now that Gorbachev failed to realize these goals. The gains made in boosting Japanese trade and investment and securing Japanese aid were modest at best. Contrary to conventional wisdom, this was not because of the roadblock erected by the Northern Territories dispute, but because the incentives for Japan to increase economic ties with the USSR were outweighed by the disincentives even in terms of pure economic logic.[29] The vision of a grand partnership to tap Siberian oil and natural gas resources, combining Japanese capital and technology and Russian labor, proved far less alluring by the latter part of the 1980s than in the 1970s. True, Siberia is closer to Japan than the Middle East is, but by 1985, Japan was less dependent on Middle Eastern oil, and its more energy-efficient economy, which featured the increasing saliency of the service sector, was using less raw material per unit of output. The Soviet market was potentially vast, as was the Soviet need for technology. But the USSR's indebtedness and political instability, both of which increased under Gorbachev, perturbed Japan. Japanese capitalists, like their counterparts elsewhere, are fundamentally risk-averse. Because trade with the Soviet Union accounted for less than two percent of all Japanese trade, the influence of those industries and institutions in Japan that had a stake in expanding economic ties with the USSR was marginal at best; and it was negated by the more powerful national security groups and institutions (particularly the *Gaimusho* and the Japanese Defense Agency) that emphasized the conflictual reality, as opposed to the cooperative potential, of relations with the Soviet Union. Moreover, insofar as investment and trade in Northeast Asia were concerned, China, Taiwan, and South Korea had more to recommend themselves to Japan: their economies were more robust, their polities more stable, their militaries less threatening.

The effort to remake the Soviet image in Japan was somewhat more successful: Japanese public opinion polls, scholarly writings, and press reports (and, to a much lesser extent, the pronouncements of Japanese officials) showed that a more favorable view of the USSR was forming as a result of Gorbachev's policies.[30] Visits by senior Soviet leaders (Shevardnadze in 1986, 1988, and 1990; Aleksandr Yakovlev and Anatolii Lukianov in 1990; and Gorbachev himself in 1991) certainly helped in this regard. Yet an improved Soviet image could not substitute for concrete achievements. Tokyo, true to form, followed the American lead and remained distinctly unreceptive to Soviet proposals for naval CBMs and a regional security regime. The traditionally conservative Japanese Defense Agency, as reflected in its annual White Paper, failed to make any fundamental reassessment of the Soviet military threat, "new thinking" and "reasonable sufficiency" notwithstanding. Even Soviet force reductions were interpreted in ways consistent with the traditional view: they were duly noted but qualified with the caveat that Moscow now sought leaner, meaner, more modern forces.[31] For all of Gorbachev's efforts, by the end of his tenure, Japan and the USSR had still not signed a postwar peace treaty.

The third goal—making headway on the dispute over the Northern Territories —proved elusive as well. Soviet diplomacy, featuring tantalizing hints of compromise from visiting officials, senior scholars, and diplomats based in Tokyo, as well as "good cop–bad cop" strategies, proved far more agile than in the Brezhnev era. (Granted, this was not a difficult accomplishment.) There is little doubt that Moscow was serious about a settlement involving *mutual* compromise. Important steps were taken to facilitate progress: visa-free visits by Japanese to the islands were approved in 1986; Moscow acknowledged, albeit obliquely, the existence of a territorial dispute; and the Soviet-Japanese working groups set up in 1988 to conduct negotiations on a peace treaty included the Northern Territories on their agenda. But despite Gorbachev's reputation for effecting dramatic diplomatic breakthroughs, his visit to Japan in 1991 left the territorial dispute intact. By then, the political and economic chaos in the USSR and Gorbachev's increased dependence on the military and the party apparatus left him with little political capital to expend on selling a controversial territorial compromise at home. Nor did Tokyo's unwillingness to accept a less-than-full-loaf solution help his position.

Each of these goals—expanding economic ties, improving the political aura of bilateral relations, and addressing the territorial dispute—remains central to Yeltsin's policy toward Japan. But the impediments that prevented Gorbachev from realizing them also remain. In the economic sphere, there is no doubt that opening up the Russian economy to foreign trade and investment is of paramount importance to Yeltsin; his future, and that of Russian democracy, hinges upon transforming the economy under the adverse circumstances of rising unemployment, high inflation, and divisive nationalism. Enticing Japan into an economic partnership is part of Yeltsin's strategy for the success of that transformation.

But Japan's government and businesses are not any more eager to participate than they were in the Gorbachev years. True, Russia's economic difficulties and political instability make the strategic rationale for Japanese involvement more crucial than ever before: Tokyo has much to lose from the failure of Russian democracy and the rise of a nationalist-authoritarian regime in Moscow; the chances for resolving the Northern Territories dispute would surely diminish, as would Japan's security. Yet the economic disincentives remain just as compelling as before, at a time when the economic constraints on Japan to take the lead in a multilateral effort to aid the Russian economy are much greater.

For its part, Russia has taken steps that indicate its interest in increasing economic contacts with Japan and the other countries of Northeast Asia. It has expressed enthusiasm for the Tiumen River Project (which envisages Japanese participation), and it has opened Vladivostok to foreign economic activity and sought UN and Japanese assistance to establish SEZs around the city.[32] Additional forms of economic cooperation are also possible. One case in point is the idea of a Sea of Japan Rim Economic Zone involving Japan, South Korea, North Korea, the Russian Maritime Provinces (Khabarovsk, Primorskii, Sakhalin, and Amur), and the northern Chinese provinces of Heilongjiang, Jilin, and, Liaoning.[33] Its proponents envision a zone of economic growth created by Chinese labor, Russian natural resources, and Japanese and South Korean technology and capital.

Russian experts recognize that Japanese involvement is key to the realization of schemes such as the Tiumen River Project and the Sea of Japan Rim Economic Zone. But while they remark on the untapped potential for Japanese-led multilateral economic cooperation in Northeast Asia, they are well aware of the reasons for Japan's reluctance, from Russia's political instability and the unresolved Russo-Japanese territorial dispute to the scarcity of infrastructure and skilled labor and the preponderance of military industries in the Russian Far East.[34] Indeed, one Russian scholar has acknowledged that the hesitation of investors is hardly surprising given this "sober reality," while the Russian deputy foreign minister, Georgii Kunadze, remarked that, without a change in these conditions, "purely diplomatic efforts [to integrate the Russian Far East with the Asia-Pacific economic subsystem] will remain in the air."[35]

Undoubtedly, a settlement of the dispute over the Northern Territories would help to foster economic ties with Japan (although it would not guarantee a qualitative change in bilateral economic relations). While visiting Japan in January 1990 as president of the Russian Republic, Yeltsin outlined a four-stage solution to be implemented over a span of some twenty years.[36] It involved moving from a formal acknowledgment of the dispute by Moscow to demilitarization and joint economic development of the islands and to a peace treaty. From the standpoint of the Japanese, the plan had two decisive flaws: its schedule was too long, and it was vague about the key issue of sovereignty over the islands. As the abortive Gorbachev visit of 1991 had demonstrated, the Japanese government had made the territorial dispute a major domestic political issue over the years, and even were it so inclined, cannot accede to an agreement that at a minimum does not acknowledge Japanese sovereignty and transfer at least some of the islands quickly.

But Yeltsin has even less room to maneuver for acceptance of such an agreement than Gorbachev had. The influence of Russia's conservative-nationalist forces (the Civic Union, former Communist Party members in the parliament, the military, the managers of state enterprises) increased during the course of 1992. Yeltsin's (lost) battles with the Russian parliament over the composition of his cabinet and the pace of economic reforms at the end of that year demonstrated this all too vividly. These are the very forces that would lead the charge against any accord that surrendered Russian land to Japan. Ironically, Yeltsin, the symbol of heroic resistance during the August 1991 coup, must now contend with the limitations on his power imposed by the democratic polity he helped to protect. A deal involving the transfer of territory to Japan would have to be approved by an intractable legislature, defended before the rising tide of nationalism, and insulated from legal challenges by local authorities and the 50,000 residents of the islands. These difficulties may be regarded as part of the routine hurly-burly of democratic politics. But Yeltsin's weakened political position and the Russian economic crisis will incline him, as an astute politician, to defer them. His visit to Japan, which had been scheduled for September 1992, was canceled precisely because he lacked the political resources necessary to address the territorial dispute in a way that was both acceptable to the Japanese government and defensible at home (at a time when the campaigns of nationalists had turned public opinion sharply against transferring territory to Japan).[37] Realizing that the economic returns from a visit to Japan would be meager and symbolic unless Tokyo could be satisfied on the territorial issue, Yeltsin chose wisely to avoid controversy that could not be balanced with tangible gains.

If the territorial dispute is to be addressed, several conditions are needed. First, Japan must rethink its policy of insisting that this problem be settled before any substantive cooperation with Russia in the economic and security realms is possible. A case can be made that a network of mutually beneficial measures to build economic interdependence, promote trust, and reduce the historical legacy of suspicion will, over time, create a political climate in which controversial compromises can be rendered acceptable in both Russia and Japan. In the aftermath of the cancellation of Yeltsin's visit, the decision of Moscow and Tokyo to consider the broad range of bilateral issues instead of highlighting the territorial problem is an encouraging development in this regard. Second, each government must shape domestic opinion more effectively so that the idea of compromise is not viewed as tantamount to treason. One way to do so is to develop models for a settlement that incorporate clear, demonstrable benefits to each side. Third, Tokyo must reconsider its all-or-nothing approach that rests upon the (dubious) assumption that sheer economic desperation will ultimately force Moscow to settle on Japan's terms. By appearing to seek unilateral concessions unaccompanied by economic incentives, Japan may well create a consensus in Russia that a settlement that affords it some dignity and gain is impossible.

Against this background of Russo-Japanese relations, several implications for U.S. policy emerge. For a variety of reasons, both Japan and the United States have an overriding interest in sustaining democracy and a successful economic transition in Russia. Neither country has the power to ensure these outcomes, but both can do much more to organize an Asia-Pacific coalition that creates a regional environment that contributes to Russia's stability and economic recovery. In economic terms, the United States, Japan, South Korea, and Taiwan could increase loans and investment to Russia, provide technical and financial support for the all-important task of converting defense industries to nonmilitary production, and supply commodities to alleviate politically explosive shortages. Both Japan and the United States (as well as South Korea) face their own economic constraints, but a coordinated plan would reduce the burden on each. Such support for Russia's fledgling democracy would also obviate the need to increase military spending in the event that upheaval in Russia brings a chauvinistic regime into being. As such, it is a prudent investment that will prove cost-effective in the long term.

What is required is not so much mobilizing additional resources, but redirecting the purely military expenditures that a post–Cold War environment makes less essential into a program of assistance to Russia. This would promote regional security in a way more appropriate to the new environment in Northeast Asia. American security policy in Northeast Asia cannot ignore the traditional task of marshaling appropriate amounts and types of military force to maintain regional equilibrium; but it must also now be reconceptualized to serve the new imperative of promoting regional security by influencing the evolution of Russia. Ultimately, what matters is not the military power Russia wields, but the nature of the regime that wields it.

While U.S.-led regional economic diplomacy can shape domestic trends in Russia, so too can the nature of U.S. strategic planning in Northeast Asia. The two central and interconnected elements of such planning are the level of future U.S. deployments in the region and its effect on Japan's regional military role. Economic problems at home make a reduction in the U.S. military presence in Northeast Asia inevitable. But reductions so severe as to generate Japanese insecurity and sharply increased Japanese military spending will inevitably strengthen the influence in Russia of those who oppose cuts in Russian military might. A motif of Soviet strategic thinking, even with the advent of "new thinking," was apprehension and suspicion about U.S.-Japanese military cooperation.[38] But the leaders of independent Russia are apt to regard the continuation of the U.S. security treaty with Japan as a means to keep Japanese military power within acceptable bounds. (Similar logic led to Moscow's ultimate acceptance of a unified Germany within NATO.) Japan, after all, is a country against which Russia, both tsarist and Soviet, has fought three wars in this century. It already has the third largest defense budget in the world and a military that "must be rated first-class in regional, as well as global, terms."[39] It leads the world in many of the technologies that have revolutionized warfare in the late twentieth century, and the appropriations for research and development in its defense budget, as well as the efforts of its civilian corporations in research and development with military applications, have increased since the early 1980s.

A restructuring of the U.S.-Japanese security relationship could reassure Moscow and dampen the influence of Russia's nationalists who warn that reductions in military spending and deployments would make the country more vulnerable to U.S. and Japanese power. The treaty as it exists was constructed in the environment of the Cold War. It now requires a new rationale. Transforming it from a Russia-centered bilateral mechanism to one that focuses on emerging problems in East Asian security—and does so through an institutionalized procedure for consultation with the other states of the region—would be wise in four respects. First, the treaty would be severed from its linkage to the Cold War and made more relevant to new regional security challenges, among them, nuclear proliferation and safety, environmental mishaps, runaway arms transfers, and conflicts over maritime resources. Second, it would constitute the first step toward a multilateral regional security regime that involves the United States (and thus calms fears about an independent, expanded Japanese military posture), but devolves more of the burden and responsibility on the region's states. Third, it would create a climate in which Russian leaders feel more comfortable reducing their own military expenditures and defending their actions before critics at home. Existing defense agreements would no longer be seen as hostile arrangements forged to deter and fight Russia. Instead, they would be seen as means to a partnership toward an inclusive security which, while stopping short of a regional security regime, initiates movement toward it. Fourth, Washington's effort to encourage Japan to do more for regional security in the name of burden-sharing would be more palatable not only in Russia (and China and the Korean states), but also in Japan itself.

The Korean Peninsula:
The Primacy of Pragmatism

Perestroika and "new thinking" were designed to revitalize the Soviet economy, promote trade and investment with the world's most developed countries, reduce Soviet military burdens and the risks of conflict, and create trust and rapprochement with the West. Not surprisingly, these objectives radically changed Moscow's policy toward the two Korean states. In essence, Gorbachev concluded that South Korea was the far more important of the two. If North Korea was still mired in the neo-Stalinist quagmire from which he sought to extract the USSR, South Korea was making the difficult transition from authoritarianism to democracy. If North Korea was a burdensome economic dependent, South Korea, with twice its population and ten times its GNP, was potentially an asset to *perestroika* as a source of investment and technology. If North Korea's clandestine efforts to build nuclear weapons and resort to terrorism gave it the international reputation of a rogue elephant, South Korea's economic model and its rising profile in the international marketplace were widely admired.

The change in Moscow's policy was not sudden. In the early Gorbachev years, Soviet officials denied that drastic change in relations with North Korea was in the offing. High-level contacts with Pyongyang continued (including a visit to Moscow in 1986 by Kim Il-Sung); so did arms sales and visits to North Korean ports by vessels of the Pacific Fleet.[40] The ritualized praise of the 1961 Soviet–North Korean security treaty continued; so did support for Pyongyang's calls for the withdrawal of U.S. forces from South Korea and Korean unification on a confederal basis.[41]

But before long, unmistakable signs emerged that economic self-interest and pragmatism—the driving forces of Gorbachev's reforms—would alter Moscow's Korean policy. In 1988, the USSR failed to display solidarity with Pyongyang and boycott the Seoul Olympics; indeed, it used the occasion to engage in cultural diplomacy aimed at the hearts and minds of South Koreans. The Soviet government not only lent encouragement as Hungary and South Korea established diplomatic relations in 1989, but it also allowed South Korea to open a trade mission in Moscow that year. Economic contacts and trade between the Soviet Union and South Korea grew as well, with South Korean conglomerates such as Daewoo, Samsung, and Lucky Goldstar probing the Soviet market. While senior Soviet officials stuck to their traditional rejection of the concept of "cross recognition" of North Korea and South Korea by the major powers and the admission of the two states to the UN, influential commentators began to explore such ideas in the Soviet press. Thus, when the Soviet decision to establish full diplomatic relations with South Korea was announced in 1990, it was somewhat anticlimactic. This, in brief, was the situation Yeltsin inherited at the end of 1991.

The continuity with Gorbachev's policies, evident in Yeltsin's policies toward China and Japan, has also characterized his diplomacy toward the Korean peninsula. But it has been marked by a more rapid pace of change. The cold-eyed willingness to pursue economic self-interest with Seoul at the expense of Pyongyang is particularly striking—and was evident during Yeltsin's November 1992 visit to South Korea. Yeltsin sought to obliterate whatever inclination may remain among South Koreans to see Russia through the prism of Soviet policies and the Cold War. As if to bury the past, he observed that, in Soviet policy toward South Korea, "dogmas came before common sense" and that Russia now sought a "new era" in relations.[42] The return of the black box from the Korean Airlines plane shot down in 1983 over Soviet air space was a tangible demonstration of this, as was Yeltsin's expression of regret over the incident.[43] So was his condemnation of the forcible resettlement in 1937 of the Korean population of the Soviet Far East and the repression that it was subjected to in the years thereafter.[44] Yeltsin clearly wanted the South Koreans to understand that the agreement he signed with them on principles of bilateral relations was not mere window dressing.

But Yeltsin was, and is, interested in far more than demonstrating that the difference between the communist Soviet Union and democratic Russia is real. He and his advisers admitted freely during the visit to South Korea that they sought, above all, to increase the level of economic interchange between the two countries. They noted that the interest of South Korean corporations in the Russian market "has noticeably diminished as of late" due to fears of instability, a lack of governmental guarantees for trade and investment, and Russia's default in 1992 on its share of loans extended to the USSR.[45]

To pave the way to reignite economic cooperation, an agreement was reached on resuming loan payments (in cash and kind) before Yeltsin's arrival.[46] To spark South Korean interest, Yeltsin brought along many representatives from Russian industry and a list of twenty-three projects in which Moscow sought South Korean involvement. Among them: an industrial complex around Nakhodka; the conversion of defense industries; and a $50 billion project for exploiting Yakutia's oil and gas and constructing pipelines, roads, and rail links between South Korea and Yakutia via North Korea. This last project was given particular emphasis and heralded as one that could mesh with and stimulate the Tiumen River Project. Yeltsin also reiterated Russia's interest in a regional zone of economic cooperation around the Sea of Japan. In the course of his visit, agreements were signed in principle (though the fine print is unknown) to explore seventy-four projects, and South Korea agreed to resume the loans that had been frozen because of Russia's failure to make interest payments.[47]

Developments in the security realm were even more dramatic. Yeltsin's goal was to demonstrate that Russia was not, as the USSR had traditionally been, the patron and protector of North Korea. Russia, he proclaimed, had no interest in "exporting ideology or exporting revolution." By noting the removal of tactical nuclear weapons from surface ships and many submarines and the cuts that had been made in defense spending (18 percent in 1992), the rates of submarine construction, and the size of the Pacific Fleet, Yeltsin sought to underscore that Russia posed no military threat to South Korea. Reverting to Gorbachevian lexicon, he emphasized the importance of "reasonable sufficiency" and stated that Russia's armed forces would be oriented toward "exclusively defensive tasks."[48]

An agreement was signed between the defense ministries of both countries, providing for the exchange of delegations, joint exercises on a small scale, and the dispatch of observers to military maneuvers.[49] Alluding to the possibility of arms and defense technology being provided to South Korea, Yeltsin noted wryly that these were fields in which Russia "has quite enough brains and ability."[50] The significance for the military-strategic equation on the Korean peninsula cannot be overestimated: Yeltsin was saying not just that Russian power would not be a detriment to South Korea, but that it would, for the first time, be a supplement.

This theme was developed in Yeltsin's surprising comments regarding the change of Russian policy in military relations with North Korea. He announced that Russia had "completely halted any kind of military aid to North Korea" and had also terminated technical assistance to its nuclear industry, adding that the latter step would "freeze" North Korean nuclear technology.[51] He called for North Korea to permit the International Atomic Energy Agency (IAEA) to inspect its nuclear facilities and underscored the importance of a nuclear-free Korean peninsula. Yeltsin thus made it amply clear that Russia would oppose North Korean efforts to build nuclear weapons and circumvent IAEA inspections. Indeed, he stated that Russia would use "political measures to bring pressure" on Pyongyang to accept inspections.[52] In a move perhaps even more disconcerting to Pyongyang, Yeltsin argued that the 1961 security treaty with North Korea needed to be "canceled completely or drastically revised" on the grounds that it had been signed with the Soviet Union, not Russia. He objected specifically to the treaty's first article that required Russia, as the successor state of the USSR, to support North Korea in the event of war.[53]

These shocks ended whatever comfort North Korea may have received from comments by Yeltsin and other Russian officials that Moscow would not seek better ties with South Korea at the expense of North Korea—for this was precisely what was happening. To add to this, Yeltsin left little doubt of his disdain for North Korea's political model, although he did so not by direct criticism but by referring to Russia's own experience with communism as a "perverted lie, a monstrous violence . . . and a desecration of nature." In contrast, the attempt at solidarity with South Korea was obvious: Russia, Yeltsin said, sought "a market economy" and an "effective democracy" and had much to learn from South Korea.[54] That North Korea had little to offer, apart from complications, was implied.

The Gorbachev revolution, South Korea's successful policy of detente with Moscow and Beijing (initiated by President Roh Tae-Woo in 1988), the Soviet collapse, and Russia's policies under Yeltsin have transformed the strategic environment of the Korean peninsula. In particular, North Korea's adroit policy of extracting economic and military resources from the USSR and China, while preserving its autonomy by manipulating their rivalry, is now unworkable. In 1992, Beijing followed Moscow in establishing full diplomatic relations with South Korea, and both supported the admittance of South Korea into the UN in that year. Both have expanded economic ties with it while trying to reduce the North Korean burden. Aid from Moscow to North Korea tapered off under Gorbachev and ended under Yeltsin. For their part, the Chinese announced in December 1992 that North Korea would henceforth have to pay for its imports in hard currency.[55]

In response to these jolts, North Korea has sought to improve relations with Japan and the United States. Talks with both countries were held (with the United States from 1988 to 1991, in unofficial form below the ambassadorial level; with Japan between 1991 and 1992), but several obstacles emerged, among them, Pyongyang's reluctance to allow unobstructed IAEA inspections of its nuclear facilities and its demands for Japanese reparations not only to cover the years of occupation and war, but also in compensation for Japan's unfriendly policies since World War II.[56]

Pyongyang also began negotiations with Seoul: five rounds of prime-ministerial talks were held from September 1990 to December 1991.[57] Unlike the atmosphere around previous talks between the two Koreas, the new global conditions induced North Korean flexibility and produced important results. In December 1991, the two countries signed the Agreement on Reconciliation and Non-Aggression, providing for CBMs, cultural and economic contacts, and a reduction of tensions. The following month, North Korea—which had signed the Non-Proliferation Treaty in 1985 but had not followed up with an agreement with the IAEA on inspections—accepted the principle of IAEA checks. By June, the North Korean legislature had ratified an agreement on IAEA inspections and the first inspections of facilities on a list provided by Pyongyang had been conducted.[58] In sum, by the middle of 1992, important steps had been taken to address two principal security problems on the Korean peninsula: war between the two Korean states; and the acquisition by North Korea of nuclear weapons.

The changes in Soviet/Russian and Chinese policies toward the Korean peninsula have several implications for the United States. The traditional American policy toward North Korea—minimal political contact, economic boycott, and military containment—needs to be reconsidered. Continued isolation of North Korea may, under the new circumstances, prove counterproductive. That country has now been deprived of its principal sources of external support; its economy is in dire straits; and it is being bypassed by South Korea economically and technologically in a world that has witnessed communist regimes falling for lack of legitimacy and economic effectiveness. As well, it faces the retirement or demise before long of Kim Il-Sung, and thus the prospect of a difficult transition of power to his son, Kim Jong-Il.

These circumstances virtually ensure that North Korea will soon face either domestic upheaval or debates and power struggles within a new leadership divided over the appropriate responses to deepening economic problems and the new, post-Soviet external environment. U.S. policies that diminish North Korea's sense of vulnerability and create an external setting conducive to reform and evolution within the country should now be considered. Concretely, the United States should use political engagement and economic incentives to facilitate reform and reduce the dangers of nuclear proliferation and war at a particularly sensitive time in North Korean history. The continuation of xenophobic, hard-line policies after the passing of Kim Il-Sung will only increase both dangers, while upheaval and collapse in North Korea could well heighten the risk of war: on the Korean peninsula, civil war can easily mutate into interstate war. Alternatively, a North Korean collapse could saddle South Korea with sudden and enormous burdens that prove destabilizing, particularly given the country's recent and hesitant march toward democracy. Thus an evolutionary path to Korean reunification is far more preferable, as is change in North Korea through the medium of reform rather than disintegration.

U.S. willingness in principle to increase political contacts and forge economic ties with North Korea and to withdraw ground forces from South Korea should be announced. But implementation should be linked to verifiable changes in the nuclear and conventional arms equation on the Korean peninsula. The United States should expand the level and scope of contacts as North Korea gives evidence over time of allowing IAEA safeguards in a way that does not suggest deception or circumvention.[59] Such an approach could also be used to reshape the military situation on the Korean peninsula, where the overriding problem arises from North Korea's force structure, its numerical advantage in weaponry, and its deployment patterns, all of which provide the basis for a short-warning attack (I refer here not to intentions, but to capabilities). Mechanized and armored North Korean divisions are stationed close to the demilitarized zone (DMZ) such that a *blitzkrieg* could be attempted against front-line South Korean forces before reservists could be mobilized or U.S. forces from within or outside Korea could be brought to the front.[60] The implicit objective of this strategy is to neutralize Seoul's key advantages in a protracted war: a larger, more robust economy and the availability of U.S. assistance. Washington's willingness to expand ties with Pyongyang, as well as to remove ground forces from South Korea, should be tied to the alteration of this situation. This could be done if the two Korean states design and implement a regime of arms control and CBMs. It should rest on equal numbers for both North Korea and South Korea in the key offensive categories of weaponry (tanks, armored personnel carriers, strike aircraft, and artillery tubes) and the creation of a no-weapons zone in a broad swath on either side of the DMZ.[61] The system for arms reduction and control should be created in phases and be subject to strict verification and guaranteed by the United States, Russia, and China. If established—and fostered by a joint U.S.-Japanese carrot-and-stick approach toward North Korea—such a security arrangement would remove the most important conditions that create the danger of war on the Korean peninsula.

The policy of linking U.S. and Japanese economic and political ties to demonstrable progress in creating a security regime and implementing IAEA inspections in North Korea would address both aspects of military stability on the peninsula—nuclear proliferation and conventional war. It would also help create external conditions that maximize the prospects for reform and stability and reduce the dangers of turmoil and militancy in North Korea after Kim Il-Sung's departure. Such a policy would be consistent with both the desire of Russia and China to avoid instability, war, and nuclear proliferation on the Korean peninsula and the tenor of their recent policies toward the two Korean states. It would also be a more creative response to the new circumstances of Northeast Asian security in the aftermath of the Gorbachev revolution and to Washington's declining ability to muster economic resources and domestic political support for military deployments overseas. The discussions for a new security regime on the Korean peninsula could be begun through multilateral consultations within the frameworks of the U.S.-Japanese security treaty—as suggested in the previous section of this essay—and the U.S.-South Korean defense treaty. This would modify the bilateral, anti-Soviet framework of U.S. security commitments in the region and, as I have already noted, initiate the transition toward a multilateral regional security system.

The suggestion to withdraw U.S. ground forces from South Korea is a radical one,[62] but several factors should be kept in mind before it is rejected solely for that reason. First, although a commitment in principle to withdraw ground troops could be made once the two Korean states accept a security regime of force reductions, CBMs, and verifications, actual disengagement should be deferred until implementation is complete, verification provisions are in place, and multilateral guarantees have been secured. Second, in both the United States and South Korea, it will become increasingly problematic to find political support for a U.S. military presence at substantially the same levels as existed during the Cold War. U.S. budgetary constraints in particular make a reduced military profile in the Pacific inevitable. The real question is not whether reductions will occur, but whether a security regime can be created to ensure stability when they do take place. Third, the proposal made here for withdrawing ground forces from South Korea does not extend to a total disengagement from East Asia. As I have noted earlier, a U.S. military presence in East Asia is needed for the foreseeable future. This need stems from a variety of conditions: the threat of instability on the Korean peninsula; the prospect of rising Chinese power in East Asia; the decline of Russian power owing to economic weakness and instability and the possible emergence of hypernationalism and authoritarianism there if democracy fails and disintegration looms; regional fears of Japan's military resurgence; and unresolved disputes over the ownership of the Paracel, Senkaku, and Spratly islands. A naval presence using South Korean and Japanese ports could be maintained, and Japanese bases could be used to maintain ground forces (at reduced levels) and naval and air forces for deployment in the region. Indeed, with the Japanese now paying $3 billion a year of the costs of U.S. military forces in their country,[63] this is a cost-effective way to contribute to Northeast Asian stability in the post–Cold War era.

Conclusion: Trends in Post–Cold War Northeast Asia

The policies of Gorbachev and Yeltsin, the unraveling of the USSR, and economic crisis and political instability in Russia have recast the geopolitical situation in Northeast Asia. Emerging strategic trends are distinctly different from those that shaped American interpretations and policies during the Cold War. The past focus was on fencing in Soviet power. The future of Northeast Asia will be marked by a decline of Russian influence, American disengagement, and the consequent increase in Chinese and Japanese power. Even a Russia in which democracy fails and a nationalistic, authoritarian regime emerges will face severe economic constraints that will limit its military-political influence in the region. These shifts in the regional balance of power require that U.S. strategic planning, deployments, and defense commitments be refashioned so that far less attention is given to the traditional problem of Moscow's military might. To be sure, events in Russia still matter for regional equilibrium. A Russia in which democracy can be sustained and economic desperation does not compel the sale of vast quantities of weapons to China will make for greater security in Northeast Asia. So will a Russia that remains unified and sufficiently robust to balance the relative increase in Chinese and Japanese might, particularly as the U.S. reduces its military presence because of its own economic limitations.

But there are new challenges that are only tangentially related to the policies of Moscow that have traditionally been the focus of U.S. scholarship and policy concerning Northeast Asian security. One is the effect of rising Chinese economic and military power on regional stability, particularly given China's unresolved territorial disputes with a number of East Asian countries and the uncertainties about the direction of its policies after the death of Deng Xiaoping. A second is the influence on Japanese defense policy of this expansion of China's power: growing economic frictions with Washington and budget-driven cuts in the U.S. military presence could raise questions in Japan about the continued viability of relying on the United States as the ultimate source for security. A radical change in Japan's military role would have repercussions in China, Russia, and the two Korean states. A third is upheaval on the Korean peninsula. The source of this problem is not likely to be a premeditated North Korean attack (the traditional scenario), but turmoil within an isolated North Korea rendered unstable by economic crises and a conflict-ridden political succession that creates the danger of inter-Korean war.

Notes

1. Moshe Lewin, *The Gorbachev Phenomenon* (Berkeley, CA: University of California Press, 1989).

2. In addition to the continuing reduction of 120,000 troops from the Russian Far East, the Pacific Fleet has also been reduced and its operations scaled back. In December 1992, Admiral Gennady Khvatov, commander of the Pacific Fleet, told a group of visiting U.S. Senators that it had been reduced by seventy ships in 1992. It was also revealed that operations at sea had been cut back and patrols of the U.S. coast by nuclear submarines eliminated. Interfax in English, December 2, 1992; in FBIS-SOV, December 3, 1992, p. 1.

3. Yet as late as 1991, an analysis of Pacific security incorporated many of the traditional concepts of the Soviet threat. See William J. Crowe and Alan Romberg, "Rethinking Security in the Pacific," *Foreign Affairs*, vol. 70, no. 2 (Spring 1991), pp. 124–26. Despite this, Crowe and Romberg made several innovative suggestions for refashioning U.S. security policy in the Pacific based on the reduced saliency of Soviet power.

4. On this issue, see David Sanger's article in *The New York Times*, February 14, 1993, p. 4.

5. See Nancy Bernkopf Tucker, "China and America: 1941–1991," *Foreign Affairs*, vol. 70, no. 5 (Winter 1991/92), pp. 75, 92.

6. *The Economist*, November 28, 1992, p. 4; *The New York Times*, February 14, 1993, pp. 1, 12.

7. On the tension between China's economic reforms and the preservation of the Communist Party's monopoly of power, see Roderick MacFarquhar, "Deng's Last Campaign," *New York Review of Books*, December 17, 1992, pp. 22–28.

8. Quoted in Stephen Uhalley, Jr., "Sino-Soviet Relations: Continued Improvement Amidst Tumultuous Change," *Journal of East Asian Affairs*, vol. VI, no. 1 (Winter-Spring, 1992), p. 104.

9. This was an important aspect of a joint declaration on Russo-Chinese relations that, prior to Yeltsin's visit to Beijing in December 1992, was being crafted by the foreign ministers of both countries. Interfax in English, 1653 GMT, November 20, 1992; in FBIS-SOV, November 23, 1992, p. 16.

10. *Izvestiia*, December 3, 1992, p. 5, trans. in FBIS-SOV, December 4, 1992, p. 2.

Russia, Kazakhstan, Kyrgyzstan, and Tajikistan (these three Central Asian countries also have common borders with China) formed a joint delegation at the talks.

11. *The Washington Post* (National Weekly Edition), July 20–26, 1992; *The New York Times*, October 18, 1992, pp. 1, 14.

12. Samuel S. Kim, "China as a Regional Power," *Current History*, vol. 91, no. 566 (September 1992), pp. 248–49.

13. In May 1992, China granted—despite Vietnamese opposition—a contract to an American firm, the Crestone Energy Corporation, to explore the Tu Chinh bank, "located some 80 nautical miles off the coast of southern Vietnam." *Far Eastern Economic Review*, December 17, 1992, p. 23.

14. *The New York Times*, January 11, 1993, pp. 1, 8.

15. According to several reports, China and Ukraine discussed the purchase by China of the *Variag*. Work on the ship was halted because of a shortage of funds. Future arms transfers from Ukraine to China cannot be ruled out, even though the *Variag* sale has not proceeded, primarily because of the technical and financial difficulties that the Chinese would encounter in completing and maintaining the ship. While no formal agreements were signed on military sales during Ukrainian President Leonid Kravchuk's visit to Beijing in October 1992, Kravchuk pointedly mentioned they might prove possible in the future. On the reports regarding the *Minsk* and the *Novorossiisk*, I am grateful to Charles E. Ziegler.

16. Guocang Huan, "The New Relationship with the Former Soviet Union," *Current History*, vol. 91, no. 566 (September 1992), p. 255.

17. See *Far Eastern Economic Review*, January 7, 1993, pp. 16–17, for an account of the economic links between Manchuria and the Russian Far East.

18. See Charles E. Ziegler, "Russia and the Emerging Asian-Pacific Economic Order," in Ramesh Thakur and Carlyle A. Thayer, eds., *Reshaping Regional Relations* (Boulder, CO: Westview Press, 1993), pp. 514–15.

19. This has been noted by Russia's Deputy Foreign Minister Georgii Kunadze. See his interview with the Mayak Radio Network in Russian, 06300 GMT, December 5, 1992; trans. in FBIS-SOV, December 8, 1992, p. 11.

20. For an excellent account of the contention between these two perspectives within China's ruling group, see MacFarquhar, "Deng's Last Campaign."

21. Urban cooperatives and private enterprises in towns and villages, together with enterprises involving foreign investment, now employ 60 percent of China's industrial workforce, while village industries alone employ more than the 70 million individuals working in state-owned industries. Whereas central government investment accounted for 90 percent of industrial output in 1979, the figure is now 20 percent. Half of China's exports now come from the nonstate sector. A significant percentage (about 36 percent) of state sector industries tend to operate at a loss. These details are based on Jan Prybyla, "China's Economic Dynamos," *Current History*, vol. 91, no. 556 (September, 1992), pp. 263–64; and Thomas Gottschang, "The Economy's Continued Growth," ibid., p. 271.

22. MacFarquhar, "Deng's Last Campaign,"; David Shambaugh, "Regaining Political Momentum: Deng Strikes Back," *Current History*, vol. 91, no. 566 (September, 1992), pp. 257–61.

23. Ziegler, "Russia and the Emerging Asian-Pacific Economic Order," p. 508.

24. My discussion here derives from Nicholas Kristof's informative dispatch in the *The New York Times*, September 5, 1991, p. 16.

25. *Komsomol'skaia pravda*, June 26, 1992, p. 3, trans. in FBIS-SOV, June 30, 1992, pp. 6–7; *Nezavisimaia gazeta*, July 29, 1992, p.3, trans. in ibid., July 30, 1992, 49.

26. The head of the Xinjiang region's government warned in March 1992 that "the changed international situation is having an adverse influence on social stability in the

[Xinjiang] autonomous region." *Komsomol'skaia pravda*, March 12, 1992, p. 3, trans. in FBIS-SOV, March 16, 1992, p. 14.

27. In a speech smuggled out of Tibet and ascribed to him, Chen Kuiyuan, the newly appointed Communist Party head in Tibet, is said to have noted that there was insufficient attention by local party officials to Tibetan nationalism and warned that "separatist activities are rampant." *The New York Times*, February 14, 1993, p. 11.

28. Itar-TASS World Service in Russian, 1300 GMT, November 25, 1992; trans. in FBIS-SOV, November 27, 1992, p. 9.

29. See Rajan Menon, "Gorbachev's Japan Policy," *Survival*, vol. 31, no. 2 (March–April, 1991), pp. 165–66.

30. For details, see Gilbert Rozman, *Japan's Response to the Gorbachev Era, 1985–1991: A Rising Superpower Views a Declining One* (Princeton, NJ: Princeton University Press, 1992).

31. Menon, "Gorbachev's Japan Policy," p. 159.

32. Ibid.

33. See Valery K. Zaitsev, "Problems of Russian Economic Reforms and Prospects for Economic Cooperation Between the Russian Far East and Northwest Pacific Countries," *Journal of Northeast Asian Studies*, vol. 10, no. 4 (Winter, 1991–92), pp. 38–39.

34. Ibid., pp. 37–39.

35. Ibid., p. 39. Kunadze's comment appears in his interview with Mayak Radio Network (in Russian), 0630 GMT, December 5, 1992; trans. in FBIS-SOV, December 8, 1992, p. 11.

36. Vladimir Ovsyannikov, "USSR-Japan," *New Times* (Moscow), no. 6 (February, 1990), pp. 20–21.

37. In November 1992, the head of the Interfax news agency made this observation in an interview with Japan's Kyodo news service. Kyodo in English, 0934 GMT, November 24, 1992; in FBIS-SOV, November 24, 1992, pp. 11–12.

38. See Menon, "Gorbachev's Japan Policy," pp. 166–68.

39. Reinhard Drifte, *Japan's Foreign Policy* (New York: Royal Institute of International Affairs and the Council on Foreign Relations, 1990), p. 35.

40. See Rajan Menon, "New Thinking and Northeast Asian Security," *Problems of Communism*, vol. 38, nos. 2–3 (March–June 1989), pp. 25–26.

41. Ibid., p. 25

42. Address to the South Korean National Assembly, Russian Television Network in Russian, 112 GMT, November 19, 1992; trans. in FBIS-SOV, November 19, 1992, pp. 11–14. The words quoted appear on p. 11.

43. It should be noted here that what was turned over were copies of the flight tapes, not the complete and original recordings, which, Russian officials said, would be turned over to the ICAO. Itar-TASS in English, 1323 GMT, December 1, 1992; in FBIS-SOV, December 2, 1992, pp. 5–6.

44. This was mentioned in the text of the Russian–South Korean joint statement issued at the end of Yeltsin's visit. Text in Itar-TASS World Service in Russian, 0802 GMT, November 20, 1992; trans. in FBIS-SOV, November 20, 1992, pp. 9–11. The portion dealing with the forced resettlement of Koreans from the Soviet Far East appears on p. 10.

45. Interfax in English, 1707 GMT, November 16, 1992 (summarizing the remarks of a Russian Foreign Ministry official), ibid., November 17, 1992, p. 5.

46. Details in Itar-TASS World Service in Russian, 0640 GMT, November 13, 1992; trans. in ibid., November 16, 1992, p. 11.

47. For the economic projects put forward, discussed, and agreed to during Yeltsin's visit, see the texts of his speech to the South Korean Parliament and his press conference with Roh Tae-Woo as cited in note 42. Also see the joint statement issued at the conclu-

sion of Yeltsin's visit in Itar-TASS World Service in Russian, 0802 GMT, November 20, 1992; trans. in FBIS-SOV, November 20, 1992, pp. 911.

48. The comments about exporting revolution and the details about Russia's defense cuts appeared in Yeltsin's speech before South Korean Parliament and in the joint news conference he held with Roh Tae-Woo.

49. Itar-TASS in English, 0810 GMT, November 25, 1992; in FBIS-SOV, November 25, 1992, p. 9, citing a representative of China's Foreign Ministry.

50. Speech before the South Korean parliament. Russian Television Network in Russian, 1122 GMT, November 19, 1992; trans. in FBIS-SOV, November 19, 1992, p. 11.

51. The quote regarding the ending of military supplies to North Korea is from Yeltsin's speech to the South Korean parliament. Russian Television Network in Russian, 1122 GMT, November 19, 1992; trans. in FBIS-SOV, November 19, 1992, p. 13. The comment on ending assistance to North Korea's nuclear industry was made during a joint press conference with South Korean President Roh Tae-Woo. Itar-TASS World Service in Russian, 1412 GMT, November 20, 1992; trans. FBIS-SOV, November 20, 1992, p. 14.

52. Comment at joint press conference. Itar-TASS World Service in Russian, 1412 GMT, November 20, 1992; trans. in FBIS-SOV, November 23, 1992, p. 14.

53. Yeltsin's remarks at Seoul press conference quoted in Itar-TASS in English, 1015 GMT, November 20, 1992; in FBIS-SOV, November 20, 1992, p. 11.

54. These remarks were made in Yeltsin's speech to the South Korean parliament.

55. *The New York Times*, December 30, 1992, p. 2.

56. See Kim Hong-Nack, "North Korea's Policy Toward Japan and the United States in the Post Cold War Era," *Journal of Northeast Asian Affairs*, vol. 6, no. 2 (Summer-Fall 1992), pp. 259–83. After preliminary meetings, the Japanese–North Korean talks were held between January 1991 and May 1992. Thirteen unofficial meetings below the ambassadorial level had been held between the United States and North Korea (in Beijing) from 1988 to 1991.

57. Kwak Tae-Hwan, "Korean Reunification: Problems and Prospects," in ibid., pp. 334–63; International Institute for Strategic Studies (IISS), *Strategic Survey, 1991–92* (London, IISS: 1992), pp. 140–42.

58. By February 1992, six inspections of installations at the Yongbyon nuclear complex had taken place. *The New York Times*, February 14, 1992, p. 10.

59. It should be noted that a mutually acceptable arrangement between North Korea and the IAEA has not been worked out. Although North Korea has accepted the principle of IAEA inspections and allowed several inspections of its declared nuclear facilities, it rejected an IAEA request to inspect two sites at the Yongbyon nuclear complex that were not declared and proclaimed that it would resist any effort to carry out inspections under the IAEA's "special inspection" provisions. The IAEA has maintained that tests on the nuclear waste at these two sites are needed to determine if North Korea has extracted weapons-grade plutonium from its reactors. *The New York Times*, February 14, 1992, p. 10.

60. See James C. Wendt, "Conventional Arms Control for Korea: A Proposed Approach," *Survival*, vol. 34, no. 4 (Winter, 1992–93), pp. 110–12.

61. For a similar, albeit more detailed, proposal, see ibid., pp. 113–23.

62. It is in this respect that the proposal outlined here differs fundamentally with that offered by Wendt. Wendt argues the need for retaining U.S. ground forces both in the interest of stability on the Korean peninsula and in East Asia as a whole. See ibid., pp. 109–11.

63. Richard Holbrooke, "Japan and the United States: Ending the Unequal Partnership," *Foreign Affairs*, vol. 70, no. 5 (Winter, 1991/92), p. 49.

11

The Russian Federation and the Middle East: An Evolving Relationship

Oles M. Smolansky

In his January 1992 analysis of his country's geopolitical position, Foreign Minister Andrei Kozyrev distinguished among three spheres of the Russian Federation's national interests. The first and the most important was the sphere of the former union republics, most of which had joined the Commonwealth of Independent States (CIS). Though weak initially, Kozyrev hoped that in time the CIS would become a "fairly powerful, integrated association." To the argument that the foreign ministry was paying insufficient attention to it, Kozyrev countered that some 80 percent of his time was devoted to CIS affairs.

To describe the second sphere, Kozyrev evoked the image of the imperial twin-headed eagle, whose one head was turned west and the other, east. In this sphere are located Eastern and Western Europe as well as Japan and South Korea. The "band of developed democratic countries" was once divided by the "Communist empire." After its demise, the Russian Federation assumed the role of a "natural communication link" between the eastern and western parts of this "northern hemisphere" band. Finally, and by implication of less importance, were the "southern countries," which comprised the third sphere of Russia's national interests. Included in this category were such "direct neighbors . . . [as] China, Turkey, Pakistan, and Afghanistan" (though not, surprisingly, Iran) as well as "other countries that are fairly close to us." Many of them were "long-standing economic partners," hence good relations had to be maintained with them as well.[1]

As defined in this chapter, the Middle East covers the territory between the Atlantic Ocean and the Indian subcontinent and consists of four subregions: the "Northern Tier" (Turkey, Iran, Afghanistan); the Persian Gulf and the Arabian peninsula; the Arab-Israeli sector; and North Africa.

Using Kozyrev's classification, it is obvious that the Middle East was initially relegated to the third sphere of Russia's national interests. For analytical purposes, these interests may be divided into three distinct but interrelated categories: military-strategic, political, and economic.

Military-Strategic Interests

National Security

In February 1992, the Russian Ministry of Foreign Affairs issued a document, "On Basic Principles of Russian Federation Foreign Policy Concept." It was argued that Russia's national security was to be promoted by means of a "reduction of military potentials in the world, the elimination of military presence abroad, and a strengthening of a 'belt of good-neighborliness' along the entire perimeter of our borders." In addition, the document recommended developing "ties of alliance with the United States and other Western countries . . . and [to work] for the establishment of a global security system and its regional analogues."[2]

The thrust of the Yeltsin–Kozyrev foreign policy was challenged not only by the Russian nationalist and communist groupings but also by the CIS (and subsequently the Russian) military establishment. Writing in *Krasnaia zvezda*, Colonel S. Pechorov noted that "arguments that Russia is threatened by no one and from nowhere can hardly be taken seriously." Viewed from this perspective, the United States had retained its capacity to destroy the CIS and was on record wishing to prevent Russia from ever becoming a menace to the West again. Moreover, NATO was very much alive, while other threats were looming on the Asian horizon. Hence, Pechorov concluded that Russia continued to have potential adversaries and that the very idea of an alliance with the West ran against Russia's national interests.[3] Kozyrev countered: "To place an enemy image in the way of Russia's integration into the democratic world would spell a return to confrontation."[4]

However, the military remained unconvinced. One of the strongest public indictments of the Yeltsin–Kozyrev approach to foreign policy as well as to national security was offered by Colonel-General I. Rodionov, whose position as head of the General Staff's military academy lent a high-level military *imprimatur* to the view held by Pechorov and others. In supporting the views expressed by Pechorov, Rodionov argued that, being "one of the world's largest states," Russia had both "global and regional national interests." In the global context, he spoke generally about Russia's interest in "strengthening economic, political, cultural [and] scientific . . . ties with all states," and in creating a world order based on "collective resolution of . . . [existing] problems under the aegis of the UN."[5]

With respect to regional interests, Rodionov was much more explicit about the "nearby foreign countries" (*blizhnee zarubezh'e*) than he was about the "distant foreign countries" (*dal'nee zarubezh'e*). Most important in the former category were "all the countries of the CIS." He was particularly concerned about attempts by "certain domestic and external forces to enflame artificially the . . . separatist and nationalist moods" in the former Soviet republics. Such activities and the resulting temptation on the part of any "European, American or Asian states . . . to strengthen their influence" on the territory of the former USSR represented an "infringement on [Russia's] national interests" and affected its national security.[6] Disagreeing with those who argued that "all former enemies . . . [were now] friends," Rodionov maintained that "such an approach [to the problem] is deeply mistaken."[7] Threats to Russia's security, he said, definitely did exist. Nor was this surprising, because "national interests of various states often do not coincide, creating among them certain contradictions. . . . If one takes the interests of Russia in any . . . [given region, such as the Baltics, Eastern Europe, the Middle East, or the Far East], they are, to an extent, contrary to the interests . . . of other states, above all the U.S.A."[8]

A more detailed account of possible military threats to Russia's security emanating from the Middle East was contained in Pechorov's *Krasnaia zvezda* article. With regard to the "southwestern sector" of the CIS, he noted that Turkey had exhibited "increased interest in regions that are either a part of or border on Russia. The extension of Turkey's economic, and . . . politico-military influence over these regions may have negative consequences for Russia's geostrategic positions—the neutralization of its naval presence in the Black Sea and the Mediterranean and the disruption of maritime communications in the southern waters." Pechorov also saw "Iran and, to a lesser extent, Afghanistan and Pakistan" as neighbors determined "to include the states of Transcaucasia and Central Asia within their spheres of interest." These ambitions, he said, were detrimental to Russia's interests. Success on the part of the neighbors in establishing their influence in the former southern republics of the USSR would "result inevitably in the weakening of the traditionally strong Russian positions in those regions." It would also "intensify centripetal tendencies among the Muslim peoples of Russia itself, creating a threat to the maintenance of its territorial integrity."

Pechorov cited other potential dangers looming on the horizon. One possible scenario was a "confrontation between Russia and the Islamic world." Russia could be drawn into a "confrontation along its north-south axis" and risk being transformed into a "buffer separating the 'flourishing West' from the 'seething East.' " Moreover, Pechorov—again in contradicting the Yeltsin–Kozyrev line—expressed concern about the "increased activity of U.S. diplomacy in the Muslim republics of the former USSR." He was particularly apprehensive that, "along with Washington's desire to prevent the spread of Iranian-style Islamic fundamentalism, . . . the U.S. leadership [also] nurtures the hope of replacing Russian regional influence with its own."[9]

Most Russian analysts agree that the Federation's security is being threatened by the explosive situation which has developed along the southern fringes of the CIS. Some of these conflicts, which have occurred within or between various republics, have the potential of drawing in outside powers. Because most of the former Soviet republics are members of the CIS, the security of their frontiers is technically still Moscow's responsibility. Moreover, the Russian military as well as many Russian politicians regard the territory of the former USSR as an exclusive sphere of the Federation's national interests, in part because of the presence in many of the newly independent republics of a sizable Russian population, and argue that Russia is obligated to play an important role in the affairs of its southern neighbors. As for the latter, they have differed in their responses to Moscow's attitude and actions. Some have favored Russian peacekeeping operations, while others have not.

In the Nagorno-Karabakh conflict, the Soviet government initially supported Azerbaijan, on the ground that Armenian demands for self-determination in the contested region challenged the existing—and therefore legal—border separating the two republics. Gorbachev's attitude was met with an outburst of indignation in Erevan and, since the dissolution of the USSR, the Yeltsin government has informally shifted its sympathy from Azerbaijan to Armenia. As a result, the latter now regards the presence of CIS (i.e., Russian) troops in the Caucasus as a "stabilizing factor" and favors their continued deployment in the region. Azerbaijan, in contrast, has resented the change in Moscow's position and has no interest in the continued presence of CIS forces in its territory. As for Russia, it is unlikely to sanction an active involvement of its troops in the Nagorno-Karabakh imbroglio because it represents no immediate threat to the relatively small Slavic population in the Transcaucasus.

In the conflict between Georgia and Abkhasia, Tbilisi claimed that tanks, surface-to-air missiles, and other types of equipment had been delivered to the Abkhasian militias from the Russian armories. At the time of this writing, it is impossible to ascertain whether these assertions are justified. Even if they are, it should be borne in mind that the transfer of arms could have taken place without Moscow's direct involvement or orders. Whatever the truth of the matter, Georgia formally requested the withdrawal of CIS forces from its territory.[10] It did so in spite of the fact that Moscow and Tbilisi had cooperated in efforts to settle the South Ossetian conflict. Finally, Russian troops have intervened, on the Kremlin's orders, in the fighting between the North Ossetian and Ingush militias. (Both regions are situated in the Russian Federation.) In sum, Moscow has apparently decided that restoration and maintenance of peace along (or near) its Caucasian border—a vital national interest—can be secured only by selective use of force. As noted, this conclusion does not seem to apply to the Transcaucasus and, in particular, to the conflict between Armenia and Azerbaijan. At the same time, it stands to reason that Moscow watches the situation carefully and is likely to resist any outside intervention in Nagorno-Karabakh.

The situation in Central Asia differs markedly from that in the Caucasus. Kazakhstan and the other four republics (Uzbekistan, Turkmenistan, Tajikistan, and Kyrgyzstan) have not only joined the Commonwealth of Independent States but are (with the exception of Turkmenistan and to a lesser extent Uzbekistan) among its staunchest supporters. Units of the CIS armed forces are stationed in all of their territories and their presence is welcomed by most republican governments, whose attitude is dictated by considerations of strategic security as well as of local stability. Tajikistan, currently engulfed in a civil war, is a case in point, with forces of the anticommunist opposition fighting the supporters of the former president, Rakhman Nabiev. It is no secret that the opposition enjoys the support of the Tajik anticommunist Islamic groups operating across the Afghan border. According to unconfirmed reports, military and logistical backing has also been provided by Iran and Pakistan. True or not, the Russian military establishment seems convinced that "powerful outside interests" are exploiting for their own purposes the "political rivalries, regional differences . . . [as well as] the religious factor," features that are typical of the Tajik situation but are also present in virtually all the Central Asian republics.[11] In any event, CIS troops have patrolled Dushanbe and parts of the Tajik-Afghan border—an involvement justified by the concern for the safety of some 300,000 Slavs who reside in Tajikistan.[12] For the foreseeable future, and for the same reasons, they are likely to stay there and elsewhere in Central Asia.

Proliferation of Weapons of Mass Destruction

Many Russian military and civilian analysts have expressed serious concern about what Colonel Pechorov termed the "proliferation of nuclear missile weaponry to the countries of the Near and Middle East and South Asia." In their view, the spread of these weapons represented an "undoubted threat to Russia in the southern sector, as does, in the long run, the potential formation of a bloc of these states to counterbalance the 'nuclear' North, or a confrontation among these states themselves." Russia felt threatened also because deterioration of its relations with new members of the "nuclear club" might result in a nuclear war and because launchings of nuclear weapons might occur accidentally or be ordered by unauthorized personnel. Finally, "potential ecological disasters" in the Middle East or South Asia were also cited as a great concern to Russia.[13]

Interestingly, Yeltsin's prolific foreign minister did not disagree. In an article published in August 1992, Kozyrev addressed the question of the spread of weapons of mass destruction in the Middle East and singled out the Persian Gulf as an area where large amounts of Western and Soviet-made arms had been amassed and used in two major regional conflicts. Kozyrev described the USSR as having been an important contributor to the arms race in the Persian Gulf and went on to say that "even today, the urgent task is to remove once and for all the threat of a repetition of the Iraqi aggression and to secure guarantees for the elimination of chemical and . . . [bacteriological] weapons of mass destruction from the Iraqi arsenals." (In contrast to Kozyrev, the military professed concern mainly about the spread of nuclear weapons.) But it was not just Iraq and its capabilities and intentions that perturbed the military and civilian officials of the Russian Federation. As explained by Kozyrev, "destabilization in . . . [the Persian Gulf] and activation of extremist forces there, whether of the pseudo-revolutionary or Islamic fundamentalist ilk, and even more their possession of very destructive weapons and the means to deliver them over great distances, are capable of spreading with dizzying speed to the vulnerable regions of the Caucasus and Central Asia."[14] In short, the respective military and civilian approaches to the problem of proliferation of weapons of mass destruction in the Middle East and elsewhere represented an area of overlapping agreement between two groups that agreed on little else. In this instance, both were in favor of preventing the spread of nuclear weapons and their means of delivery on the ground that they represented a major destabilizing threat to the territory of the former USSR, widely regarded as a vital national interest.

Political Interests

Yeltsin's and Kozyrev's approach to Russia's foreign policy, with its emphasis on close cooperation with the industrial West, has reflected the viewpoint of the so-called Atlanticists who have been opposed by the so-called Eurasians. The latter have complained that preoccupation with the Western democracies runs counter to Russia's national interests. One of the problems, as they see it, is that Russia's interests in the "South"—which includes the Middle East—are being neglected, an argument that Kozyrev has gone out of his way to refute. In the spring of 1992, he reminded his critics that the Yeltsin government was engaged in preparing a wide-ranging treaty with Turkey and in negotiating an improvement in Russo-Iranian relations.[15] Kozyrev was also very much in favor of improving relations with the "Muslim states of the Persian Gulf and some of our other neighbors to the south."[16] In any event, the Russian Federation did indeed pursue a number of foreign policy initiatives in the Middle East, and it is to this subject that we now turn.

Russia's Status in the Middle East

The USSR's military, political, and economic rivalry with the United States—one of the cornerstones of Soviet foreign policy before 1985—was substantially reduced by Gorbachev. Normalization of relations between Moscow and Washington was reflected in the Middle East as well, except, initially, in the Persian Gulf area. Even there, however, the Kremlin eventually sided with the United States and its allies following the Iraqi attack on Kuwait. Subsequently, Yeltsin's policy of close cooperation with the West officially eliminated superpower competition as one of Moscow's major political interests in the Middle East. Nevertheless, Kozyrev has insisted that Russia must retain its status as an "independent great power" with legitimate interests in the region and must be recognized as such by the West.[17]

In abandoning the concept of superpower rivalry while simultaneously insisting on Western recognition of Russia's legitimate interests in the Middle East, has Kozyrev pursued what might appear to be a contradictory policy? This question must be answered in the negative, because he has made it clear that the desire to play the role of a great power excluded competition with the Western powers, except as regards the arms trade (more on this below). In any event, this approach has resulted in a number of changes in Russian policy and, where no major changes have occurred, has provided new stimuli for some of the policies initiated by Gorbachev.

New Relations with Former
Antagonists and Friends

The most dramatic manifestation of this trend has occurred in the Arab-Israeli sector, following the resumption of diplomatic relations between Moscow and Jerusalem and the active (though admittedly limited) participation with Washington in efforts to resolve the Arab-Israeli conflict. Yeltsin has built on Gorbachev's initiatives, leading to further improvements in the cordial relations between Russia and Israel. In the Persian Gulf, too, Moscow has gone out of its way in attempts to broaden cooperation with the member states of the Gulf Cooperation Council (GCC). It did so, in part, by fully supporting UN efforts to force Iraq to comply with the Security Council resolutions. In the "Northern Tier," Russia has been working to improve relations with Turkey and Iran, and, in North Africa, with Egypt.

Parallel to these initiatives, the Yeltsin administration has also continued the process of distancing itself from some of the USSR's former friends and clients. This shift in Moscow's position, which affected mainly such old-time Soviet favorites as Iraq, Libya, and, to a lesser extent, Syria, goes back to the Gorbachev period. But to Yeltsin belongs the credit for dropping the pretense of an independent superpower policy and for basically agreeing to follow Washington's lead in efforts to help resolve some of the region's knottiest problems in which the USSR's clients had been involved.

In this respect, Iraq has been ostracized, in spite of the spirited objections from some of Moscow's military hard-liners and the ultranationalist–Communist opposition. The same is true of Libya. In mid-1992, the Russian Federation voted for the imposition of sanctions on Tripoli in an attempt to force it to comply with the UN resolutions pertaining to the investigation of terrorist attacks against French and American aircraft in 1988 and 1989. In the case of Syria, Yeltsin has upheld Gorbachev's insistence that, in the Arab-Israeli conflict, the military option was no longer applicable and that a solution must therefore be found in the political-diplomatic sphere. Nevertheless, unlike in the respective Iraqi and Libyan cases, Moscow has expressed a strong interest in improving political and economic cooperation with Damascus.

Regional Stability and Security in the Middle East

The change in its basic approach to international politics enabled the USSR/Russia to take a much more relaxed view of the problems of stability and security in the Middle East. Thus, in the Persian Gulf, Moscow offered virtually no objections to the August 1991 security agreement between Kuwait and the United States or to the subsequent accords with Great Britain and France. Moreover, in the heated regional arguments as to who was responsible under what circumstances for maintaining order in the Gulf, Kozyrev offered the Kremlin's "partnership in defending security and stability in the Persian Gulf" and intimated that the "guarantees of security that Russia may provide have met with a favorable response from a number of Gulf leaders."[18] But in the ensuing regional debates on the subject, Moscow has remained wisely on the sidelines.

Nor did the Kremlin take a stand on the border disputes among various GCC states or in the Gulf islands controversy between Iran and the United Arab Emirates (UAE). On the latter issue, a foreign ministry official argued that "the growth of tension in this region" ran counter to "the interests of states located" in the Gulf and expressed hope that the conflict would be resolved by means of a "constructive dialogue on the basis of the appropriate norms of international law."[19] But, as of this writing, Moscow has not taken any official steps to help defuse the Iran-UAE dispute. In the Arab-Israeli sector, the emphasis has remained on the application of the "land for peace" formula. Otherwise, Moscow is content to follow Washington's lead while retaining a flexible position on the details of the various arrangements. This is not surprising, since the details of the future settlement do not affect Russia's national interests.

Dissolution of the USSR

Closer to home, the breakup of the Soviet Union has created a number of new political problems for Yeltsin's Kremlin. As mentioned earlier, the emergence of six Muslim republics to Russia's south has brought onto the scene Turkey, Iran, Afghanistan, and Pakistan, as well as Saudi Arabia, Egypt, and even Israel. Of these, Turkey and the Islamic Republic of Iran are clearly the major outside actors. This turn of events has presented Moscow with two important questions: What should its attitude be toward the growing Turkish and Iranian inroads into the Transcaucasus and Central Asia? And how should the Kremlin react to the reawakening of Islam (and to the possible spread of Islamic fundamentalism) in the Muslim republics?

With respect to the first question, since the Russian Federation is eager to secure the economic cooperation of Saudi Arabia and Iran—the chief respective Sunni and Shi'a propagators of Islam—Yeltsin and his associates have not publicly objected to Riyadh's and Tehran's activities in the Muslim republics. And since they have not said much about Saudi Arabia and Iran, it has made no sense to complain about the efforts exerted by secularist Turkey. Moreover, Moscow has been trying to avoid the appearance of interference in the internal affairs of nominally independent states. Privately, there has been considerable concern and the Kremlin's sympathies have invariably been on the side of Turkey.

With regard to the second question, in contrast, Moscow has not remained silent. Rather, not bothering to distinguish between the Shi'a and Sunni brands of fundamentalism, the Kremlin has publicly condemned what Kozyrev described as "proliferation of extremism, disguised as Islam." In commenting on his late spring 1992 visit to the Persian Gulf, the foreign minister noted that "true Islam has nothing to do with aggression, violence, or obscurantism." The whole problem was of great importance to his government, Kozyrev added, because of the Russian Federation's own huge Muslim population.[20] It is relevant to note in this connection that King Fahd of Saudi Arabia as well as other monarchs in the Persian Gulf had assured Kozyrev that they supported Yeltsin's struggle to preserve the unity of the Russian Federation and were therefore opposed to the efforts of "Chechnia, Tatarstan, and other Muslim republics to secede from Russia. . . ."[21] In any event, in the sense that Istanbul's position is similar to that held by Moscow, a commonality of interests has emerged between them—both favor containment of Islamic fundamentalism and oppose the emergence of theocratic regimes in the Muslim republics of the former USSR.[22]

Turkey and Iran

Rapprochement between the Soviet Union and Turkey began long before the collapse of the USSR. In the more recent past, President Turgut Ozal visited Moscow in the spring of 1991 and signed a pact of friendship and neighborly relations as well as an agreement on Soviet-Turkish cooperation.[23] The trend continued in 1992. In February, Kozyrev and his Turkish counterpart, Hikmet Cetin, "initialed a treaty on the fundamentals of relations" between the two states. Kozyrev used the occasion to note, "The epoch of confrontation in Russo-Turkish relations has ended. We have renounced the struggle for influence in the Black Sea region and prefer to put a stake on cooperation and partnership."[24]

In May, Prime Minister Suleyman Demirel and President Yeltsin concluded a friendship and cooperation agreement which reportedly covered "all spheres" of bilateral relations, "including military-political questions." They also discussed their governments' relations with the states of the CIS, especially the Central Asian republics, and expressed their "mutual desire to act as partners and to contribute to the economic and social development of Commonwealth countries." Finally, they noted their "profound regret" over the situation in Nagorno-Karabakh,[25] and renounced acquisition of territory by military means as unacceptable.[26]

In June, Yeltsin attended a summit of Black Sea heads of state, which was held in Istanbul on Turkey's initiative. Commenting on the declaration issued by the conference, he noted that, economics aside, Moscow was determined "to strengthen peace and stability" in the Black Sea region. Yeltsin also noted the significance of the participants' agreement on "principles that correspond entirely to the provisions of the CSCE Final Act and the Paris Charter for a new Europe." This meant that cooperation among the Black Sea states had become "a highly important part of the European process."[27] Yeltsin's statement was later amplified by one of his closest advisers, Gennadii Burbulis, who visited Ankara in August 1992 and noted that one of the concrete aims of Russo-Turkish cooperation was "the settlement of the conflicts in Abkhasia and Nagorno-Karabakh." Burbulis went on to say that the political situation in Central Asia, too, would "improve considerably if Russia and Turkey exercise joint influence on the region, both directly and via European and other international organizations."[28]

In contrast, the USSR and Iran disagreed on a number of important political issues in the late 1980s and early 1990s. Paramount among them were the problems of Afghanistan, of Gulf security, and of the Arab-Israeli peace process. Specifically, Iran had strongly and consistently opposed the Soviet invasion of Afghanistan and did its best, politically and logistically, to hasten the Russian departure from that country. Only after Gorbachev had ordered the withdrawal of Soviet forces did Tehran change its tune and, in fact, express its appreciation of Moscow's and Washington's September 1991 decision to stop arms deliveries to the warring factions in Afghanistan.[29]

In a similar fashion, Moscow and Tehran disagreed on the general issue of regional security in the Persian Gulf. Iran was strongly opposed to the U.S.-Kuwait defense pact, which it interpreted as a move to solidify Washington's position in the Gulf. Instead, Tehran recommended the establishment of regional security on the basis of what it called the "six plus one" formula, meaning the six members of the Gulf Cooperation Council and itself. Iran's proposal was rejected by the GCC. Traditionally wary of both Iran and Iraq, the council was unwilling to accept what it perceived as Tehran's attempt to dominate the Gulf. Given this situation, and because of its heavy involvement with the West, Gorbachev's Kremlin adopted an attitude of what might be called benign neglect. Thus, the Soviet media reported Iran's opposition to the U.S. military presence in the Persian Gulf as well as its desire to establish a regional security system in which Tehran would play an important role. Radio Moscow noted without comment that this ambition was not acceptable to the GCC.[30] Finally, on the subject of Arab-Israeli relations, Iran strongly disapproved of the rapprochement between Jerusalem and Moscow and of the Kremlin's cosponsorship of the Madrid peace process.[31]

In 1992, relations between the Russian Federation and Iran improved somewhat. Some of the problems had lost much of their former urgency—for example, Afghanistan—while others, like the issue of regional security, had retained their importance for Tehran but were no longer regarded as highly significant by

Moscow. On the Arab-Israeli conflict, Russia and Iran have apparently agreed to disagree. Finally, no major differences between Moscow and Tehran have surfaced with respect to Libya. While Russia officially favored economic sanctions against Tripoli, Iran did not. Nevertheless, as a member of the United Nations and in accordance with its charter, Tehran promised to abide by them.[32]

Among the problems emerging since the dissolution of the USSR, none has been more important to Moscow than the future of the Muslim republics. Tehran recognized them as well as the other independent states in late December 1991 and proceeded to establish diplomatic relations with them.[33] Some of the problems which emerged between the Russian Federation and Iran in this connection have been referred to earlier. Suffice it to add that, while Moscow welcomed Iranian efforts to find a political solution to the conflict in Nagorno-Karabakh,[34] the Kremlin has been wary about Tehran's meddling in the affairs of the autonomous Muslim republics within the Russian Federation[35] and those of the Central Asian republics. For instance, Uzbek President Islam Karimov's "direct accusation" of Iran's alleged intervention in Tajik affairs was reported in Moscow and his concerns appeared to be shared there.[36]

In sum, in examining the Russian Federation's relations with Turkey and Iran, it would appear that, on the political plane, Moscow was able to strengthen its ties with both Ankara and Tehran. Turkey's sentiments toward the emergence of a democratic Russia have been presented above. As for Iran, Deputy Foreign Minister Mahmud Vaezi has insisted that his government is "emphatically in favor of developing cooperation" with Moscow; that it sees the Russian Federation as its "main partner in the CIS."[37] Moreover, all three attempted to solve the problems of Nagorno-Karabakh. However, progress has been slow, caused, in part, by some conflicts of interests—while Moscow is backing Armenia, Istanbul's sympathies are clearly on the side of the Turkic-speaking Azeris. Only Tehran may have been trying hard, but without success, to reach a compromise that would be acceptable to both contending parties. Its efforts have foundered partly because of the mistrust with which the Iranian initiatives have been viewed in both Russia and Turkey.

Moscow and Ankara have also opposed Tehran's efforts to expand relations with the Central Asian republics. Nevertheless, in spite of the Kremlin's preference for the Turkish model of development, some mistrust concerning Ankara's motives remains deeply embedded in those Russian circles which regard the territory of the former USSR as the zone of Russia's vital national interests.

Economic Interests

Continuation of Conventional Arms Sales

When the USSR first became involved in the arms business, armaments were delivered at concessionary prices to Third World clients who, for reasons of their own, were willing to help Moscow expand its political and military influence in the Cold War competition with the United States. Under Gorbachev, with the importance of superpower rivalry gradually receding, the Soviets began to decrease their foreign arms sales. Affected by this trend were such old-time clients as Saddam Hussein, Muammar al-Qaddafi, and Hafiz al-Asad. But under Yeltsin, weapons sales for hard currency have once again been elevated to a high priority on Moscow's foreign policy agenda.

The decision to step up the arms trade has not come as a surprise. As early as February 1992, Yeltsin himself announced that "weapons exports would be a cushion for the Russian arms industry as the country tried to make the transition to a civilian economy." And, as subsequently explained by a foreign ministry official, "Russia cannot, . . . taking into account the economic situation in the country, give up the receipts of freely convertible currency through the sales of armaments abroad."[38] Nevertheless, pursuit of hard cash did not mean that arms would be sold indiscriminately to everyone willing and able to pay for them. As noted by Kozyrev, weapons would be made available only to what he termed "normal partners" and not to "belligerent regimes." Although he did not say so, the latter clearly included the governments of Iraq and Libya.[39] Interestingly, Kozyrev's indictment did not apply to Iran, which, along with China and India, has emerged as one of Moscow's main arms customers.

In 1992–93, Moscow made persistent efforts to sell military equipment in the Third World, particularly in the Middle East. Thus, during his visit to the Persian Gulf states, Kozyrev made overtures to Kuwait as well as to the United Arab Emirates. The former, having concluded security agreements with the United States, Great Britain, and France, seems to have side-stepped the issue. The UAE, in contrast, was more receptive, due to its vulnerability vis-à-vis Iran in connection with the developing dispute over the Persian Gulf islands. Subsequently, during his June 1992 visit to Abu Dhabi, Defense Minister Pavel Grachev expressed Russia's readiness to supply the UAE with armored personnel carriers (APCs). The initial shipment of twenty-seven vehicles would be followed by Russian military specialists who would train UAE military personnel in their use. Also discussed were possible purchases of the Russian "military aviation equipment" as well as joint production of "various armaments systems." The discussions were apparently inconclusive, because, according to Grachev, these subjects required "deeper study."[40] Elsewhere on the Arab side of the Gulf, Russia has not had much success in selling military equipment.

Traditionally, Syria had been one of Moscow's main arms purchasers in the Third World, accumulating a huge arsenal of Soviet weapons, including T–72 tanks as well as SU–24 and MiG–29 fighter aircraft (twenty-four planes of the former variety and forty-eight of the latter were reported in Syrian possession at the time of the dissolution of the USSR). In January 1992, London's *al-Hayah* reported that Damascus and Moscow had negotiated a new agreement, "estimated at $2 billion to complete the development of . . . [Syria's] air force and defenses." Russia reportedly agreed to the deal on condition that Damascus pay "in cash and in hard currency." The transaction was said to involve MiG–29s, Sukhoi–24s, as well as "long-range SAM–10 surface-to-air ... and SAM–11 medium-range missiles."[41]

Moscow refused to discuss the details of the Syrian negotiations, but the chief of the General Staff's department involved in foreign arms trade stated that the Russian Federation had assumed all the commitments entered into by the USSR under the terms of its treaty of friendship and cooperation with Syria. He said that Russia continued "to deliver weapons and render services on technical aid" but went on to note that "now defensive weapons, rather than offensive, predominate in our supplies." Moreover, "the volume of deliveries" was "declining notably."[42] Al-Hayah disagreed. A follow-up story, published in November 1992, quoted "Western and Israeli defense sources" as saying that the January deal provided for the delivery of 24 MiG–29s, 12 advanced SU–27 interceptors, 300 T–72 and –74 tanks as well as SAM–10 and SAM–16 shoulder-carried missiles. With their arrival, scheduled to be completed by the end of 1992, the Syrian air force would consist of 120 MiG–29s, 48 SU–24s, and 12 SU–27s. The ground forces would possess 3,200 T–72 and –74 tanks.[43]

Among the "Northern Tier" countries, Turkey has emerged as one of the Russian Federation's new customers—in August 1992, the Turkish minister of interior announced that Ankara was interested in acquiring Soviet-made helicopters and APCs for use by its internal security forces. The deal, worth $300 million, had apparently just been struck.[44] It might be noted here that the agreement was being "sold" in Russia on the additional ground that it entitled Moscow "to openly ask Turkey whether it has any secret interests in Azerbaijan the pursuit of which would be harmful to Armenia."[45]

However, Moscow's main partner in the Middle East—which now finds itself in the same league with China and India—has been Iran. Tehran began purchasing Soviet weapons long before 1992, with some arms reaching Iran even during the Iran–Iraq war, when the USSR maintained a generally pro-Baghdad stance. Later, during Russian Vice President Aleksandr Rutskoi's December 1991 visit to Tehran, a great deal of attention was devoted to Iran's purchase of Soviet weapons.[46] Military cooperation between the two states intensified in 1992. As of this writing, Iran has reportedly received (or has been promised the delivery of) three diesel submarines, one of which has been delivered,[47] and a number of advanced fighter aircraft. Among them are SU–24s as well as MiG–29s.[48] Iran has also placed a large order for spare parts. In addition, both the USSR/Russia and China agreed to sell nuclear plants to the Islamic Republic. Though intended for peaceful purposes only, some Western observers fear that use of this equipment will enhance Tehran's ability to produce nuclear weapons.[49] Finally, it was reported that USSR/Russia has also delivered to Iran T–72 tanks, two AWACS-type reconnaissance planes, missile launchers, and long-range artillery.[50]

It might be noted in passing that the question of Moscow's arms deliveries to

Iran had been raised in most (if not all) of the Persian Gulf's Arab capitals during Kozyrev's spring 1992 visit to the region. Since one of the tour's themes was the search for markets for Russian armaments, it was not surprising that the delivery of large quantities of sophisticated weapons to Iran would create anxiety on the Arab side of the Gulf. According to *Izvestiia*, Kozyrev's assurances that Moscow was not selling the "latest models" to Tehran's armed forces "did not reassure his interlocutors."[51]

The reasons for Yeltsin's determination to increase Russia's share in the lucrative international arms market are not difficult to understand in view of some of the major problems his government has had to deal with: the reduction in military spending that has resulted in the curtailment of orders for new weapons, which has affected the economically vital military-industrial complex; the desperate need for hard currency; and, last but not least, the fact that conversion of military industries to civilian production has not been cost-effective and has proved very difficult to achieve.

The Search for Financial Assistance and for Investments in the Russian Economy

As a result of Gorbachev's anti-Iraq stance after the occupation of Kuwait, the USSR was successful in securing large-scale credits and loans from Kuwait, Saudi Arabia, and the UAE. While no precise figures are available, it is generally assumed that financial assistance extended to Moscow prior to 1992 exceeded $5 billion. The quest for credits, loans, and grants continued under Yeltsin, but the going got appreciably tougher. In retrospect, this was not surprising. The GCC states no doubt feel that they rewarded Moscow handsomely for its assistance in their time of need (especially in view of the fact that the USSR did not directly participate in the liberation of Kuwait) and that, by 1992, the Kremlin needed the GCC more than the GCC needed the Kremlin. This did not mean that Russia would be dropped as a political and economic partner, but simply that the time of extravagant largess had come to an end. This attitude on the part of the GCC was probably reinforced by the fact that the Western powers, and particularly the Group of Seven, have not been in any hurry to advance billions of dollars in support of their beleaguered Kremlin ally.

It appears that Kozyrev had grasped the situation even prior to his spring 1992 visit to the Persian Gulf states. Commenting on the trip after his return to Moscow, the foreign minister stated that he had not gone to the GCC capitals in pursuit of credit: "A policy calculated only to secure financial assistance is virtually worthless." Instead, he said, it was imperative for Russia to "establish a foot-hold in the region and [to] demonstrate that . . . [it] is still a great power that wants mutually beneficial cooperation," rather than appearing as a pauper with an outstretched hand. "If we are acknowledged as a great neighbor, there will be credit." How was this goal to be achieved? According to Kozyrev, Russia must continue to play a "stabilizing role" in the Persian Gulf and in the Middle East generally.[52]

As events bore out, Kozyrev's evaluation of the attitude adopted by the GCC governments was essentially correct. Kuwait, busy with its own reconstruction program, was not inclined to part with large sums of money. In fact, "the question of granting the Russian Federation a loan of $500 million," discussed during the February 1992 visit to Moscow by Kuwait's minister of finance,[53] does not seem to have been raised during Kozyrev's visit to the emirate. Saudi Arabia and the UAE were prepared to discuss only "the timing of the payment of the credits promised earlier." Bahrain welcomed Moscow's idea of creating a joint bank, while Qatar, whose emir was perturbed by Kozyrev's late arrival, offered nothing. Only Oman, one of the poorer members of the GCC, promised to invest $500 million in the development of Russia's oil and gas industry and an additional $100 million in the modernization of its oil fields.[54] Otherwise, as noted earlier, some Gulf states, above all Abu Dhabi, expressed an interest in military conversion projects and certain high-tech programs.

Nevertheless, the quest for credits continued. Soon after Kozyrev's departure, Russian Minister of Foreign Economic Relations Petr Aven arrived in Kuwait. One of the purposes of his visit, according to Moscow's media, was to secure new credits to finance various economic projects in Russia. His hosts reportedly agreed in principle to increase Kuwait's investment in the Russian economy, but no specific deals appear to have been struck on that occasion. A similar reaction awaited Aven in Riyadh as well.[55]

Debt

At the time of the dissolution of the USSR, several Middle Eastern states owed Moscow a combined total of some $15 billion. Much of the debt had been incurred in the process of equipping the armed forces of these countries with Soviet-made weapons. The biggest debtor by far was Iraq, which owed the Soviet Union $7 billion, followed by Libya, with a debt of approximately $3.5 billion. Because of the deterioration of Moscow–Baghdad relations and of the economic blockade, no attempt has been made to try to collect money from Iraq. Prior to the imposition of the sanctions against it, Libya was slowly repaying its debt by shipping oil to the USSR/Russia.[56] Some progress has been achieved in negotiations with other states as well. Thus Algeria, which owed Moscow $1 billion, has agreed to repay some of it by delivering various kinds of goods. (However, the question of payment for spare parts, needed to maintain previously purchased military equipment, remains unresolved because of Russia's insistence on payment in cash and in hard currency.)[57] Positive results have marked negotiations with Egypt as well. In an attempt to improve bilateral relations, Vice President Rutskoi visited Cairo in May 1992 and reached a compromise settlement of the two countries' claims.[58]

Negotiations have also been conducted with Syria and Jordan, which owe Russia approximately $1 billion and $750 million, respectively. When the question of the Syrian debt was examined during negotiations between Rutskoi and Syrian Foreign Minister Faruq al-Shar' in Moscow in September 1992,[59] no agreement appeared to have been reached. In contrast, a short while later, Jordan settled its debt on a part cash, part exports basis.[60]

Conflicting claims have complicated the settlement of the Iranian debt. According to Russian sources, by the end of 1991, Tehran owed the USSR approximately $600 million for what was described as "deliveries ... of 'special property.' " However, this debt was offset by what was described as "$270 million for consumer goods and $150 million for gas which Iran supplies to Azerbaijan." But Azerbaijan had proclaimed its independence and refused to join the CIS, so Moscow refused to foot Baku's gas bill. The situation is confounded by the fact that, having proclaimed itself the legal heir to the USSR, Russia may be responsible for the debt anyway. That, in any event, seems to be the Iranian position.[61] Negotiations have been held, but no solution has yet been found.

Economic Cooperation and Trade

With respect to economic cooperation and trade with the states of the Middle East, Russia, following in the footsteps of the USSR, has been very active. By Moscow's standards, the volume of Middle Eastern trade has not been insignificant; but because of Russia's steadily and sharply declining productivity, it has had no major impact on its economy.

One of the important decisions made by the Kremlin in mid-1992 was to continue what an official in the Ministry of Foreign Economic Relations described as "investment cooperation in the Arab states, either with government guarantees, or through trade, or in cash." He admitted that, in pursuing this course, Moscow had run into difficulties, among them "the lack of organization in the overall economic machinery of our country and the economic chaos." Nevertheless, Russia decided "to allocate funds in rubles and in hard currency" to complete some of the North African projects that had been begun by the USSR. Among them were construction projects—water installations and a power station in Egypt; dams in Tunisia; and a steel and iron plant in Algeria. In addition, the Kremlin agreed to "guarantee ... a loan to execute a project for a hydroelectric complex in Morocco."[62]

Otherwise, the USSR/Russia has paid particular attention to the oil-producing states of the Persian Gulf. In September 1991, Gorbachev's personal emissary, Evgenii Primakov, visited several Gulf states (Saudi Arabia, Kuwait, the UAE, Iran) as well as Egypt and Turkey. One of the major purposes of this and of his follow-up trip in December was to replace the ideological underpinnings of USSR–Middle Eastern relations with practical, mutually beneficial bilateral cooperation.[63] Though noncommittal on specifics, most Middle Eastern governments were receptive to Moscow's overtures. This was particularly true of Kuwait, whose emir thanked the USSR for its support and said that his government "would welcome the Soviet Union's involvement in plans to rehabilitate" Kuwait.[64] Similarly, during his November 1991 visit to Moscow, the emir spoke to Gorbachev of the "need to expand bilateral economic relations."[65] Similar sentiments were expressed by the governments of Saudi Arabia and the UAE.

By late 1991, Kuwait had emerged as Moscow's most active GCC economic partner. According to reports on Radio Moscow, the USSR was exporting "machinery, equipment, ferrous rolled stock, timber and other goods" to Kuwait. Plans had also been approved for Soviet-Kuwaiti economic cooperation in "oil and gas extraction [and] irrigation" and for the construction of "ophthalmological and orthopaedic centers in Kuwait." Last but not least, Soviet specialists helped "to extinguish wells ... [and were] ready to contribute to the restoration of the oil industry." All was not roses, however. During a visit to the Gulf, Arkadii Vol'skii, deputy head of the State Committee for the Management of the National Economy, was reportedly told by "business leaders" in Dubai that economic relations between the USSR and the UAE had been "poorly developed." Vol'skii agreed, noting that the Kremlin had not had "the correct picture of the Persian Gulf Arab states" or of the "broad opportunities" which they provided for "state and private businesses of the Union and of the republics." He then called for increased cooperation with the Persian Gulf states,[66] but no major economic breakthroughs were achieved in 1992 with either the Gulf states or for that matter with Syria, Egypt, Libya, or Iran. Only with Turkey was Russia able to expand its economic relations significantly.

In late spring 1992, a Russian parliamentary delegation visited several Arab capitals, including Damascus. One of the questions raised during the negotiations was the Syrian debt to the USSR. The Russian legislators suggested that part of it could be paid off by means of "agricultural joint enterprises" that could be set up in Syria to grow such scarce items as citrus fruit which would then be sold on the Russian market. In addition to reducing the debt, such enterprises would also stimulate the growth of further Russian-Syrian economic cooperation. Damascus was reportedly receptive to the proposals, but the project never got off the ground. The problems of economic cooperation and of trade were also raised during al-Shar's visit to Moscow, but no details were disclosed at the time,[67] suggesting that little or no progress was made in this regard.

In North Africa, as noted above, the Russian government decided to go through with a number of major projects that had been approved by the USSR. In addition to Tunisia, Algeria, and Morocco, this decision also affected Egypt. In fact, improvement in economic relations with Cairo has been high on Moscow's agenda. This was demonstrated during Rutskoi's spring 1992 visit to Cairo. His discussions with the Egyptian leaders resulted in an agreement on economic, scientific, and technical cooperation between the two states. A short while later, they entered into an accord providing for Russian assistance in extracting phosphate.[68]

While economic relations with Egypt were gradually expanding, the exact opposite was true of its neighbor Libya. In the spring of 1992, Russia voted in favor of UN sanctions against Libya, in spite of its extended military and technical cooperation with Libya and in spite of the fact that a large contingent of Russian military and civilian advisers (more than 3,000) had been employed by the Libyan government. The Kremlin's position was criticized by the nationalist–Communist opposition and by the Russian media.[69] In fact, Radio Moscow complained that "sanctions against Libya will turn out to be trade sanctions against the CIS on the arms market." It also pointed out that the vote in favor of the sanctions would result in the stoppage of Libyan oil shipments which were intended to help pay off Tripoli's debt to Russia.[70] Radio Moscow was correct. As thousands of Russian advisers and their families left Libya in late spring 1992, economic cooperation between the two states came to a virtual halt.

Both before and after the dissolution of the USSR, Iran—an important purchaser of Soviet weapons—was seen in Moscow as potentially a major contributor to Russia's economic development. During his September 1991 visit to Tehran, Primakov reminded Rafsanjani that Iran "can play an effective role in alleviating the Soviet Union's economic problems." The Iranian president replied that Tehran would attempt to assist its struggling northern neighbor. A few months later, during a visit to Moscow that was designed to lay the groundwork for direct Iranian participation in the affairs of the Muslim republics, Iranian Foreign Minister Velayati discussed with his hosts "ways to activate long-term commercial-economic and scientific-technical agreements envisaging cooperation until the year 2000."[71] Similar sentiments were expressed by both sides during Rutskoi's December 1991 visit to Tehran. Rafsanjani, in particular, was interested in creating "an economic market in the zone of the Caspian Sea." Rutskoi supported Iran's initiative and was otherwise pleased with the results of the visit: "Particular attention ... [had been] devoted to trade and economic relations," and the sides agreed to increase their scope.[72]

In 1992, representatives of both governments continued to favor expanding relations. Iranian Deputy Foreign Minister Vaezi, in particular, stated to a visiting Russian official that the "Iranian government is emphatically in favor of developing cooperation with the Russian Federation." He added that although Iran had established separate ties with several of the other former Soviet republics, it "sees Russia as its main partner in the CIS and as the successor to the economic agreements that were concluded previously."[73] In March, the two states discussed ways to increase "cooperation in trade, transportation and development projects" and "worked out the details of a barter trade agreement."[74] A few days later, they "signed a letter of understanding on transport cooperation and transit of cargo and passengers," and, in April, along with Azerbaijan, Kazakhstan, and Turkmenistan, Iran and Russia participated in a conference on maritime cooperation in the Caspian Sea.[75] However, actions have not always matched the oratory. As the Iranian ambassador to Moscow noted: "We think that our relations with Russia should be better than they are at present."[76] One of the problems has been their inability—briefly mentioned above—to resolve the debt issue.

In contrast, Turkey moved swiftly to exploit the opening provided by the end of the Cold War and the ensuing demise of the Soviet Union. As early as December 1990, President Ozal proposed the creation of what he called a Black Sea cooperation area, which, in addition to Turkey, would also embrace the USSR, Romania, and Bulgaria. In an attempt to sweeten the deal, Ankara offered commercial credits to its three northern neighbors. In the meantime, economic cooperation between Turkey and the Soviet Union continued to expand: in 1985, the value of their trade was estimated at $410 million. It rose to $1.7 billion in 1990 and to some $2 billion in 1991.[77] The trade was regulated by several economic and commercial agreements concluded during Ozal's March 1991 visit to Moscow, and, after the breakup of the USSR, approximately 90 percent of it was with Russia.[78]

The idea of Black Sea economic cooperation was resurrected after the dissolution of the Soviet Union, when Turkish Foreign Minister Cetin, during his January 1992 visit to Moscow, declared that Ankara continued to place "special hopes on the creation of a zone of economic cooperation of the Black Sea countries" in which Russia would "serve as a link between Turkey and other states in that region." In February, a conference of representatives from Turkey, Russia, Ukraine, Romania, Bulgaria, Moldova, Georgia, and Armenia took place in Istanbul. Its stated purpose was "to discuss the plan for economic cooperation" in the Black Sea region.[79] The participants issued a joint declaration calling for a "multifaceted partnership . . . in the Black Sea area" and agreed to broaden their "cooperation in matters pertaining to the economy, trade, science and technology, and environmental protection."[80]

The conference was followed by a summit meeting in June 1992 of the heads of states who had initialed the February declaration. On this occasion, they were joined by the presidents of Albania, Greece, and Azerbaijan. The June declaration noted that "the Black Sea must become a sea of peace, stability, and prosperity," and that regional conflicts should be resolved by peaceful means. Yeltsin said in particular that Russia was very much interested in stimulating economic cooperation among the Black Sea countries and suggested the creation of a "customs union for the towns on the Black Sea coast" and of "transnational stock exchanges."[81]

Additional negotiations were conducted both before and after the June summit. In May, as noted above, Turkish Prime Minister Demirel traveled to Moscow to negotiate a friendship and cooperation agreement. According to Radio Moscow, the sides were particularly interested in a "substantial increase in trade turnover . . . and the joint implementation of new, large-scale economic projects."[82] In August, Gennadii Burbulis arrived in Ankara and signed an agreement on the modernization and construction of natural gas pipelines and on cooperative air, automobile, and ferry transportation. Turkey also expressed readiness to grant more than $1 billion in credit to Moscow and to expand Turkish construction projects in Russia. The latter reciprocated by agreeing to an increase in the supply of Russian natural gas to Turkey beginning in 1996.[83]

Conclusion

The post-1985 reformist elements in Moscow believed that success in revitalizing the Russian economy was predicated on Western technical, political, and, above all, economic and financial support. They were also convinced that the West would seriously consider extending such a backing only in the context of close cooperation in the military and political spheres. This, in a nutshell, was the position held by Gorbachev and Shevardnadze. It was subsequently accepted by Yeltsin and the "Atlanticists," led by Foreign Minister Kozyrev. According to them, relations with the West were of paramount significance to Russia while all the other problems (and, by implication, all the other geographic regions) were to be relegated to secondary (or lower) importance.

In retrospect, the Atlanticists were almost destined to fail. Although no one could have foreseen it in early 1992, the Western powers, preoccupied with their own problems, found it impossible to extend Russia the kind and the volume of financial and economic support needed to enable the Yeltsin–Gaidar team to move ahead successfully with rapid privatization. The result was growing disappointment with the West and a corresponding decline in the influence that could be exerted by Gaidar's reform team. As the prestige of Yeltsin, Gaidar, and Kozyrev decreased, so did the popularity of the Atlanticists who, in 1992, had shaped Russia's domestic and foreign policies. Opposition to them came mainly from the Communist-nationalist right as well as from Russia's military establishment, the military-industrial complex, and some centrists.

In a parallel development, the disintegration of the USSR was accompanied by the intensification of interethnic and political conflicts in the southern republics of the former union, much of it adjacent to the Middle East and inhabited by an indigenous Muslim population. The gaining of nominal independence by six Muslim republics could not but attract the attention of their coreligionists from across the border. Since Russia's own national security, its economy, and even its politics are closely intertwined with and affected by the situation that has developed in the Caucasus and Central Asia, the Kremlin could not continue indulging in its Western fantasies indefinitely while it disregarded the turmoil in its southern "backyard."

Over and beyond these important, if not vital, national interests, the Russian Federation has also been obliged to pay attention to the Middle East for other distinct but interrelated reasons. Economically and militarily, several Middle Eastern states had been among the major traditional purchasers of Soviet weapons. As Yeltsin has never tired of pointing out, since the military industry is one of the few branches of the Russian economy still capable of turning out high-quality products, the sale of arms for hard currency represents an important national economic interest. And as wealthy customers are few, holding on to old markets (Iran, Syria) and developing new ones (the Arab Gulf states, Turkey), has also become a very important Kremlin concern. Moreover, the oil-rich states of the Middle East remain significant potential sources of capital, credits, and loans.

Finally, the Russian Federation—democratic or otherwise—is determined to play the role of a great power in international politics. The Middle East—situated in the immediate vicinity of Russia and adjacent to the territory stretching from the Caucasus through Central Asia—is one important part of the world where this claim will be put to a test. Hence, Moscow has endeavored to keep itself involved in regional and subregional politics, particularly in the Persian Gulf but also in the Arab-Israeli sector and even in North Africa. This trend is likely to continue in the years ahead.

How does Russia's developing stance in the Middle East affect U.S. interests and policy? From Washington's point of view, the major breakthrough occurred with the end of the Cold War and of the competition for the allegiance of the various Middle Eastern states that accompanied it. Subsequently, in the last stages of the Soviet Union's existence and after its downfall, Gorbachev and Yeltsin initiated a process of active cooperation with the United States in an effort to resolve some of the regional conflicts which had previously been used by the superpowers to undermine each other's positions. This has been true with respect to the Arab-Israeli conflict, Saddam Hussein's Iraq, and Qaddafi's Libya. It is therefore no exaggeration to say that, especially under Yeltsin, the Kremlin not only relinquished the initiative in dealing with regional conflicts to Washington but was also, in fact, supporting American initiatives, having taken the back seat to the United States. Needless to say, this change in Moscow's position was highly welcome in Washington. However, it also set off a chorus of loud criticism of the Yeltsin–Kozyrev team by Russia's communist and nationalist hardliners, as well as by many representatives of the political center.

Partly in response to the attacks by the opposition and partly as a reflection of the Kremlin's dissatisfaction with Western insensitivity and unwillingness to contribute significantly to the rebuilding of the Russian economy, the Yeltsin government has recently adopted a more assertive approach to the country's role in international politics. Specific to this change was Yeltsin's announcement that, as a great power, the Russian Federation had its own interests and that it would pursue them more vigorously than before. This applied above all to Moscow's determination to keep its military-related industries going and to compete with other producers in the international arms market. The same determination holds with respect to Russia's other economic and political interests. Since the Middle East has figured prominently in all of these endeavors, Yeltsin has made it clear that Moscow's position on Middle Eastern issues (military, political, and economic) will be arrived at, and its interests there will be pursued, independently.

Is Yeltsin's "new look" in the Middle East something for the West, and Washington in particular, to worry about? It would seem not, because the positive elements in Moscow's overall position (from the Western point of view) clearly outweigh the negative. Commonality of interests exists on such issues of overriding significance to the West as the prevention and punishment of terrorism and aggression in the Middle East, the curtailment of the spread of weapons of mass destruction, the peaceful resolution of conflicts, and, closer to home for Moscow, limiting the spread of Islamic fundamentalism and restoring stability in the former republics of the USSR. On these issues, the West and Russia find themselves in outright or at least relative agreement. This commonality of interests forms a solid foundation upon which cooperation can be built, and, barring the collapse of the democratic experiment in Moscow, it should contribute to meaningful interaction between the West and Russia in the years to come.

Notes

1. Interview with *Rossiiskaia gazeta* (Moscow), January 21, 1992.
2. As quoted by Iu. Leonov in *Nezavisimaia gazeta* (Moscow), February 20, 1992.
3. Colonel S. Pechorov in *Krasnaia zvezda* (Moscow), March 20, 1992.
4. *Nezavisimaia gazeta*, April 1, 1992.
5. I. Rodionov, "Nekotorye podkhody k razrabotke voennoi doktriny Rossii," *Voennaia mysl'* (Moscow), July 1992, p. 7.
6. Ibid., p. 8.
7. Ibid., p. 9.
8. Ibid., p. 8.
9. Pechorov in *Krasnaia zvezda*.
10. Serge Schmemann in *The New York Times*, October 18, 1992.
11. Ibid.
12. *The Economist* (London), November 14, 1992, p. 60.
13. Pechorov in *Krasnaia zvezda*.
14. *Nezavisimaia gazeta*, August 20, 1992.
15. *Nezavisimaia gazeta*, April 1, 1992.
16. *Nezavisimaia gazeta*, August 20, 1992.
17. See Kozyrev's comments in *Rossiiskaia gazeta*, May 8, 1992.
18. As quoted by Iu. Kashin in ibid.
19. Radio Moscow, September 15, 1992, as quoted in FBIS-SOV, September 16, 1992, p. 12.
20. Radio Moscow, April 30, 1992, as quoted in FBIS-SOV, May 1, 1992, p. 18.
21. M. Iusin in *Izvestiia* (Moscow), May 6, 1992.
22. For more details, see M. Iusin in *Izvestiia*, February 5, 1992.
23. Ibid., March 13, 1991.
24. Radio Moscow, February 4, 1992, as quoted in FBIS-SOV, February 5, 1992, p. 33; and M. Iusin in *Izvestiia*, February 5, 1992.
25. Radio Moscow, May 25 and 26, 1992, as quoted in FBIS-SOV, May 27, 1992, p. 17 and pp. 17–18.
26. Radio Ankara, May 26, 1992, as quoted in FBIS-SOV, May 29, 1992, p. 21.

27. Radio Moscow, June 25, 1992, as quoted in FBIS-SOV, June 25, 1992, p. 9.

28. Radio Moscow, August 26, 1992, as quoted in FBIS-SOV, August 27, 1992, p. 27.

29. See statement by Foreign Minister Velayati, Radio Moscow, September 27, 1991, as quoted in FBIS-SOV, September 30, 1991, p. 8.

30. Radio Moscow (in Persian), September 30, 1991, as quoted in FBIS-SOV, October 2, 1991, p. 20.

31. See Radio Moscow's commentary on a speech by President 'Ali Akbar Rafsanjani, October 21, 1991, as quoted in FBIS-SOV, October 23, 1991, p. 9.

32. Statement by Velayati. Radio Tehran, April 17, 1992, as quoted in FBIS-NES, April 17, 1992, p. 40.

33. *Radio Tehran*, December 24, 1991, as quoted in FBIS-NES, December 26, 1991, p. 38.

34. See K. Eggert, *Izvestiia*, February 27, 1992.

35. See *Radio Moscow*'s transmission of Iran's denial of any contacts with Chechnia on July 1, 1992, as quoted in FBIS-SOV, July 2, 1992, p. 13.

36. See *Nezavisimaia gazeta*, September 17, 1992. For a more detailed analysis of Iran's policy in Central Asia, see I. Rotar´ in *Nezavisimaia gazeta*, May 29, 1992.

37. Radio Moscow, July 3, 1992, as quoted in FBIS-SOV, July 10, 1992, p. 29.

38. As quoted by Michael R. Gordon, *The New York Times*, October 18, 1992.

39. Kozyrev's Moscow television interview of May 6, as quoted in FBIS-SOV, May 8, 1992, pp. 23–24.

40. Radio Moscow, June 5, 1992, as quoted in FBIS-SOV, June 5, 1992, p. 19. For more details (but, evidently, not more progress), see the account of the visit to Moscow of the UAE foreign minister. Radio Moscow, June 27, 1992, as quoted in FBIS-SOV, June 29, 1992, p. 21.

41. For more details, see *al-Hayah* (London), January 11, 1992, as quoted in FBIS-SOV, January 15, 1992, pp. 20–21.

42. Radio Moscow, January 17, 1992, as quoted in FBIS-SOV, January 21, 1992, p. 7.

43. *Al-Hayah,* November 1, 1992, as quoted in FBIS-NES, November 12, 1992, pp. 43–44.

44. Radio Moscow, August 13, 1992, as quoted in FBIS-SOV, August 13, 1992, p. 11.

45. Gennadii Burbulis, according to Radio Moscow, August 26, 1992, as quoted in FBIS-SOV, August 27, 1992, p. 27.

46. For more details, see Radio Moscow, December 19, 1991, as quoted in FBIS-SOV, December 19, 1991, p. 32.

47. Gordon in *The New York Times*, October 18, 1992.

48. *Al-Hayah,* January 11, 1992.

49. Gordon in *The New York Times*, October 18, 1992.

50. See *Sawt al-Kuwayt al-Duwali* (London), January 12, 1992, as quoted in FBIS-NES, January 16, 1992, p. 40. The value of the contracts signed in 1992 has been estimated at $600 million. *The Economist*, January 16, 1993, p. 36.

51. M. Iusin in *Izvestiia*, May 6, 1992.

52. As quoted by Iu. Kashin in *Rossiiskaia gazeta*, May 8, 1992.

53. Radio Moscow, February 13, 1992, as quoted in FBIS-SOV, February 14, 1992, p. 29.

54. Iusin in *Izvestiia*, May 6, 1992.

55. Radio Moscow, May 18, 1992, and Radio Riyadh of the same day, as quoted in FBIS-SOV, May 19, 1992, p. 17, and FBIS-NES of the same date, p. 15.

56. V. Skosyrev in *Izvestiia*, March 24, 1992.

57. Radio Moscow (in Arabic), July 6, 1992, as quoted in FBIS-SOV, July 10, 1992, p. 32.

58. For details, see *al-Ahram al-Masa'i* (Cairo), May 19, 1992, as quoted in FBIS-NES, May 27, 1992, p. 8.

59. Radio Moscow, September 11, 1992, as quoted in FBIS-SOV, September 14, 1992, p. 17.

60. For more details, see Radio Amman, October 13, 1992, as quoted in FBIS-NES, October 16, 1992, p. 26.

61. V. Litovkin, *Izvestiia*, July 29, 1992.

62. Radio Moscow (in Arabic), July 6, 1992, as quoted in FBIS-SOV, July 10, 1992, p. 32.

63. Radio Manama, September 14, 1991, as quoted in FBIS-NES, September 16, 1991, p. 14.

64. Radio Moscow, September 16, 1991, as quoted in FBIS-SOV, September 17, 1991, p. 12.

65. Radio Moscow, November 18, 1991, as quoted in FBIS-SOV, November 19, 1991, p. 13.

66. Radio Moscow, November 15, 1991, and December 4, 1991, as quoted in FBIS-SOV, November 18, 1991, p. 15 and December 5, 1991, p. 16.

67. *Rossiiskaia gazeta*, June 3, 1992; and Radio Moscow, September 11, 1992, as quoted in FBIS-SOV, September 14, 1992, p. 17.

68. Radio Cairo, May 14 and June 11, 1992, as quoted in FBIS-NES, May 20, 1992, p. 6, and June 12, 1992, p. 9.

69. For some details, see V. Skosyrev, *Izvestiia*, March 24, 1992.

70. Radio Moscow, April 1, 1992, as quoted in FBIS-SOV, April 2, 1992, p. 8.

71. Radio Tehran, September 18, 1991, and Radio Moscow (in Persian), November 26, 1991, as quoted in FBIS-NES, September 18, 1991, p. 62, and FBIS-SOV, December 3, 1991, pp. 22–23.

72. Moscow Central Television, December 19, 1991, and Radio Moscow, December 23, 1991, as quoted in FBIS-SOV, December 20, 1991, p. 48, and December 24, 1991, p. 54.

73. Radio Moscow, July 3, 1992, as quoted in FBIS-SOV, July 10, 1992, p. 29.

74. Radio Tehran, March 3, 1992, as quoted in FBIS-SOV, March 3, 1992, p. 22.

75. Radio Tehran, March 6 and April 26, 1992, as quoted in FBIS-NES, March 12, 1992, p. 36 and April 27, 1992, p. 55.

76. In an interview with *Nezavisimaia gazeta*, June 16, 1992.

77. See Alan J. Day, ed., *The Annual Register: A Record of World Events, 1990* (London: Longman, 1991), p. 194; and Iu. Glukhov, *Pravda* (Moscow), January 22, 1992.

78. See *Izvestiia*, March 13, 1991, and January 22, 1992.

79. See *Commonwealth of Independent States and the Middle East* (Jerusalem), 1992, no. 1 (January), p. 19; and *Izvestiia*, February 3, 1992.

80. See *Bakinskii rabochii* (Baku), and *Krasnaia zvezda*, both of February 5, 1992.

81. *Radio Moscow*, June 25, 1992, as quoted in FBIS-SOV of the same date, p. 9.

82. Radio Ankara, May 26, 1992, and Radio Moscow of the same day, as quoted in FBIS-SOV, May 29, 1992, p. 21, May 27, 1992, p. 17.

83. Radio Moscow, August 26, 1992, as quoted in FBIS-SOV, September 1, 1992, p. 12.

F

OVERVIEW

12

Russia and America in Strategic Perspective

Alvin Z. Rubinstein

For both the United States and Russia, the future has come like an unwelcome guest. The strategic perspective and foreign policy that each fashioned at the end of World War II and that were galvanized by their sense of threat and their incompatible aims have become irrelevant with stunning suddenness. Unanticipated change demands new strategies, new priorities. Each power now faces very different kinds of problems. These cannot but affect their attempts to develop a new, nonadversarial relationship unlike any they had in the past.

There is a devilish contradiction besetting their strategic reconciliation. On the one hand, the end of the Cold War and the dissolution of the Soviet Union provide the United States with an international environment more congenial to its long-term interests than any that has existed in this century: it no longer faces a serious military threat or a defining ideological enemy; and, despite its ambivalence toward the disappearance of once predictable relationships in Europe and the Far East, it has a welcome flexibility in diplomatic-political maneuvering, greater than at any time since 1945. On the other hand, Russia now confronts greater threats to its longtime status as a great power, indeed, to its very survival as a coherent society than it has at any time since its period of troubles in the early seventeenth century, when internal chaos, civil war, and external enemies were clear and present dangers. The collapse of communist rule has left an economy and society in shambles. All of Russia's institutions, values, and elite relationships are in crisis. Moreover, Russia faces not only trouble with the fourteen independent republics of the former Soviet Union, but also increasing challenges within the Russian Federation itself from the non-Russian ethnic groups whose separatist impulses threaten its territorial integrity. In such an environment, the quest for security cannot be calculated in traditional military terms. Whereas America's uncertainty as to its future involves no major choices that pose immediate threats to its security or survival, Russia's choices go directly to the very heart of both.

By all the conventional criteria of foreign policy analysis, the United States and Russia should be friends; and if less than friends, assuredly not adversaries or major rivals. Historically, the United States and Russia (or the Soviet Union) never fought a war against one another. Given the vagaries of international politics over the past two hundred years and the crises that strained their relationship in the post-1945 period—Berlin, Korea, Hungary, Cuba, the Middle East—their avoidance of war is remarkable. One explanation for it is the absence of irredentist compulsions: unlike most great power rivalries, theirs never resulted in a quest to possess the other's real estate. As a consequence, chauvinistic passions were never mobilized for the achievement of nationalist ambitions, and each could more easily accept the other's limited gains. Even during the worst days of the Cold War, political tensions were compartmentalized because there was no tradition of hostility between the American and Russian peoples, but instead a shared, mutually reinforcing positive image of each other's literature, music, theater, and art.

The two powers have never been serious economic rivals. Each is a continental power of enormous land mass and potential wealth, with more than the usual motivation to look inward for development and growth rather than abroad in search of colonies. Militarily, until the advent of the nuclear-missile age, neither posed a direct threat to the security of the other. Indeed, except for the period from 1945 to 1990, instead of regarding one another as potential enemies, both sensed that the real enmity came from their neighbors, who disliked and mistrusted them, fearing their power and restless expansionism. And strategically, both powers had reasons to view with suspicion the hegemonic aspirations of Germany in Europe and of Japan in the Far East.

Looked at in this perspective, the Cold War seems almost an aberration. Yet it was real, and it did dominate the relationship between these two powers and between them and every other country in the world from 1945 to 1990. The more ideologically inclined would date the antagonism from the coming to power of the Bolsheviks in November 1917 and insist that its cause was systemic. But it is important for the future relationship of our two countries that we not oversimplify or demonize the recent past. Examination of the successive ups and downs between Washington and Moscow reveals that they had little to do with the antithetical nature of capitalism and communism; that the actual determinants of specific policy shifts and turns were far more complex. The Cold War between the United States and the USSR emerged at the end of World War II. It was generated and sustained by five broad developments. They varied over time in intensity but were manifest for more than four decades.

The key catalysts of the Cold War were the advance of Soviet military power into the center of Europe and Moscow's pressure on Turkey and Iran for strategic advantage. To the West, the Soviet military presence in a sovietized East

Germany and Eastern Europe constituted an ever-present threat and gave rise to the establishment of NATO and the institutionalization of a strategy of containment. Although the Soviet Union had suffered enormous wartime losses, its conventional forces were more than a match for the thinly defended perimeter manned largely by U.S. replacement troops, the experienced combat-tested divisions having been for the most part demobilized by early 1946. Moreover, the defense capability of Western Europe was minimal, as the recovery from defeat, occupation, and war proceeded slowly.

Reinforcing the antagonism that attended the advance of Soviet military power into Europe was the heavily ideological dimension of Stalin's approach to ensuring the USSR's security. Not content with interlocking alliances and pro-Soviet leaderships to assure Eastern Europe's adherence to a Moscow-dominated sphere of influence, Stalin insisted also on communization. By eradicating all noncommunist elites and institutions, by imposing pro-Moscow indigenous Communists as satraps, and by insisting on total control over these societies, he went far beyond the bounds of what the West might have accepted as legitimate Soviet security needs. In the process of equating Soviet security with the export of communism, Stalin precipitated a countervailing anticommunist animus in U.S. policy. This ideological divide sustained misperceptions on both sides.

Another development that hardened Cold War divisions in the decade following the wartime victory over the Axis Powers was the Soviet Union's nuclear capability. Technological advances heightened security concerns and marginalized political attempts to foster meaningful detente. Worst-case scenarios affected military-strategic thinking on both sides.

Two other Soviet policies helped perpetuate East-West tensions and globalize the U.S.-Soviet rivalry: Khrushchev's "forward policy" in noncontiguous areas of the Third World that lay far beyond the realm of Soviet security interests, and his decision to press ahead with the construction of an oceanic naval force, which was perceived by the United States as a threat to its maritime supremacy. Khrushchev shifted Soviet foreign policy from a continental strategy in world affairs to a global one, thereby extending the rivalry with the United States to all regions and accelerating the polarization of international alignments. Starting with the decision to sell arms to Egypt in 1955 and on up to the commitment of 30,000 troops to Cuba in the months before the Cuban missile crisis, Khrushchev showed himself far more of an activist and risk-taker than Stalin. Ironically, it was the U.S. decision to globalize its policy of containment to include the Third World during the premissile era, when U.S. nuclear superiority was unquestioned, that facilitated the USSR's entry into and courtship of key Third World countries such as India, Egypt, Iraq (after 1958), and Ghana. The U.S. policy of ringing the Soviet Union with military and refueling bases in nearby states in order to enhance the nuclear strike effectiveness of its Strategic Air Command's long-range bomber force was perceived by the Soviet leadership as a threat to their national security. Even more important in terms of the reactions of Third

World nations to the superpower rivalry, and ultimately their ability to exploit it, the ensuing polarization ran counter to the forces of nationalism in the Third World, which aspired to shed all traces of former Western overlordship and to steer an independent course in world affairs. By applying its containment policy uncritically to the Third World, the United States paved the way for Khrushchev's "ruble diplomacy," the principal aim of which was strategic denial. Over the years, his successors refined, extended, and developed this policy into one that sought strategic advantage. Not until Gorbachev's time was it reversed.

These five prominent military-strategic sources of the Cold War have either disappeared (witness the end of Moscow's projection of military power into the center of Europe, the emergence to independence of Eastern Europe, the unification of Germany, and the collapse of the Moscow-centered world communist movement) or have sharply diminished (as with the threat of nuclear war, challenge to U.S. naval supremacy, or rivalry in the Third World). These developments do more than confirm the end of the Cold War; when considered in conjunction with three additional factors, they strongly suggest that the past rivalry was unique in character and that the new conditions the two countries find themselves in may well foreshadow an essential convergence of their basic national interests.

In retrospect, it is also possible to discern in the U.S.-Soviet Cold War three factors that distinguished it from previous great power rivalries of the nineteenth and twentieth centuries. First, there were the constraints imposed by the nuclear dimension. In projecting their power into the "gray" areas of the Third World that lay outside their respective security communities, both the United States and the Soviet Union exercised care not to exceed the bounds of what could be done without precipitating a superpower confrontation that might turn nuclear. Whereas incremental gains were accepted as appropriate to the rivalry, attempts to effect a significant shift in the central strategic balance of power—such as Moscow's attempt to implant nuclear-armed missiles in Cuba—were not; and each came to terms with setbacks as a necessary part of the process of engaging in comprehensive competition in the Third World.

Second, the U.S.-Soviet global rivalry unfolded in a tight bipolar world. But in the aftermath of decolonization, clients in the Third World, though dependent, were nevertheless sovereign states, which gave them enough leverage to pursue their own foreign policy goals and sufficient international legitimacy to fend off excessive intrusiveness by their patrons. Washington and Moscow, utterly fascinated by each other, underestimated the extent to which they were manipulated by their clients who used a rival's alignment with one superpower as a way of eliciting generous economic and military backing for themselves from the other. In their quest for advantage vis-à-vis one another, the United States and the Soviet Union adopted a de facto deideologization that led them to take on whatever clients became available instead of seeking out the most preferable ones. Except when prepared to impose arbitrary military control, as Moscow did in

Afghanistan in December 1979, neither superpower could take for granted the loyalty or deference of a dependent client regime.

Finally, and startling in its departure from previous imperial rivalries, the U.S.-Soviet struggle focused on the quest for a combination of strategic denial and strategic advantage; in the Third World, their rivalry was akin to a chess game in which the premium was on maneuver and position, not on holding on to a particular piece of territory.

As Russia looks ahead to a new century, the government of Boris Yeltsin seems intent on reconciliation with the West. Moscow's attitude is no longer considered hostile by the United States, though its nuclear forces and military-industrial complex remain formidable reminders of the era of antagonism. Diplomatic relations with the United States have altered beyond even the most optimistic projections of a few years ago, when Mikhail Gorbachev embarked the Soviet Union on a course of internal reform, imperial retrenchment, and detente, a policy Yeltsin has continued since the dissolution of the Soviet Union in December 1991, notwithstanding some vocal domestic opposition.

On June 17, 1992, during a state visit to Washington, President Yeltsin joined with President Bush in signing the Charter of Russo-American Partnership and Friendship. The agreement affirmed their commitment to the establishment of "a reliable and durable basis" for relations resting on partnership and friendship, to "democratic principles and practices," and to the quest for a strengthening of international peace and security.[1] Yeltsin committed the Russian Federation to accelerate the processes "of privatization and demonopolization" and to implement extensive structural reforms in all sectors of society and the economy. Bush acknowledged "the courage with which the Russian Government embarked on the path of reform" and pledged "continuing support ... on a bilateral and multilateral basis, including through the 'Group of Seven,' international financial institutions, and the process of the coordinating conference to provide humanitarian and technological aid."

The efforts of Moscow and Washington to forge a new relationship are rooted in a number of congruent concerns and aims. The former global rivals find themselves in an emerging loosened multipolar world in which their security interests show a growing complementarity. Their agenda of accommodation has been significantly carried forward under Yeltsin. Among the issues that hold out the promise of sustained U.S.-Russian cooperation are the following:

- nuclear arms control;
- strengthening and enhancing the viability of the Commonwealth of Independent States (CIS);
- strategic stability in Europe;
- Russian integration into the network of international organizations and the world trading system;

- Russia's continuation of the reform process and move toward a market economy;
- environmental cooperation;
- conflict containment and resolution in the Third World.

Nuclear Arms Control

The centerpiece of U.S.-Russian cooperation is nuclear arms control. Above all, this entails sharp reductions in strategic nuclear forces.[2] On May 23, 1992, in Lisbon, the United States, Russia, Ukraine, Belarus, and Kazakhstan signed a protocol in which they committed themselves to nuclear arms reductions in accordance with the broad provisions of the strategic arms reduction agreement concluded the previous year between Soviet President Mikhail Gorbachev and U.S. President George Bush. At the June 1992 summit, Yeltsin and Bush agreed in broad terms to the provisions of a follow-up START II treaty.

Over the period of the coming decade, U.S. and Russian nuclear arsenals are to be reduced by about two-thirds, each ultimately retaining about 3,500 strategic nuclear warheads. In the final stage, land-based, MIRVed ICBMs will be eliminated by the year 2003 and SLBM (submarine-launched ballistic missile) warheads will be limited to 1,750. According to Aleksei G. Arbatov, a leading Russian military analyst at the Institute of World Economy and International Relations (Russian Academy of Sciences), the readiness to ban MIRVed ICBMs, "traditionally the backbone of Soviet strategic offensive power," represents a significant concession by President Yeltsin and "is certainly opening him to fierce attacks of conservatives and nationalists at home."[3] By moving to diminish and contain the nuclear threat, Moscow and Washington have cleared the way for a profound transformation of their relationship. A SALT II treaty is expected to be ratified by both parties in 1993 or 1994.

However, as the danger of nuclear war between the former Soviet Union and the United States recedes, the difficulties facing strategists and decision-makers on both sides become more prominent and more complex. There is, of course, the challenge of shaping a strategic-military environment that gives each confidence in its deterrent capability, fosters political stability, and copes with technological aspects of arms reduction and arms control. As has frequently been noted, the devil is in the details, and verification of the SALT II accords will be extraordinarily difficult. According to General Colin L. Powell, chairman of the U.S. Joint Chiefs of Staff, "there are over 80 different kinds of notifications which cover each system and facility from cradle to grave," and more than "a dozen different kinds of inspections." These include on-site inspections that would monitor missile plants, share data, ensure a ban on encrypting radio signals, and oversee the dismantling of warheads and missiles.[4] The downsizing of nuclear arsenals will be far more demanding an enterprise than their creation. By comparison, the task of persuading Ukraine and Kazakhstan to forgo membership in the nuclear club, denuclearize, and adhere to the Nuclear Non-Proliferation Treaty, though not without its knotty, frustrating aspects, should be manageable with a firm mixture of blandishment and pressure.[5]

Strengthening the CIS

With the dissolution of the Soviet Union, Moscow lost an empire, and with it 40 percent of its population and GNP and almost a third of its territory. On the eve of dissolution, the three Slavic republics—Russia, Ukraine, and Belarus— created the Commonwealth of Independent States. Gavriil Popov, the former mayor of Moscow, derided it as "a fig leaf pasted over chaos."[6] Kazakhstan promptly insisted on admission, and very soon thereafter the four Muslim republics of Central Asia (Turkmenistan, Uzbekistan, Tajikistan, and Kyrgyzstan), Moldova, Armenia, and Azerbaijan joined as well. While the key question concerning the CIS's future is whether Russia and Ukraine can avoid conflict, in a broader sense it is whether Russia will continue to accept the independence of its former imperial domains. The shedding of 450 years of empire cannot, under the best of circumstances, be easy for any leadership. It is even more of a problem for a weak government beset by economic privation, threats of coups, and sociopolitical disintegration.

During the first year of the post-Soviet era, Yeltsin and his foreign minister, Andrei Kozyrev, spent more time on CIS relations than on relations with all of the rest of the world. That the CIS survives is testament to its important role, even if only during the transitional years ahead. It was unable to prevent serious ethnic conflicts, resolve disputes between Russia and Ukraine over the Crimea and the disposition of the Black Sea Fleet, or forge a coherent agreement on economic relationships and claims. Still, it has been very active, holding frequent summits, repeatedly affirming a shared commitment to a strengthened commonwealth, and groping for ways of reconciling and coordinating economic, political, and military issues.

Yeltsin's priority is a viable CIS. However, although he "has said repeatedly that he believes in the commonwealth," the issue of viability is moot "without a charter and coordinating structures."[7] Continued efforts to strengthen the CIS would reassure Western nations and reinforce their moves toward conciliation. Given Yeltsin's policy objectives, there is no reason to anticipate any clash of interests that could derail progress toward nuclear arms control or U.S.-Russian cooperation. The United States should deepen its relations with all CIS members. Indeed, expanded U.S. (and West European) ties with CIS members might help Yeltsin in his struggle with hard-liners who envisage a reincorporation of many of the republics into a reconstituted Russian empire.

Strategic Stability in Europe

Moscow and Washington seem to have parallel views of the evolving strategic situation in Europe: acceptance of the territorial integrity of existing

European borders; a thus far muted concern over Germany's diplomacy; and a suspicion that Western Europe's integration will inevitably entail difficult compromises.

Russia seeks close ties to Germany, but another Rapallo-type relationship is unlikely.[8] True, Germany is once again Russia's main European trading partner, its principal source of credits, investment, and technology, and its long-term geopolitical competitor in the diverse ethnic-linguistic-cultural swath of border-lands extending from the Baltic Sea to the Black Sea. However, Russia is no longer a pariah nation estranged from Europe; for the foreseeable future, its security can best be assured by good relations with the United States, not Germany; and its concern over Germany's revived economic presence in the Baltics and Eastern Europe and emerging intrusiveness in Ukraine can be countered more by cooperation with the United States than by recreating spheres of influence with Germany. Moreover, Russia now has alternatives which it once lacked.

In the past, friendship with Germany was a necessity for Russia, not a preference. Indeed, ever since Germany unified in 1870, the particular character of Russo-German relations has been a function primarily of German policy: Bismarck's courtship of Russia was overturned by a Kaiser with a flawed sense of how to secure Germany's dominance in Europe and an over-weening ambition to play a global as opposed to a European role; Rapallo was discarded because Hitler did not need to adhere to the prohibitions placed on German rearmament by the Treaty of Versailles; and the 1939 Nazi-Soviet Pact was cast aside because Hitler's expansion was determined more by a Wagnerian *Weltanschauung* than by historical perspective or strategic logic.

But in the future, Russia's leaders may prefer to develop a special relationship with the United States. Nuclear capability may be the catalyst for cooperation. It has introduced new calculations into Russian thinking about national security that mark a break with Russia's past reliance on establishing an alliance with one or more European powers in order to ensure itself of favorable balance of power. To secure its status as a great power and prevent Germany from again emerging as Europe's preeminent military actor and threat, Russia needs to keep Germany denuclearized. A denuclearized Germany eases Moscow's anxiety—and probably Paris's and London's as well—over Germany's growing economic power. Its continued denuclearization and containment within the NATO framework, which are basic to Russia's security, depend on the United States' continuing to see its security in similar terms. As long as it functions as a partner in a U.S.-dominated NATO, and as long as it wields its economic clout within the European Community and does not seek to go it alone, Germany will be constrained from seeking a special relationship with Russia and, perhaps as important, it will not be likely to find Russia prepared to jeopardize its improved relationship with the United States.

Russian Integration into the Network of
International Organizations and
the World Trading System

Russia's integration into the international community's network of global organizations came of age in 1992. Of particular importance was its admission to the International Monetary Fund (IMF) and the International Bank for Reconstruction and Development (IBRD). Both organizations symbolized integration into the global capitalist system that had been anathema to Stalin and his successors, who had attempted to create, through COMECON, an alternative trading and financial bloc. For Yeltsin, membership in the IMF and the IBRD has facilitated the mobilization of economic assistance to Russia from the Group of Seven industrial nations (the United States, Germany, Japan, France, Britain, Italy, and Canada), and it has enabled Russia to gain access to foreign investment and trade in ways previously impossible.

Moscow's coming to terms with the United Nations began under Gorbachev. On September 17, 1987, in a major article in *Pravda*, Gorbachev advanced sweeping proposals for revitalizing UN functions, in particular a wider use of "UN military observers and UN peacekeeping forces in disengaging the troops of warring sides, and observing ceasefire and armistice agreements." He called on the permanent members of the UN Security Council to act as guarantors of regional security, to cooperate in "uprooting international terrorism," and to make greater use of the International Court of Justice. This "new thinking" gained prompt credibility when the Soviet government announced its readiness to pay its long overdue assessments for peacekeeping operations and for the regular UN budget.[9] It was also under Gorbachev that Moscow opened negotiations to join the IMF, IBRD, and GATT, among others; jointly sponsored a substantive resolution calling for the United States and the Soviet Union to shape their policies in accordance with the UN Charter;[10] joined Interpol (after having long criticized it as a bourgeois organization); and pioneered concrete steps to cooperate with the United States and other Western powers in policing crime on a transborder scale.[11] Yeltsin is reaping what Gorbachev sowed. In these functional spheres, Russia and America are pursuing policies that could, if continued and deepened, significantly extend the activities of international organizations.

Russia's Continuation of the Reform Process

The U.S. government is committed to Russia's efforts to promote economic and political reforms and to the historic attempt to establish a market-oriented economy. It (along with the West European powers) has provided substantial food aid; credits needed to meet debt payments, encourage investment, and expand trade; and extensive technical assistance. It has also granted most-favored-nation trading status. Overall, in 1992 alone, the West committed more than $30 billion in assistance, although there is no plan or timetable that ties future aid to actual reform. The United States seeks to help, but some analysts wonder whether it is doing all it can—whether, for example, it should greatly expand its aid and be more active in helping Yeltsin push reform.[12] There is no agreement among U.S. or Western policy-makers on what would be the best ways to go about this. The U.S. private sector, which accounts for only about ten percent of the joint ventures in Russia and other CIS states, is far less engaged than its European counterparts.

Still, the more important question may be how much Russia is prepared to do to help itself transform its institutions, practices, and priorities. We must not underestimate the enormous hurdles. Russia has no democratic tradition and has never been able to sustain a liberalizing process. Its conversion to a capitalist market economy may prove a problematic process: "at every decisive turning in the road there will be Russian voices urging the people to turn back, repent, find a Father Czar and disdain the decadent West."[13] Already there are "rhetorical echoes of an older reform tradition as well. The terminology of the bureaucratic reformers" in Russia of the 1840s and in the Soviet Union of the late 1980s is being repeated: "Interdependence of free and open access to information (*glasnost*) and the reconstruction of society (*preobrazovanie*) under a rule of law (*zakonnost*). The earlier reformers not only had been partisans of reform initiated and implemented from above—a modern version of enlightened despotism —but also had favored the introduction of representative forms of self- government at the local and provincial levels in order to draw the mass of the population, including the peasantry, into the reforming process."[14]

The postcommunist effort to modernize and transform Russia is conceptually more ambitious and systemic in character, but it must surmount an unpromising array of problems, ranging from a weak civic culture to rampant political fragmentation and corruption, and from the absence of an entrepreneurial tradition among Russians (as distinct from non-Russian nationalities) to an ideological antipathy to individualism, private ownership of the means of production, and the operational imperatives essential to a market economy. Yeltsin has barely scraped the surface of the calcified guideposts of previous plans for Russia's development and democratization. Indeed, on December 14, 1992, under pressure from a hostile, anti–market-oriented parliament, he succumbed and accepted the resignation of his staunchly reform-minded but extremely unpopular acting prime minister, Egor Gaidar, and the appointment of a long-time Communist Party apparatchik/manager, Viktor Chernomyrdin, whose specialty had been running the state's oil and natural gas industry. This does not bode well for Yeltsin's reform package, which, in any event, may well be undeliverable.

Against this background, helping on the margins and buying time may be as much of a policy as the United States, itself burdened by profound domestic problems, can manage. One can be alert to the cautionary admonitions of those who note that "there are no grounds for supposing that the political conditions requisite for establishing private ownership of the means of production, distributing state assets into competent hands and abandoning dysfunctional state regulations" have been significantly enhanced thus far under Yeltsin;[15] but one can also grant that there is a political payoff with regard to our own national interest in staying involved in Russia's reform process and ensuring that credits are targeted for particular projects and recipients whose "general goal should be to foster competition and therefore to shore up those elements of the system—small- and medium-size business, independent banks, and so on—that would contribute to that goal. It makes no sense whatsoever to give general-purpose, untied loans to the central government; but it does make good sense to get funds into the hands of small businesses starved for capital and foreign exchange."[16]

Environmental Cooperation

Russia is an ecological disaster area. Like the other countries of the former Soviet Union (FSU) and Eastern Europe, it will long remember the more than seven decades of communist despotism and centrally controlled economic planning as a time of unparalleled despoliation and destruction of the nation's natural and human resources There is no more polluted part of the world than the FSU.

One catalyst for Gorbachev's *perestroika* was the world's worst nuclear accident, which took place on April 26, 1986, at the Chernobyl nuclear power station north of Kiev in Ukraine. The full truth about the radioactive contamination that forced the evacuation of thousands of people from within a twenty-mile radius of the accident is still not known. But present knowledge indicates that Chernobyl is the FSU writ large. Other Chernobyls are waiting to happen. There are about sixty nuclear reactors operating in the FSU and virtually none of them meet minimal U.S. or West European safety standards. All sixteen of the large graphite Chernobyl-type reactors that provide almost 50 percent of the nuclear-generated electricity of the FSU are in need of extensive work to equip them with improved safety features. A sum of $20 billion for this item alone has been projected by the UN International Atomic Energy Agency.[17] In addition, the extensive dumping of radioactive waste in the Arctic, revealed by the Yeltsin government, raises fears for the future of the rich fishing grounds in the Barents and Norwegian seas.

The nuclear issue alone mandates concerted action by Russia and the other afflicted states on the one hand, and the West European nations and the United States on the other. Yet little has been done and precious time has been lost. The United States should be drawing on the ever larger pool of nuclear scientists and engineers who are available for civilian employment as a result of the drastic decline in military expenditures on nuclear weapons; and it should help to create multinational special action SWAT teams to work with the Russians on improving the safety of their nuclear reactors. No one could question the cost effectiveness or mutual self-interest of such investment or preventive environmental protection.

Other types of pollution, equally in need of attention and expertise, are easy to identify: coal-belching plants without industrial scrubbers; chemical wastes dumped into rivers and lakes; overuse of dangerous pesticides; outmoded agricultural techniques; and impure drinking water. Russia has the need, the United States the know-how. The conditions for long-term collaboration to raise minimal health and environmental standards are ripe for translation into activities with important political implications.

Conflict Containment and Resolution in the Third World

Moscow's accommodation with the United States in the Third World, inaugurated by Gorbachev and continued by Yeltsin, is seen in its shift away from sustaining regional conflicts to cooperation in resolving them. Thus, in Afghanistan, Angola, Cambodia, Nicaragua, and the Horn of Africa, Moscow and Washington negotiated, cajoled clients, and fashioned interim settlements, ending their competitive military involvement. Gorbachev also helped to persuade PLO Chairman Yasir Arafat to state publicly, as he did in Geneva in December 1988, his acceptance of Israel's right to exist and his renunciation of terrorism. In the United Nations, Gorbachev's cooperation enabled the Security Council to pass Resolution 598, which served as the basis for the ceasefire that ended the Iran–Iraq War in August 1988; and in the 1990–91 Gulf crisis, Moscow's support of various UN resolutions made possible the U.S.-organized international coalition that defeated Saddam Hussein, long a prized Soviet client. Under Yeltsin, Moscow has retrenched even more and, pressured by resource constraints, has discontinued the aid that Gorbachev had until the very end never withdrawn from ideological allies such as Afghanistan.

Yet, probably because of the Russian military's insistence, Moscow has held on to the Lourdes electronic intelligence-gathering station in western Cuba, which continues to monitor U.S. transmissions (after all, the United States has similar spy stations near Russia) and to facilitate communications with Latin America and the Far East. Also, despite greater openness than ever before, not very much beyond the obvious is being made available about Russia's Third World policy: Moscow provides little information about new Russian-Iranian ties, the status of Russian military personnel in Syria and elsewhere in the Middle East, or its connections with the Indian military. For a combination of political, economic, and military reasons, Moscow is trying to maintain good relations with India and Cuba and to develop a comprehensive diplomatic relationship with Iran, Turkey, and the Gulf states. Although its capability to act as a patron-protector or to deliver large-scale economic credits has been severely diminished as a consequence of the collapse of the USSR and the need to put its own house in order, Russia has a major arms industry and is actively selling weapons to nations that can afford to pay for them. This places it in open competition with the United States and other arms sellers and could prove to be a source of tension, particularly if Washington sees the buildup of Iran, Syria, or China as destabilizing. In a world without a consensus on arms transfers, residual strains are inevitable, but they need not become irreconcilable sources of conflict.

Russia is adjusting to the loss of empire. Yeltsin has accepted the independence of the states that emerged from the former Soviet Union, and his goals in foreign policy are modest. The ambitions that generated the Cold War are nowhere in evidence, and this circumstance needs our unequivocal encouragement.

However, the process of becoming a normal great power will not be an easy one. Several developments have the potential for disrupting the improvement and deepening of Russian-American relations:

- a return to domestic repression and an authoritarian system;
- resurgent militarization and an imperial-minded policy;
- tensions over territorial claims;
- ethnic strife.

A Return to Domestic Repression and an Authoritarian System

Yeltsin's commitment to a market economy and democratization is being sorely tested. A generally unsympathetic parliament has been fighting his reforms with considerable success. In the process, the mélange of conservative and ultranationalist forces has been strengthened: the Civic Union, a coalition of managers of the still formidable military-industrial complex, led by Arkadii Vol'skii and Nikolai Travkin; the Russian National Assembly (*Sobor*), a magnet for former Communists, writers, and advocates of a return to the old Soviet borders, led by Aleksandr Sterligov, an ex-KGB officer; and the Liberal-Democratic Party, an extreme right-wing group, headed by Vladimir Zhirinovskii.

The threat of a coup from the right is ever present. But perhaps an even greater threat is Yeltsin's inability, or unwillingness, to fight to the hilt for the reforms and liberalization of Russian life that he advocates. During the year that he possessed emergency powers to decree reforms without parliament's approval, from December 1, 1991, to December 1, 1992, Yeltsin tinkered with privatization and overhauling the legal system and tax codes, but overall he reminded us of G.K. Chesterton's observation about Christianity: "The trouble is not that it was tried and found difficult, but that it was found difficult and not tried."

The United States could make a difference in such a situation. In the past, the White House was able to seize on dramatic developments abroad to persuade a divided U.S. Congress and the public that changing policy and becoming heavily involved in support of a foreign power (or powers) was in America's national interest. Woodrow Wilson was able to get Congress to declare war on Germany in April 1917, in part because the February Revolution in Russia, which had overthrown the tsarist autocracy, permitted him to solemnly declare that the war was being fought to make the world safe for democracy. Franklin D. Roosevelt could paper over Stalin's horrendous tyranny because of the growing realization in the country that Nazi Germany, along with perfidious Japan, had to be defeated. In the absence of a major war, or the threat of one, Bill Clinton must somehow demonstrate that timely political and economic support of Russia can have a major impact in terms of reduced military expenditures and enhanced national security. Whether he can provide significant aid to reinforce Yeltsin's reformist efforts may depend on the case for it that can be made to an increasingly skeptical America that wants domestic priorities and not foreign policy to be the center of his presidency. He will have to demonstrate that channeling resources to Russia, though a long-term enterprise, will move it toward privatization, encourage a trend toward self-help, and advance democratization; and that reversion to a centrally controlled, bureaucratically ruled, autocratic society would be detrimental to U.S. investment and trade, not to mention defense interests.

Russia's ambassador to the United States, Vladimir Lukin, captured the sense of Russia's urgency and of America's opportunity, observing that "democracy in Russia is greatly needed by the West, but it is needed even more by ourselves." The West's support, "although not resolving our [Russia's] problems for us, is very, very important. If we lose it, we will once again find ourselves behind a Great Wall of China of isolation, only on this occasion this wall will run far closer to Moscow than before."[18]

Resurgent Militarization and an Imperial-Minded Policy

Like domestic policy, foreign policy is in flux in Russia. Outsiders trying to find a logic in the chaotic conditions search for data that will reveal a trend. Internally, there are ongoing disagreements over what Russia's national interests are. The tone for Yeltsin's foreign policy was set early on by Foreign Minister Kozyrev in his statement that "joining the civilized world" is in Russia's national interest. His views were fleshed out in a report drafted by the Russian Ministry of Foreign Affairs in February 1992. According to *Nezavisimaia gazeta*, the document, "On Basic Principles of the Russian Federation's Foreign Policy Concept," stressed the need to devise "a constructive, low cost, and high payoff foreign policy" that would be based "on the principles of democracy and the unconditional supremacy of human rights." National security would be fostered by reducing military arsenals, eliminating a military presence abroad, and strengthening relations with Russia's neighbors. A key aim envisages "the development of ties of alliance with the United States and other Western countries, with NATO, and with the West European Union, as well as the maximum use of multilateral agreements for creating both a global security system and its regional analogues. Russia acts on the assumption that no country is its enemy; thus, it does not intend to use force other than for the purpose of repelling aggression."[19]

Kozyrev's blueprint was quickly challenged by Sergei Stankevich, another Yeltsin adviser. The focus on "Atlanticism"—that is, gravitating toward Europe, entering the world economy quickly, and concentrating attention on the United States and Germany—is, he conceded, "rational, pragmatic and natural: That is where the credits are, that is where the aid is, that is where the advanced technology is." But that ignores, he argued, the unique historical and cultural alloy of Slavic and Turkic, Orthodox and Moslem, elements that must constitute an integral part of Russia's policy. "Eurasianism" must be nurtured to provide a complementarity to relations with the West; and Russia should work to expand ties with "second-echelon countries," which are situated to the south of former Soviet republics: "in Latin America, there are Mexico, Brazil, Chile, and Argentina; in Africa, there is the Republic of South Africa; closer to Europe, there is Greece; then Turkey; and in Asia, there are India, China, and the countries of Southeast Asia."[20] Stankevich's exposition remains more of a countervailing concept to Kozyrev's pro-Western orientation than a clearly developed "Eastern" complement or alternative. However, it has stimulated discussions in the parliament, the media, academic circles, and the Ministry of Foreign Affairs itself on how to develop a security policy and foreign policy suited to a great power.[21]

But a very different position may be forming, one that could coalesce support from those still entrenched elements in Russian society that believe in a militarily strong Russia and an autocratic centralism of some kind. In parliament, its advocates are evident, though their strength is uncertain. In the military, the leadership is worried over the decline in morale, combat efficiency, and national unity of the armed forces, as well as the decrease in defense spending and what it sees as a pell-mell rush to conclude arms-reduction agreements without regard for Russia's security needs. An unusual, blunt statement on the threats Russia faces received little attention in the West. It was made by General I.N. Rodionov, head of the military academy of the General Staff, at a conference convened in July 1992 by the Russian Ministry of Defense:

> The military threat to the national interests of Russia exists, and it is unlikely that it will vanish in the near future. This is proved by the conclusions of the analysis of likely enemies and allies, which are very important in the formulation of the state's military doctrine. . . .
>
> It is impossible to agree with the opinion that nobody threatens us now, and that the danger of war for Russia no longer exists as a result of the disappearance of ideological differences with foreign countries—which in the past was the source of the danger of war. This is completely false. . . .
>
> *The military-technical side of military doctrine* in the most general sense of the question must answer the following basic problems: What is the strategic

character of a possible war for which we must prepare; what are the methods of waging it and what armed forces must we have for this. . . .

First of all, as long as other states possess nuclear arms and the ability to use them, the global nuclear threat remains. This is a reality which cannot be ignored. The statements of the leaders of these states about not using these weapons against Russia cannot be sufficient basis for our nuclear disarmament. Moreover, the Americans are in no hurry to make a similar statement with regards to Russia. Everything seems quite the opposite. For example, in the directive on the problems of the defense of the United States for 1994–98 it is noted that American nuclear weapons will remain targeted at their military objectives as usual. The directive states that "American rockets will continue to hold the most significant targets under threat . . . Russia and other possible enemies. . . .

Second, major aggression against Russia using conventional means of attack is possible in the future. The beginning of such a war can differ, but its distinguishing characteristic consists in that the enemy's invasion will, most likely, begin in air and sea strikes, and in the future, with strikes from space. It is possible that as a result of the political-military, military-strategic, and military-technological situation which has developed (for Russia and for the CIS as a whole), this scenario of an enemy conducting a war will become the most realistic one. This is also borne out by the fact that developed countries possess strong and effective means of highly accurate air-strike capability and these have priority in the development of their military capability. . . . Respecting the reality of these scenarios, Russia must openly declare that to deter aggression it is lawful for her to use all her arsenal of weapons, including nuclear weapons.

Third, in the future there might emerge local wars and military conflicts which affect the national interests of Russia. Such wars are possible near the borders of Russia and of other countries of the CIS, as well as in other areas. They may be waged with limited involvement of the armed forces and projection of military actions to relatively small areas of land. However, local wars and military conflict are rife with the potential of developing into major military conflicts both as a result of escalation and as a result of the aims of the governing circles of different countries to use these wars as an excuse for the implementation of large-scale aggression.

Fourth, the internal situation of the country may be destabilized by conflicts on national or religious grounds, by civil war, and by the involvement of the armed forces in such instances. It is interesting to note that the concept of using the armed forces to resolve internal problems is rejected by opposition forces fighting for power, that is, until they get power—after which they begin to look at the armed forces in a different manner.

In this way, *the armed forces of Russia must be capable of carrying out military actions of any nature and on any scale.*[22]

Rodionov's assessment, with its concerns over national security and the very territorial integrity of Russia, is increasingly reflected in analyses of Russia's unique geopolitical situation: not only does Russia border on sixteen countries (compared to eight in 1991), but arbitrary internal delineations established by

Stalin and Khrushchev have become borders with foreign countries.[23] Adding to the sense that the military is receiving greater political and economic attention was President Yeltsin's announcement at the end of November 1992 that he intended to maintain the military's budget in 1993 and increase spending on arms and equipment by ten percent.[24] To what extent this amount represents an adjusted-for-inflation figure is not clear. Nor is the proposed expenditure on weapons, given the apparent decrease of arms production in 1992 "by about 60 percent as compared to 1991," as reported by Egor Gaidar to the Supreme Soviet on September 22, 1992.[25] The message, though, seems to be that the military's needs will not be shortchanged in the period of adversity ahead. A decision to strengthen Russia militarily at this time will inevitably have political and diplomatic implications for U.S.-Russian relations.

Tensions Over Territorial Claims

The breakup of the Soviet Union left many complex, potentially explosive territorial claims on Russia. The Russian Federation itself is beset by strong separatist movements in a number of the twenty republics located within its territorial boundaries. During the Soviet period, these non-Russian areas enjoyed a considerable measure of cultural and linguistic autonomy. From December 15, 1990, when the Russian Constitution was amended and deleted the word "autonomous" before "republic," manifestations of independence in the non-Russian republics have grown, intensifying the pressure on Moscow to resist, negotiate, or accept the virtual fragmentation of the Russian Federation. In Tatarstan, in Ingushetia, in Chechnia, in Ossetia, and elsewhere, indigenous leaders are seeking greater control of their republics. Yeltsin has tried to defuse each situation case by case, using a combination of diplomacy and permissive decentralization to buy time. His ultranationalist rightist opposition is waiting to parlay this issue into a virtual referendum on what defines Russia.

Russia also has territorial disputes with its neighbors. Most of them, as with Ukraine over the Crimea or Lithuania over the Kaliningrad enclave, involve both territory and the issue of social protection of Russian minorities. With Japan, the issue is the "Northern Territories," a group of islands in the southern Kuriles seized by the Soviet Union in 1945. Militarily and diplomatically, Yeltsin is in a difficult position. He cannot indefinitely keep the lid on the crises over real estate on his periphery, in part because of domestic pressures. Yet a resort to force in any of these trouble spots could damage relations with the West.

The danger is real that ethnonationalistic militancy, whose success would diminish the Russian Federation, will trigger a major Russian military build-up, and a commensurate response; and that in the process, an already well-developed Russian paranoia will be heightened. As one Western analyst has noted, Russia's rearming to defend its territorial integrity could result in "a paranoid, insecure state, bounded by hostile republics, that over-arms against all of them in response. An over-armed Russia would once again raise the specter of a threat to Western security that the collapse of the Soviet Union was to have forever ended."[26] Andrei Kozyrev himself, though deploring all talk of or recourse to the use of force to keep any territory part of Russia, on one occasion indicated that it "cannot be ruled out" that the Trans-Dniester would someday become part of Russia and not remain part of Moldova.[27]

Ethnic Strife

The potential for conflict between Russia and its neighbors and for the disruption of U.S.-Russian reconciliation that exists in Moscow's efforts to maintain the territorial integrity of the Russian Federation inheres ever more in the precarious situation of the 25 million ethnic Russians living outside of Russia itself, in other republics of the former Soviet Union. There are already more than 800,000 refugees in Russia from the other republics, and the number may well increase to two million by the end of 1993.[28]

Russians are leaving Tajikistan, Georgia, and Moldova to escape civil wars and endemic domestic instability. Their situation in the Baltic states is fraught with dire political consequences. Lithuania's 20 percent Russian population was granted citizenship, on request, when the country became independent, though there have been reports of lagging administrative implementation. But Latvia and Estonia, each with Russian minorities constituting about 40 percent of the population, have placed barriers to citizenship, including a requirement that "aliens" need to show a knowledge of Latvian or Estonian, respectively. Compounding the tension, Yeltsin suspended Russian troop withdrawals in late October 1992, citing a need to conclude agreements that would safeguard the remaining Russian military personnel based in these countries and a "profound concern over numerous infringements of rights of the Russian-speaking population in the Baltic countries."[29] The issue festers, with no solution in sight. Should Moscow renege on its commitment to withdraw its troops by the end of 1993, relations with the West would suffer.

One of Kozyrev's deputy foreign ministers, Fedor Shelov-Kovediaev, noted that Russia could not intervene militarily on the spur of the moment, as the United States did in Grenada and Panama on behalf of relatively small numbers of its citizens, without incurring international isolation and possible sanctions; nor could it bring beleaguered nationals home immediately, as the United States did, because Russia lacks adequate housing and employment for them: "We will have to remain, lingering on as we did in Afghanistan."[30] The way to protect ethnic Russians living in the former Soviet republics (the *blizhnee zarubezh'e*, or "near abroad"), he argued, was to draw attention to violations of their human rights and to negotiate agreements with the governments concerned. The process will be time-consuming and in need of constant monitoring, but only it can avoid destabilization and nationalist conflicts.

In his speech to the UN General Assembly in September 1992, Foreign Minister Kozyrev suggested that the United Nations could play an important role in guaranteeing the rights of minorities in countries of the former Soviet Union. The suggestion, little noticed at the time, merits exploration. One of the most effective means available to the United States for helping Yeltsin and nurturing democratization in Russia might be to make the fair treatment of minorities in Estonia, Latvia, Lithuania, and Ukraine a prerequisite for closer ties and expanded assistance.

Concluding Comments

In the waning days of the Gorbachev era, when the worst of the Cold War was over and prospects between Washington and Moscow were clearly brightening, George F. Kennan made an observation that is even more pertinent for Russia today:

> That country should now be regarded essentially as another great power, like other great powers—one, that is, whose aspiration and policies are conditioned outstandingly by its own geographic situation, history and tradition, and are therefore not identical with our own, but are also not so seriously in conflict with ours as to justify any assumption that the outstanding differences could not be adjusted by the normal means of compromise and accommodation.[31]

We may not be moving into the best of times, but we are assuredly not entering the worst. The challenges facing Russia and America are far different from any they have ever known. Though asymmetrical and defined by different philosophical traditions, values, and aims, there is no reason they should not foster irenic rather than conflictual relations. There are certain common needs underlying their challenges: the achievement of a security that both realize must be mutual; time to look inward to urgent domestic problems, even as pressures build to act abroad in their national interests; the shedding by their imperial and global-minded elites of past ideologically engendered perceptions and ambitions; a reordering of foreign policy priorities with greater logic and attention to resource constraints; and the indispensable discarding of the enemy image that each has held of the other.

With so much still in flux, it is premature to be either overly optimistic or unduly pessimistic about the future of U.S.-Russian relations. But it would not be unreasonable to note that the conditions that gave rise to the Cold War at the end of World War II are gone and unlikely to reappear in a way that would again pit Russia and the United States against each other as global rivals. This alone recommends a modicum of optimism. If, in the past, Russia and America had little to link them in friendship, in the future there are really few good reasons they ought not achieve a state of amity. It all depends on the choices they will make. Machiavelli said it well: "There is nothing more difficult to take in hand, more perilous to conduct, or more uncertain in its success, than to take the lead in the introduction of a new order of things."

Notes

1. FBIS-SOV, June 18, 1992, pp. 18–21.

2. For details, see the essay in this volume by David T. Twining.

3. Alexei G. Arbatov, "Sizing an Adequate Defense Establishment for Russia," paper prepared for the Rand-Hoover Symposium on the Role of the Military Sectors in the Economics of the Republics (Washington, DC), November 16–17, 1992, p. 18.

4. "Cheney Urges Swift OK of Nuclear Pacts," *Air Force Times*, August 10, 1992, p. 22.

5. For example, William Walker, "Nuclear Weapons and the Former Soviet Republics," *International Affairs*, vol. 68, no. 2 (1992), pp. 255–277.

6. *The New York Times*, December 31, 1991.

7. Ann Sheehy, "The CIS: A Progress Report," *RFE/RL Research Report*, vol. 1, no. 38 (September 25, 1992), p. 6.

8. See the essay in this volume by Yaroslav Bilinsky.

9. See Andrei V. Kozyrev, "The New Soviet Attitude Toward the United Nations," *The Washington Quarterly*, vol. 13, no. 3 (Summer 1990), pp. 41–53. At the time, Kozyrev was director of the Department of International Organizations of the USSR Ministry of Foreign Affairs. Six months later, as minister of foreign affairs of the RSFSR under the newly elected president of Russia, Boris Yeltsin, he espoused an even stronger defense of UN peacekeeping operations. See Andrei Kozyrev and Gennadi Gatilov, "The UN Peace-Making System: Problems and Prospects," *International Affairs* (Moscow), no. 12 (December 1990), pp. 79–88.

10. The resolution proposed on November 3, 1989, was called "Enhancing International Peace, Security and International Cooperation in All of Its Aspects in Accordance with the Charter of the United Nations." FBIS-SOV, November 6, 1989, pp. 8–9.

11. See the essay in this volume by George Ginsburgs.

12. For example, see Jeffrey Sachs, "How to Save Yeltsin's Reforms: Home Alone 2," *The New Republic*, December 21, 1992, pp. 23–25; and for a contrary assessment, Steven S. Rosefielde, "Russian Aid and Western Security," *Global Affairs*, vol. 7, no. 4 (Fall 1992), pp. 105–119.

13. Michael Ignatieff, "Falling Apart and Coming Together: Russia and Europe in the 1990s," *Queens Quarterly*, vol. 98, no. 4 (Winter 1991), p. 811.

14. Alfred J. Rieber, "The Reforming Tradition in Russian History," in Alfred J. Rieber and Alvin Z. Rubinstein, eds., *Perestroika at the Crossroads* (Armonk, NY: M.E. Sharpe, 1991), p. 23.

15. For example, Steven Rosefielde, "The Grand Bargain: Underwriting Catastroika," *Global Affairs*, vol. 8, no. 1 (Winter 1992), p. 28.

16. For example, Ed. A. Hewett, *Open For Business: Russia's Return to the Global Economy* (Washington, DC: The Brookings Institution, 1992), pp. 155–56.

17. Paul Lewis, *The New York Times*, May 21, 1992, p. 16; also, Malcolm W. Browne, "Russia Will Continue Operating Its Notorious Types of Reactors," *The New York Times*, November 8, 1992.

18. FBIS-USR-Russia, October 2, 1992, pp. 52–53.

19. As quoted in FBIS-SOV, March 3, 1992, p. 32.

20. *Nezavisimaia gazeta*, March 28, 1992, p. 4.

21. This emerging debate has been evident in *Mirovaia ekonomika i mezhdunarodnye otnosheniia*, the journal of the Russian Academy of Sciences Institute of World Economy

and International Relations; for example, the October 1992 issue, and in *Mezhdunarod-naia zhizn'*, which is closely linked to the Russian Ministry of Foreign Affairs.

22. I.N. Rodionov, "Nekotory podkhody k razrabotke voennoi doktrina Rossii," *Voennaia mysl'*, July 1992, pp. 9–12.

23. Sergei Rakovsky, "New Neighbors, New Problems: Russia's Geopolitical Situation is Undergoing Profound Change," *New Times*, no. 34 (August 1992), pp. 19–21.

24. Serge Schmemann, "Yeltsin to Keep Military Budget at Same Level," *The New York Times*, November 24, 1992.

25. FBIS-SOV, September 24, 1992, p. 29.

26. Ted Hopf, "Managing Soviet Disintegration," *International Security*, Summer 1992, p. 44.

27. FBIS-SOV, June 9, 1992, p. 14.

28. FBIS-SOV, December 1, 1992, p. 13.

29. Serge Schmemann, *The New York Times*, October 30, 1992; also, Steven Erlanger, *The New York Times*, December 27, 1992.

30. FBIS-USR-Russia, September 11, 1992, p. 31. Shelov-Kovediaev, who has been responsible for Russian policy toward "near abroad" countries, was forced to resign in mid-October 1992, apparently as a concession to Yeltsin's right-wing opponents.

31. George F. Kennan, "Just Another Great Power," *The New York Times*, April 9, 1989.

International Politics and U.S.-Russian Relations

Henry Trofimenko

I

Relations between the Russian Federation and the United States entered a new phase after the demise of the Soviet Union in December 1991. If until the end of 1991 there was still talk about relations between the two *superpowers* (with due understanding that the USSR was weakened by internal strife and deep economic and political crises), then after the disintegration of the Soviet Union it became patently clear to everyone that the only superpower remaining on earth was the United States.

Unanimous opinion in the West is that Russia, constituting half of the population of the former Soviet Union and still a nuclear giant, is no longer a threat to the United States or to the West in general and can no longer be rated as a superpower. It is also no longer on the offensive in the Third World, is itself on the verge of economic collapse with hat in hand outstretched toward the West, and is in total political disarray.

Despite all its troubles, however, it is still a great power: demographically, territorially, even economically. But it is so deep in malaise, so weakened physically and morally that it can be put out of focus of American security concerns and primary attention in general. The Cold War has been won by the West, the main long-term strategic goal of the United States—incapacitating or mellowing the Soviet system—has been achieved, and the best policy for the observable future toward Russia should be benign neglect.

Such is the advice to the government of the United States coming from American conservative, isolationist quarters. Of course, not many advocates of such a point of view have the guts to air the advice publicly in such a stark, cynical way. Like

Russians, when Americans are suggesting something totally negative, they are prone to wrap it in glib phraseology. But it is clear that such a position is strongly shared by quite an influential sector of the U.S. establishment. The more enlightened ones among them, like Henry Kissinger, add that if Washington still wants to be involved with the former Soviet Union then it ought to concentrate its attention on developing relations with the other states, besides Russia: the newly independent Baltic republics, Ukraine, and the Central Asian republics. Such an involvement would mean practicing an active balance-of-power politics in that region of the world, would contribute to some deterrence of Russia "just in case of misbehavior," and would best protect American interests.

The other point of view (widely shared by political forces that brought President Clinton to the White House) is that the United States should be closely involved in the developments in Russia, and that it should exert concerted efforts to help save "fledgling Russian democracy" from the onslaught of a mounting red-brown nationalistic coalition which threatens to turn Russia again toward some form of dictatorship and rabid antiwesternism. They rightly argue that the fate of democracy in the territories of the former Soviet Union depends first of all on Russia and its progressive internal reform. One can also agree with their arguments that the United States has been spending around $300 billion a year to defend itself against a hostile Soviet communist regime. So now, when communism has been unseated in Russia, one should be more generous—financially and otherwise—than President Bush's government was, to help stabilize the Russian economy and make the Yeltsin government's choice of a road leading to a free market and real democracy irreversible.

That is the thrust of three of the four essays under review here: "Russia and America in Strategic Perspective," by Alvin Z. Rubinstein; "The Russian Federation and the Middle East: An Evolving Relationship," by Oles M. Smolansky; and "Russia, America, and Northeast Asia After the Cold War," by Rajan Menon.

The fourth essay—"Germany as a Factor in U.S.-Russian Relations: An Essay on a Growing 'Invisible' Challenge," by Yaroslav Bilinsky—does not deal with the problem of help to Russia. Its thrust is the growing rapprochement between Germany and Russia that may undermine and replace the American predominance in Europe (that danger, suggests the author, can be averted through skillful balance-of-power politics from Washington).

Essentially, I agree with the analysis of situations and policies made in these four excellently researched and well-argued essays. So my critique will deal mostly with particulars, not more general statements.

However, before dealing with particulars one has to establish the starting ground: What kind of regime in Russia has the United States to deal with for the time being?

II

The essays tacitly or explicitly proceed from the assumption that the present regime in Russia is actually democratic, while the authors are concerned with a possibility, under certain circumstances, of the regime backsliding into authoritarianism. And they see as America's main task the prevention of such an eventuality, while again perfectly understanding that the scope of U.S. influence with regard to the internal developments in Russia cannot but be limited.

According to Professor Rubinstein, one of the developments that have "the potential for disrupting the improvements and deepening of Russian-American relations" is "a return to domestic repression and an authoritarian system." True, Professor Rubinstein does not state anywhere in his paper that there is now a full-fledged democracy in Russia; but by warning about the danger of a return to an authoritarian system, he implies that there already exists some kind of a democracy in Russia.

I agree that some traces of democracy can be found in the present Russian political set-up in the same way as intoxicating substances can sometimes be found in the blood of a drug user. But until private property is really entrenched in Russia, the country will continue to be conceptually a totalitarian system, although in practice it is a severely crippled one nowadays.[1] It cannot function for the time being in a truly totalitarian mode because of (a) a duality of power at the top and (b) the absence of effective political control over the military by either of the two competing branches of power (the parliament and the president). At the moment, however, there are no real barriers against a slide back toward full-scale totalitarianism if power were again to become concentrated in the hands of a strong, charismatic, and unscrupulous leader. Such a potentiality will loom if the present presidential draft of Russia's constitution is adopted unchanged as the law of the land.

After the August 1991 suppression of the so-called putsch in Moscow, there was a lot of writing in Russia and in the West about a "new Russian revolution" (called a second, third, or fourth revolution, depending on the historical outlook of the author). But while one can agree that the demise of the Communist Party of the Soviet Union as an institution that maintained a tight grip on the jugular vein of every living person in the country (and even on the images of those who passed away) might be called a revolution, it is still far from finished.

The class structure of the society has not yet undergone significant change. The same *camarilla* of Communist *apparatchiki* (albeit "progressive" ones) and their progeny rule the country. Those "presently at the helm of power" are "graduates of the Soviet regime, of the Communist system and its political culture of thought and of action."[2] The same communist mugs can also be seen in the local organs of power in the provinces. The masses, as usual, are mute, watching and suffering in perplexed bewilderment every new brutal experiment the "people's power" continues to perform on them.

President Yeltsin rules by decree. His government consists of veterans of the CPSU, some with younger faces. The new non-*nomenklatura* businessmen are not represented, though it is difficult to say whether one should be sorry or grateful for the fact. The Russian Congress of People's Deputies, as well as the smaller Russian Supreme Soviet, are still the products of the CPSU-managed elections, and the majority of their deputies are old party stalwarts turned "democrats." Many of them, racing ahead of all reforms and "revolutions," managed de facto to appropriate virtually as their private property a lot of Russian industrial enterprises and farms that still formally belong to the state.

This is the parliament that refused to ratify a new Russian-Hungarian treaty on friendly relations and cooperation only because the preamble to it contained the sentence that both sides denounced the intervention of 1956![3] Speaker of the parliament Ruslan Khasbulatov, though his mandate was revoked by the secessionist republic of Chechnia (whence he was elected), rules parliament like an absolute autocrat, while maintaining his own praetorian armed guard and a tremendous apparatus of assistants and researchers who work exclusively for him, not for the deputies.

There are no independent political parties in Russia except the Civic Union, which has its roots in the industries its bosses control. All other political groupings and associations exist only through the benevolence of the present ruler and can be dismissed overnight by a presidential decree. The "freedom of the press" is also sustained through the leniency of the government, and not because the mass media has a base independent of the powers that be.[4]

Moreover, all the old organs of suppression and repression that were at the service of the CPSU Politburo, first and foremost the infamous KGB, still function and prosper under new official signboards and the patronage of the Russian president and his inner circle of advisers.

So there is not a final answer yet to the question of whether the collapse of Communist rule has really occurred, despite the formal banning of the old Communist Party and the expropriation of its holdings by the current government.

This state of internal affairs has a direct bearing on the problem of U.S.-Russian relations. The fact is that almost everything of importance in Russian life is still controlled (de jure, though not always de facto, given the spreading anarchy) by the central government. But unlike in the "good old days" when it was so easy for Washington to deal with Moscow, it is now very difficult for any outsider to work through "democratic institutions" because those institutions and the individuals who represent them are hardly capable of delivering anything. The only matter that really interests them and at which they have become professionals is the art of skimming additional cream from Americans or other holders of hard currency for their personal gain.[5]

That is why to be effective, at least to some extent, one has to work through the president of Russia and his enormous and utterly corrupted administrative apparatus. But working through this apparatus helps to entrench and strengthen the semitotalitarian rule that still exists in Russia. That apparatus demonstrates a tendency, even without any real involvement of the "red-brown" forces, for evolution in the direction that leads farther away from and not toward democracy.

Another more general problem is that of the limits of U.S. intervention into Russian affairs and the effects of such an intervention.

It is true that any private intervention in the form of investments, joint ventures, technical assistance, humanitarian aid, and so on, is always beneficial, whether totally successful or not. But in the essay by Dr. Rubinstein, as in some of the others, a more general problem of U.S.-Russian relations in the light of military developments in Russia is raised.

I fully agree with the statement by Professor Rubinstein that "a decision [by the Russian authorities] to strengthen Russia militarily at this time will inevitably have political and diplomatic implications for U.S.-Russian relations." It is also certain that "an over-armed Russia would once again raise the specter of a threat to Western security that the collapse of the Soviet Union was to have forever ended." The Yeltsin government does not want to make such an impression and scare the West. More than that, while it struggles to continue to produce arms, especially for export, it definitely does not want to overarm, as was once again demonstrated by Moscow's concerted efforts to finalize and sign the START II Treaty before changes in the government in Washington took place.

It is probably inevitable that resort to force by Russia in certain trouble spots within the former Soviet Union "could damage relations with the West" and it is also true that "the potential . . . for the disruption of the U.S.-Russian reconciliation . . . exists in Moscow's efforts to maintain the territorial integrity of the Russian Federation." However, paraphrasing the well-known statement by General Haig when he was U.S. secretary of state that "there are things more important than peace," one can say that there are things more important to Russians than good relations with the United States. One such thing is preserving the integrity of the traditional Russian state. If the United States in its imperial hubris could lightly invade Panama, breaking all the solemn obligations that it assumed under the Stockholm agreements just for the sake of apprehending a ruler that it did not particularly like, how can one expect a Russian leader not to react to the activities of those forces *inside* Russia that would seek to reduce it to the boundaries of pre–Ivan III Muscovy?

No president of Russia—be he Yeltsin or, as a Russian would say, the Almighty himself—can expect to hold the job for any length of time if he does not react vigorously and forcefully to check challenges by the Chechen, Tatar, Bashkir, Yakut, or any other small national minority group that threaten to dismember the great country and turn it into a conglomerate of medieval fiefdoms. It is one thing for Russia to be restrained in the dispute with Ukraine over the Crimea (however illegal its transfer to the jurisdiction of Ukraine may have been), or with Lithuania over the Kaliningrad enclave which never before belonged to Russia. It is quite another not to confront decisively attempts by a leader of some small minority group (all of which presently enjoy complete autonomy over their internal affairs) to break the Russian state apart in order to become a "sovereign member of the international community" and a "full member of the United

Nations." No comparisons with the disintegration of the Soviet Union into national republics have any relevance here, because the atomizing of the country
has to stop at some point. The final point concerning Russia is the territorial
space of a modern Russian state—not of the Russian empire, but of modern
Russia proper, as delineated by the borders of the Russian Federation inside the
former Soviet Union. Russia would definitely react to such challenges the same
way as the U.S. administration would predictably react if, say, Navajos or Chero-
kees declared total independence, or a Vietnamese group in a California county
attempted to create "a sovereign and independent republic of Vietnamstan" and
asked the world to accord it full diplomatic recognition.

By implying that any attempt on the part of the Russian central government to
secure the integrity of Russia would disrupt reconciliation between Russia and
the United States, American scholars not only do a disservice to improved Russian-American understanding; they also add fuel to the flames of resurgent Russian militant nationalism. The latter is thriving on every chance to demonstrate to
the Russian masses that the prime goal of Russia's Western partners is to humili-
ate it as much as possible and to squeeze out of Russia's present predicament
maximum geopolitical gain for themselves. That is why anyone who is really
concerned with establishing a real democracy in Russia should be very careful in
touching the raw nerve of Russian patriotic feeling. Especially so when quite a
few foreigners in Russia by their very behavior, albeit often unwittingly, and
through sheer negligence, daily remind Russian citizens that their country is
defeated, lying prone, and too ill to be reckoned with, despite all the diplomatic
assurances to the contrary.

Of course, one might retort: "And why not show those communist scoundrels
that they have to pay for years of scare tactics against the West and all the
dangers the Western public had to live with because the Moscow chieftains were
busy preparing to bury capitalism, if not in the holocaust of nuclear war, then
through the political-psychological war of attrition and gradual expansion into
the Third World?"

Such an argument has some merit. But the trouble is that the former communist scoundrels in the Russian establishment are meek now. They do not want to
fight anyone, they just want to make friends and money. That is why arrogant,
imperial behavior by foreigners inside Russia affects not so much those former
and present bosses who would sell their own mothers for greenbacks, but the
broad masses of still downtrodden people. For them, nationalistic protest, heated
up by demagogues striving for power, is a natural course nowadays for venting
their pent-up indignation against everything they deem repulsive: ever more
dominating and unbridled foreigners, thieving and corrupted officials, shameless
speculators, deceitful and bankrupt "architects of *perestroika*," who are still living off people's backs, and against all the mess that is called reform.[6]

Many Eastern states, by the way, understand Moscow's predicament with the
nationalities problem much better than the West does. To quote Oles Smolansky,

"King Fahd of Saudi Arabia as well as other monarchs in the Persian Gulf had assured [Russian Foreign Minister] Kozyrev that they supported Yeltsin's struggle to preserve the unity of the Russian Federation and were therefore opposed to the efforts of 'Chechnia, Tatarstan, and other Muslim republics to secede from Russia.' "

III

There are quite a few penetrating observations in Professor Rubinstein's paper about the main factors that led to the Cold War; about the "enlightened despotism" of all Russian reformers, who are usually prone to gratify people with schemes, rather than doing what people really need; about President Yeltsin, who "barely scraped the surface of the calcified guideposts of previous plans for Russia's development and democratization"; about the paranoia of the military, which, like one of modern Russia's military strategists, the butcher of Tbilisi, General Rodionov, again frightens the Russian people with "governing circles of different countries" that aim to use local wars "as an excuse for implementation of large-scale aggression"; and about Khrushchev's policy in noncontiguous areas of the Third World, which alarmed the United States and other Western countries.

However, it was not Khrushchev but Brezhnev, his successor, who gave the green light to construction of the Soviet ocean-going surface navy. (Khrushchev, enchanted with nuclear missiles, ordered some of the newer Soviet warships to be turned into scrap iron because he believed that in transcontinental missile warfare surface ships would have no role to play.)

Professor Rubinstein says that "by applying its containment policy uncritically to the Third World, the United States paved the way for Khrushchev's 'ruble diplomacy,' the principal aim of which was strategic denial." While in agreement with such an observation, I would put it slightly differently. The United States did not initially apply its containment policy *to* the Third World; it tried to restrain Russia *from* venturing into the Third World, using American bases in that region, especially during the time before the United States possessed intercontinental means of nuclear weapons delivery. Nikita Khrushchev started with a strategy of denial, which grew into the strategy of concerted offensive against "imperialism" by the "back door." And then U.S. containment began to be applied *in* the Third World. Gorbachev, while making peace with the United States, continued this offensive policy for a number of years, albeit in curtailed form. Only Yeltsin finally put a stop to it.

Professor Rubinstein is absolutely correct in his statement that "the U.S.-Soviet global rivalry unfolded in a tight bipolar world." However, one should probably add that such a world ceased to exist almost a quarter-century ago, with the defection of China in 1969 from the "global communist monolith." Bipolarity was never restored. That epochal phenomenon gave rise to the first true détente between the Soviet Union and the United States (as well as between the

United States and the People's Republic of China). In a way, Gorbachev emerged from the cradle of that détente and global realignment of power.

I also concur with Professor Rubinstein's observation that in a loosened multipolar world the security interests of the former global rivals "show a growing complementarity." As indicated in the other essays under review, this complementarity is of an uneven nature. In certain cases, there is a definite convergence of security interests between the two countries due to change in the international situation and the radical reassessment by Moscow of its strategic needs. All the cases mentioned in Professor Rubinstein's essay fall into this category.

In certain situations, however, their convergence is more imaginary than real, because it is the result of Russia's inability to affirm its specific interests due to its present political, diplomatic, economic, and, to a certain extent, military weaknesses. I doubt that Russian security interests vis-à-vis the so-called *blizhnee zarubezh'e* ("near abroad,") are really compatible with the U.S. geopolitical posture. It is also painful to watch the twists of Russian diplomacy in the Middle East: trying at one and the same time to combine the role of a loyal supporter of the United States with attempts to map out its own independent strategy in the region.

Professor Smolansky asserts in his essay that there is no contradiction between Russia's desire to pursue its legitimate aims in the Middle East and its declarations that such a policy excludes competition with the West, except as regards the arms trade. I believe the contradiction exists and very much so.

There is no doubt that "under Yeltsin, the Kremlin not only relinquished the initiative in dealing with regional conflicts to Washington but was also, in fact, supporting American initiatives, *having taken a back seat to the United States*" (emphasis mine). Oppositionist *Pravda*—formerly the official newspaper of the CPSU Central Committee and now the mouthpiece for all the dissatisfied elements—cynically explains such taking of a back seat by the fact that Russia simply cannot pursue an independent foreign policy:

> This deplorable fact, carefully hidden by the leadership of the Ministry of Foreign Affairs, has unexpectedly been documented by the spokesman for Smolensk-Sennaia Square himself. . . .
> In explaining the reasons for our country's support of the UN sanctions against Libya, Iraq, and Yugoslavia, he [Mr. S. Yastrzhembskii, director of the information and press department] noted that we lost nearly $5 billion in 1992–93 as a result of severing economic ties with them. Apparently, this should not be viewed as a bad thing. For the Foreign Ministry spokesman said that if we hadn't joined the sanctions, we could not have expected either credits from the West (on the order of $15 billion in 1991–92) or the deferment of payments on the Russian debt (as a result of the latter, we managed to save $18 billion for the treasury this year alone), much less the long-term restructuring of our debts that is currently under discussion in Paris. . . .

Such is the nature of "cooperation" with democratic countries that [Foreign Minister] Kozyrev so zealously propagandizes.[7]

Taking the back seat in this fashion is untenable not only to the Russian right-wing opposition; it very much bothers the Russian government itself, which felt uneasy about supporting the January 1993 bombing of Iraq by the United States and some of its allies. Its position is also made awkward by the constantly increasing pressure from the Western countries on Serbia, which, despite its behavior, Moscow still considers to be Russia's natural ally. However, the Russian government is too involved with the West, too dependent on it to lodge either a really vigorous protest or to start going its own way. Hence, Yeltsin's feeble accusations of the United States' tendency to "dictate terms" in places like Iraq and the former Yugoslavia.[8] Lately, such criticism is usually softened by the expressed hope that the Clinton government will behave differently. And if not, what then?

It is necessary to emphasize again and again that the pivotal change in the Soviet Union's policy in the Third World, and in the Middle East in particular, happened in August-September 1990, when Moscow unequivocally joined the anti-Iraq coalition. Against the background of the entire previous Soviet policy in the Third World, it was an exceedingly difficult and agonizing decision to make. And the moment it was made, Moscow actually started to have second thoughts about its appropriateness, as was vividly demonstrated by the two visits which Evgenii Primakov, then Gorbachev's adviser, paid to Saddam Hussein during the Persian Gulf crisis with "dubious mediation efforts that would have saved Hussein from defeat (serving Soviet interests and not the coalition's)."[9]

The government of Russia continues mechanically to follow Gorbachev's line in the Middle East, with questions constantly arising in the back of its mind regarding its neglect of Russia's specific interests in that region. The larger problem is that the traditional boundaries of what was once defined as the Middle East are now blurred: as it clearly follows from Professor Smolansky's essay, the Muslim republics of the former Soviet Union are becoming an integral part of the true Middle East. (Israel and the adjacent Arab states are better described as belonging to the Near East—all the traditional geographical terms measured by the distance of these locations from Great Britain.)

It is clear, as Professor Smolansky's essay convincingly confirms, that Iraq, Iran, Turkey, Saudi Arabia, and some other Persian Gulf states are becoming ever more active players in this wider region (not to mention Afghanistan, Pakistan, India, and China). In this new game of nations, the interests and tasks of Russia are very complex and ipso facto different from those of the United States and other Western powers. This is first and foremost because Russia, with all due notice of the demise of the Soviet Union and the ineffectiveness of the CIS, has truly organic ties with these former Soviet republics and will be bound to them for a long time to come. And as President Yeltsin has emphasized, Russia will pursue its own interests "regardless of other considerations."

What are those interests? I believe they are the following:

- to insure the security of Russia and other republics of the CIS that ask for Moscow's help;
- to uphold the existing common market with other republics of the CIS (including united electric energy, transportation, and communication systems);
- to prevent any other power from using these republics as anti-Russian bridgeheads;
- to prevent a triumph of xenophobic Islamic fundamentalism in the republics of the former Soviet Union;
- to prevent the spread of politicomilitary conflagrations in the Middle East and to extinguish existing conflicts;
- to strengthen economic ties with Turkey, Iran, Saudi Arabia, and some other Arab countries in the Gulf;
- to make effective use of the Arab countries' considerable potential to help solve Russia's economic problems;
- to show solicitude for friendly ties (with certain Arab countries) established over a period of decades;[10]
- to cultivate relations with Israel, whose former Soviet citizens are no longer considered traitors or enemies but friendly compatriots who can do much to help revive Russia; one can even see a developing competition among the various republics of the former Soviet Union toward improving economic and other ties with Israel;
- to participate actively in the stabilization of the situation in the region by promoting Israeli–Arab peace negotiations, UN peacekeeping missions, and the CIS's own efforts in this regard;
- to supplement state-to-state contacts with private entrepreneurial activity in the region;
- to continue military-technical cooperation with Arab countries.

Of course, selling armaments to the Middle East is not going to contribute to decreasing tensions in the region. But Russia, starved for hard currency, has no option but to sell, and is encouraged by the multi-billion-dollar arms deals of the United States with Arab countries and Taiwan. Professor Smolansky rightly notes that "as Yeltsin has never tired of pointing out, since the military industry is one of the few branches of Russian economy still capable of turning out high-quality products, the sale of arms for hard currency represents an important national interest."

Such sales have already for quite a long time been stimulated by purely economic considerations and have nothing to do with the ideological competition of the past.[11] If and when Russia gets out of the present political and economic crises, it might become a competitor of the industrial countries of the West and the East not only in armaments but in other manufactured goods. However, such a time is very far away. And that situation is once again confirmed by the analysis in Professor Rajan Menon's essay.

IV

One cannot but agree with Professor Menon that "overwhelming economic constraints of any future Russian government will limit considerably its ability to maintain current military force levels—let alone add to them—as well as its ability to project military power far beyond its borders."

This appraisal of the sad state of the Russian economy for some time to come contradicts his further statement that a possible emergence of authoritarian rule in Russia may spur an accelerated Chinese and Japanese build-up. First of all, whatever the nature of the Russian regime's evolution, its dire economic and social situation will definitely preclude, for the observable future, any use of its "vast military assets" for actions outside the boundaries of the CIS.[12] Second, these assets are rapidly shrinking as is vividly demonstrated by the growing numbers of rusting Russian Navy submarines and surface vessels moored in Vladivostok and elsewhere in the region. Third, Japan and, especially, China are continuing their military build-up now not in response to some future Russian threat but due to other considerations.

China's military construction has in fact accelerated with the demise of Soviet communism, not slowed down. China's official military budget for 1992 was $6.8 billion, up 52 percent from 1989. "But that official figure vastly understates real military spending, because it does not include capital expenditures, research and development, or even procurement of weapons."[13]

It puzzles many observers that, in the face of the deterioration of Russia's geopolitical situation in Asia, Moscow is overzealous in supplying China with the most modern weaponry and military gadgets, including "technology to improve the accuracy of its surface-to-surface and air-to-air missiles." Professor Menon does not delve into the reasons why Russian inhibition against building up China's military might seems to have disappeared. One can hardly accept as an explanation his remark that "alteration of bilateral political relations removes Russian inhibition about building Chinese military might." That reason might suffice to explain the Russian military cutback on the border with China, but not Moscow's active contribution to the build-up of China's military potential.

Is it done to placate China in a situation where Russia's defenses in its sparsely populated Asian domain are weakened and the separatist tendencies of some of its far eastern provinces are growing? Or is it the result of a long-term vision of an emerging new world bipolarity (the United States versus China) and Russia's belief that it would fare better as a junior partner of China in a new global confrontation? Or is it simply a manifestation of strategic cretinism, proof that Moscow has been intellectually blinded by the craze for getting dollars by any means? These questions ought to be debated seriously some day, at least in Russia. The answers that will emerge surely will have some direct bearing on the problem of U.S.-Russian relations in Asia.

It is absolutely clear that present global developments, stemming from the end of the Cold War, plus the needs of America's domestic economy, will require further curtailments in the U.S. military presence in the Asian-Pacific basin. But this trend is in direct contraposition to the U.S. policy of continuing the role of global policeman, which the new Clinton administration does not yet seem ready to abandon. Professor Menon favors the curtailment of U.S. military involvement in Asia. "Washington," he says, "must orchestrate a security policy that looks beyond traditional military instruments, containment, and balance-of-power principles." But that is easier said than done in view of the fact that any security policy or peace-keeping operation in our day and age still requires a sizable military presence (Cambodia, Somalia, and Yugoslavia are good examples). It seems premature to write off balance-of-power politics in Asia and the Pacific, and the curious thing about Professor Menon's essay is that, while registering his opposition to balance-of-power politics, he structures his analysis of regional and local situations in Northeast Asia around balances of power there. Further, his query about who precisely needs to be balanced (and, I would add, by whom?) needs serious elaboration. He himself recognizes that "the extent to which China is now the entity to be balanced" is a key question to be addressed.

"A resurgent China in a region from which the United States is disengaging . . . could increase the sense of vulnerability in Japan and Southeast Asia." This, intimates Professor Menon, is a special question for the Clinton administration. But, contradicting his own advice to Washington to look beyond balance-of-power politics, he admits that "American security policy in Northeast Asia cannot ignore the traditional task of marshaling appropriate amounts and types of military force to maintain regional equilibrium."

In the political-military field, Professor Menon believes, "a restructuring of the U.S.-Japanese security relationship could reassure Moscow and dampen the influence of Russia's nationalists who warn that reductions in military spending and deployments would make the country more vulnerable to U.S. and Japanese power." As a way of such restructuring, he suggests transforming the U.S.-Japanese bilateral security treaty into some medium of "institutionalized procedure for consultation with the other states of the region," so that it might be, say, "the first step toward a multilateral regional security regime." This suggestion and its more detailed elaboration in the essay strike me as highly contrived: some abstract scheme aimed at preserving the current military arrangements between the United States and Japan under a new signboard of multilateral security.

I think that some sort of real multilateral security arrangements will be welcomed by Moscow, which has repeatedly advanced proposals for such arrangements in the past several years. However, attempts to salvage the instruments of the Cold War under new guises are hopeless. Even such truly multilateral Cold War institutions as NATO seem rather inadequate to cope with problems for which they were not designed (for example, European Balkanization). What can one then expect from a refurbished bilateral Cold War arrangement, especially if such refurbishing would still entail—according to Professor Menon—continuing encouragement of Japan by Washington "to do more for regional security"?

Only real demilitarization of politics in the region, which ought to include drastic curtailment of the American military presence and the slowing down of military build-up by Japan and China, would really usher in a new quality of relations in the Asian-Pacific region. Otherwise, everything will boil down to new realignments in a multipolar military competition from which one of the former principal players has actually withdrawn.

All the problems between Russia and Japan are tied into a tight knot around the Northern Territories issue. Until that knot is cut or untied to the satisfaction of Tokyo, nothing of substance will happen in relations between Japan and Russia. Grand projects of economic development in the Russian Far East and Siberia with the help of foreign investors (like the Tiumen River project) will remain mere pipe dreams. The Republic of Korea might get involved, but on a small scale, specifically limited to some raw materials and energy projects. Tokyo—and in this I disagree with Professor Menon—does not have much to lose by waiting and now it can outwait anybody in the region except China. But that is a separate story.

I think that the present Russian regime—whose president failed to deliver on his own promise to return to Seoul the black-box recorder from the tragic KAL 007 flight during his official visit to the Republic of Korea in November 1992 and even did not dare punish those who intentionally caused him a humiliation unprecedented in recent diplomacy—hardly evokes much enthusiasm in Asian business circles to deal with Russia, all other obstacles notwithstanding.[14]

Because all four principal powers in the region—the United States, Japan, Russia, and China—now have diplomatic relations with South Korea and are working more or less in consonance (though separately) to persuade North Korea to stop being an international brigand and outlaw, the situation on the Korean peninsula holds considerable promise of evolving in a positive way, especially once the Great Leader of North Korea has left the scene. Professor Menon, however, is not so sure that the situation will remain under control during the period of political succession in North Korea. Otherwise, I am in full agreement with his essay's conclusions.

V

One of the topics broached in two of the essays (those by Professor Rubinstein and Dr. Yaroslav Bilinsky) is the problem of stability in Europe and the role of Russian-U.S. relations in insuring it. This problem deserves special consideration, if only for the fact that the two authors treat it differently.[15]

For Professor Rubinstein, ensuring European stability through Russian-American cooperation is a typical example of the convergence of the strategic interests of both countries. Though Russia, he says, is no longer estranged from Europe "its security can best be assured by good relations with the United States, not Germany." He argues that in the future, "Russia's leaders may prefer to develop a special relationship with the United States" for quite a few reasons. One of the most compelling is to keep Germany denuclearized and contained within the NATO framework.

Dr. Bilinsky, on the other hand, is most worried by possible connivance between Russia and Germany and the prospect of a future "German-Russian condominium." And he evidently strongly doubts that "Russia and the United States [will] come together to effectively enforce the denuclearization of Germany in ten or twenty years." Evidently—to stretch Dr. Bilinsky's argument a bit—the will of both sides to do that will be played out: by a United States withdrawal into its trans-Atlantic shell and by Russia's strong involvement with Germany as a partner in managing European affairs, or something similar. He also says that "one need not be an absolute contrarian to realize that staying nuclear-free is a luxury that new Germany will not be able to afford in the long run." In such a way we have two potential courses juxtaposed: either Russia and the United States cooperate to prevent a German-dominated Europe, or Russia closely allies itself with the new Germany to dominate Europe, both Eastern and Western, and—in the final analysis—to fight whatever is left of American influence there.

There are too many imponderables at this time, when the whole European situation is in flux, to permit one to be definite one way or another regarding the possible outcome. However, the situation has the intrinsic capacity to develop as a self-fulfilling prophecy, depending on the courses of action each of those three powers will now take. My feeling is that the events, as they may be shaping, could embrace elements of both trends.

I strongly disagree with Dr. Bilinsky that Germany cannot afford not to be nuclear. What will the acquisition of nuclear weapons give Germany that it does not already have, powerful as it is in possessing the most effective—that is, economic—tools that a democratic country can wield nowadays in the international arena? Germany attained this kind of pan-European and emerging global influence by renouncing (like Japan) excessive militarization, not by practicing it. On the other extreme, we now have the example of Russia and other former Soviet republics in a tailspin under the weight of excessive armaments—"an Upper Volta with missiles," Dr. Bilinsky quotes Chancellor Helmut Schmidt as saying of Brezhnev's Soviet Union. (I would dare guess, however, that if Herr Schmidt came to that discovery at the time of Brezhnev, the boldest thing he could have done was to share this observation with his wife, Loki—in the middle of the night and under the blanket to cheer her up.)

The urge to get nuclear weapons can only be entertained by some German neo-Nazis, but I think everybody will agree that their chances of regaining power in present-day Germany are near zero. It is another story if Russia stops nuclear disarmament and itself turns neofascist, or if Ukraine—by renouncing all its international commitments and turning itself into an international pariah—sticks to its nuclear status and manages to master the launching procedures for ICBMs on its territory while neutralizing beforehand Russian electronic command over those weapons and Russian measures to block such developments.

One cannot forget, however, that while all the former victors in World War II acquiesced with varying degrees of enthusiasm in the reunification of Germany, one can hardly be sure that they would accept the nuclear armament of Germany with equanimity—the way the big powers allowed Hitler to reoccupy the Rhineland in 1936. It is also clear that in order to really start misbehaving again, Germany must shed dozens of visible and invisible ties that strongly connect it to the European Community, the Western European Union, NATO, and so forth. This is hardly feasible in the foreseeable future and—most important— absolutely unnecessary for Germany in the quest "to expand its political and economic influence both west and east."

It will surely do the latter and, just as surely, it will strive to be more closely allied with Russia and the countries of Eastern Europe in order to continue to be *primus inter pares* on the European continent.

Although Gorbachev's version of a "common European home" was an absolute sham (because he was interested not in sincerely cooperating with Europe but in lulling West European leaders during a brief period, as he thought, of Soviet weakness), Russia's interest in merging with Europe, or getting as much into a democratic Europe as it can, is genuine. The most realistic path to such an integration is by working in close cooperation with Germany. Even so, this does not mean that Russia (and I am speaking of some sane Russian leadership in the Kremlin, whatever its colors) cannot but be forever supersensitive to any military build-up in Western Europe and especially in Germany. That is why it will increase its cooperation with the United States and other European powers in the theater of pan-European security, whatever its differences with Washington or Paris with regard to former Yugoslavia.

Speaking of such differences, as a Russian who for many years was involved in the foreign policy process, I cannot treat the so-called Kozyrev escapade at the December 1992 Stockholm conference of CSCE foreign ministers as lightly as it was finally treated by European and American statesmen.[16] One can stage a prank like that at a small seminar—and I have been guilty of performing some such mystifications. But one cannot act like this at a pan-European ministerial conference. Evidently, Kozyrev had some directive approved at a high level under pressure from Russia's parliamentary opposition to "firmly present" Moscow's position in the terms that he did. And his warnings were actually substantiated by the recent and not-so-recent moves of Russian diplomacy.

Tilt to the east? It is evident from the direction of President Yeltsin's foreign travels. Special Russian position on former Yugoslavia? Who can doubt that now? Worries that the withdrawal of Russian forces from the Baltic states will give NATO a chance to make its influence felt in those countries? What is particularly outrageous about such anxiety on the part of the Russian military command?[17] I think that Mr. Eagleburger's reaction to Mr. Kozyrev's statement was typical of an American official who sees Russia as an Upper Volta!

Russia's international stands on certain issues will definitely differ from those of its present Western friends and partners—it cannot be otherwise if one is dealing with a country that is pursuing its own policies and not with an errand boy of Washington. Only if Washington accepts such unity in diversity (to use Palmiro Togliatti's phrase, stolen by Gorbachev without attribution)—unity in common understanding of and adherence to universal human values and democratic institutions with inevitable differences in approaches to concrete problems —will Russian-American cooperation be really honest, strong, and durable.

In summary, then: from a strategic perspective, Russian-American relations will be influenced first and foremost by the developments inside Russia and the CIS. Russia is not a great player on the international arena for the time being, though it is trying now to establish its new international identity. This, to a great extent, depends on the elaboration of its national interests in the new international environment and of its military doctrine, based on the principle of "minimum sufficiency for defense."

Russia's definition of its national interests will be vague and even confusing for some time, not in the least because of continuing internal struggle over national goals among the various political forces. The struggle can be diversely defined as nationalists versus internationalists, marketeers versus statists, Russian separatists versus empire-builders (imperialists), democrats versus authoritarian centralists, Westernizers versus Slavophiles, "Atlanticists" versus Easterners, military industrialists versus the rest of society. I wanted to add "crooks versus honest people," but evidently, at this stage of Russian "reform," it is mandatory for society to pass through a stage in which everybody is a crook before the majority realizes that it pays more to play by the rules.

The results of these struggles will be strongly influenced by the policies of foreign powers, the United States in particular, by their willingness or unwillingness to take into consideration in their dealings with Russia the specifics of the Russian national character, by their ability or inability, to quote George Kennan, "to envisage and apprehend the spirit of another society,"[18] and to treat Russia as an equal partner and not as a prostrate foe to whom anything can be done.

Notes

1. With all due respect to Hannah Arendt, I would define totalitarian rule generally as one based on a one-party system and total government control over real estate. Though private property theoretically existed in Nazi Germany, the control by Hitler's government over it was almost as total as the control over property by the Soviet government where all the real estate (except some small houses—without the land they were built on) belonged to the state. In any other country with a strong and even dictatorial central authority, but with private property fully legalized and functioning—as in the Republic of Korea until 1992 or in Chile under the rule of General Pinochet—the system can be defined as authoritarian.

2. Alexei Murzhenko, "Dissidents and Nomenclature at Opposite Sides of a Barricade," *Novoe Russkoe Slovo*, February 3, 1993, p. 6.

3. *Izvestiia*, January 22, 1993.

4. The media are now managed by two (!) ministries: the Ministry of the Press and Information and the newly created (December 25, 1992) Russian Federal Information Center. Commenting on the creation of the latter, which had Yeltsin's crony Mikhail Nikiforovich Poltoranin at the head, *Nezavisimaia gazeta* wrote: "There are historical precedents [for the new Federal Information Center]—for example, the ministry of propaganda. Because when information is concentrated in a single pair of hands, propaganda is exactly what it becomes.... We have to call a spade a spade: Mikhail Nikiforovich doesn't want to disappear into political oblivion. He wants to keep his office, his government phone, his car and his other nomenklatura accessories. And the President wants to control the press—especially the electronic press" (*Nezavisimaia gazeta*, December 29, 1992, as quoted in *The Current Digest of the Post-Soviet Press*, January 27, 1993, p. 24). In addition to the two above-mentioned watchdogs, there exists also a parliamentary committee on the mass media, which the speaker of the parliament wants to turn into a de facto censorship body.

5. "The deputies have already announced the main thing about themselves: greed is above party affiliations. Mass cupidity is much more important than conceptual differences," writes well-known Moscow political analyst Albert Plutnik about the collusion between democrats and conservatives in the Russian parliament in promoting their personal self-interest. See *Novoe Russkoe Slovo*, February 2, 1993, p. 6.

6. At the end of January 1993, the right-wing Russian newspaper *Den'* published what it said was a transcript of a private conversation between President Bush and President Yeltsin at their meeting in Moscow on January 3 under the headline "Your Commands Have Been Fulfilled, Mr. Bush." Among the passages that the newspaper underlined as especially objectionable was one in which Mr. Yeltsin allegedly said to Mr. Bush, "You asked that we keep Kozyrev in place, and we met your request," *The New York Times*, January 27, 1993, p. A6.

7. *Pravda*, December 4, 1992, as quoted in *The Current Digest of the Post-Soviet Press*, January 6, 1993, p. 19. By the way, Russian Minister of Foreign Economic Relations Sergei Glazev claimed that, as a result of international sanctions against the three states in question, Russia lost not $5 billion but $16 billion. See *Izvestiia*, January 22, 1993.

8. *The New York Times*, January 26, 1993, p. A6.

9. Peter W. Rodman, "Middle East Diplomacy after the Gulf War," *Foreign Affairs*, Spring 1991, p. 11.

10. This and some other points are taken from a paper prepared by the Russian Ministry of Foreign Affairs in concert with scholarly institutions and concerned circles in parliament and approved by the president of the Russian Federation. The document sets guidelines regarding Russia's relations with the Arab world. Commenting on this particular point, *Pravda*'s analyst pointed out that this "correct position" cannot be reconciled with the current Russian policy toward Iraq which was called by President Yeltsin a "common enemy" of Russia and the West during his visit to London in 1992. See *Pravda*, November 14, 1992.

11. Once, in the mid-1980s, I asked one of the big bosses of the Soviet agency that dealt with arms sales what were the official guidelines with regard to selling heavy weaponry to foreign countries, to what kind of buyer it could be sold. "For what currency?" he asked. "For a hard one." "We'll sell to anyone," was his unequivocal answer. At the peak of such sales at the end of the 1980s, the Soviet Union held first place in the trade, providing $23 billion worth of weapons deliveries in 1989. In 1991–92 the

deliveries were much lower, though the president of the Russian League of Defense Enterprises thinks the industry is in a position to increase the total volume of exports to $12–$14 billion a year if Russia preserves the best part of its defense potential. See *Nezavisimaia gazeta*, September 29, October 1, 1992.

12. Actually, this is the conclusion Professor Menon draws at the end of his paper: "Even a Russia in which democracy fails and a nationalistic, authoritarian regime emerges, will face severe economic constraints that will limit its military-political influence in the region."

13. *The New York Times*, June 7, 1992, p. A20.

14. It was only natural for the Korean authorities (like everyone else) to assume that the black box was being returned with all its original recordings intact—not simply as a silent memento of a past misdeed, an empty souvenir without real recordings, as it turned out to be after the floodlights of international television cameras were switched off.

15. There are many other points in Dr. Bilinsky's paper which are interesting and also deserve to be scrutinized. But I am limited by space from arguing at length. Still, as a person who was involved in preparing position papers for the top leadership, I would like to confirm Dr. Yurii Davidov's claim in *Europa Archiv* that there were no diplomatic position papers on the German question until the end of 1989. Eduard Shevardnadze's assertion that he debated this problem with someone in 1986 might be correct, but it is unverifiable. As late as December 1989, Mikhail Gorbachev was insisting that it was for "our grandchildren" to try to reopen the problem. "It is necessary to proceed from realities that have been in place since the war—the existence of two sovereign German states" (*Pravda*, December 12, 1989). Polemicizing with Jeremy Azrael and Stephen Sestanovich in August 1988, I wrote that "the time to liquidate the Berlin Wall will come. Only one must not pretend today that it is just the Berlin Wall alone that is a problem." See *SShA: Ekonomika, politika, ideologiia* [USA: Economics, Politics, Ideology] (published by the Institute of the USA and Canada), August, 1988, p. 48.

16. "Ultimatum by Andrei Kozyrev. European Political Beaux Monde in a Shock." Under such a heading, Moscow's *Nezavisimaia gazeta* in its issue of December 15, 1992, issue printed the talk of the Russian foreign minister at the conference.

17. It is not for nothing that on December 18, 1992, commenting on the resolution on Yugoslavia adopted by the Russian Supreme Soviet the previous day, *Izvestiia* wrote: "Andrei Kozyrev's Stockholm speech, which shocked the world and the country, has proved to be a great deal more prophetic than it initially seemed."

18. George F. Kennan, *Russia and the West under Lenin and Stalin* (New York: New American Library, 1961), p. 142.

Index